Oracle9*i* PL/SQL:
A Developer's Guide

BULUSU LAKSHMAN

Apress™

Oracle9*i* PL/SQL: A Developer's Guide

ISBN (pbk): 1-59059-049-X

Printed and bound in the United States of America 12345678910

Technical Reviewer: Martin Reid
Editorial Directors: Dan Appleman, Gary Cornell, Jason Gilmore, Simon Hayes, Karen Watterson, John Zukowski
Managing Editor: Grace Wong
Project Manager and Developmental Editor: Tracy Brown Collins
Copy Editors: Nicole LeClerc, Ami Knox
Production Editor: Laura Cheu
Compositor and Artist: Impressions Book and Journal Services, Inc.
Cover Designer: Kurt Krames
Indexer: Valerie Robbins
Marketing Manager: Stephanie Rodriguez
Manufacturing Manager: Tom Debolski

Distributed to the book trade in the United States by Springer-Verlag New York, Inc., 175 Fifth Avenue, New York, NY, 10010 and outside the United States by Springer-Verlag GmbH & Co. KG, Tiergartenstr. 17, 69112 Heidelberg, Germany.

In the United States, phone 1-800-SPRINGER, email orders@springer-ny.com, or visit http://www.springer-ny.com.

Outside the United States, fax +49 6221 345229, email orders@springer.de, or visit http://www.springer.de.

For information on translations, please contact Apress directly at 2560 9th Street, Suite 219, Berkeley, CA 94710. Phone 510-549-5930, fax 510-549-5939, email info@apress.com, or visit http://www.apress.com.

The source code for this book is available to readers at http://www.apress.com in the Downloads section.

With love to my parents, Professor B.S.K.R. Somayajulu and Smt. B. Sita.

Contents at a Glance

Contents

Chapter 7: Native Dynamic SQL and Dynamic PL/SQL 291

Chapter 8: Autonomous Transactions 315

Chapter 9: Native Bulk Binds 333

Part Three: Object-Oriented Features in PL/SQL 9i 359

Chapter 10: The World of Objects 361

Foreword

I HAD ALREADY READ a couple of chapters of Bulusu Lakshman's book on Oracle9*i*
PL/SQL when I was asked to write this Foreword. I immediately accepted
because of the strong impression the book made on me.

There have been several PL/SQL titles published over the years, but I think
Bulusu's book is the best Oracle PL/SQL book ever written. There are several reasons for this emphatic declaration, one of them being that *Oracle9*i *PL/SQL:
A Developer's Guide* is the most comprehensive book on the subject, period. It
takes readers from the basics to the most complex techniques. Moreover, what's
most important is that Bulusu doesn't just "cover" the topics—he leads readers
step by step through the various techniques. The examples in this book use an
actual Oracle9*i* database and some sample schemas, and the data is all right
there for you to learn or verify the techniques. Like mathematics, PL/SQL is an
endeavor in which you need to practice the examples to get good at the game.
You don't have to know any PL/SQL to start using this book, and if you persevere
and try the multitude of tested examples Bulusu provides, you might very well
become an expert in PL/SQL in short order.

Bulusu has set himself a lofty goal: to write a comprehensive book on PL/SQL
that is technically complete and accessible to even the beginner. I am glad to
confirm that Bulusu has succeeded in achieving his goal. Oracle professionals at
various career stages, from fledgling newbies to seasoned veterans, will find this
book a treasure trove of useful examples and lucidly explained concepts.

The very first chapter, which introduces PL/SQL, sets the tone for the book,
and Bulusu carefully and painstakingly builds on this chapter. The next chapter
(Chapter 2) covers cursors, and it provides the best treatment of the subject
that I've seen in any book. The chapter on record types and index-by tables
(Chapter 3) is also excellent. Bulusu takes care throughout the book to provide
useful information to his readers. Two examples of this are the tips for PL/SQL
error messages in Chapter 4 and the performance-improving tips in Chapter 15.
The chapter on triggers (Chapter 6) is another good example of how this book
stands out from many of the other titles on the market: You not only learn about
all there is to learn about creating and deploying triggers, but you also learn
about the dba_tables that contain pertinent information for managing triggers,
details about enabling and disabling triggers, and the privileges you need to be
able to use triggers. Typically, authors explain a concept, provide some examples,
and move on, but Bulusu consistently endeavors to provide a complete treatment of each topic so readers can not only learn what the concept means, but
also implement the concept successfully in the real world.

Oracle provides its own manuals, but they do not always offer a fruitful way for developers to learn new and complex techniques. Bulusu takes you beyond what any Oracle manual can show you about using the innovations in Oracle9*i* PL/SQL. Chapter 7, which covers native dynamic SQL, is a good example of this. The chapter is a very useful yet simple and systematic tutorial-like introduction to complex topics such as dynamic bulk SQL and dynamic PL/SQL. Bulusu covers a lot of ground in this book and includes solid treatments of topics such as Java stored procedures (Chapter 13) and PL/SQL and the Web (Chapter 14). The latter chapter shows you how to Web-enable your PL/SQL code. Chapter 15 alone makes the book an indispensable volume for any professional who uses or intends to use PL/SQL—in it, Bulusu provides the most comprehensive set of PL/SQL performance-enhancing hints and guidelines that you can find anywhere. And Bulusu's chapter on PL/SQL coding standards (Chapter 16) contains the most comprehensive coding guidelines that you can find. In fact, most PL/SQL books give short shrift to this very important part of PL/SQL implementation. It is chapters like these that make Bulusu's book a standout among the current crop of Oracle books.

Bulusu's book is an important addition to the Oracle9*i* literature, and it will remain a favorite book on many a developer's desk in the years to come. Enjoy your voyage through the new Oracle9*i* PL/SQL world, with Bulusu's book by your side!

Sam Alapati
October 4, 2002

About the Author

 **Bulusu Lakshman** is an experienced Oracle developer with more than 10 years of extensive software design and development experience in using Oracle and its related tools, including PL/SQL and Java. He's the author of *Oracle Developer Forms Techniques* and *Oracle and Java Development*, both of which have been well received. He also has an Oracle Master credential from Oracle Corporation, is an Oracle Certified Professional (OCP) application developer, and is a double honors graduate in computer science and engineering and mathematics. He has presented at numerous international and national conferences on Oracle and its tools and published articles in various technical magazines and journals in the United States and the United Kingdom. He is currently employed by Compunnel Software Group Inc., a leading technical consulting firm based in New Jersey.

About the Technical Reviewer

 **Martin W.P. Reid** is currently employed at Queen's University Belfast, where he is responsible for staff and student computer training, teaching everything from Windows to Web authoring to database design. He is also employed by the faculty of computer science as a part-time lecturer in database design and teaches several courses using Microsoft Access for other areas of the university.

Martin particularly enjoys the contact with staff and students, and one of his biggest thrills was when two of his part-time students—who had previously never been near a database—started to work as developers.

Martin is married with six children. He credits his wife, Patricia, with keeping the whole show on the road while he plays with databases.

About the Foreword Writer

Sam R. Alapati is an experienced Oracle database administrator who holds the Oracle OCP DBA and the Hewlett Packard UNIX System Administrator certifications. He currently manages Oracle databases at the Boy Scouts of America's National Office in Los Colinas, Texas. Sam has been dealing with databases for a long time, including the Ingres RDBMS in the mid-1980s. In addition, he is well versed in the Sybase and IBM DB2 database management systems. Sam has also taught Oracle DBA classes for system administrators.

Acknowledgments

I THANK MY WIFE, Anuradha, for her consistent endeavor in creating a positive atmosphere throughout the writing period of my book.

I thank my brother B. Rama for his constant encouragement throughout.

I thank Mr. Paul Wu, director of MIS at Associated Press, the client company for which I am consulting, for providing me with necessary resources to write this book.

I thank my friends V. Satya Prasad and Devendra Trivedi for their help in preparing part of the manuscript and providing valuable suggestions.

I thank Mr. Vinayak Rampalli and Mr. Rakesh Shah of Compunnel Software Group Inc. for letting me use the name of the mail server as an example for one of the programs in my book.

I thank Apress' publisher, Gary Cornell, and the various editors at Apress for their help in editing and publishing my book.

Introduction

ORACLE9*i* IS THE major relational database management system (RDBMS) for developing and running a wide variety of applications, starting from creating and maintaining simple databases in client/server environments to conducting e-business on the Web. PL/SQL is the primary procedural component of Oracle9*i*'s server-side programming and is regarded as the primary language for developing applications on the database and middle tiers using Oracle9*i*. PL/SQL in Releases 1 and 2 of Oracle9*i* has incorporated new features that take programmers to a higher level of coding, especially with its true object-relational capabilities. Also, Oracle9*i* provides for support of Java in the database, and PL/SQL 9*i* provides this capability by means of Java stored procedures and their new functionality in 9*i*, to build highly scalable applications.

What This Book Covers

This book covers the techniques of using PL/SQL in Oracle9*i* Releases 1 and 2 for server-side applications. It covers PL/SQL 9*i* in exhaustive detail and provides the methodology for implementing robust applications of exceptional quality. This book will assist programmers in implementing techniques that are effective for real-world and code-centric Oracle applications. This saves time and effort on the part of the PL/SQL developer in addition to increasing his or her level to that of an advanced developer. Also, PL/SQL is widely used by many organizations, and the combination of Oracle9*i* and PL/SQL provides a robust and effective environment for development of mission-critical applications. This book is a source for development of such applications by companies incorporating these technologies as well as those organizations migrating from earlier versions.

How This Book Is Organized

This book is divided into 6 parts containing 16 chapters and 1 appendix, as follows.

Part One: Introduction

This part, which consists of Chapter 1, introduces you to the fundamental constructs of the PL/SQL language and the development and execution environments for PL/SQL programs.

Part Two: Non-Object-Oriented Features in PL/SQL 9i

This part presents the non-object-oriented features in PL/SQL 9*i* and is composed of eight chapters. It covers details about cursors in Chapter 2, index-by tables and PL/SQL records in Chapter 3, error message handling in Chapter 4, stored subprograms (specifically, procedures, functions, and packages) in Chapter 5, database triggers in Chapter 6, native dynamic SQL and dynamic PL/SQL in Chapter 7, autonomous transactions in Chapter 8, and native bulk binds in Chapter 9.

Part Three: Object-Oriented Features in PL/SQL 9i

This part explains the ins and outs of using objects in PL/SQL and is composed of three chapters. Chapter 10 explains the use of different types of objects. Chapter 11 explains collections and their use in PL/SQL in detail. Chapter 12 highlights the use of large objects in PL/SQL.

Part Four: PL/SQL with Java and the Web

This part, which consists of two chapters, deals with using PL/SQL in conjunction with Java and using PL/SQL applications on the Web. Specifically, Chapter 13 covers using PL/SQL with Java by means of Java stored procedures, and Chapter 14 covers Web-enabling PL/SQL applications.

Part Five: PL/SQL Performance and Standards

This part outlines some methods of improving the performance of PL/SQL applications and certain standards to follow when coding using PL/SQL. It is composed of two chapters. Chapter 15 presents performance considerations, and Chapter 16 presents some coding standards to keep in mind when writing PL/SQL programs.

Part Six: Appendix

This part, which consists of Appendix A, provides the case studies and some of the schema objects necessary to run programs provided in this book.

Prerequisites and Intended Audience

This book is targeted toward intermediate-level Oracle developers who are designing or coding applications in SQL and PL/SQL. It assumes a working knowledge of Oracle SQL, PL/SQL, and Java. This book is also a guide for programmers who intend to use advanced PL/SQL 9*i* features. It discusses Oracle9*i* PL/SQL from an application developer's perspective.

Part One
Introduction

CHAPTER 1

Introduction to PL/SQL

ORACLE FIRST INTRODUCED Procedural Language/Structured Query Language (PL/SQL) in version 6.0 of its relational database management system (RDBMS). As its RDBMS evolved, Oracle made developmental changes to the PL/SQL language by introducing new features and enhancing existing features. As of Oracle9*i*, the version of PL/SQL is PL/SQL 9.2 or 9.0 depending on whether it is Oracle9*i* Release 2 (9.2.*x*) or Oracle9*i* Release 1 (9.0.*x*). In this book, I refer to both versions collectively as PL/SQL 9*i*.

PL/SQL incorporates third-generation language (3GL) structures otherwise unavailable in Structured Query Language (SQL). SQL is a fourth-generation language (4GL), meaning it uses constructs and elements that specify "what to do" without having to specify "how to do it." It's a major language for the Oracle RDBMS (as well as for other RDBMSs), and it's used for data definition, database querying, and data manipulation and control. However, there are situations that demand the use of 3GL constructs, such as conditional or iterative execution of SQL and the like. This kind of logic and control flow can be achieved only in a 3GL language such as Java, C++, or C. To accommodate 3GL features, Oracle designed and implemented the PL/SQL language as a procedural extension to SQL. PL/SQL is integrated with SQL, and both SQL and PL/SQL serve as the major database server-side languages, with each language complementing the other. You can also use PL/SQL in client-side environments.

Table 1-1 offers a comparison of PL/SQL with other 3GLs such as Java, C++, and C.

Table 1-1. Comparison of PL/SQL with Other 3GLs

FEATURE	PL/SQL	OTHER 3GLS (JAVA, C++, C)
Ease of use	Fairly easy	Difficult; requires a steep learning curve
Portability of applications	Highly portable	Portable except for system calls
Integration with SQL	Tightly integrated	Integrated to a lesser degree than PL/SQL; access by means of SQLJ or JDBC
SQL-intensive operations	Well suited	Not well suited
Compute-intensive operations	Not well suited	Well suited (e.g., for sorting of large arrays)
Object orientation	Object oriented to a certain extent	Truly object oriented (like Java and C++)

In this chapter, I describe the building blocks of PL/SQL and discuss the various PL/SQL environments. I also highlight the new features of PL/SQL 9*i*.

A Brief History of PL/SQL

PL/SQL was first introduced in 1991 with Oracle 6.0. It was provided as the "procedural option" on the server side. At the same time, it was subsequently introduced on the client side with SQL*Forms version 3.0 having a PL/SQL engine of its own. The first version of PL/SQL, PL/SQL 1.0, had very limited procedural features. But one of its strong points was its capability to process multiple SQL statements mixed with procedural constructs.

PL/SQL has its roots in ADA, a high-level programming language. The concept of the PL/SQL block resembles the concept of block structure in ADA using BEGIN and END blocks. PL/SQL shares other features with ADA such as the syntax "=" used for comparison and ":=" used for assignment, exception handling, and the declarative syntax of defining stored subprograms.

Over the years, Oracle came up with new releases of PL/SQL. With Oracle 7.0, Oracle released PL/SQL 2.0, which turned Oracle into an active database with the capability to store business and application logic in the database in the form of stored procedures, functions, and packages. It also defined the capability to declare programmer-defined records and arrays in the form of PL/SQL tables. PL/SQL 2.1 came into existence with Oracle 7.1 and enabled the use of stored functions in SQL statements. Also, dynamic SQL was introduced in

PL/SQL for the first time with the DBMS_SQL package. Oracle 7.2 was released subsequently, and along with it came PL/SQL 2.2. It had the capability to define binary wrappers for PL/SQL stored subprograms, thus hiding code from other developers. Also, the DBMS_JOB package was introduced, which enabled programmers to submit jobs from within the database. The next release of PL/SQL was PL/SQL 2.3, which was introduced with Oracle 7.3. It enhanced the capabilities of PL/SQL tables with the ability to define new methods, and it also enabled programmers to access the file system from within the database. File I/O could be done using the UTL_FILE package.

Oracle 8.*x* was a major breakthrough in the Oracle database history with the introduction of objects and Java in the database. PL/SQL 8.*x* was released along with Oracle 8.*x* and included major features such as native dynamic SQL, Java stored procedures, and system- and schema-level database triggers.

Finally, Oracle9*i* was released and along with it came PL/SQL 9.2 and 9.0, corresponding to Releases 2 and 1 of Oracle9*i*. This release saw the introduction of native compilation of PL/SQL code, enhancement to PL/SQL cursors in the form of cursor expressions, new data types, enhancements to bulk binding, pipelined table functions, true inheritance among objects, and more.

Advantages of Using PL/SQL

PL/SQL is a block-structured language that enables you to encapsulate business logic in one place. This is by far the greatest advantage of PL/SQL that I've leveraged. Also, PL/SQL code runs on the server side, thus providing direct interaction with the database and the SQL engine. Other advantages of using PL/SQL are outlined in the following sections.

Procedural Capabilities

The primary advantage of PL/SQL is its capability to define and implement 3GL constructs with embedded SQL statements. Using PL/SQL, you can implement standard 3GL capabilities, such as support for BOOLEAN data types; sequential, conditional, and iterative logic; arrays and subprograms; and object-oriented features. And you can do this side by side with SQL. This support for SQL in PL/SQL makes PL/SQL powerful. The capability to define 3GL constructs is primarily beneficial when you use PL/SQL in writing applications that mix and match business logic that's complicated and necessary. Also, PL/SQL is the primary procedural language for Oracle client-side tools such as Oracle Forms and Oracle Reports.

Portability

Programs written in PL/SQL are hardware independent and operating system independent. They are highly portable and work well on any platform where an Oracle server and an integrated development environment (IDE) are installed.

Tight Integration with SQL

Oracle has integrated SQL and PL/SQL. Programs written in PL/SQL can make use of almost all SQL features such as SQL data types and the NULL construct. Also, as of Oracle9*i*, there's an integrated SQL and PL/SQL parser. This means the same parser is used for SQL and PL/SQL code, which results in more efficient performance.

Modularity

PL/SQL enables you to write programs as independent modules that you can integrate. You can implement this modularity by using features such as procedures, functions, and packages.

Better Performance

PL/SQL offers better performance for three main reasons:

1. Data type conversion isn't needed on input and output. When data is retrieved into PL/SQL variables or when data is input into Oracle using PL/SQL variables, PL/SQL takes care of the appropriate conversion between the Oracle server and PL/SQL by means of the same internal database format. Other 3GL programs written in C++ or Java to access an Oracle database are required to convert data to and from Oracle format to C++/Java format.

2. Generally, database applications run in a client-server environment are deployed in either a two-tier architecture (Oracle RDBMS on the server and the PL/SQL application on the client) or a three-tier structure (a database server layer, an application server layer on an application server, and a presentation layer on a client). With PL/SQL, you can group a set of SQL statements (along with application logic) into a PL/SQL block and you can submit the entire block over to the Oracle server. This reduces network traffic in a two-tier or three-tier application structure

and thus improves performance. This concept of block structuring also means fewer database calls, which results in better performance.

3. PL/SQL 9*i* introduces native compilation of PL/SQL code, and subsequent conversion to C and storage in machine code. This results in faster execution. Prior to Oracle9*i*, the interpreted versions of PL/SQL code, known as *p-code*, exhibited only fairly fast execution of PL/SQL.

Object Orientation

PL/SQL provides object-oriented features such as encapsulation, abstraction (the ability to define abstract data types), data and information hiding, reusability, inheritance, polymorphism, and dynamic method dispatch. Various features introduced in PL/SQL, from its earlier versions to PL/SQL 9*i*, enable object orientation to be defined and implemented in PL/SQL. I discuss these features throughout this book.

Building Blocks of PL/SQL

The basic coding element of PL/SQL is the *block*. A PL/SQL block imitates the concept of block structuring inherent in structured programming languages such as Pascal. Each block is a discrete set of code that would normally perform a certain function. A PL/SQL block also provides modularization of code into logically related units of code. A typical PL/SQL block begins with a BEGIN statement and ends with an END statement followed by a semicolon (;). There are three types of PL/SQL blocks:

1. *Anonymous block:* This is a section of code enclosed within BEGIN and END statements. It has no name associated with it.

2. *Labeled block:* This is a PL/SQL block identified by a label. It starts with a PL/SQL label followed by a BEGIN and an END statement.

3. *Named block:* This is a PL/SQL block stored in the database as a subprogram and identified by a unique name. This block is implemented by means of stored subprograms and database triggers.

Whatever the type, a PL/SQL block consists of the following sections defined within it:

- *Declaration section:* This section begins with the DECLARE keyword and contains declarations of variables, constants, cursors, and local subprograms. This section is optional for a block.

- *Executable section:* This section begins with a BEGIN statement and consists of procedural logic and SQL statements. It ends with an END statement.

- *Exception handling section:* This section begins with the EXCEPTION WHEN keywords and contains logic for handling PL/SQL and/or Oracle server errors. Although this section is optional, it's a recommended programming practice to always include an exception handling section.

A PL/SQL Block Example

Here's an example of a PL/SQL block. You should create the following table before you execute this PL/SQL block.

```
CREATE TABLE items_tab (item_code varchar2(6) PRIMARY KEY,
                       item_descr varchar2(20) NOT NULL);
```

Listing 1-1 shows the sample PL/SQL block.

Listing 1-1. A Sample PL/SQL Block

```
DECLARE
     v_item_code VARCHAR2(6);
     v_item_descr VARCHAR2(20);
BEGIN
     v_item_code := 'ITM101';
     v_item_descr := 'Spare parts';
     INSERT INTO items_tab VALUES (v_item_code, v_item_descr);
EXCEPTION WHEN OTHERS THEN
     dbms_output.put_line(SQLERRM);
END;
/
```

The program in Listing 1-1 declares two PL/SQL variables named v_item_code and v_item_descr to store the item code and description, respectively. It initializes these two variables with specific values and then inserts into the items_tab table with values held in these two variables. Any errors that occur in the process are output to the screen buffer with a corresponding error message. This is done by a call to a special procedure named dbms_output.put_line, a packaged procedure that outputs to the SQL*Plus screen with a corresponding message passed as input to it. To make this procedure work, the SQL*Plus environment variable SERVEROUTPUT should be set to ON. Here's the code to do this in SQL*Plus:

```
SQL> set serveroutput on;
```

A Nested Block Example

You can nest PL/SQL blocks, and the level of nesting is arbitrary. Listing 1-2 is an example of the PL/SQL code in Listing 1-1 modified to include a nested block.

Listing 1-2. The Modified PL/SQL Code That Uses a Nested Block

```
DECLARE
     v_item_code VARCHAR2(6);
     v_item_descr VARCHAR2(20);
     v_num NUMBER(1);
BEGIN
     v_item_code := 'ITM101';
     v_item_descr := 'Spare parts';
     BEGIN
         SELECT 1
         INTO    v_num
         FROM    items_tab
         WHERE item_code = v_item_code;
     EXCEPTION
         WHEN NO_DATA_FOUND THEN
            v_num := 0;
         WHEN OTHERS THEN
                dbms_output.put_line('Error in SELECT: '||SQLERRM);
                RETURN;
     END;
     IF (v_num = 0) THEN
        INSERT INTO items_tab VALUES (v_item_code, v_item_descr);
     END IF;
     dbms_output.put_line('Successful Completion' ) ;
EXCEPTION WHEN OTHERS THEN
     dbms_output.put_line(SQLERRM);
END;
/
```

Note the following with regard to this example PL/SQL block:

- There's an inner PL/SQL block nested in the outer PL/SQL block. This inner block begins with the second BEGIN statement.

- Each PL/SQL block starts with a BEGIN statement and ends with an END statement.

- SQL statements are embedded within 3GL constructs.

- Any PL/SQL block can have an optional declaration section. In the preceding example, the outer block has a declaration section but the inner block doesn't.

- Each PL/SQL block has its own exception handling section. It's up to the program to handle exceptions in each block. Any uncaught exceptions in the nested block propagate to the exception handler in the immediate outer block. If an exception isn't caught at all in any of the blocks, it results in an unhandled exception, and control transfers out of the program.

 TIP   *Always define an exception handling section in each PL/SQL block—even in the case of nested blocks.*

The next section highlights the various procedural constructs available in PL/SQL.

Procedural Constructs in PL/SQL

The 3GL features available in PL/SQL are as follows:

- Support of the BOOLEAN data type, reference cursor (REF CURSOR) types, and user-defined subtypes (not available in the Oracle server)

- New data types introduced in Oracle9*i* such as TIMESTAMP and INTERVAL, as well as user-defined types and conditional constructs such as IF THEN ELSE

- CASE statements and expressions (as of Oracle9*i*)

- Iterative constructs such as loops (LOOP . . . END LOOP, FOR LOOP, and WHILE LOOP), single-dimensional arrays, and records

- Collection types (nested tables and varrays)

- Subprograms such as procedures, functions, and packages

- Object-oriented features

This section covers conditional constructs, CASE statements and expressions, and iterative constructs. I discuss arrays, records, and collections, subprograms, and object-oriented features in later chapters.

Conditional Constructs

A *conditional construct* executes a set of statements based on a condition being true. It's specified by the IF statement. Here's the syntax:

```
IF (condition1) THEN
    [action1]
ELSIF (condition2) THEN
    [action2]
ELSIF (condition3) THEN
  [action3]
 . . . . . .
ELSE
  [actionN]
END IF;
```

In the preceding code, condition1, condition2, and condition3 evaluate to BOOLEAN TRUE or FALSE. If a condition evaluates to TRUE, the action under it is performed. If one condition evaluates to TRUE, the other conditions in the IF chain aren't checked.

The order in which the IF or ELSIF branches are written is important, as this determines which one of the actions is to be executed.

Here's an example of the IF statement:

```
DECLARE
    a number := 50;
    b number := -20;
BEGIN
    IF (a>b) THEN
        dbms_output.put_line('A is greater than B');
```

```
  ELSIF (a<b) THEN
      dbms_output.put_line('A is less than B');
  ELSE
      dbms_output.put_line('A is equal to B');
  END IF;
```

You can nest the IF statement. However, good programming practice recommends that you avoid nested IFs wherever possible and use ELSIF instead.

> **TIP**   *Using ELSIF instead of nested IFs wherever possible eliminates the confusion of an IF . . . ELSE mismatch, and it's less error-prone. It also improves performance because only a specific leg of the IF statement is executed in the case of ELSIF as opposed to nested IFs.*

CASE Statements and Expressions

The *CASE statement* is a conditional construct first introduced in PL/SQL 9*i*. It is an alternative to the IF statement, but it's more elegant. There are two types of CASE statements: the normal CASE statement and the searched CASE statement. Similarly, CASE expressions are analogues of CASE statements when used in an expression. I discuss them in the section "New Features of PL/SQL 9*i*" later in this chapter.

Iterative Constructs

Iterative constructs are specified by means of loops. There are three types of loops that perform repetitive control flow, namely the simple LOOP, the numeric FOR LOOP, and the WHILE LOOP. Each of these loops ends with an END LOOP ' statement.

The Simple LOOP

Here's the syntax of the simple LOOP:

```
LOOP
      [statement1]
      [statement2]
      . . . . . .
```

```
    EXIT WHEN (condition);
END LOOP;
```

In the preceding code, statement1, statement2, and so forth refer to the executable statements constituting the body of the loop, and condition refers to the EXIT condition for the loop when the control exits the loop. If the EXIT condition isn't specified, the execution would result in an infinite loop. Here's an example of the simple LOOP:

```
DECLARE
    line_length  NUMBER := 50;
    separator VARCHAR2(1) := '=';
    actual_line VARCHAR2(150);
    i NUMBER := 1;
 BEGIN
    LOOP
        actual_line := actual_line || separator;
        EXIT WHEN i = line_length;
        i:= i + 1;
    END LOOP;
    DBMS_OUTPUT.PUT_LINE(actual_line);
END;
/
```

This program displays a line made of equal signs (=) whose length equals 50.

The index of the loop has to be explicitly defined, initialized, and incremented. The body of the loop must have an explicit EXIT condition specified.

The FOR LOOP

You can write the same simple LOOP as a numeric FOR LOOP or a WHILE LOOP. The FOR LOOP has the following syntax:

```
FOR index IN initialval..finalval LOOP
    [statement1]
    [statement2]
    . . . . . .
END LOOP;
```

In the preceding code, index refers to a variable that increments the count for the duration of the loop, and initialval and finalval refer to the initial and final values that the index will take when looping. The difference between these two values plus 1 gives the number of times the control repetitively executes the statements in the body of the loop—that is, between FOR LOOP and END LOOP.

Here's the line display example written using a numeric FOR LOOP:

```
DECLARE
    line_length  NUMBER := 50;
    separator VARCHAR2(1) := '=';
    actual_line VARCHAR2(150);
BEGIN
    FOR idx in 1..line_length LOOP
        actual_line := actual_line || separator;
    END LOOP;
    DBMS_OUTPUT.PUT_LINE(actual_line);
END;
/
```

You don't need to declare the index of the FOR LOOP. Also, you don't need to initialize the index, and you need not increment the index for each iteration of the loop. You don't need an EXIT condition for the loop.

The WHILE LOOP

Next, I discuss the WHILE LOOP. Here's the syntax:

```
WHILE (condition) LOOP
    [statement1]
    [statement2]
    ... ...
END LOOP;
```

Here's the same line display example using a WHILE LOOP:

```
DECLARE
    line_length  NUMBER := 50;
    separator VARCHAR2(1) := '=';
    actual_line VARCHAR2(150);
    idx NUMBER := 1;
```

```
BEGIN
    WHILE (idx<=line_length) LOOP
        actual_line := actual_line || separator;
        idx := idx +1 ;
    END LOOP;
    DBMS_OUTPUT.PUT_LINE(actual_line);
END;
/
```

The index of the WHILE LOOP must be declared and initialized. The index should be incremented programmatically. The condition is evaluated first, and if it results to be TRUE, then only the body of the loop is executed. There's no need for an explicit EXIT condition for the loop.

PL/SQL Environments

To develop and execute 3GL programs, you need a development environment in which you can write and execute the programs. This is called an *integrated development environment,* or IDE. Most popular 3GLs such as Java, C++, and so forth provide such IDEs as IBM's Visual Age for Java, Visual C++, and so on.

There are typically three types of environments necessary for any programming language, and PL/SQL is no exception:

1. Development environment

2. Execution environment

3. Debugging environment

Oracle provides two major development environments for the development and execution of PL/SQL programs: SQL*Plus and Procedure Builder. These IDEs not only enable development and execution, but they also assist in debugging PL/SQL programs. However, the interface for each of these environments is different. Both are interactive, with Procedure Builder providing a greater degree of debugging functionality.

Figure 1-1 shows an example of the SQL*Plus environment.

```
Oracle SQL*Plus                                              _ □ x
File  Edit  Search  Options  Help

SQL*Plus: Release 9.2.0.1.0 - Production on Mon Oct 7 21:31:19 2002

Copyright (c) 1982, 2002, Oracle Corporation.  All rights reserved.


Connected to:
Oracle9i Enterprise Edition Release 9.2.0.1.0 - Production
With the Partitioning, OLAP and Oracle Data Mining options
JServer Release 9.2.0.1.0 - Production

SQL> set serverout on;
SQL> DECLARE
  2     line_length NUMBER :=50;
  3     separator VARCHAR2(1):='=';
  4     actual_line VARCHAR2(150);
  5  BEGIN
  6    FOR idx in 1..line_length LOOP
  7       actual_line :=actual_line ||separator;
  8    END LOOP;
  9    DBMS_OUTPUT.PUT_LINE(actual_line);
 10  END;
 11  /
=====================================================

PL/SQL procedure successfully completed.

SQL> |
```

*Figure 1-1. The SQL*Plus development and execution environment*

Oracle Procedure Builder is more of a GUI tool and has a more powerful debugging capability than SQL*Plus. For instance, you can set breakpoints and you can define the functions of step in, step into, and step out to debug a PL/SQL subprogram. Figures 1-2 and 1-3 show the typical Procedure Builder development and debugging environments, respectively. The debugging environment has certain breakpoints to track the execution of programs. *Breakpoints* are points of control in a PL/SQL program where execution of the program pauses and the user can interactively know the value of runtime variables and decide whether to halt execution by stepping out of the program or resume execution by stepping into the code.

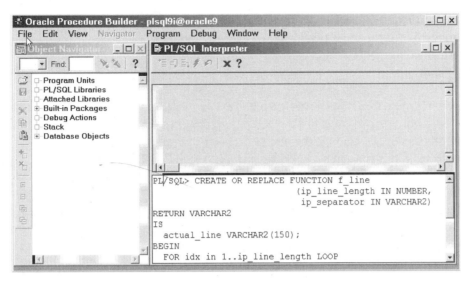

Figure 1-2. The Procedure Builder development and execution environment

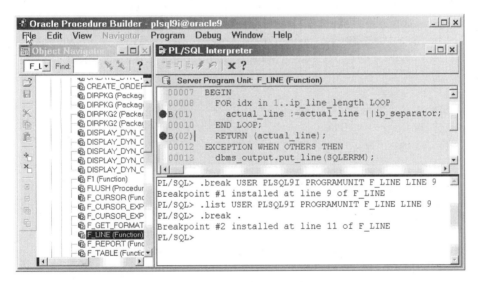

Figure 1-3. The Procedure Builder debugging environment

New Features of PL/SQL 9*i*

A number of new features have been added to PL/SQL in Oracle9*i*. Some are new features of the language itself, some are enhancements made to existing features, and still others are added functionality with regard to how PL/SQL has been implemented. This section presents in some detail the major new features of

PL/SQL 9*i* and broadly categorizes them into two groups: namely, non-object-oriented features and object-oriented features. Details of each feature are explained throughout the book.

Non-Object-Oriented Features Exclusive to PL/SQL 9i

In this section, I introduce the new non-object-oriented features of PL/SQL 9*i* such as CASE statements and expressions, searched CASE statements and expressions, cursor expressions, native compilation of PL/SQL code, data manipulation language (DML) operations (specifically, INSERT, UPDATE, and SELECT) involving entire PL/SQL records (as of Oracle9*i* Release 2), associative arrays (as of Oracle9*i* Release 2), new PL/SQL packages and enhancements to existing packages, new SQL features in PL/SQL, and miscellaneous enhancements.

CASE Statement

Oracle9*i* introduces the CASE statement as an improved alternative to the IF . . . ELSIF . . . statement. The use of CASE statement provides more compact code and increased usability on the part of the programmer, and increased readability on the part of the code reviewer. Here's the syntax of the CASE statement:

```
CASE    selector
   WHEN value1 THEN action1;
   WHEN value2 THEN action2;
   WHEN value3 THEN action3;
   . . . . . .
   ELSE        actionN;
END CASE;
```

In the preceding code, selector is a variable or expression, and value1, value2, and value3 are the values of the selector. The selector is evaluated only once. In the case of a CASE statement, this is immediately evident to the compiler, as the selector is specified only once in the beginning.

The order in which the WHEN branches are written is important, as it determines which one of the actions is to be executed.

Here's an example of a CASE statement:

```
CASE report_choice
     WHEN 1 THEN p_proc_report1;
     WHEN 2 THEN p_proc_report2;
     WHEN 3 THEN p_proc_report3;
```

```
    WHEN 4 THEN p_proc_report4;
    ELSE  dbms_output.put_line('Invalid option.');
END CASE;
```

In the preceding example, depending on the value of the report_choice variable, the corresponding procedure is executed. The same code segment written as an IF . . . ELSIF chain would have the condition repeated for each choice, as shown here:

```
IF (report_choice=1) THEN
    p_proc_report1;
ELSIF (report_choice=2) THEN
    p_proc_report2;
ELSIF (report_choice=3) THEN
    p_proc_report3;
ELSIF (report_choice=4) THEN
    p_proc_report4;
ELSE
    dbms_output.put_line('Invalid option.');
END IF;
```

This method is more error-prone than the CASE statement.

CASE Expression

You can use the CASE construct in an expression and assigned it to a variable to generate a value. Here's the syntax of the CASE expression:

```
var := CASE selector
    WHEN value1 THEN assigned_value1
    WHEN value2 THEN assigned_value2
    WHEN value3 THEN assigned_value3
    . . . . . .
    ELSE assigned_valueN;
END CASE;
```

In the preceding code, var is a declared variable that receives a value. value1, value2, and value3 are the values of the selector, and assigned_value1, assigned_value2, assigned_value3, and assigned_valueN are the values that are assigned to the variable var depending on the value of the selector.

As an example, consider the following code segment, which is part of a program that converts digits to words:

```
temp := CASE i
                        WHEN 0 THEN 'Zero'
                        WHEN 1 THEN 'One'
                        WHEN 2 THEN 'Two'
                        WHEN 3 THEN 'Three'
                        WHEN 4 THEN 'Four'
                        WHEN 5 THEN 'Five'
                        WHEN 6 THEN 'Six'
                        WHEN 7 THEN 'Seven'
                        WHEN 8 THEN 'Eight'
                        WHEN 9 THEN 'Nine'
                        ELSE
                               NULL
                    END;
```

Searched CASE Statement

The searched CASE statement is a variant of the CASE statement and has no
selector defined. Instead of testing on the equality of the selector, the searched
CASE statement tests a boolean expression for a truth value. Here's the syntax of
the searched CASE statement:

```
CASE
  WHEN (boolean_condition1) THEN action1;
  WHEN (boolean_condition2) THEN action2;
  WHEN (boolean_condition3) THEN action3;
  . . . . . .
  ELSE          actionN;
END CASE;
```

Here's an example of the previously presented CASE statement rewritten
using the searched CASE statement:

```
CASE
      WHEN (report_choice = 1) THEN p_proc_report1;
      WHEN (report_choice = 2) THEN p_proc_report2;
      WHEN (report_choice = 3) THEN p_proc_report3;
      WHEN (report_choice = 4) THEN p_proc_report4;
      ELSE  dbms_output.put_line('Invalid option.');
END CASE;
```

TIP *Always specify the ELSE part explicitly when you use a searched CASE statement.*

Searched CASE Expression

The searched CASE expression is a variant of the CASE expression, and it omits the selector. Like the searched CASE statement, it tests for the truth value of a boolean condition instead of the equality of a single selector common for all WHEN clauses. It's used in assignment statements. Here's the example of the previously presented CASE expression rewritten using a searched CASE expression:

```
temp := CASE
                WHEN (i=0) THEN 'Zero'
                WHEN (i=1) THEN 'One'
                WHEN (i=2) THEN 'Two'
                WHEN (i=3) THEN 'Three'
                WHEN (i=4) THEN 'Four'
                WHEN (i=5) THEN 'Five'
                WHEN (i=6) THEN 'Six'
                WHEN (i=7) THEN 'Seven'
                WHEN (i=8) THEN 'Eight'
                WHEN (i=9) THEN 'Nine'
                ELSE
                        NULL
        END;
```

Searched CASE expressions are more powerful than ordinary CASE expressions because you can use them to evaluate multiple conditions involving multiple variables rather than basing conditions on a single variable. For instance, consider the example of comparing two numbers as greater than, less than, or equal to that I presented earlier in the chapter when I covered IF statements. You can implement this comparison more elegantly using a searched CASE expression. Here's the corresponding code (you should set the SERVEROUTPUT environment variable to ON before executing this code):

```
declare
  a number := 20;
  b number := -40;
  string varchar2(50);
```

```
begin
  string := case
              when (a>b) then 'A is greater than B'
              when (a<b) then 'A is less than B'
            else
              'A is equal to B'
            end;
  dbms_output.put_line(string);
end;
/
```

Here's the output of this program:

```
A is greater than B
PL/SQL procedure successfully completed.
```

Cursor Expressions

Oracle9*i* has incorporated the facility to nest cursors in PL/SQL cursor declarations in the form of *cursor expressions*. Cursor expressions eliminate the use of declaring and using multiple cursors, and hence result in a more effective optimization scheme by the SQL engine (only one SQL statement) than in the case of multiple cursors (multiple SQL statements). Also, cursor expressions eliminate the use of the complicated joins involved in SQL SELECT statements. As a third benefit, Oracle9*i* removes the limitation of using cursor expressions in SQL embedded in PL/SQL code. Now you can use cursor expressions as part of PL/SQL cursors. Also, when you use dynamic SQL, you can use and fetch cursor expressions into REF cursor variables. In this case, they support the complex binds and defines needed for REF cursors. This is not supported by DBMS_SQL.

 CROSS-REFERENCE   *I discuss cursor expressions in detail in Chapter 2.*

Native Compilation of PL/SQL Code

PL/SQL 9*i* allows native compilation of PL/SQL packages, procedures, and functions, and the subsequent conversion to native C code and storage in machine code. The PL/SQL is translated into C code rather than p-code, which is in interpreted mode, and it's compiled using the C compiler on the given platform and then linked directly into Oracle processes. When the particular stored subprogram is invoked, the natively compiled program is mapped to the Program Global Area (PGA). This native compilation of PL/SQL code is most effective when you're writing compute-intensive PL/SQL subprograms that perform database-independent tasks. In this case, native compilation results in faster execution of PL/SQL.

DML Operations Involving Entire PL/SQL Records

PL/SQL 9*i* as of Oracle9*i*, Release 2 allows the INSERT and UPDATE operations involving entire PL/SQL records. Instead of specifying a list of individual record attributes, you can insert records into the database using a single variable of type RECORD or %ROWTYPE. The same is allowed for the UPDATE operation. Also, you can do bulk binding operations involving SELECT, FETCH, INSERT, UPDATE, and RETURNING INTO using a single variable of type PL/SQL table of records instead of specifying individual PL/SQL tables for each SQL column.

CROSS-REFERENCE   *I discuss enhancements related to DML operations involving entire PL/SQL records further in Chapter 3.*

Associative Arrays

In line with index-by tables, Oracle9*i* Release 2 enables definition of index-by tables that are indexed by VARCHAR2 values instead of BINARY_INTEGER. The VARCHAR2 index serves as a primary key of a database table and improves performance by enabling fast lookup of individual array elements, eliminating the need for you to know the position of the individual element, and avoiding looping through all array elements.

CROSS-REFERENCE   *I discuss associative arrays in detail in Chapter 3.*

New PL/SQL Packages and Enhancements to the Existing Packages

PL/SQL 9*i* incorporates a lot of new packages and provides enhancements to existing packages. The new packages deserving mention are dbms_xmlgen, which you use to create an XML document from any SQL query (in the form of a character large object, or CLOB), and dbms_metadata, which has the application programming interface (API) for extracting complete definitions of database objects in XML format or as SQL data definition language (DDL). Other new packages are as follows:

dbms_transform

dbms_xmlquery

dbms_xmlsave

dbms_aqelm

dbms_encode

dbms_fga

dbms_flashback

dbms_ldap

dbms_libcache

dbms_logmnr_cdc_publish

dbms_logmnr_cdc_subscribe

dbms_odci

dbms_outln_edit

dbms_redefinition

dbms_url

dbms_wm

dbms_types

utl_encode

In addition, Oracle9*i* has three new special SQL data types that enable dynamic encapsulation of and access to type descriptions, data instances, and sets of data instances of any other SQL type, including object and collection types. In addition, you can use these three special types to create anonymous (i.e., unnamed) types, including anonymous collection types. The three special types are SYS.ANYTYPE, SYS.ANYDATA, and SYS.ANYDATASET.

Of the enhanced packages, the UTL_FILE package, which provides the API for file input/output (I/O), also has some enhancements with regard to enabling opening, reading, and writing files in Unicode format. And as of Oracle9*i* Release 2, the UTL_FILE package has the API to read and write binary data and perform functions on files such as autoflush, seek, delete, copy, and rename from within PL/SQL. The UTL_HTTP package has new features to support authentication, cookies, and sending large messages and persistent connections.

New SQL Features Available in PL/SQL

The new SQL features, such as the new date/time data types TIMESTAMP and INTERVAL (and their variants), the MERGE statement, and the nullif and coalesce functions, are automatically available for use in PL/SQL 9*i*.

You can use TIMESTAMP with two variants such as TIMESTAMP WITH TIME ZONE and TIMESTAMP WITH LOCAL TIME ZONE. TIMESTAMP offers a higher level of granularity in the time component in addition to the capability to deal with time zones. You can use INTERVAL with two variants: INTERVAL YEAR TO MONTH and INTERVAL DAY TO SECOND. Also, Oracle9*i* has defined a set of built-in functions associated with TIMESTAMP and INTERVAL, and you can invoke all of these functions in PL/SQL.

The MERGE statement enables you to combine the insert and update functions into a single operation.

Miscellaneous Enhancements

Other new features (in addition to the ones I described in the previous sections) that are significant to SQL and/or PL/SQL performance and usability are as follows:

- *Integration of the SQL and PL/SQL parser:* The integration of SQL and PL/SQL is tighter with SQL and PL/SQL sharing a parser. This enables features implemented in SQL to be automatically available in PL/SQL.

- *Reduced overhead of calling PL/SQL subprograms from SQL:* This enables faster execution of SQL that references PL/SQL subprograms.

- *Seamless integration of CLOB with VARCHAR2:* Assignment of VARCHAR2 to CLOB and using string functions on CLOB and NCLOB are now possible in PL/SQL 9*i*. Also, 9*i* now provides implicit data conversion between VARCHAR2 and NVARCHAR2.

- *Autogeneration of PL/SQL call specs for Java stored procedures while loading Java classes into the database:* This feature is available as of Oracle9*i* Release 2. I discuss this feature further in Chapter 13.

Object-Oriented Features Exclusive to PL/SQL 9i

This section introduces the new object-oriented features of PL/SQL 9*i*, such as bulk dynamic SQL and exception handling with bulk binding, pipelined table functions, multilevel collections, object type inheritance and dynamic method dispatch, and SQLJ object types and type evolution. It also presents the new feature of user-defined constructors and a new API to load large objects from external files, which are introduced in Oracle9*i* Release 2.

Bulk Dynamic SQL and Exception Handling with Bulk Binding

Oracle9*i* PL/SQL allows *dynamic bulk binding,* which is the use of the BULK COLLECT construct for SELECT statements, the FORALL . . .USING construct for INSERT, and the UPDATE and DELETE statements with the EXECUTE IMMEDIATE construct so that bulk binding can be done with native dynamic SQL in PL/SQL. Dynamic bulk binding is also supported for implicit query in a DML statement via the RETURNING keyword.

A second new feature of PL/SQL 9*i* is the capability to bulk fetch from a cursor variable using native dynamic SQL.

Oracle9*i* introduces the SAVE EXCEPTIONS clause with bulk binding to enable continuation of the bulk binding operation in case of row-wise exceptions. For example, in the case of a FORALL statement, the error information pertaining to the exception resulting rows is saved and execution continues. This clause is also available in native dynamic SQL.

CROSS-REFERENCE   *I explain the concepts of bulk dynamic SQL and exception handling with bulk binding in detail in Chapter 9.*

Pipelined Table Functions

A *table function* is a PL/SQL function that returns a resultset and can be called in the FROM clause of a SQL SELECT clause. Prior to Oracle9*i*, PL/SQL supported table functions but in an elementary form in that they could return only collections of schema-level types and not PL/SQL types. Also, you had to use the CAST operator in the syntax of calling a table function. In addition, the entire collection had to be materialized before it could be used. As of PL/SQL 9*i*, a table function can

- Return a PL/SQL type (i.e., a packaged PL/SQL type) based on a table of records.

- Be pipelined so that rows of data can be returned incrementally rather than waiting for the function to execute completely and an entire set of rows to be stored in memory. The entire collection need not be instantiated in memory. This results in better response time and less memory consumption.

- Be passed from one table function to the next in a pipelined fashion without the need to store data in intermediate tables.

- Be parallelized for execution, which improves speed and scalability.

CROSS-REFERENCE   *I further discuss table functions in Chapter 11.*

Multilevel Collections

PL/SQL 9*i* introduces the concept of *nested collections*, or collections of collections. The level of nesting can be to an arbitrary depth. This is true for both schema-level collection types and PL/SQL collection types. Also, relational tables can now have multilevel collection columns. Multilevel collections constitute part of the features that provide object-model completeness in Oracle9*i* Object-Relational Technology.

CROSS-REFERENCE   *Chapter 11 covers multilevel collections.*

Object Type Inheritance and Dynamic Method Dispatch

PL/SQL 9*i* supports object type inheritance as part of the object-model completeness features in Oracle9*i* Object-Relational Technology. *Object type inheritance* refers to the capability to organize objects as types, and types as type hierarchies. The hierarchy so formed constitutes a supertype/subtype hierarchy with subtypes inheriting attributes (data) and methods (behavior) from their supertypes. In fact, a subtype inherits all of the attributes and methods from all its supertypes in the resulting object type hierarchy and not just the immediate subtype.

Inheritance leads to substitutability and dynamic method dispatch, or dynamic polymorphism as it is often called. PL/SQL 9*i* also supports *substitutability,* which is the capability to use the value of a subtype where a supertype is expected. It also supports *dynamic method dispatch,* which is the capability to determine at runtime and execute the most specific method in the object hierarchy that corresponds to the instance of the object type that invokes the method.

CROSS-REFERENCE   *Chapter 10 examines object type inheritance and dynamic method dispatch in detail.*

SQLJ Object Types and Type Evolution

Oracle9*i* now supports features for operational completeness, such as Java object persistence with SQLJ object types and type evolution. *SQLJ object types* are SQL object types of the Java language. You can use these types wherever you can use a SQL object type such as the type of an object table, an attribute of a type, or a column of an object-relational table. You can query and manipulate using SQL schema objects of SQLJ object types.

Type evolution refers to the capability to change the attributes and methods of an existing object type without having to re-create the type and its data, and all of its dependent types. You can add attributes and methods to and drop attributes and methods from existing object types. In addition, the changes you make can be explicitly propagated to the dependent types and tables.

CROSS-REFERENCE   *I discuss SQLJ object types and type evolution further in Chapter 10.*

These new PL/SQL features together with the existing ones provide better performance and functionality for applications designed and developed using PL/SQL 9*i* as well as improved usability for the PL/SQL programmer.

User-Defined Constructors

As of Oracle9*i* Release 2, the introduction of *user-defined constructors* for object types allows you to override the default constructor for object types with a customized function.

CROSS-REFERENCE   *Chapter 10 covers user-defined constructors.*

New API to Load Large Objects from External Files

Oracle9*i* Release 2 introduces two functions to load binary and character data into binary large objects (BLOBs) and character large objects (CLOBs) from external files. These functions have been added to the PL/SQL API package DBMS_LOB and are as follows:

- *DBMS_LOB.LOADBLOBFROMFILE:* Loads binary data from a binary file (BFILE) into a BLOB

- *DBMS_LOB.LOADCLOBFROMFILE:* Loads character data from a BFILE into a CLOB

 CROSS-REFERENCE   *Chapter 12 covers DBMS_LOB.LOADBLOBFROMFILE and DBMS_LOB.LOADCLOBFROMFILE in detail.*

Summary

This chapter gave you a brief introduction to PL/SQL and its elements. I discussed the pros and cons of using PL/SQL as a 3GL in an Oracle environment, and I outlined two PL/SQL environments. Finally, I presented the new features of PL/SQL 9*i*.

The next chapter discusses cursors and related features in detail.

Part Two

Non-Object-Oriented

Features in PL/SQL 9i

CHAPTER 2

Cursors

THINK OF THIS CHAPTER as Cursors 101 and 201 combined. I start with a quick overview of cursors and how to use them in PL/SQL. Next, I cover the methods for processing multirow resultsets with cursors. Then I tackle cursor variables and their uses, and I wrap up with a discussion of Oracle9*i*'s new cursor expressions.

I illustrate the concept of cursors, cursor variables, and cursor expressions by taking into account an organizational hierarchy system. The case study I present uses the data model shown in Figure 2-1. The schema objects to be created are listed in Appendix A.

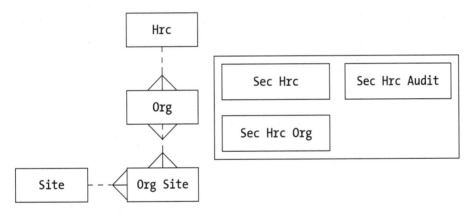

Figure 2-1. The data model of an organizational hierarchy system

Introducing Cursors

As described in Chapter 1, PL/SQL interacts with SQL by combining SQL statements with PL/SQL constructs inside a PL/SQL block. Cursors are one more PL/SQL feature that exhibits interaction with SQL by using SQL within PL/SQL. A *cursor* is a handle to a work area that holds the resultset of a multirow SQL query. Oracle opens a work area to hold the resultset of multirow queries. A cursor gives this work area a name and can be used to process the rows returned by the multirow query.

There are two types of cursors: explicit and implicit. The cursors defined earlier for handling multirow resultsets are called *explicit* cursors. *Implicit* cursors are those defined by Oracle and are associated with single-row SELECT . . . INTO statements and INSERT, UPDATE, and DELETE statements. These statements are also executed within the context of a work area and the Oracle PL/SQL engine automatically opens a cursor that points to this work area. This work area identifies the rows to be modified with the INSERT, UPDATE, DELETE, or SELECT . . . INTO statement. There's no need to declare the cursor explicitly, hence the name "implicit."

This section begins with a discussion of explicit cursors and then moves on to cover implicit cursors in detail.

Explicit Cursors

In an explicit cursor's definition, the cursor name is explicitly associated with a SELECT statement. This is done using the PL/SQL CURSOR . . . IS SELECT . . . statement. Explicit cursors can be associated with a SELECT statement only.

You can use an explicit cursor to process multirow queries, including queries that fetch one row.

Defining an Explicit Cursor

You declare an explicit cursor using the CURSOR . . . IS SELECT . . . statement in PL/SQL. Here's the syntax:

```
CURSOR cursor_name IS
    SELECT_statement ;
```

where cursor_name is the name of the cursor and SELECT_statement is any valid SQL SELECT statement without the INTO clause.

When you use a PL/SQL block, you need to declare an explicit cursor in the declaration section after the DECLARE keyword. The following is an example of an explicit cursor:

```
DECLARE
    CURSOR csr_org IS
        SELECT h.hrc_descr, o.org_short_name
        FROM   org_tab o, hrc_tab h
        WHERE o.hrc_code = h.hrc_code
         ORDER by 2;
         v_hrc_descr VARCHAR2(20);
```

```
            v_org_short_name VARCHAR2(30);
    BEGIN
      /* ... <Process the cursor resultset> ... */
      null;
    END;
  /
```

When naming a cursor, you should follow the standard PL/SQL variable naming conventions. Other declarations can follow or precede a CURSOR declaration. The order of declaring cursors and other variables is immaterial. The SELECT statement associated with a cursor can't contain an INTO clause. It may, however, have GROUP BY and ORDER clauses, as well as joins and set operators such as UNION, INTERSECT, and MINUS. The scope of a cursor is the PL/SQL block in which it is defined or any of its nested blocks. Enclosing (outer) blocks can't reference a cursor defined within them.

Using an Explicit Cursor

Once you've defined a cursor, you can use it for processing the rows contained in the resultset. Here are the steps:

1. Open the cursor.

2. Fetch the results into a PL/SQL record or individual PL/SQL variables.

3. Close the cursor.

There are two ways to use an explicit cursor once it has been defined: using OPEN, FETCH, and CLOSE, and using a cursor FOR LOOP. You can do this in the executable section of a PL/SQL block in between BEGIN and END.

Using OPEN, FETCH, and CLOSE

After declaring the cursor, you have to open it as follows:

```
OPEN cursor_name;
```

where cursor_name is the name of the declared cursor.

Here's an example that illustrates opening the cursor csr_org declared previously:

```
DECLARE
    CURSOR csr_org IS
        SELECT h.hrc_descr, o.org_short_name
        FROM   org_tab o, hrc_tab h
        WHERE o.hrc_code = h.hrc_code
         ORDER by 2;
         v_hrc_descr VARCHAR2(20);
         v_org_short_name VARCHAR2(30);
  BEGIN
      OPEN csr_org;
     /* ... <Process the cursor resultset> ... */
    null;
  END;
/
```

Once opened, the resultset returned by the associated SELECT statement is determined and fixed. This is often termed the *active set* of rows. Also, the cursor pointer points to the first row in the active set.

CAUTION   *Don't open an already opened cursor. This raises the predefined PL/SQL exception CURSOR_ALREADY_OPEN.*

The next step is to fetch the cursor into PL/SQL variables. This retrieves individual rows of data into the PL/SQL variables for processing. You fetch a cursor using the FETCH statement, which has four forms. Here's the syntax:

```
FETCH cursor_name INTO var1, var2, ... , varN;
```

or

```
FETCH cursor_name INTO cursor_name%ROWTYPE;
```

or

```
FETCH cursor_name INTO table_name%ROWTYPE;
```

or

```
FETCH cursor_name INTO record_name;
```

Here, var1, var2, and varN represent PL/SQL variables having data types identical to the cursor SELECT columns. cursor_name%ROWTYPE represents a PL/SQL record type with attributes implicitly defined that are identical to the cursor SELECT. In this case, the record type needs to be defined explicitly. table_name%ROWTYPE represents a similar record type, but one that has attributes as the column names of the table identified by table_name. In this case, the columns in table_name should exactly match in number and data type the columns in the cursor SELECT statement. Lastly, record_name is a variable of a PL/SQL record type that's explicitly defined. In this case also, the number and data types of the individual attributes of the record should be a one-to-one match with the columns in the cursor SELECT.

Here's an example that extends the previous example of csr_org to fetching rows:

```
DECLARE
    CURSOR csr_org IS
        SELECT h.hrc_descr, o.org_short_name
        FROM    org_tab o, hrc_tab h
        WHERE o.hrc_code = h.hrc_code
        ORDER by 2;
        v_hrc_descr VARCHAR2(20);
        v_org_short_name VARCHAR2(30);
  BEGIN
      OPEN csr_org;
      FETCH csr_org INTO v_hrc_descr, v_org_short_name;
     -- This fetch fetches the first row in the active set.
      null;
  END;
/
```

Here, the first row in the active set is fetched into two PL/SQL variables named v_hrc_descr and v_org_short_name. Once the first row in the active set is fetched, it's up to the program to process the data in whatever manner desired.

Alternatively, you can declare a record variable of type cursor_name%ROWTYPE and then fetch the cursor into it. This is recommended and eliminates the use of multiple variables. Here's an example:

```
DECLARE
    CURSOR csr_org IS
        SELECT h.hrc_descr, o.org_short_name
        FROM    org_tab o, hrc_tab h
        WHERE o.hrc_code = h.hrc_code
        ORDER by 2;
```

```
            v_org_rec csr_org%ROWTYPE;
     BEGIN
        OPEN csr_org;
        FETCH csr_org INTO v_org_rec;
        -- This fetch fetches the first row in the active set.
        null;
     END;
   /
```

In this case, you can access the individual columns in the record type using the same column names as in the CURSOR SELECT statement.

Note that a single FETCH fetches only one row at a time. The first FETCH statement fetches the very first row, the second FETCH statement fetches the second row, and so on. To fetch all the rows, you have to use a single FETCH statement in a loop. Each iteration of FETCH advances the cursor pointer to the next row. Once fetched, the individual rows can be processed in whatever manner desired. You can fetch sets of rows at one time by repeating the definition of the FETCH statement. For example, to fetch two rows at a time, just repeat the FETCH statement twice.

TIP   *A single FETCH always fetches only one row (the current row) from the active set. To fetch multiple rows, use the FETCH statement in a loop.*

You can fetch a cursor only after you open it. The number and data types of the individual variables should exactly match the columns list in the cursor SELECT statement. In the case when the cursor is fetched into a record type (either cursor_name%ROWTYPE, table_name%ROWTYPE, or record_name), the number and data type of each attribute in the record should exactly match the columns list of the cursor SELECT statement.

CAUTION   *Don't fetch from an already closed cursor. Doing so results in an "ORA-01001: invalid cursor" error or an "ORA-01002: Fetch out of sequence" error.*

 h into a record type of
WTYPE, or, at least fetch into a record type
e cursor SELECT rather than into indi-
is is less error-prone and also improves

completed, you have to close the cursor.
e cursor, such as the memory required for
using the CLOSE statement. Here's the

ys close an opened cursor. If you don't
a "too many open cursors" error. The
en cursors is determined by the
rameter open_cursors. The default
in Oracle9i is 50. Don't close an

nt should always appear after the
u use a loop to fetch the rows
sert the CLOSE statement after
e, it results in an illegal fetch.

not, you have to use *cursor attri-*
"Explicit Cursor Attributes."
_org cursor involving all the steps

```
    ARE
/* Declare a cursor explicitly */
    CURSOR csr_org IS
        SELECT h.hrc_descr, o.org_short_name
```

```
                FROM    org_tab o, hrc_tab h
                WHERE o.hrc_code = h.hrc_code
                 ORDER by 2;
                  v_org_rec csr_org%ROWTYPE;
        BEGIN
            /* Open the cursor */
            OPEN csr_org;
            /* Format headings */
            dbms_output.put_line('Organization Details with Hierarchy');
            dbms_output.put_line('-----------------------');
            dbms_output.put_line(rpad('Hierarchy',20,' ')||' '||
                                            rpad('Organization',30,' '));
            dbms_output.put_line(rpad('-',20,'-')||' '||rpad('-',30,'-'));
            /* Fetch from the cursor resultset in a loop and display the results
*/
            LOOP
                FETCH csr_org INTO v_org_rec;
                EXIT WHEN csr_org%NOTFOUND;
                dbms_output.put_line(rpad(v_org_rec.hrc_descr,20,' ')||' '||
                            rpad(v_org_rec.org_short_name,30,' '));
            END LOOP;
        /* CLose the cursor */
            CLOSE csr_org;
    END;
    /
```

Here's the output of this program:

```
Organization Details with Hierarchy
-----------------------------------------------
Hierarchy            Organization
------------------   ---------------------------
CEO/COO              Office of CEO ABC Inc.
CEO/COO              Office of CEO DataPro Inc.
CEO/COO              Office of CEO XYZ Inc.
VP                   Office of VP Mktg ABC Inc.
VP                   Office of VP Sales ABC Inc.
VP                   Office of VP Tech ABC Inc.

PL/SQL procedure successfully completed.
```

The code in this program opens the cursor, fetches the rows one by one until no more rows are found, displays the information in a formatted manner, and then closes the cursor. The one thing to note here is the EXIT condition for the cursor loop. This is determined by a cursor attribute %NOTFOUND, which is defined in the statement

```
EXIT WHEN csr_org%NOTFOUND;
```

%NOTFOUND returns a boolean true when the last row has been fetched and there are no more rows left in the active set. This tells PL/SQL to stop executing the fetch loop and exit the cursor loop. Fetching past the last row results in an "ORA-01002: Fetch out of sequence" error.

> **TIP**   *Always check for the attribute %NOTFOUND* immediately after *the FETCH statement to terminate a cursor FETCH loop normally. When you use multiple FETCH statements to fetch a row set at a time, specify the EXIT WHEN cursor_name%NOTFOUND condition* immediately after every FETCH statement. *This ensures avoidance of the ORA-01002 error.*

The program in this example used a simple LOOP . . . END LOOP to fetch rows from a cursor. This serves the purpose very well. However, a WHILE LOOP can replace the simple LOOP if desired. Using a WHILE LOOP, however, demands greater caution in using the FETCH statement and specifying the EXIT condition for the loop. Here are the rules of the thumb to keep in mind when you use WHILE LOOP for FETCHing:

- FETCH once before the beginning of the LOOP.

- Specify a condition of cursor_name%FOUND as the condition of the WHILE LOOP.

- Inside the loop, process the row first and then include a second FETCH after the processing logic.

- Don't specify an EXIT condition after the FETCH statement inside the LOOP, such as EXIT WHEN . . .

Here's the same example presented previously rewritten using a WHILE fetch loop:

```
DECLARE
    CURSOR csr_org IS
            SELECT h.hrc_descr, o.org_short_name
            FROM   org_tab o, hrc_tab h
            WHERE o.hrc_code = h.hrc_code
             ORDER by 2;
             v_org_rec csr_org%ROWTYPE;
    BEGIN
        OPEN csr_org;
        dbms_output.put_line('Organization Details with Hierarchy');
        dbms_output.put_line('------------------------');
        dbms_output.put_line(rpad('Hierarchy',20,' ')||' '||
                                            rpad('Organization',30,' '));
        dbms_output.put_line(rpad('-',20,'-')||' '||rpad('-',30,'-'));
        FETCH csr_org INTO v_org_rec;
        WHILE (csr_org%FOUND) LOOP
                dbms_output.put_line(rpad(v_org_rec.hrc_descr,20,' ')||' '||
                                            rpad(v_org_rec.org_short_name,30,' '));
                FETCH csr_org INTO v_org_rec;
        END LOOP;
        CLOSE csr_org;
    END;
/
```

The following points are worth noting:

- The first FETCH before the beginning of the WHILE LOOP is necessary to make sure the condition for the WHILE LOOP evaluates to TRUE. You do this by using the %FOUND cursor attribute, which evaluates to TRUE if at least one row is present in the active set.

- If the active set contains no rows, the WHILE LOOP isn't executed. This is in contrast to a simple LOOP . . . END LOOP, where the control enters the loop even before the first fetch.

- The processing of the data fetched by the first FETCH (outside the WHILE LOOP) is done first and then the successive row(s) are fetched.

- There is no need for an EXIT condition after the second FETCH (inside the loop).

Using a Cursor FOR LOOP

You can also use a declared cursor using a cursor FOR LOOP instead of explicitly using OPEN, FETCH, and CLOSE. A cursor FOR LOOP takes care of cursor processing using an implicit OPEN FETCH and CLOSE. Here are the steps:

1. Declare a cursor FOR LOOP. Here's an example:

```
FOR idx in cursor_name LOOP
 . . .
 . . .
END LOOP;
```

Here, cursor_name is the name of the cursor and idx is the index of the cursor FOR LOOP and is of type cursor_name%ROWTYPE.

 TIP   *Using a cursor FOR LOOP doesn't make the cursor an implicit cursor. It's still an explicit cursor and has to be declared explicitly.*

2. Process the data in the active set. Here's the example of the csr_org cursor modified using a cursor FOR LOOP:

```
DECLARE
    CURSOR csr_org IS
        SELECT h.hrc_descr, o.org_short_name
        FROM   org_tab o, hrc_tab h
        WHERE o.hrc_code = h.hrc_code
         ORDER by 2;
BEGIN
        dbms_output.put_line('Organization Details with Hierarchy');
        dbms_output.put_line('------------------------');
        dbms_output.put_line(rpad('Hierarchy',20,' ')||' '||
                                        rpad('Organization',30,' '));
        dbms_output.put_line(rpad('-',20,'-')||' '||rpad('-',30,'-'));
        FOR idx IN csr_org LOOP
                dbms_output.put_line(rpad(idx.hrc_descr,20,' ')||' '||
```

```
                                      rpad(idx.org_short_name,30,' '));
                END LOOP;
        END;
        /
```

The following points are worth noting:

- The index of the cursor FOR LOOP isn't declared. It's implicitly declared by the PL/SQL compiler as type csr_org%ROWTYPE.

> **TIP**   *Never declare the index of a cursor FOR LOOP.*

- You can access the individual columns in the cursor SELECT using the "." (dot) notation of accessing record type attributes by succeeding the index name with a dot followed by the column name in the cursor SELECT.

- There is no need to OPEN, FETCH, and CLOSE the cursor.

> **TIP**   *An important use of the cursor FOR LOOP is when you process* all *the rows in a cursor unconditionally. This is a recommended practice and is in contrast to the conventional method of OPEN, FETCH, and CLOSE, which is used to process some of the rows or to skip some rows on a certain condition.*

Avoiding Declaration of an Explicit Cursor with a Cursor FOR LOOP

In the earlier example, although the cursor FOR LOOP was used, the cursor csr_org was still declared in the declaration section of the PL/SQL block. However, you can wholly specify the cursor SELECT in the specification of the cursor FOR LOOP itself instead of an explicit declaration. This improves readability and is less error-prone. Here's the csr_org cursor rewritten in this way:

```
BEGIN
        FOR idx in (SELECT h.hrc_descr, o.org_short_name
                        FROM   org_tab o, hrc_tab h
                        WHERE o.hrc_code = h.hrc_code ORDER by 2) LOOP
                dbms_output.put_line(rpad(idx.hrc_descr,20,' ')||' '||
                                rpad(idx.org_short_name,30,' '));
        END LOOP;
END;
/
```

Specifying a cursor as presented in this code still comes under the explicit category, as you have to specify the cursor SELECT explicitly.

 TIP   *Always avoid declaration of cursors in the declaration and specify them in the cursor FOR LOOP itself when dealing with cursors to process all of the rows unconditionally.*

Explicit Cursor Attributes

Every explicit cursor has four attributes associated with it that you can use to determine whether a cursor is open or not, whether a fetch yielded a row or not, and how many rows have been fetched so far. Table 2-1 lists these attributes.

Table 2-1. Explicit Cursor Attributes

ATTRIBUTE	USE
%FOUND	Indicates whether a FETCH yielded a row or not
%ISOPEN	Indicates whether a cursor is OPEN or not
%NOTFOUND	Indicates if a FETCH failed or if there are no more rows to fetch
%ROWCOUNT	Indicates the number of rows fetched so far

To use these four cursor attributes, you prefix the cursor name with the corresponding attribute. For example, for the csr_org cursor defined earlier, these four attributes can be referenced as csr_org%FOUND, csr_org%ISOPEN, csr%NOTFOUND, and csr%ROWCOUNT. The %FOUND, %ISOPEN, and %NOTFOUND attributes return a boolean TRUE or FALSE, and the %ROWCOUNT attribute returns a numeric value. The following sections describe these attributes in more detail.

%FOUND

You use %FOUND to determine whether a FETCH returned a row or not. You should use it after a cursor is opened, and it returns a value of TRUE if the immediate FETCH yielded a row, and a value of FALSE if the immediate FETCH did not fetch any row. Using %FOUND before opening a cursor or after closing a cursor raises the error "ORA-01001: invalid cursor" or the predefined exception INVALID_CURSOR.

I presented an example of using %FOUND during the discussion of using the WHILE LOOP to fetch multiple rows. Here's the same example repeated for illustration:

```
DECLARE
    CURSOR csr_org IS
        SELECT h.hrc_descr, o.org_short_name
        FROM   org_tab o, hrc_tab h
        WHERE o.hrc_code = h.hrc_code
         ORDER by 2;
         v_org_rec csr_org%ROWTYPE;
  BEGIN
      OPEN csr_org;
      dbms_output.put_line('Organization Details with Hierarchy');
      dbms_output.put_line('------------------------');
       dbms_output.put_line(rpad('Hierarchy',20,' ')||' '||
                                       rpad('Organization',30,' '));
      dbms_output.put_line(rpad('-',20,'-')||' '||rpad('-',30,'-'));
      FETCH csr_org INTO v_org_rec;
      WHILE (csr_org%FOUND) LOOP
            dbms_output.put_line(rpad(v_org_rec.hrc_descr,20,' ')||' '||
                          rpad(v_org_rec.org_short_name,30,' '));
            FETCH csr_org INTO v_org_rec;
      END LOOP;
      CLOSE csr_org;
  END;
  /
```

The following points are worth noting regarding the statement

```
WHILE (csr_org%FOUND) LOOP
```

- The statement appears after the first FETCH statement, and it should always appear after a FETCH statement. If %NOTFOUND is referenced before the first FETCH, it returns NULL.

- The condition csr_org%FOUND evaluates to TRUE if the first FETCH returned a row; otherwise, it evaluates to FALSE and the WHILE LOOP is never executed.

%ISOPEN

You use %ISOPEN to check if a cursor is already open or not. You use it to prevent an already opened cursor from opening or an already closed cursor from closing. It returns a value of TRUE if the referenced cursor is open; otherwise, it returns FALSE. Here's the previous example modified to use the %ISOPEN attribute:

```
DECLARE
    CURSOR csr_org IS
        SELECT h.hrc_descr, o.org_short_name
        FROM   org_tab o, hrc_tab h
        WHERE o.hrc_code = h.hrc_code
         ORDER by 2;
         v_org_rec csr_org%ROWTYPE;
  BEGIN
        IF (NOT csr_org%ISOPEN) THEN
          OPEN csr_org;
        END IF;
        dbms_output.put_line('Organization Details with Hierarchy');
        dbms_output.put_line('------------------------');
        dbms_output.put_line(rpad('Hierarchy',20,' ')||' '||
                                        rpad('Organization',30,' '));
        dbms_output.put_line(rpad('-',20,'-')||' '||rpad('-',30,'-'));
        FETCH csr_org INTO v_org_rec;
        WHILE (csr_org%FOUND) LOOP
            dbms_output.put_line(rpad(v_org_rec.hrc_descr,20,' ')||' '||
                          rpad(v_org_rec.org_short_name,30,' '));
            FETCH csr_org INTO v_org_rec;
        END LOOP;
        IF (csr_org%ISOPEN) THEN
          CLOSE csr_org;
        END IF;
  END;
/
```

Note the following points about %ISOPEN:

- csr_org%ISOPEN is negated in the beginning to check that the cursor isn't already open.

- At the end, the cursor csr_org is closed only if it's open.

- %ISOPEN can be referenced after a cursor is closed, and it returns FALSE in this case.

%NOTFOUND

You use %NOTFOUND to determine if a FETCH resulted in no rows (i.e., the FETCH failed) or there are no more rows to FETCH. It returns a value of TRUE if the immediate FETCH yielded no row and a value of FALSE if the immediate FETCH resulted in one row. Using %NOTFOUND before opening a cursor or after a cursor is closed raises the error "ORA-01001: invalid cursor" or the predefined exception INVALID_CURSOR. I presented an example of using %NOTFOUND during the discussion of using the simple LOOP to fetch multiple rows. Here's the same example repeated for illustration:

```
DECLARE
    CURSOR csr_org IS
        SELECT h.hrc_descr, o.org_short_name
        FROM   org_tab o, hrc_tab h
        WHERE o.hrc_code = h.hrc_code
        ORDER by 2;
        v_org_rec csr_org%ROWTYPE;
BEGIN
    OPEN csr_org;
    dbms_output.put_line('Organization Details with Hierarchy');
    dbms_output.put_line('------------------------');
    dbms_output.put_line(rpad('Hierarchy',20,' ')||' '||
                                    rpad('Organization',30,' '));
    dbms_output.put_line(rpad('-',20,'-')||' '||rpad('-',30,'-'));
    LOOP
        FETCH csr_org INTO v_org_rec;
        EXIT WHEN csr_org%NOTFOUND;
        dbms_output.put_line(rpad(v_org_rec.hrc_descr,20,' ')||' '||
```

```
                              rpad(v_org_rec.org_short_name,30,' '));
        END LOOP;
        CLOSE csr_org;
 END;
/
```

The following points are worth noting:

- Note the statement

  ```
  EXIT WHEN csr_org%NOTFOUND;.
  ```

  It appears after the first FETCH statement, and it should always appear
  after a FETCH statement. If %NOTFOUND is referenced before the first
  FETCH or after a cursor is opened, it returns NULL.

- The condition csr_org%NOTFOUND is used as the EXIT condition for
  the loop. It evaluates to TRUE if the first FETCH didn't return a row and the
  loop is exited. If the first FETCH resulted in at least one row, it evaluates to
  FALSE and the loop is executed until the last row is fetched. After the last
  row is fetched, %NOTFOUND evaluates to TRUE and the loop is exited.

%ROWCOUNT

You use %ROWCOUNT to determine the number of rows fetched from a cursor. It
returns 1 after the first fetch and is incremented by 1 after every successful fetch.
It can be referenced after a cursor is opened or before the first fetch and returns
zero in both cases. Using %ROWCOUNT before opening a cursor or after closing
a cursor raises the error "ORA-01001: invalid cursor" or the predefined exception
INVALID_CURSOR. The best use of this attribute is in a cursor FOR LOOP to
determine the number of rows returned by the cursor. Since a cursor FOR LOOP
is used to process *all* the rows of the cursor unconditionally, the value of this
attribute after the cursor FOR LOOP is executed gives the total number of rows
returned by the cursor.

In the following example, I've modified the cursor FOR LOOP presented earlier to include %ROWCOUNT:

```
DECLARE
    CURSOR csr_org IS
        SELECT h.hrc_descr, o.org_short_name
        FROM   org_tab o, hrc_tab h
        WHERE o.hrc_code = h.hrc_code
         ORDER by 2;
```

```
        num_total_rows NUMBER;
BEGIN
    dbms_output.put_line('Organization Details with Hierarchy');
    dbms_output.put_line('------------------------');
    dbms_output.put_line(rpad('Hierarchy',20,' ')||' '||
                                        rpad('Organization',30,' '));
    dbms_output.put_line(rpad('-',20,'-')||' '||rpad('-',30,'-'));
    FOR idx IN csr_org LOOP
            dbms_output.put_line(rpad(idx.hrc_descr,20,' ')||' '||
                                rpad(idx.org_short_name,30,' '));
            num_total_rows := csr_org%ROWCOUNT;
    END LOOP;
    IF num_total_rows > 0 THEN
      dbms_output.new_line;
      dbms_output.put_line('Total Organizations = '||to_char(num_total_rows));
    END IF;
END;
/
```

Here's the output of this program:

```
Organization Details with Hierarchy
----------------------------------------------
Hierarchy            Organization
-------------------- ------------------------------
CEO/COO              Office of CEO ABC Inc.
CEO/COO              Office of CEO DataPro Inc.
CEO/COO              Office of CEO XYZ Inc.
VP                   Office of VP Mktg ABC Inc.
VP                   Office of VP Sales ABC Inc.
VP                   Office of VP Tech ABC Inc.
Total Organizations = 6

PL/SQL procedure successfully completed.
```

%ROWCOUNT is an incremental count of the number of rows, and hence you can use it to check for a particular value. In this example, the first three lines after the BEGIN and before the cursor loop are displayed, irrespective of the number of rows returned by the cursor. This is true even if the cursor returned no rows. To prevent this, you can use the value of %ROWCOUNT to display them only if the cursor returns at least one row. Here's the code to do so:

```
DECLARE
     CURSOR csr_org IS
           SELECT h.hrc_descr, o.org_short_name
           FROM   org_tab o, hrc_tab h
           WHERE o.hrc_code = h.hrc_code
            ORDER by 2;
          num_total_rows NUMBER;
BEGIN
        FOR idx IN csr_org LOOP
             IF csr_org%ROWCOUNT = 1 THEN
                 dbms_output.put_line('Organization Details with Hierarchy');
                 dbms_output.put_line
                 ('------------------------');
                 dbms_output.put_line(rpad('Hierarchy',20,' ')||' '||
                              rpad('Organization',30,' '));
                 dbms_output.put_line(rpad('-',20,'-')||' '||rpad('-',30,'-'));
             END IF;
             dbms_output.put_line(rpad(idx.hrc_descr,20,' ')||' '||
                              rpad(idx.org_short_name,30,' '));
              num_total_rows := csr_org%ROWCOUNT;
        END LOOP;
        IF num_total_rows > 0 THEN
          dbms_output.new_line;
          dbms_output.put_line('Total Organizations = '||to_char(num_total_rows));
        END IF;
END;
/
```

The following points are worth noting:

- The %ROWCOUNT is checked inside the cursor FOR LOOP.

- After the first row is fetched, the value of %ROWCOUNT is 1 and the headings are displayed. Successive fetches increment the value of %ROWCOUNT by 1 so that %ROWCOUNT is greater than 1 after the first fetch.

- After the last fetch, the cursor FOR LOOP is exited and the value of %ROWCOUNT is the total number of rows processed.

Parameterized Cursors

An explicit cursor can take parameters and return a data set for a specific parameter value. This eliminates the need to define multiple cursors and hard-code a value in each cursor. It also eliminates the need to use PL/SQL bind variables.

In the following code, I use the cursor example presented earlier in the section to illustrate parameterized cursors:

```
DECLARE
    CURSOR csr_org(p_hrc_code NUMBER) IS
        SELECT h.hrc_descr, o.org_short_name
        FROM    org_tab o, hrc_tab h
        WHERE o.hrc_code = h.hrc_code
            AND h.hrc_code = p_hrc_code
        ORDER by 2;
        v_org_rec csr_org%ROWTYPE;
BEGIN
    OPEN csr_org(1);
    dbms_output.put_line('Organization Details with Hierarchy 1');
    dbms_output.put_line('------------------------');
    dbms_output.put_line(rpad('Hierarchy',20,' ')||' '||
                    rpad('Organization',30,' '));
    dbms_output.put_line(rpad('-',20,'-')||' '||rpad('-',30,'-'));
    LOOP
        FETCH csr_org INTO v_org_rec;
        EXIT WHEN csr_org%NOTFOUND;
        dbms_output.put_line(rpad(v_org_rec.hrc_descr,20,' ')||' '||
                        rpad(v_org_rec.org_short_name,30,' '));
    END LOOP;
    CLOSE csr_org;
    OPEN csr_org(2);
     dbms_output.put_line('Organization Details with Hierarchy 2');
     dbms_output.put_line('------------------------');
     dbms_output.put_line(rpad('Hierarchy',20,' ')||' '||
                    rpad('Organization',30,' '));
    dbms_output.put_line(rpad('-',20,'-')||' '||rpad('-',30,'-'));
    LOOP
        FETCH csr_org INTO v_org_rec;
        EXIT WHEN csr_org%NOTFOUND;
        dbms_output.put_line(rpad(v_org_rec.hrc_descr,20,' ')||' '||
```

```
                    rpad(v_org_rec.org_short_name,30,' '));

      END LOOP;
```

                                         1

                                         BC Inc.
)ataPro Inc.
                                         YZ Inc.
                                         2

                                         ----
                                         tg ABC Inc.
                                         les ABC Inc.
                                         ch ABC Inc.

                                         ted.

s immediately after the cursor name by
and its data type within parentheses. These
are referred to as the *formal parameters*. The actual parameters (i.e., the actual data values for the formal parameters) are passed via the OPEN statement as shown in the previous example. Notice how the same cursor is used twice with different values of the parameters in each case.

You can rewrite the same example using a cursor FOR LOOP. In this case, the actual parameters are passed via the cursor name referenced in the cursor FOR LOOP. Here's the code:

```
DECLARE
    CURSOR csr_org(p_hrc_code NUMBER) IS
        SELECT h.hrc_descr, o.org_short_name
        FROM   org_tab o, hrc_tab h
        WHERE o.hrc_code = h.hrc_code
            AND h.hrc_code = p_hrc_code
        ORDER by 2;
        v_org_rec csr_org%ROWTYPE;
    BEGIN
```

```
            dbms_output.put_line('Organization Details with Hierarchy 1');
            dbms_output.put_line('------------------------');
            dbms_output.put_line(rpad('Hierarchy',20,' ')||
                                     ' '||rpad('Organization',30,' '));
            dbms_output.put_line(rpad('-',20,'-')||' '||rpad('-',30,'-'));
            FOR idx in csr_org(1) LOOP
                  dbms_output.put_line(rpad(idx.hrc_descr,20,' ')||' '||
                              rpad(idx.org_short_name,30,' '));
            END LOOP;
             dbms_output.put_line('Organization Details with Hierarchy 2');
             dbms_output.put_line('------------------------');;
            dbms_output.put_line(rpad('Hierarchy',20,' ')||' '||
                                              rpad('Organization',30,' '));
            dbms_output.put_line(rpad('-',20,'-')||' '||rpad('-',30,'-'));
            FOR idx in csr_org(2) LOOP
                  dbms_output.put_line(rpad(idx.hrc_descr,20,' ')||' '||
                              rpad(idx.org_short_name,30,' '));
            END LOOP;
      END;
      /
```

The output of this program is the same as the output of the earlier one.

Parameterized cursors are very useful in processing nested cursor loops in which an inner cursor is opened with data values passed to it from an outer opened cursor.

SELECT FOR UPDATE Cursors

You use SELECT FOR UPDATE cursors for updating the rows retrieved by a cursor. This is often required when there's a need to modify each row retrieved by a cursor without having to refetch that row. More often, SELECT FOR UPDATE cursors are required to update a column of the table defined in the cursor SELECT using a complex formula.

Defining a SELECT FOR UPDATE Cursor

A SELECT FOR UPDATE cursor is defined using the FOR UPDATE OF clause in the cursor SELECT statement, as follows:

```
DECLARE
     CURSOR csr_1 IS
           SELECT * FROM sec_hrc_tab FOR UPDATE OF hrc_descr;
BEGIN
     /* ... Open the cursor and process the resultset ... */
     null;
END;
/
```

> **NOTE**   *Notice how the column name to be updated is specified in the FOR UPDATE OF clause. If no column name is specified in the FOR UPDATE OF clause, any column of the underlying cursor table can be modified.*

Using a SELECT FOR UPDATE Cursor

Once you've defined a SELECT FOR UPDATE cursor, you use the WHERE CURRENT OF clause to process the rows returned by it. You can use this clause in an UPDATE or DELETE statement. It has the following syntax:

```
WHERE CURRENT of cursor_name;
```

where cursor_name is the name of the cursor defined with a FOR UPDATE clause.

The following is a complete example of using SELECT FOR UPDATE cursors. I use the sec_hrc_tab table to demonstrate this. First, this table is populated using an INSERT statement as follows:

```
BEGIN
     INSERT INTO sec_hrc_tab
         SELECT * FROM hrc_tab;
     COMMIT;
END;
/
```

The output can be verified as follows:

```
SQL> select * from sec_hrc_tab;

  HRC_CODE HRC_DESCR
```

```
----- -------------
         1 CEO/COO
         2 VP
         3 Director
         4 Manager
         5 Analyst
```

Then I define a SELECT FOR UPDATE cursor and use the WHERE CURRENT OF clause to update the rows retrieved by this cursor in a particular fashion. Here's the program for this:

```
DECLARE
     CURSOR csr_1 IS
           SELECT * FROM sec_hrc_tab FOR UPDATE OF hrc_descr;
           v_hrc_descr VARCHAR2(20);
BEGIN
     FOR idx IN csr_1 LOOP
           v_hrc_descr := UPPER(idx.hrc_descr);
           UPDATE sec_hrc_tab
            SET        hrc_descr = v_hrc_descr
            WHERE CURRENT OF csr_1;
     END LOOP;
     COMMIT;
END;
/
```

This program updates the hrc_descr column of each row retrieved by csr_1 with its value converted to uppercase. The output can be verified as follows:

```
SQL> select * from sec_hrc_tab;

  HRC_CODE HRC_DESCR
  -------- ----------
         1 CEO/COO
         2 VP
         3 DIRECTOR
         4 MANAGER
         5 ANALYST
```

The mechanism of SELECT FOR UPDATE cursors works as follows:

1. The SELECT FOR UPDATE cursor puts a lock on the rows retrieved by the cursor. If it's unable to obtain a lock because some other session has placed a lock on the specific rows, it waits until it can get a lock. A COMMIT or ROLLBACK in the corresponding session frees the locks held by other sessions.

2. For each row identified by the cursor, the cursor updates the specified column of that row. That is, it keeps track of the current row and updates it, and then fetches the subsequent row and updates it. It does this without scanning the same table again. This is unlike an ordinary UPDATE or DELETE statement inside the loop, where the cursor scans the updated table again to determine the current row to be modified.

Although you could achieve the same function by using a simple UPDATE statement, this example is meant to illustrate the use of SELECT FOR UPDATE cursors.

To use WHERE CURRENT OF, you have to declare the cursor using FOR UPDATE. The reverse is not true. That is, you can use a SELECT FOR UPDATE cursor to modify the rows without using the WHERE CURRENT OF clause. Then, you have to update or delete the cursor rows using the primary key.

A SELECT FOR UPDATE cursor offers two important advantages: Namely, it locks the rows after opening the cursor and the resultset rows are identified for update, and it eliminates a second fetch of the rows for doing the update and preserves the current row by the WHERE CURRENT OF clause.

You have to do a COMMIT outside of the cursor loop when you use WHERE CURRENT OF in processing the rows of a SELECT FOR UPDATE cursor. This is because a COMMIT releases the lock on the rows that the SELECT FOR UPDATE has put a lock on, and this causes a subsequent fetch to fail.

Implicit Cursors

Of all the types of DML statements, the explicit cursors discussed previously are used for processing multirow SELECT statements. To keep track of other types of DML statements, such as INSERT, UPDATE, DELETE, and single-row SELECT . . . INTO statements, Oracle PL/SQL provides the implicit cursor, also known as the SQL cursor. Just as a SELECT statement points to a work area whether it returns a single row or multiple rows, even INSERT, UPDATE, and DELETE statements are executed within the context of a work area, and the Oracle PL/SQL engine automatically opens the implicit or SQL cursor that points to this work area. Also, after the execution of the DML statements, the implicit cursor is automatically closed. Hence, there's no such thing as OPEN, FETCH, and CLOSE. These operations are only valid for an explicit cursor. Here's an example of an implicit cursor:

```
BEGIN
        DELETE sec_hrc_org_tab WHERE hrc_code = 1;
        INSERT INTO sec_hrc_org_tab
                SELECT h.hrc_code, h.hrc_descr,
                               o.org_id, o.org_short_name, o.org_long_name
                FROM   org_tab o, hrc_tab h
                WHERE o.hrc_code = h.hrc_code
                      AND h.hrc_code = 1;
        IF (SQL%FOUND) THEN
           dbms_output.put_line(TO_CHAR(SQL%ROWCOUNT)||
                   ' rows inserted into secondary table for hierarchy 1');
        END IF;
        COMMIT;
END;
/
```

The output of this code can be verified as follows:

```
3 rows inserted into secondary table for hierarchy 1

PL/SQL procedure successfully completed.

SQL> select * from sec_hrc_org_tab;

  HRC_CODE HRC_DESCR                   ORG_ID ORG_SHORT_NAME
----- ----------       -----  -------------
ORG_LONG_NAME
---------------------------------------------
         1 CEO/COO                      1001 Office of CEO ABC Inc.
Office of CEO ABC Inc.

         1 CEO/COO                      1002 Office of CEO XYZ Inc.
Office of CEO XYZ Inc.

         1 CEO/COO                      1003 Office of CEO DataPro Inc.
Office of CEO DataPro Inc.
```

This code refreshes a secondary table named sec_hrc_org_tab with new rows. It first deletes all rows from the sec_hrc_org_tab table where the hrc_code matches 1. It then inserts new rows into the same table. Now the question is, did the INSERT succeed? That is, did it insert zero or more rows? This is determined by an implicit cursor attribute, SQL%FOUND, which is defined in the statement

```
IF (SQL%FOUND) THEN
```

SQL%FOUND returns a boolean true when at least one row has been inserted into the temp_hrc_org_tab. When this happens, the code inside the IF condition is executed and the given output appears. Also note the use of the SQL%ROWCOUNT attribute. This gives the numbers of rows inserted into the sec_hrc_org_tab table. Note that the SQL%ROWCOUNT gives the number of rows affected by the immediately preceding DML statement.

Implicit Cursor Attributes

Although an implicit cursor is opened and closed automatically by the PL/SQL engine, the four attributes associated with an explicit cursor are also available for an implicit cursor. You can reference these attributes by prefixing the keyword SQL with the particular attribute. Table 2-2 lists the four attributes of the implicit cursor.

Table 2-2. Implicit Cursor Attributes

ATTRIBUTE	USE
SQL%FOUND	Indicates whether an INSERT, UPDATE, or DELETE affected any row(s) or not.
SQL%ISOPEN	Indicates whether the cursor is OPEN or not. This is FALSE always, as the implicit cursor is closed after the DML statement is executed.
SQL%NOTFOUND	Indicates if a DML statement failed to modify any rows.
SQL%ROWCOUNT	Indicates the number of rows affected by the DML statement.

Note that the name of the cursor in this case is "SQL" instead of a programmer-defined cursor name.

The SQL%FOUND, SQL%ISOPEN, and SQL%NOTFOUND attributes return a boolean TRUE or FALSE, and the SQL%ROWCOUNT attribute returns a numeric value. The following sections describe these attributes in detail.

SQL%FOUND

You use SQL%FOUND to determine whether an INSERT, UPDATE, or DELETE affected any row(s) or not, or a SELECT . . . INTO returned a row or not. You should use it immediately after the DML statement, and it returns a value of TRUE if the INSERT, UPDATE, or DELETE affected one or more rows, or the SELECT . . . INTO fetched a row. Otherwise, it returns a value of FALSE. Using SQL%FOUND before defining any DML statement yields NULL.

I provided an example of using SQL%FOUND during the discussion of implicit cursors. I repeat it here for illustration:

```
BEGIN
        DELETE sec_hrc_org_tab WHERE hrc_code = 1;
        INSERT INTO sec_hrc_org_tab
              SELECT h.hrc_code, h.hrc_descr,
                               o.org_id, o.org_short_name, o.org_long_name
              FROM    org_tab o, hrc_tab h
              WHERE o.hrc_code = h.hrc_code
                    AND h.hrc_code = 1;
        IF (SQL%FOUND) THEN
           dbms_output.put_line(TO_CHAR(SQL%ROWCOUNT)||
                    ' rows inserted into secondary table for hierarchy 1');
        END IF;
        COMMIT;
END;
/
```

The following points are worth noting:

- The statement IF (SQL%FOUND) THEN appears immediately after the INSERT statement and it always should. If SQL%FOUND is referenced before the INSERT statement, it returns NULL.

- The condition SQL%FOUND evaluates to TRUE if the INSERT succeeded in creating one or more rows; otherwise, it evaluates to FALSE and the code inside the IF is never executed.

SQL%ISOPEN

SQL%ISOPEN is always FALSE because the implicit cursor is closed after the DML statement is executed. Hence, it's not useful to check this attribute for the same.

SQL%NOTFOUND

You use SQL%NOTFOUND to determine if an INSERT, UPDATE, or DELETE failed to modify any rows. It returns a value of TRUE if no rows were modified by the INSERT, UPDATE, or DELETE, and a value of FALSE if at least one row was modified. Using SQL%NOTFOUND before executing any DML statement yields a NULL value. Here's an example of using SQL%NOTFOUND:

```
DECLARE
    v_num_rows NUMBER;
BEGIN
        DELETE sec_hrc_org_tab WHERE hrc_code = 1;
        INSERT INTO sec_hrc_org_tab
            SELECT h.hrc_code, h.hrc_descr,
                            o.org_id, o.org_short_name, o.org_long_name
            FROM    org_tab o, hrc_tab h
            WHERE o.hrc_code = h.hrc_code
                AND h.hrc_code = 1;
    v_num_rows := SQL%ROWCOUNT;
    IF (SQL%FOUND) THEN
        UPDATE sec_hrc_audit
        SET num_rows = v_num_rows
        WHERE hrc_code = 1;
        IF (SQL%NOTFOUND) THEN
          INSERT INTO sec_hrc_audit(hrc_code, num_rows) VALUES (1, v_num_rows);
        END IF;
        END IF;
        COMMIT;
  END;
/
```

The output of this program can be verified as follows:

```
PL/SQL procedure successfully completed.

SQL> select * from sec_hrc_org_tab;

  HRC_CODE HRC_DESCR                  ORG_ID ORG_SHORT_NAME
------ ---------- ------ ---------------
ORG_LONG_NAME
--------------------------------------------
        1 CEO/COO                      1001 Office of CEO ABC Inc.
Office of CEO ABC Inc.
```

```
          1 CEO/COO                      1002 Office of CEO XYZ Inc.
Office of CEO XYZ Inc.

          1 CEO/COO                      1003 Office of CEO DataPro Inc.
Office of CEO DataPro Inc.

SQL> select * from sec_hrc_audit;

  HRC_CODE    NUM_ROWS
  -----  -----
    1      3
```

This code first deletes all rows from the sec_hrc_org_tab table where the hrc_code matches 1. It then inserts new rows into the same table. Now the question is, did the INSERT succeed? That is, did it insert zero or more rows? This is determined by the implicit cursor attribute SQL%FOUND, which is defined in the statement

```
IF (SQL%FOUND) THEN
```

SQL%FOUND returns a boolean true when at least one row has been inserted into the sec_hrc_org_tab. When this happens, the code inside the IF condition is executed and the UPDATE statement against the sec_hrc_audit table is executed.

Now the second question is, did this update succeed or fail? This is determined by the implicit cursor attribute SQL%NOTFOUND. If the update failed, SQL%NOTFOUND returns TRUE and a record is inserted into the sec_hrc_audit table. Notice the use of SQL% attributes immediately after each DML statement. The use of SQL%FOUND refers to its immediately preceding DML statement—that is, the first INSERT statement. The use of the SQL%NOTFOUND attribute refers to its immediately preceding DML statement—that is, the UPDATE statement. Also note the use of the SQL%ROWCOUNT attribute. This attribute gives the numbers of rows inserted into the sec_hrc_org_tab table, as it's used immediately after the INSERT statement.

SQL%ROWCOUNT

You use %ROWCOUNT to determine the number of rows affected by a DML statement. It returns a value greater than zero if the DML statement succeeded; otherwise, it returns zero. It's a good alternative to SQL%NOTFOUND. Since %NOTFOUND returns TRUE if the DML statement failed, it's equivalent to use

```
IF (SQL%ROWCOUNT = 0) THEN . . .
```

instead of

```
IF (SQL%NOTFOUND) THEN . . .
```

Here's the previous example modified to use %ROWCOUNT:

```
DECLARE
    v_num_rows NUMBER;
BEGIN
        DELETE sec_hrc_org_tab WHERE hrc_code = 1;
        INSERT INTO sec_hrc_org_tab
            SELECT h.hrc_code, h.hrc_descr,
                         o.org_id, o.org_short_name, o.org_long_name
            FROM    org_tab o, hrc_tab h
            WHERE o.hrc_code = h.hrc_code
                AND h.hrc_code = 1;
        v_num_rows := SQL%ROWCOUNT;
        IF (SQL%FOUND) THEN
           UPDATE sec_hrc_audit
           SET num_rows = v_num_rows
           WHERE hrc_code = 1;
           IF (SQL%ROWCOUNT=0) THEN
             INSERT INTO sec_hrc_audit(hrc_code, num_rows) VALUES (1, v_num_rows);
           END IF;
         END IF;
         COMMIT;
END;
/
```

The output of this program is same as the output of the previous example. The following points are worth noting:

- The first SQL%ROWCOUNT returns the number of rows affected by the very first INSERT statement—that is, the number of rows inserted into the sec_hrc_org_tab table.

- The second SQL%ROWCOUNT returns the number of rows affected by the UPDATE statement against the table sec_hrc_audit.

> **TIP**   *Always check for the attributes SQL%FOUND,*
> *SQL%NOTFOUND, and SQL%ROWCOUNT immediately*
> *after the DML statement.*

How Using SQL%FOUND, SQL%NOTFOUND, or SQL%ROWCOUNT Replaces a SELECT COUNT(*)

Using SQL%FOUND, SQL%NOTFOUND, or SQL%ROWCOUNT replaces
a SELECT COUNT(*), as you can see from the previous example. Notice the IF
statement after the first statement. If this weren't there, the way to check whether
the insert succeeded or not is to do a SELECT COUNT(*) from the
sec_hrc_org_table into a variable and explicitly check for its value to be greater
than zero. The same is true for the sec_hrc_audit table. Hence, the program will
be as shown here:

```
DECLARE
    v_num_rows NUMBER;
    v_cnt NUMBER;
BEGIN
        DELETE sec_hrc_org_tab WHERE hrc_code = 1;
        INSERT INTO sec_hrc_org_tab
            SELECT h.hrc_code, h.hrc_descr,
                            o.org_id, o.org_short_name, o.org_long_name
            FROM    org_tab o, hrc_tab h
            WHERE o.hrc_code = h.hrc_code
                AND h.hrc_code = 1;
    SELECT COUNT(*)
    INTO        v_num_rows
    FROM    sec_hrc_org_tab
    WHERE hrc_code = 1;
 IF (v_num_rows >0) THEN
    SELECT COUNT(*)
    INTO      v_cnt
    FROM   sec_hrc_audit
    WHERE hrc_code = 1;
    IF (v_cnt > 0) THEN
        UPDATE sec_hrc_audit
        SET num_rows = v_num_rows
        WHERE hrc_code = 1;
```

```
        ELSIF (v_cnt=0) THEN
            INSERT INTO sec_hrc_audit(hrc_code, num_rows) VALUES (1, v_num_rows);
          END IF;
        END IF;
        COMMIT;
  END;
  /
```

The output of this program is same as the output of the previous example.

Even if you don't use a SELECT COUNT(*), at least use a SELECT . . . INTO instead. Using implicit cursor attributes saves this overhead.

Cursor Variables

As mentioned in the earlier section, "Introducing Cursors," an explicit cursor once declared was associated with a specific query—only the one specific query that was known at compile time. In this way, the cursor declared was static and couldn't be changed at runtime. It always pointed to the same work area until the execution of the program completed. However, you may sometimes want to have a variable that can point to different work areas depending on runtime conditions. PL/SQL 2.2 onward offers this facility by means of cursor variables.

A *cursor variable* is a single PL/SQL variable that you can associate with different queries at runtime. The same variable can point to different work areas. In this way, cursor variables and cursors are analogous to PL/SQL variables and constants, but from a cursor perspective. A cursor variable acts like a pointer that holds the address of a specific work area defined by the query it's pointing to.

Before PL/SQL 2.3, cursor variables were available for use in host environments such as Pro*C. As of PL/SQL 2.3 onward, cursor variables are available for use in both server- and client-side PL/SQL as well as in host environments.

Why Use Cursor Variables?

The primary advantage of using cursor variables is their capability to pass result-sets between stored subprograms. Before cursor variables, this wasn't possible. Now, with cursor variables, the work area that a cursor variable points to remains accessible as long as the variable points to it. Hence, you can point a cursor variable to a work area by opening a cursor for it, and then any application such as Pro*C, an Oracle client, or another server application can fetch from the corresponding resultset.

Another advantage of cursor variables is their introduction of a sort of dynamism, in that a single cursor variable can be associated with multiple queries at runtime.

Defining a Cursor Variable

Defining a cursor variable consists of defining a pointer of type REF CURSOR and defining a variable of this type. These steps are outlined in the following sections.

Defining a Pointer of Type CURSOR

In PL/SQL, a pointer is declared using the syntax

```
REF type
```

The keyword REF implies that the new type so defined is a pointer to the defined type.

PL/SQL offers two types of REF types: CURSOR and an object type. So, the definition of a cursor variable involves the definition of a REF CURSOR first, as shown here:

```
TYPE rc IS REF CURSOR;
```

Defining a Variable of Type REF CURSOR

Once you've defined a REF CURSOR type, the next step is to declare a variable of this type. Here's the code for this:

```
v_rc rc;
```

So the complete declaration of a cursor variable is as follows:

```
TYPE rc IS REF CURSOR;
v_rc rc;
```

This code suggests that rc is a pointer of type CURSOR and v_rc (in fact, any variable) defined of type rc points to a SQL cursor.

Strong and Weak REF CURSOR Types

The REF CURSOR type defined earlier is called a *weak* REF CURSOR type. This is because it doesn't dictate the return type of the cursor. Hence, it can point to any SELECT query with any number of columns. Weak cursor types are available in PL/SQL 2.3 and higher versions.

PL/SQL lets you define a *strong* REF CURSOR having a return type using the following syntax:

```
TYPE ref_type_name IS REF CURSOR RETURN return_type;
```

Here, ref_type_name is the name of the new pointer name and return_type is a record type of either %ROWTYPE or a user-defined record type. For example, you can declare strong REF CURSORS as follows:

```
TYPE rc is REF CURSOR RETURN hrc_tab%ROWTYPE;
v_rc rc;
```

or

```
TYPE hrc_rec is RECORD (hrc_code NUMBER, hrc_name VARCHAR2(20));
TYPE rc IS REF CURSOR RETURN hrc_rec;
```

In the case of a strong REF CURSOR, the query that's associated with it should be type-compatible one to one with the return type of the corresponding REF CURSOR.

Using a Cursor Variable

Once you've defined a cursor variable, you can use it to associate it with a query. Here are the steps:

1. Allocate memory.

2. Open the cursor variable for a query.

3. Fetch the results into a PL/SQL record or individual PL/SQL variables.

4. Close the cursor variable.

The following sections provide more detail about each step in the process.

Allocate Memory

Once you declare a cursor variable in PL/SQL, the PL/SQL engine in PL/SQL 2.3 and higher versions automatically allocates memory for storage of rows. Prior to PL/SQL 2.3, a host environment was needed to explicitly allocate memory to a cursor variable.

Opening the Cursor Variable

Once you've defined a cursor variable, you have to open it for a multirow query, either with an arbitrary number of columns in the case of a weak REF CURSOR or with a type-compatible query in the case of a strong REF CURSOR. Opening the cursor variable identifies the associated query, executes it, and also identifies the resultset.

You open a cursor variable using the OPEN-FOR statement. Here's the syntax:

```
OPEN {cursor_variable_name | :host_cursor_variable_name} FOR
{  select_query
 | dynamic_string [USING bind_variable[, bind_variable] ... ] };
```

where cursor_variable_name is the name of the declared cursor variable and select_query is the SELECT query associated with the cursor variable. Also, host_cursor_variable_name is the name of the cursor variable declared in a PL/SQL host environment (such as Pro*C), and bind_variable represents the name of a PL/SQL bind variable. dynamic_string represents a dynamic SQL string instead of a hard-coded SELECT statement. You open cursor variables for dynamic strings using native dynamic SQL.

CROSS-REFERENCE   *Chapter 7 covers opening cursor variables for dynamic strings using native dynamic SQL.*

Here's an example that illustrates opening the cursor variable for the previously declared weak cursor variable v_rc:

```
DECLARE
    TYPE rc is REF CURSOR;
    v_rc rc;
BEGIN
```

```
    OPEN v_rc FOR SELECT * from hrc_tab;
    /* ... FETCH the results and process the resultset */
    null;
END;
/
```

TIP *You can't define any parameters while opening a cursor variable for a query. However, the associated query can reference PL/SQL variables, parameters, host variables, and functions.*

Fetching the Results into a PL/SQL Record or Individual PL/SQL Variables

The next step is to fetch the cursor variable into a PL/SQL record or individual variables. This retrieves individual rows of data into the PL/SQL variables for processing. You fetch a cursor variable using the FETCH statement, which has three forms. Here's the syntax:

```
FETCH cursor_variable_name INTO var1, var2, ... , varN;
```

or

```
FETCH cursor_variable_name INTO table_name%ROWTYPE;
```

or

```
FETCH cursor__variable_name INTO record_name;
```

Here, var1, var2, and varN represent PL/SQL variables having data types identical to the cursor variable query. table_name%ROWTYPE represents a PL/SQL record type with attributes implicitly defined as the column names of the table identified by table_name, which are identical to the cursor variable SELECT. In this case, you need to explicitly define the record type. Lastly, record_name is a variable of a PL/SQL record type that's explicitly defined. In this case also, the number and data types of the individual attributes of the record should exactly match the columns in the cursor variable SELECT.

Here's an example that extends the previous example of v_rc to fetching rows:

```
DECLARE
    TYPE rc is REF CURSOR;
    v_rc rc;
```

```
        hrc_rec hrc_tab%ROWTYPE;
BEGIN
    OPEN v_rc FOR SELECT * from hrc_tab;
    LOOP
        FETCH v_rc INTO hrc_rec;
        EXIT WHEN v_rc%NOTFOUND;
        /* . . . Process the individual records */
        null;
    END LOOP;
END;
/
```

The number and data types of the individual variables should exactly match the columns list in the cursor variable's associated SELECT statement. If the cursor is fetched into a record type (either table_name%ROWTYPE or record_name), the number and data type of each attribute in the record should exactly match the columns list of the cursor variable associated SELECT statement. If this isn't the case, then PL/SQL raises an error at compile time if the cursor variable is strongly typed, and a predefined exception called ROWTYPE_MISMATCH at runtime if the cursor variable is weakly typed.

CAUTION   *Never fetch from a cursor variable before opening it.*

TIP   *Always fetch into a record type of table_name%ROWTYPE, or at least fetch into a record type compatible with the cursor SELECT rather than into individual variables. This is less error-prone and also improves program readability.*

Similar to static cursors, a single FETCH always fetches only one row (the current row) from the active set. To fetch multiple rows, use the FETCH statement in a LOOP.

Closing the Cursor Variable

Once the processing of the rows is completed, you can close the cursor variable. Closing the cursor variable frees the resources allocated to the query but doesn't necessarily free the storage of the cursor variable itself. The cursor variable is freed when the variable is out of scope. You close a cursor using the CLOSE statement. Here's the syntax:

```
CLOSE cursor_variable_name;
```

 TIP   *The CLOSE statement should always appear after the FETCH statement. When you use a loop to fetch the rows from a cursor variable, you should insert the CLOSE statement after you close the loop. Otherwise, it results in an illegal fetch. Don't fetch from an already closed cursor variable, and don't close an already closed cursor variable.*

Here's a complete example of using the v_rc cursor, involving all the steps previously covered:

```
DECLARE
     TYPE rc is REF CURSOR;
     v_rc rc;
     hrc_rec hrc_tab%ROWTYPE;
BEGIN
     OPEN v_rc FOR SELECT * from hrc_tab;
     dbms_output.put_line('Hierarchy Details');
     dbms_output.put_line('-----------------------');
     dbms_output.put_line('Code'||' '||rpad('Description',20,' '));
     dbms_output.put_line(rpad('-',4,'-')||' '||rpad('-',20,'-'));
     LOOP
          FETCH v_rc INTO hrc_rec;
          EXIT WHEN v_rc%NOTFOUND;
          dbms_output.put_line(to_char(hrc_rec.hrc_code)||' '||
                                        rpad(hrc_rec.hrc_descr,20,' '));
     END LOOP;
     CLOSE v_rc;
END;
/
```

Here's the output of this program:

```
Hierarchy Details
-----------------
Code Description
-- -----------
1 CEO/COO
2 VP
3 Director
4 Manager
5 Analyst

PL/SQL procedure successfully completed.
```

This code is similar to the code used for static cursors, except that it uses cursor variables instead of cursors.

TIP   *The scope of a cursor variable is the scope of the PL/SQL block in which it is defined.*

Cursor Variables Assignment

One way to make a cursor variable point to a query work area is to open a query for the cursor variable. You saw this earlier. Here, I describe a second way to make a cursor variable point to a query work area. Simply assign the cursor variable to an already OPENed cursor variable. Here's an example of cursor variable assignment:

```
DECLARE
     TYPE rc is REF CURSOR;
     v_rc1 rc;
     v_rc2 rc;
     hrc_rec hrc_tab%ROWTYPE;
BEGIN
     OPEN v_rc1 FOR SELECT * from hrc_tab;
     dbms_output.put_line('Hierarchy Details');
     dbms_output.put_line('------------------------');
     dbms_output.put_line('Code'||' '||rpad('Description',20,' '));
     dbms_output.put_line(rpad('-',4,'-')||' '||rpad('-',20,'-'));
     /* Assign v_rc1 to v_rc2 */
     v_rc2 := v_rc1;
```

```
    LOOP
        /* Fetch from the second cursor variable, i.e., v_rc2 */
        FETCH v_rc2 INTO hrc_rec;
        EXIT WHEN v_rc2%NOTFOUND;
        dbms_output.put_line(to_char(hrc_rec.hrc_code)||' '||
                                    rpad(hrc_rec.hrc_descr,20,' '));
    END LOOP;
    CLOSE v_rc2;
END;
/
```

The output of this program is the same as the output of the earlier example without the assignment. Note that closing v_rc2 also closes v_rc1 and vice versa.

However, if the source cursor variable is strongly typed, the target cursor variable must be of the same type as the source cursor variable. This restriction doesn't apply if the source cursor variable is weakly typed. Here's an example that illustrates this concept:

```
DECLARE
    TYPE rc1 is REF CURSOR RETURN hrc_tab%ROWTYPE;
    TYPE rc2 is REF CURSOR RETURN hrc_tab%ROWTYPE;
    TYPE rc is REF CURSOR;
    v_rc1 rc1;
    v_rc2 rc2;
    v_rc3 rc;
    v_rc4 rc;
    hrc_rec hrc_tab%ROWTYPE;
BEGIN
    OPEN v_rc1 FOR SELECT * from hrc_tab;
    /* Assign v_rc1 to v_rc2 */
    v_rc2 := v_rc1; - This causes type error.
    v_rc3 := v_rc1; - This succeeds.
    v_rc4 := v_rc3; - This succeeds.
    /* ... FETCH and process ... */
    null;
END;
/
```

CAUTION   *Don't assign an unopened cursor variable to another cursor variable. Doing so causes the error INVALID_CURSOR.*

> **TIP**   *You can't assign a null value to a cursor variable. Also, you can't test cursor variables for equality, inequality, or nullity.*

Cursor Variable Attributes

All the attributes associated with explicit cursors are available with cursor variables. You can use the four explicit cursor attributes with cursor variables by referencing them as cursor_variable_name%ISOPEN, cursor_variable_name%FOUND, cursor_variable_name%NOTFOUND, and cursor_variable_name%ROWCOUNT.

SYS_REFCURSOR Type in PL/SQL 9i

PL/SQL 9*i* makes available a type called SYS_REFCURSOR that defines a generic weak cursor. You can use it as follows:

```
DECLARE
      v_rc SYS_REFCURSOR;
BEGIN
    OPEN v_rc FOR SELECT * from hrc_tab;
    /* ... FETCH and process the resultset  ... */
   null;
END;
/
```

Before Oracle9*i* you needed to perform two steps:

1. Define a type of REF CURSOR.

2. Define the cursor variable of this type.

SYS_REFCURSOR makes it convenient to define a cursor variable in a single step. However, you can use it to define only weak cursor variables. Here's an example of using SYS_REFCURSOR for cursor variable processing:

```
DECLARE
      v_rc SYS_REFCURSOR;
      hrc_rec hrc_tab%ROWTYPE;
```

```
BEGIN
    OPEN v_rc FOR SELECT * from hrc_tab;
    dbms_output.put_line('Hierarchy Details');
     dbms_output.put_line('------------------------');
    dbms_output.put_line('Code'||' '||rpad('Description',20,' '));
    dbms_output.put_line(rpad('-',4,'-')||' '||rpad('-',20,'-'));
    LOOP
        FETCH v_rc INTO hrc_rec;
        EXIT WHEN v_rc%NOTFOUND;
        dbms_output.put_line(to_char(hrc_rec.hrc_code)||' '||
                                        rpad(hrc_rec.hrc_descr,20,' '));
    END LOOP;
    CLOSE v_rc;
END;
/
```

Dynamism in Using Cursor Variables

The real use of cursor variables is when you have a need to open multiple queries using the same cursor variable or to dynamically assign different queries to the same cursor variable depending on runtime conditions. I discuss two examples in the following sections that illustrate the dynamism involved in using cursor variables.

Example 1: Opening Multiple Queries Using the Same Cursor Variable

To open multiple queries using the same cursor variable, use this code:

```
DECLARE
    TYPE rc is REF CURSOR;
    v_rc rc;
    hrc_rec hrc_tab%ROWTYPE;
    v_hrc_descr VARCHAR2(20);
    v_org_short_name VARCHAR2(30);
BEGIN
    OPEN v_rc FOR SELECT * from hrc_tab;
    dbms_output.put_line('Hierarchy Details');
    dbms_output.put_line('------------------------');
    dbms_output.put_line('Code'||' '||rpad('Description',20,' '));
    dbms_output.put_line(rpad('-',4,'-')||' '||rpad('-',20,'-'));
    LOOP
```

```
           FETCH v_rc INTO hrc_rec;
           EXIT WHEN v_rc%NOTFOUND;
           dbms_output.put_line(to_char(hrc_rec.hrc_code)||' '||
                                          rpad(hrc_rec.hrc_descr,20,' '));
       END LOOP;
       OPEN v_rc FOR SELECT h.hrc_descr, o.org_short_name
                         FROM org_tab o, hrc_tab h
                         WHERE o.hrc_code = h.hrc_code;
       dbms_output.put_line('Hierarchy and Organization Details');
       dbms_output.put_line('-----------------------');
       dbms_output.put_line(rpad('Hierarchy',20,' ')||' '||
                                      rpad('Description',30,' '));
       dbms_output.put_line(rpad('-',20,'-')||' '||rpad('-',30,'-'));
       LOOP
           FETCH v_rc INTO v_hrc_descr, v_org_short_name;
           EXIT WHEN v_rc%NOTFOUND;
           dbms_output.put_line(rpad(v_hrc_descr,20,' ')||' '||
                                      rpad(v_org_short_name,30,' '));
       END LOOP;
       CLOSE v_rc;
END;
/
```

Here's the output of this program:

```
Hierarchy Details
---------------
Code Description
-- --------------
1 CEO/COO
2 VP
3 Director
4 Manager
5 Analyst
Hierarchy and Organization Details
--------------------------
Hierarchy           Description
---------  -----------------
CEO/COO             Office of CEO ABC Inc.
CEO/COO             Office of CEO XYZ Inc.
CEO/COO             Office of CEO DataPro Inc.
VP                  Office of VP Sales ABC Inc.
VP                  Office of VP Mktg ABC Inc.
VP                  Office of VP Tech ABC Inc.

PL/SQL procedure successfully completed.
```

The following points are worth noting:

- The same cursor variable v_rc is used to point to two different queries.

- After you open v_rc for the first query and fetch the results, v_rc isn't closed. It's simply reopened for a second query and a new resultset is identified.

TIP   *Once you've opened a cursor variable for a query, the resultset is fixed. You have to reopen the cursor variable to make it point to a different query.*

TIP   *You don't need to close a cursor variable before you reopen it for a different query.*

Example 2: Assigning Different Queries to the Same Cursor Variable Depending on Runtime Conditions

Consider a scenario where a report is required of all organizations and their hierarchy levels depending on different conditions, such as the following:

- All organizations that are located in more than one site

- All organizations that don't have a particular hierarchy level

- All organizations that belong to the highest hierarchy level

- All organizations having the same hierarchy as those in a particular site

In this case, it suffices to use a single cursor variable that can be opened for different SELECT statements depending on the report option. I implement this as a SQL procedure (a stored subprogram) that takes the report option as the parameter.

CROSS-REFERENCE   *Chapter 5 covers stored subprograms.*

Here's the code for the procedure:

```
CREATE OR REPLACE PROCEDURE p_print_report(p_report_no NUMBER, p_title VARCHAR2)
IS
  TYPE rc IS REF CURSOR;
    v_rc   rc;
    v_hrc_descr VARCHAR2(20);
    v_org_short_name VARCHAR2(30);
BEGIN
    IF (p_report_no = 1) THEN
        OPEN v_rc FOR SELECT h.hrc_descr, o.org_short_name
                           FROM   org_tab o, hrc_tab h
                           WHERE o.hrc_code = h.hrc_code
                               AND 1 < (SELECT count(os.site_no)
                                          FROM   org_site_tab os
                                          WHERE os.org_id = o.org_id);
        ELSIF (p_report_no = 2) THEN
        OPEN v_rc FOR SELECT h.hrc_descr, o.org_short_name
                           FROM   org_tab o, hrc_tab h
                           WHERE o.hrc_code = h.hrc_code
                               AND NOT EXISTS
                                       (SELECT *
                                          FROM   org_tab o1
                                          WHERE o1.org_id = o.org_id
                                              AND o1.hrc_code = 2 );
    END IF;
    dbms_output.put_line(p_title);
    dbms_output.put_line(rpad('-', length(p_title),'-'));
    dbms_output.put_line(rpad('Hierarchy',20,' ')||' '||
                                       rpad('Description',30,' '));
    dbms_output.put_line(rpad('-',20,'-')||' '||rpad('-',30,'-'));
    LOOP
        FETCH v_rc INTO v_hrc_descr, v_org_short_name;
        EXIT WHEN v_rc%NOTFOUND;
        dbms_output.put_line(rpad(v_hrc_descr,20,' ')||' '||
                                       rpad(v_org_short_name,30,' '));
```

```
      END LOOP;
      CLOSE v_rc;
END p_print_report;
/
```

You can now execute this procedure in a SQL*Plus environment by passing the report number and the corresponding title.

For the first report mentioned previously, here's the code and its output:

```
SQL> set serverout on;
SQL> exec p_print_report(1, 'List of Organizations located in more than one site')
List of Organizations located in more than one site
--------------------------
Hierarchy          Description
---------  --------------
VP                 Office of VP Sales ABC Inc.
VP                 Office of VP Mktg ABC Inc.

PL/SQL procedure successfully completed.
```

For the second report mentioned previously, here's the code and its output:

```
SQL> exec p_print_report(2, 'List of Organizations not having a VP')
List of Organizations not having a VP
------------------------
Hierarchy          Description
---------  ----------------
CEO/COO            Office of CEO ABC Inc.
CEO/COO            Office of CEO XYZ Inc.
CEO/COO            Office of CEO DataPro Inc.

PL/SQL procedure successfully completed.
```

 TIP *Cursor variables and cursors aren't interchangeable. One can't be used in place of the other.*

TIP   *Cursor variables can't be stored in the database. That is, database table columns can't be of type REF CURSOR or SYS_REFCURSOR.*

Returning Resultsets from Stored Subprograms

You can use cursor variables to return resultsets from stored functions and procedures as well as packaged functions and procedures.

CROSS-REFERENCE   *I discuss using returning resultsets from stored procedures in Chapter 5.*

Cursor Expressions

Oracle9*i* has incorporated the facility to nest cursors in PL/SQL cursor declarations in the form of cursor expressions. In this section, I discuss the method of declaring and using cursor expressions in PL/SQL 9*i*. I also outline the method of passing cursors as actual parameters to functions.

Why Use Cursor Expressions?

Cursor expressions eliminate the use of declaring and using multiple cursors and hence result in a more effective optimization scheme by the SQL engine as it involves only one SQL statement as opposed to multiple cursors, which result in multiple SQL statements. Also, cursor expressions eliminate the use of complicated joins involved in SQL SELECT statements. As a third benefit, Oracle9*i* removes the limitation of using cursor expressions in SQL embedded in PL/SQL code. Now you can use cursor expressions as part of PL/SQL cursors. Also, when you use dynamic SQL, you can use cursor expressions and fetch into REF CURSOR variables. In this case, they support complex binds and defines needed for REF CURSORS. This isn't supported by DBMS_SQL.

Declaring Cursor Expressions

Basically, a *cursor expression* is a cursor declaration in PL/SQL in which the cursor SELECT statement contains one column as a cursor. This results in the declaration of nested cursors. A cursor expression is declared using this syntax:

```
CURSOR <parent-cursor-name> is
   SELECT col_name, CURSOR (SELECT  ... ) ...
```

Here's an example of a cursor expression:

```
CURSOR csr_hierarchy IS
   SELECT h.hrc_descr,
          CURSOR(SELECT o.org_long_name
                 FROM   org_tab o
                 WHERE o.hrc_code = h.hrc_code) long_name
   FROM   hrc_tab h;
```

This provides the functionality of a single query returning sets of values from multiple tables.

Prior to Oracle9*i*, CURSOR subqueries were supported in top-level SQL SELECT statements only. For example, a SELECT statement such as this:

```
SELECT h.hrc_descr,
       CURSOR(SELECT o.org_long_name
              FROM   org_tab o
              WHERE o.hrc_code = h.hrc_code) long_name
   FROM   hrc_tab h;
```

runs perfectly well in releases prior to Oracle9*i*, with the following output in SQL*Plus:

```
SQL> SELECT h.hrc_descr,
  2            CURSOR(SELECT o.org_long_name
  3                   FROM   org_tab o
  4                   WHERE o.hrc_code = h.hrc_code) long_name
  5      FROM  hrc_tab h;

HRC_DESCR          LONG_NAME
---------- -----------
CEO/COO            CURSOR STATEMENT : 2

CURSOR STATEMENT : 2

ORG_LONG_NAME
-----------------------------
```

```
Office of CEO ABC Inc.
Office of CEO XYZ Inc.
Office of CEO DataPro Inc.

VP                     CURSOR STATEMENT : 2

CURSOR STATEMENT : 2

ORG_LONG_NAME
--------------------------------------------
Office of VP Sales ABC Inc.
Office of VP Mktg ABC Inc.
Office of VP Tech ABC Inc.

Director               CURSOR STATEMENT : 2

CURSOR STATEMENT : 2

no rows selected


HRC_DESCR              LONG_NAME
----------  ------------
Manager                CURSOR STATEMENT : 2

CURSOR STATEMENT : 2

no rows selected


HRC_DESCR              LONG_NAME
----------  ------------
Analyst                CURSOR STATEMENT : 2

CURSOR STATEMENT : 2

no rows selected
```

However, before Oracle9*i*, declaring a cursor in PL/SQL with this SELECT statement resulted in the compilation error shown here:

```
SQL> DECLARE
  2    CURSOR c1 IS
  3      SELECT h.hrc_descr,
  4            CURSOR(SELECT o.org_long_name
  5                   FROM   org_tab o
  6                   WHERE o.hrc_code = h.hrc_code) long_name
  7      FROM   hrc_tab h;
  8  BEGIN
  9    NULL;
 10  END;
```

```
 11   /
           CURSOR(SELECT o.org_long_name
                     *
ERROR at line 4:
ORA-06550: line 4, column 17:
PLS-00103: Encountered the symbol "SELECT" when expecting one of the following:
( ) - + mod not null others <an identifier>
<a double-quoted delimited-identifier> <a bind variable>
table avg count current exists max min prior sql stddev sum
variance execute multiset the both leading trailing forall
year month DAY_ HOUR_ MINUTE_ second TIMEZONE_HOUR_
TIMEZONE_MINUTE_ time timestamp interval date
<a string literal with character set specification>
<a number> <a single-quoted SQL stri
ORA-06550: line 6, column 48:
PLS-00103: Encountered the symbol "LONG_NAME" when expecting one of the
following:
; return returning and or
```

In Oracle8*i* and earlier, you could achieve the same function in PL/SQL by using two cursors with corresponding cursor FOR LOOPs. Here's the code for the same:

```
BEGIN
    FOR   i   IN (SELECT hrc_code, hrc_descr FROM hrc_tab) LOOP
       FOR   j   IN (SELECT org_long_name
                         FROM    org_tab
                         WHERE hrc_code = i.hrc_code) LOOP
            dbms_output.put_line(i.hrc_descr||' '||j.org_long_name);
       END LOOP;
    END LOOP;
END;
/
```

Using a cursor expression has the advantage of using only one SELECT statement to achieve the result. As such, it is optimized more effectively. The method of using a cursor expression in PL/SQL 9*i* is explained in the next section, "Using Cursor Expressions."

 TIP *Multiple nesting using the CURSOR (subquery SELECT) is allowed.*

A cursor expression isn't allowed for an implicit cursor, in a view declaration, or in a subquery of a parent query. It is allowed in a parent query (i.e., the outermost SELECT list of a query).

Using Cursor Expressions

As I mentioned earlier, a cursor expression enables a single query to return sets of values from multiple tables. Here are the steps for using a cursor expression:

1. Declare the cursor expression with nested cursors.

2. Open the parent cursor. There's no need to open the nested cursors.

3. Use nested loops that fetch first from the rows of the result set and then from any nested cursors within these rows.

4. Declare a REF CURSOR to hold the nested cursor resultset while fetching.

5. Close the parent cursor. There's no need to close the nested cursors.

I wrote a PL/SQL function to use the cursor expression declared here. Here's the code:

```
create or replace function f_cursor_exp return NUMBER
is
TYPE rc is REF CURSOR;
/* declare the cursor expression */
CURSOR csr_hierarchy IS
   SELECT h.hrc_descr,
          CURSOR(SELECT o.org_long_name
                 FROM   org_tab o
                 WHERE o.hrc_code = h.hrc_code) long_name
   FROM  hrc_tab h;
/* Declare a REF CURSOR variable to hold the nested cursor resultset
   while fetching. */
hrc_rec rc;
v_hrc_descr VARCHAR2(20);
v_org_long_name VARCHAR2(60);
BEGIN
   /* Open the parent cursor */
   OPEN csr_hierarchy;
   LOOP
```

```
/* fetch the column csr_hierarchy.hrc_descr,
    then loop through the resultset of the nested cursor. */
    FETCH csr_hierarchy INTO v_hrc_descr, hrc_rec;
    EXIT WHEN csr_hierarchy%notfound;
/* Use a nested loop that fetches from the nested cursor
    within the parent rows. */
    LOOP
      -- Directly fetch from the nested cursor, there is no need to open it.
      FETCH hrc_rec INTO v_org_long_name;
      EXIT WHEN hrc_rec%notfound;
      DBMS_OUTPUT.PUT_LINE(v_hrc_descr ||' '||v_org_long_name);
    END LOOP;
  END LOOP;
/* Close the parent cursor. No need to close the nested cursor. */
  close csr_hierarchy;
  RETURN (0);
EXCEPTION WHEN OTHERS THEN
  RETURN (SQLCODE);
END;
/
```

The following points are worth noting:

- There's no need to open the nested cursor. It's implicitly opened when
  a row is fetched from the parent cursor.

- There's no need to close the nested cursor. It's implicitly closed when the
  parent cursor is closed.

Cursor Expressions Using Multiple Levels of Nested Cursors

This example demonstrates multiple levels of nested cursors. In the following
code, I display the complete hierarchy, org, and org-site details:

```
create or replace function f_cursor_exp_complex return NUMBER
is
TYPE rc is REF CURSOR;
/* declare the cursor expression */
CURSOR csr_hierarchy IS
  SELECT h.hrc_descr,
```

```
                    CURSOR(SELECT o.org_long_name,
                                  CURSOR (SELECT s.site_descr
                                          FROM    org_site_tab os, site_tab s
                                          WHERE   os.site_no = s.site_no
                                          AND     os.org_id = o.org_id) as site_name
                           FROM    org_tab o
                           WHERE o.hrc_code = h.hrc_code) long_name
        FROM  hrc_tab h;
        /* Declare two REF CURSOR variables to hold the nested cursor resultset
           while fetching. */
        hrc_rec rc;
        org_rec rc;
        v_hrc_descr VARCHAR2(20);
        v_org_long_name VARCHAR2(60);
        v_site_name VARCHAR2(20);
        BEGIN
          /* Open the parent cursor */
          OPEN csr_hierarchy;
          LOOP
        /* fetch the column csr_hierarchy.hrc_descr,
            then loop through the resultset of the nested cursors. */
            FETCH csr_hierarchy INTO v_hrc_descr, hrc_rec;
            EXIT WHEN csr_hierarchy%notfound;
            LOOP
        /* Use a nested loop that fetches from the first nested cursor
            within the parent rows */
              FETCH hrc_rec INTO v_org_long_name, org_rec;
              EXIT WHEN hrc_rec%notfound;
              LOOP
          -- Directly fetch from the second nested cursor, there is no need to open it
                FETCH org_rec INTO v_site_name;
                EXIT WHEN org_rec%notfound;
                DBMS_OUTPUT.PUT_LINE(v_hrc_descr ||' '||v_org_long_name||' '||
                                                        v_site_name);
              END LOOP;
            END LOOP;
          END LOOP;
        /* Close the parent cursor. No need to close the nested cursors. */
          close csr_hierarchy;
          RETURN (0);
        EXCEPTION WHEN OTHERS THEN
          RETURN (SQLCODE);
        END;
        /
```

You can now execute this function as shown here:

```
SQL> set serverout on;
SQL>  VAR ret_code NUMBER;
SQL> exec :ret_code := f_cursor_exp_complex;
```

Cursor Expressions as Arguments to Functions Called from SQL

I mentioned earlier that you can use cursor variables as formal parameters to a function. Also, cursor expressions refer to actual cursors. Now the following question arises: Can cursor expressions be used as actual parameters to such functions having REF CURSORS or SYS_REFCURSOR as formal parameter types? The answer to this question is yes, provided the function is called in a top-level SQL statement only.

Consider the second example presented in the earlier section "Dynamism in Using Cursor Variables." It describes a scenario in which a report is required of all organizations and their hierarchy levels depending on different conditions such as

- All organizations that are located in more than one site

- All organizations that don't have a particular hierarchy level

- All organizations that belong to the highest hierarchy level

- All organizations having same hierarchy as those in a particular site

In this case, it suffices to write a function that takes a cursor expression as input along with the title of the report and generates the report. The cursor expression is passed as an actual parameter with different WHERE conditions each time, but the columns in the SELECT will be the same each time. Here's the code for this function:

```
CREATE OR REPLACE FUNCTION f_report(p_cursor SYS_REFCURSOR, p_title VARCHAR2)
RETURN NUMBER
IS
    v_hrc_descr VARCHAR2(20);
    v_org_short_name VARCHAR2(30);
    v_ret_code NUMBER;
BEGIN
```

```
        BEGIN
          dbms_output.put_line(p_title);
          dbms_output.put_line(rpad('Hierarchy',20,' ')||'  '||
                                              rpad('Organization',30,' '));
          dbms_output.put_line(rpad('-',20,'-')||'  '||rpad('-',30,'-'));
          LOOP
              FETCH p_cursor INTO v_hrc_descr, v_org_short_name;
              EXIT WHEN p_cursor%NOTFOUND;
              dbms_output.put_line(rpad(v_hrc_descr,20,' ')||'  '||
                              rpad(v_org_short_name,30,' '));
          END LOOP;
          v_ret_code := 1;
      EXCEPTION WHEN OTHERS THEN
          v_ret_code := SQLCODE;
      END;
       RETURN (v_ret_code);
END;
/
```

You can now invoke this function with a cursor expression as an actual parameter to generate the different reports mentioned previously. Here's the SELECT statement:

```
SELECT 'Report Generated on '||TO_CHAR(SYSDATE,'MM/DD/YYYY') "Report1"
FROM   DUAL
WHERE f_report(
            CURSOR(SELECT h.hrc_descr, o.org_short_name
                     FROM   hrc_tab h, org_tab o
                     WHERE o.hrc_code = h.hrc_code
                          AND 1 < (SELECT count(os.site_no)
                                     FROM  org_site_tab os
                                     WHERE os.org_id = o.org_id)
                  ),
             'List of Organizations located in more than one site'
                  ) = 1;
```

Because dbms_output.put_line is being called from inside a function used in a SQL SELECT, the output buffer should be flushed. You do this by executing a small procedure called "flush," as follows:

```
CREATE OR REPLACE PROCEDURE flush
IS
 BEGIN
      NULL;
END;
/
```

Here's the output of this SELECT statement after executing flush:

```
SQL> SELECT 'Report Generated on '||TO_CHAR(SYSDATE,'MM/DD/YYYY') "Report1"
  2  FROM    DUAL
  3  WHERE f_report(
  4            CURSOR(SELECT h.hrc_descr, o.org_short_name
  5                          FROM   hrc_tab h, org_tab o
  6                          WHERE o.hrc_code = h.hrc_code
  7                             AND 1 < (SELECT count(os.site_no)
  8                                        FROM  org_site_tab os
  9                                       WHERE os.org_id = o.org_id)
 10            ),  'List of Organizations located in more than one site'
 11                              ) = 1;

Report1
----------------
Report Generated on 02/13/2002

SQL> exec flush
List of Organizations located in more than one site
Hierarchy          Organization
--------  --------------
VP                 Office of VP Sales ABC Inc.
VP                 Office of VP Mktg ABC Inc.

PL/SQL procedure successfully completed.
```

You can use the same function to generate a different report—for example, a report that contains a list of organizations that don't have a vice president (VP). In this case, the function is invoked with a different cursor expression. Here's the second SELECT statement:

```
SELECT 'Report Generated on '||TO_CHAR(SYSDATE,'MM/DD/YYYY') "Report2"
FROM    DUAL
WHERE f_report(
        CURSOR(SELECT h.hrc_descr, o.org_short_name
                        FROM   hrc_tab h, org_tab o
                        WHERE o.hrc_code = h.hrc_code
                            AND NOT EXISTS  (SELECT *
```

```
                                    FROM   org_tab o1
                                    WHERE o1.org_id = o.org_id
                                      AND o1.hrc_code = 2 )
                ), 'List of Organizations not having a VP'
                ) = 1;
```

Here's the output of the second SELECT statement (the output buffer is flushed in this case also):

```
SQL> SELECT 'Report Generated on '||TO_CHAR(SYSDATE,'MM/DD/YYYY') "Report2"
  2  FROM   DUAL
  3  WHERE f_report(
  4        CURSOR(SELECT h.hrc_descr, o.org_short_name
  5                      FROM   hrc_tab h, org_tab o
  6                      WHERE o.hrc_code = h.hrc_code
  7                        AND NOT EXISTS  (SELECT *
  8                                          FROM   org_tab o1
  9                                          WHERE o1.org_id = o.org_id
 10                                            AND o1.hrc_code = 2 )
 11              ), 'List of Organizations not having a VP'
 12              ) = 1;

Report2
----------------
Report Generated on 02/13/2002

SQL> exec flush
List of Organizations not having a VP
Hierarchy          Organization
--------- ----------------
CEO/COO            Office of CEO ABC Inc.
CEO/COO            Office of CEO XYZ Inc.
CEO/COO            Office of CEO DataPro Inc.

PL/SQL procedure successfully completed.
```

Instead of using the function f_report with dbms_output.put_line called to display output, you can directly generate the output using a SELECT column list. For this I use the following function:

```
CREATE OR REPLACE FUNCTION f_cursor(p_cursor SYS_REFCURSOR)
RETURN NUMBER
IS
    v_org_short_name VARCHAR2(30);
    v_cnt NUMBER := 0;
    v_ret_code NUMBER;
BEGIN
        BEGIN
            LOOP
                    FETCH p_cursor INTO v_org_short_name;
                    EXIT WHEN p_cursor%NOTFOUND;
                    v_cnt := v_cnt + 1;
                END LOOP;
            IF (v_cnt  > 0) THEN
                v_ret_code := 1;
            ELSE
                v_ret_code := 0;
            END IF;
        EXCEPTION WHEN OTHERS THEN
            v_ret_code := SQLCODE;
        END;
        RETURN (v_ret_code);
END;
/
```

Then you can generate the first report by using the following SELECT statement (there's no need to flush the output buffer):

```
SELECT rpad(h.hrc_descr,20,' ') "Hierarchy",
                rpad(o.org_short_name,30,' ') "Organization"
FROM    hrc_tab h, org_tab o
WHERE h.hrc_code = o.hrc_code
      AND f_cursor(
            CURSOR(SELECT o1.org_short_name
                        FROM    org_tab o1
                        WHERE o1.org_id = o.org_id
                            AND 1 < (SELECT count(os.site_no)
                                        FROM  org_site_tab os
                                        WHERE os.org_id = o1.org_id)
                    )
                ) = 1;
```

Here's the output generated:

```
SQL> SELECT rpad(h.hrc_descr,20,' ') "Hierarchy",
  2                     rpad(o.org_short_name,30,' ') "Organization"
  3  FROM    hrc_tab h, org_tab o
  4  WHERE h.hrc_code = o.hrc_code
  5       AND f_cursor(
  6            CURSOR(SELECT o1.org_short_name
  7                     FROM    org_tab o1
  8                     WHERE o1.org_id = o.org_id
  9                       AND 1 < (SELECT count(os.site_no)
 10                                FROM  org_site_tab os
 11                                WHERE os.org_id = o1.org_id)
 12                  )
 13                         ) = 1;

Hierarchy           Organization
---------  ----------------
VP                  Office of VP Sales ABC Inc.
VP                  Office of VP Mktg ABC Inc.
```

Similarly, you can generate the second report by using the following SELECT (there's no need to flush the output buffer):

```
SELECT rpad(h.hrc_descr,20,' ') "Hierarchy",
             rpad(o.org_short_name,30,' ') "Organization"
FROM    hrc_tab h, org_tab o
WHERE h.hrc_code = o.hrc_code
       AND f_cursor(
            CURSOR(SELECT o1.org_short_name
                     FROM    org_tab o1
                     WHERE o1.org_id = o.org_id
                            AND NOT EXISTS (SELECT *
                                     FROM  org_tab o2
                                     WHERE o2.org_id = o1.org_id
                                        AND o2.hrc_code = 2 )
                  )
                    ) = 1;
```

Here's the output generated:

```
SQL> SELECT rpad(h.hrc_descr,20,' ') "Hierarchy",
  2         rpad(o.org_short_name,30,' ') "Organization"
  3  FROM   hrc_tab h, org_tab o
  4  WHERE h.hrc_code = o.hrc_code
  5        AND f_cursor(
  6              CURSOR(SELECT o1.org_short_name
  7                     FROM   org_tab o1
  8                     WHERE o1.org_id = o.org_id
  9                           AND NOT EXISTS  (SELECT *
 10                                            FROM  org_tab o2
 11                                     WHERE o2.org_id = o1.org_id
 12                                       AND o2.hrc_code = 2 )
 13                    )
 14                 ) = 1;

Hierarchy           Organization
---------  ----------------
CEO/COO             Office of CEO ABC Inc.
CEO/COO             Office of CEO XYZ Inc.
CEO/COO             Office of CEO DataPro Inc.

PL/SQL procedure successfully completed.
```

Both the functions f_report and f_cursor are invoked by passing a cursor expression as an actual parameter.

You can't use cursor expressions as actual parameters to functions with formal parameters of type REF CURSOR or SYS_REFCURSOR if the function is called in PL/SQL. For example, the following code is invalid:

```
DECLARE
     v_num NUMBER;
BEGIN
     v_num := f_report(
          CURSOR(SELECT h.hrc_descr, o.org_long_name
                 FROM   hrc_tab h, org_tab o
                 WHERE o.hrc_code = h.hrc_code
                       AND 1 < (SELECT count(os.site_no)
                                FROM  org_site_tab os
                                WHERE os.org_id = o.org_id)
                ),
              'List of Organizations located in more than one site'
          ) ;
END;
/
```

The preceding code raises the following error:

```
SQL> DECLARE
  2      v_num NUMBER;
  3  BEGIN
  4      v_num := f_report(
  5          CURSOR(SELECT h.hrc_descr, o.org_long_name
  6                    FROM   hrc_tab h, org_tab o
  7                    WHERE o.hrc_code = h.hrc_code
  8                      AND 1 < (SELECT count(os.site_no)
  9                                  FROM   org_site_tab os
 10                                  WHERE os.org_id = o.org_id)
 11                ),
 12          'List of Organizations located in more than one site'
 13                ) ;
 14  END;
 15  /
          CURSOR(SELECT h.hrc_descr, o.org_long_name
              *
ERROR at line 5:
ORA-06550: line 5, column 13:
PLS-00405: subquery not allowed in this context
ORA-06550: line 4, column 6:
PL/SQL: Statement ignored
```

Summary

This chapter thoroughly covered PL/SQL cursors. You learned the various methods of using cursors and cursor variables in a PL/SQL environment. You also learned about cursor expressions, a new feature of PL/SQL 9*i*.

The next chapter presents a discussion of user-defined record types and index-by tables in PL/SQL.

CHAPTER 3

PL/SQL Records and Index-by Tables

PL/SQL OFFERS A VARIETY of data types for use, and these data types can be categorized into four broad classes: scalar data types, composite data types, object data types, and other PL/SQL-specific data types. Of these, the scalar data types are the ones in the NUMBER family and its subtypes; the CHAR family, including the Natural Character family, and its subtypes; the DATE family and its subtypes; the INTERVAL family; the TIMESTAMP family; and MSLABEL. The composite data types include the record type, the index-by table, and collections such as nested tables and VARRAYS. The object data types include object types, object references, LOB types, and Oracle9*i*-specific object data types such as SYS.ANYTYPE, SYS.ANYDATA, SYS.ANYDATASET, and their family. In addition to these data types, there are other PL/SQL-specific data types such as BOOLEAN, BINARY_INTEGER, PLS_INTEGER, %TYPE, REF CURSOR, SYS_REFCURSOR (Oracle9*i* specific), and user-defined subtypes. Table 3-1 summarizes these data types.

Table 3-1. Summary of PL/SQL Data Types

TYPE	MEMBERS
Scalar data types	NUMBER family and its subtypes
	CHAR family and its subtypes
	DATE family and its subtypes
	INTERVAL family (Oracle9*i* specific)
	TIMESTAMP family (Oracle9*i* specific)
	MSLABEL
Composite data types	RECORD
	Index-by table
	Nested table
	VARRAY

(continued)

Table 3-1. Summary of PL/SQL Data Types (continued)

TYPE	MEMBERS
Object data types	OBJECT type
	OBJECT REF
	LOB family
	SYS.ANYTYPE, SYS.ANYDATA, and SYS.ANYDATASET (Oracle9*i* specific)
Other PL/SQL-specific data types	BOOLEAN
	BINARY_INTEGER
	PLS_INTEGER
	%TYPE
	REF CURSOR
	SYS_REFCURSOR (Oracle9*i* specific)
	User-defined subtypes

In the discussion of cursors in Chapter 2, I made mention of some of the PL/SQL-specific data types such as REF CURSOR and SYS_REFCURSOR. This chapter discusses two composite data types available in PL/SQL: the record type and the index-by table type.

CROSS-REFERENCE *I discuss other composite data types such as nested tables and VARRAYS in Chapter 11.*

Beginning with the definition and use of these data types, this chapter goes on to highlight the various features available in both types and the various PL/SQL methods that you can invoke on index-by tables. The ins and outs of using both data types are presented. I illustrate the concept of records and index-by tables by taking into account the organizational hierarchy system. You can find the schema definitions in Appendix A.

Both records and index-by tables fall under the category of user-defined data structures. Records are otherwise termed as user-defined records. Other user-defined objects fall under the following categories:

- *User-defined subprograms (functions, procedures, and packages):* I discuss user-defined subprograms in Chapter 5.

- *User-defined data types:* Chapter 10 covers user-defined data types.

- *User-defined exceptions:* I discuss user-defined exceptions in Chapter 4.

- *User-defined audits:* I discuss user-defined audits with respect to DML and DDL auditing in Chapter 6.

- *User-defined parameters:* Chapter 5 covers user-defined parameters.

- *User-defined operators:* I discuss user-defined operators in Chapter 10.

Let's begin with a discussion on records.

Records

A *record* is a composite data type consisting of individual elements that are logically related. Each element of the record is called a *field,* has a value associated with it, and can be assessed as an individual element of the record. Each field in a record has a name and is usually of the scalar data type. However, a field in a record can be another record. Using record types enables you to make use of data abstraction because you work with data as a group instead of using individual elements. This also means less code, which in turn means easy maintainability. As an example, consider that an organization can be defined as a record with fields composed of logically related information about it, such as org id, org short name, and org long name.

PL/SQL lets you define three types of records: explicitly defined records, database table-oriented records, and cursor-oriented records. I begin with a discussion of explicitly defined records and then touch on the other record types in the later part of this section.

Defining a Record

Unlike scalar variables, which you define by directly declaring the variables of the particular type, you define a record variable by first defining a record type and then declaring a variable of that type. These steps are outlined in the following sections.

Defining the Record Type

You define a record type using the TYPE statement. Here's the syntax:

```
TYPE record_type_name IS RECORD
   ( field_name1 datatype [NOT NULL] [DEFAULT value1 | := assign1],
     field_name2 datatype [NOT NULL] [DEFAULT value2 | := assign2],
     ... ...
     field_nameN datatype [NOT NULL] [DEFAULT valueN | := assignN]
);
```

where record_type_name is a name that identifies the structure of the new record containing individual fields, with the names field_name1 to field_nameN. Notice that each field has a data type specified (which can be a scalar or user-defined subtype, or another record type), an optional NOT NULL constraint, and a DEFAULT clause with initial values specified by value1 through valueN. Alternatively, initial values can be specified by an initial assignment using the := syntax followed by a value. Here, assign1 through assignN are expressions that each evaluate to a value with the same data type as the specified data type of the corresponding field.

Here's an example of a record type declaration:

```
TYPE hrc_org_rec IS RECORD
        (hrc_org_id NUMBER,
         hrc_descr VARCHAR2(20),
         org_short_name VARCHAR2(30));
```

where hrc_org_rec is a record type that has a three-field structure.

Declaring a Variable of the Record Type

Once you've defined a record type with a specific structure, you need to declare
the actual records of that type. Here's the syntax:

```
<record_var_name> <record_type_name>;
```

In this line, record_type_name is the record type defined using the TYPE . . .
RECORD specification, and record_var_name is an arbitrary variable name with
a data type of this record type. Here's an example to show this:

```
v_example_rec hrc_org_rec;
```

TIP   *A TYPE . . . RECORD definition is only abstract, and
as such, it can't be used by itself. Defining a TYPE . . .
RECORD declaration doesn't occupy any memory until you
declare variables of that type.*

A complete example combining the two preceding steps is as follows:

```
DECLARE
    TYPE hrc_org_rec IS RECORD
            (hrc_org_id NUMBER,
            hrc_descr VARCHAR2(20),
            org_short_name VARCHAR2(30));
    v_example_rec hrc_org_rec;
BEGIN
    /* Do some processing */
    null;
END;
/
```

TIP   *In addition to any scalar data types and a record
type, fields in a record can have a data type of %TYPE,
%ROWSTYPE, or an index-by table. Each field in a record
type must have a unique name. A field declared as NOT
NULL must have a default value specified.*

Using a Record Type

Once you've defined a record type and declared variables of that type, the next step is to use the record for processing data. This step usually consists of accessing the individual record elements, storing data in the record, and performing comparison operations on the record for equality.

Accessing Individual Record Elements

You access the individual elements of a record using the dot notation. Here's the syntax:

```
<record_var_name>.<field_name>
```

Note that the actual record variable name, not the record type name, is used. This syntax is similar to the syntax you use when accessing a column in a database table using the <table_name>.<column_name> syntax. This brings to light the analogy between database tables and records. However, a difference between the two is that the former are stored in a database, whereas the latter are not and cannot be stored in a database.

TIP   *When you access the individual elements of a record, use the record variable name and not the record type name. Record types are PL/SQL specific, and as such, they aren't available in SQL. Also, they can't be stored in a database.*

Here's the example for the hrc_org_rec record defined previously:

```
DECLARE
     TYPE hrc_org_rec IS RECORD
             (hrc_org_id NUMBER,
              hrc_descr VARCHAR2(20),
              org_short_name VARCHAR2(30));
     v_example_rec hrc_org_rec;
BEGIN
     v_example_rec.hrc_org_id := 1001;
     v_example_rec.hrc_descr := 'CEO/COO';
     v_example_rec.org_short_name := 'Office of CEO/COO ABC Inc.';
     dbms_output.put_line('An example record:');
     dbms_output.new_line;
```

```
    dbms_output.put_line(to_number(v_example_rec.hrc_org_id)||' '||
                                    v_example_rec.hrc_descr||' '||
                                    v_example_rec.org_short_name);
END;
/
```

Here's the output of the preceding code:

```
An example record:
1001 CEO/COO Office of CEO/COO ABC Inc.

PL/SQL procedure successfully completed.
```

In this example, the individual record elements are assigned values and then they're accessed to display these values. Notice how the record elements are referenced using the dot notation when both populating the record variable and referencing the fields in the record variable.

TIP *A PL/SQL record variable is a read-write variable. You can use it on both sides of an assignment operator.*

In addition to accessing individual elements of a record, you can access the entire record itself in some cases—for example, when you initialize a record with another record or when you pass a record as a parameter to a subprogram. Here's an example to illustrate this:

```
DECLARE
    TYPE hrc_org_rec IS RECORD
            (hrc_org_id NUMBER,
             hrc_descr VARCHAR2(20),
             org_short_name VARCHAR2(30));
    v_example_rec1 hrc_org_rec;
    v_example_rec2 hrc_org_rec;
BEGIN
    v_example_rec1.hrc_org_id := 1001;
    v_example_rec1.hrc_descr := 'CEO/COO';
    v_example_rec1.org_short_name := 'Office of CEO/COO ABC Inc. ';
    v_example_rec2 := v_example_rec1;
    dbms_output.put_line('An example record: ');
```

```
                dbms_output.new_line;
                dbms_output.put_line(to_number(v_example_rec2.hrc_org_id)|| ' '||
                                              v_example_rec2.hrc_descr||' '||
                                              v_example_rec2.org_short_name);
        END;
        /
```

Here's the output of the previous program:

```
An example record:
1001 CEO/COO Office of CEO/COO ABC Inc.

PL/SQL procedure successfully completed.
```

Notice the assignment statement

```
v_example_rec2 := v_example_rec1;
```

where the first record as a whole is referenced using the record name and used as input to a second record that's also referenced as a whole.

Testing for Equality of Records

In the previous program, two example records were defined with the same structure. The first record was populated using explicit assignment of its individual fields, and this whole record was assigned to the second record. Now, how do you test these records for equality? This section provides the answer to that question.

You test for equality of each of the individual fields one-to-one in both records. Testing for equality using the record names as a whole won't work. That means the following code results in an error:

```
IF (v_example_rec1 = v_example_rec2) THEN
    . . . . . .
END IF;
```

Instead, you have to use the following:

```
IF ((v_example_rec1.hrc_org_id = v_example_rec2.hrc_org_id) AND
    ((v_example_rec1.hrc_descr = v_example_rec2.hrc_descr) AND
    ((v_example_rec1.org_short_name = v_example_rec2.org_short_name) THEN
    . . . . . .
END IF;
```

Here's a complete example:

```
DECLARE
    TYPE hrc_org_rec IS RECORD
                (hrc_org_id NUMBER,
            hrc_descr VARCHAR2(20),
            org_short_name VARCHAR2(30));
        v_example_rec1 hrc_org_rec;
        v_example_rec2 hrc_org_rec;
BEGIN
        v_example_rec1.hrc_org_id := 1001;
        v_example_rec1.hrc_descr := 'CEO/COO';
        v_example_rec1.org_short_name := 'Office of CEO/COO ABC Inc. ';
        v_example_rec2.hrc_org_id := 1002;
        v_example_rec2.hrc_descr := 'VP';
        v_example_rec2.org_short_name := 'Office of  VP ABC Inc. ';
    IF ((v_example_rec1.hrc_org_id = v_example_rec2.hrc_org_id) AND
            (v_example_rec1.hrc_descr = v_example_rec2.hrc_descr) AND
            (v_example_rec1.org_short_name = v_example_rec2.org_short_name)) THEN
            dbms_output.put_line('Both example records are identical.');
    ELSE
            dbms_output.put_line('The two example records are different. ');
    END IF;
END;
/
```

Record Initialization

A record type is a composite data type, and as such, the rules for initializing record type variables are different from those for initializing scalar type variables. To initialize a scalar variable, you simply provide an initial value in its declaration using the DEFAULT or := syntax. To initialize a record variable, you have to assign a second record variable that's compatible with the record variable you're initializing. However, you still have to use the DEFAULT or := syntax.

Record initialization is useful when you're passing records as parameters to subprograms. You might pass a record as parameter, declare a local record variable of the same type as that of the parameter, and then initialize this local variable with the parameter you're passing.

TIP   *A* compatible record *is a record based on the same record type as the target record.*

TIP   *Initializing a record to NULL is only possible by initializing each of its individual fields to NULL. You can't assign the record as a whole to NULL, because NULL is treated by PL/SQL as a scalar value.*

Record Assignment

In the simplest terms, *record assignment* means assigning a record with values. This in turn implies two things: populating the individual fields of a record and assigning a record to another record. The latter is called *aggregate assignment*. PL/SQL 9*i* allows you to assign a record with values in the following four ways:

1. Individual field assignment

2. Populating a record with a SELECT INTO (using an implicit cursor)

3. Populating a record with FETCH INTO (using an explicit cursor)

4. Assigning a record using a second record (aggregate assignment)

I discuss each of the methods in the following sections.

Individual Field Assignment

This method consists of assigning each of the individual fields in the record with data values. The fields are referenced using the record_name.field_name notation on the left side of the assignment operator and assigned with values. In the hrc_org_rec record example presented in the section "Accessing Individual Record Elements," you learned how to assign the individual fields with values. Here's the same example reproduced for illustration:

```
DECLARE
  TYPE hrc_org_rec IS RECORD
            (hrc_org_id NUMBER,
         hrc_descr VARCHAR2(20),
         org_short_name VARCHAR2(30));
     v_example_rec hrc_org_rec;
BEGIN
     v_example_rec.hrc_org_id := 1001;
     v_example_rec.hrc_descr := 'CEO/COO';
     v_example_rec.org_short_name := 'Office of CEO/COO ABC Inc. ';
   dbms_output.put_line('An example record: ');
   dbms_output.new_line;
   dbms_output.put_line(to_number(v_example_rec.hrc_org_id)|| ' '||
                                    v_example_rec.hrc_descr||' '||
                                    v_example_rec.org_short_name);
END;
/
```

 TIP *You must explicitly assign each field of the record with a value. You can't leave out any field.*

Populating a Record with SELECT INTO (Using an Implicit Cursor)

A second way to populate a record is with a SELECT INTO statement. The INTO clause can specify the entire record name or it can specify the individual fields of the records using the dot notation. However, the structure of the SELECT column list must exactly match the record structure. This means the data type of each column and the number of columns in the SELECT list should exactly match that of the record fields. The individual column names in the SELECT list can be different. Here's an example of this:

```
DECLARE
  TYPE hrc_org_rec IS RECORD
          (hrc_org_id NUMBER,
           hrc_descr VARCHAR2(20),
           org_short_name VARCHAR2(30));
     v_example_rec hrc_org_rec;
BEGIN
```

```
SELECT hrc_org_seq.nextval, h.hrc_descr, o.org_short_name
INTO     v_example_rec
FROM    org_tab o, hrc_tab h
WHERE o.hrc_code = h.hrc_code
        AND o.org_id = 1001;
dbms_output.put_line('An example record: ');
dbms_output.new_line;
dbms_output.put_line(to_number(v_example_rec.hrc_org_id)||' '||
                                  v_example_rec.hrc_descr||' '||
                                  v_example_rec.org_short_name);
END;
/
```

Here's the output of the previous code:

```
An example record:
1 CEO/COO Office of CEO ABC Inc.

PL/SQL procedure successfully completed.
```

Populating a Record with FETCH INTO (Using an Explicit Cursor)

A third way to populate a record is with a FETCH INTO statement resulting from an explicit cursor. This was demonstrated in Chapter 2. As with the implicit cursor, the INTO clause can specify the entire record name or it can specify the individual fields of the records using the dot notation. However, the structure of the cursor SELECT column list must exactly match the record structure. This means the data type of each column and the number of columns in the cursor SELECT list should exactly match that of the record fields. However, the individual column names in the cursor SELECT list can be different. Here's an example of this:

```
DECLARE
  TYPE hrc_org_rec IS RECORD
          (hrc_org_id NUMBER,
            hrc_descr VARCHAR2(20),
            org_short_name VARCHAR2(30));
      v_example_rec hrc_org_rec;
    CURSOR csr_hrc_org IS
```

```
      SELECT hrc_org_seq.nextval, h.hrc_descr, o.org_short_name
      FROM   org_tab o, hrc_tab h
      WHERE o.hrc_code = h.hrc_code
            AND h.hrc_code = 1;
BEGIN
    OPEN csr_hrc_org;
    dbms_output.put_line('An example output: ');
     dbms_output.new_line;
    LOOP
         FETCH csr_hrc_org INTO v_example_rec;
         EXIT WHEN csr_hrc_org%NOTFOUND;
         dbms_output.put_line(to_number(v_example_rec.hrc_org_id)||' '||
                                        v_example_rec.hrc_descr||' '||
                                        v_example_rec.org_short_name);
    END LOOP;
    CLOSE csr_hrc_org;
END;
/
```

Here's the output of the previous code:

```
An example output:
2 CEO/COO Office of CEO ABC Inc.
3 CEO/COO Office of CEO XYZ Inc.
4 CEO/COO Office of CEO DataPro Inc.

PL/SQL procedure successfully completed.
```

Assigning a Record Using a Second Record (Aggregate Assignment)

This method consists of assigning the entire record with a second record, otherwise known as aggregate assignment. In this case, the individual fields of the destination record are not assigned one-to-one. Instead, you use type-compatible records on both sides of the assignment operator. The source record should already be populated before you do such an assignment. In the example of the hrc_org_rec record presented in the section "Accessing Individual Record Elements," you learned how to perform aggregate assignment. Here's the same example reproduced for illustration:

```
DECLARE
   TYPE hrc_org_rec IS RECORD
                (hrc_org_id NUMBER,
             hrc_descr VARCHAR2(20),
             org_short_name VARCHAR2(30));
      v_example_rec1 hrc_org_rec;
      v_example_rec2 hrc_org_rec;
BEGIN
      v_example_rec1.hrc_org_id := 1001;
      v_example_rec1.hrc_descr := 'CEO/COO';
      v_example_rec1.org_short_name := 'Office of CEO/COO ABC Inc. ';
      v_example_rec2 := v_example_rec1;
   dbms_output.put_line('An example record: ');
   dbms_output.new_line;
   dbms_output.put_line(to_number(v_example_rec2.hrc_org_id)||' '||
                                         v_example_rec2.hrc_descr||' '||
                                         v_example_rec2.org_short_name);
END;
/
```

In this case, the value of each field in the target record is set to the value of
the corresponding field in the source record. You could have done this with three
assignment statements using the individual fields, but aggregate assignment
enables you to do this with one statement. This involves less code and it's also
less error-prone.

TIP   *Aggregate assignment of records is only possible with
records of the same type and same structure. It's not enough
that the source and target record have the same structure.
Use aggregate assignment wherever possible instead of individual field assignment.*

Other Types of Records

The records discussed so far have been user-defined records that were declared
using the TYPE . . . IS RECORD statement. In this section, I discuss two new types
of records: table-oriented records and cursor-oriented records.

Table-Oriented Records

You've seen that a PL/SQL record is a composite data type composed of fields. These fields are arbitrarily chosen and grouped together to form part of a single record. In many cases, it may be necessary to construct a record that resembles the structure of a database table row. Such a record is called a *table-oriented record* or *table record*. In this case, the individual fields are composed of all the columns of a database table row. The fields in this record correspond one-to-one in name and structure to the columns of the database table on which the record is based.

You create a table-oriented record with the %ROWTYPE operator. Here's the syntax:

```
record_var_name table_name%ROWTYPE;
```

where record_var_name is the record variable with the same record structure as a row in the table identified by table_name. Unlike defining explicitly defined records, where you had to first define a record type and then define a record variable of that type, you directly declare table-oriented records without having to define the record type. The record type is inherited from the database table row structure.

> **TIP**   *Use a table-oriented record when you have a need to include all the columns in the underlying database table as fields in the record. You can't use a table-oriented record to include only some of the columns in the underlying table.*

> **TIP**   *When the structure of the database table is altered, the changes are automatically reflected in the table-oriented record.*

You still access the individual fields in a table-oriented record using the dot notation.

Here's a complete example of defining and using a table-oriented record:

```
DECLARE
     hrc_rec hrc_tab%ROWTYPE;
BEGIN
    SELECT *
    INTO        hrc_rec
    FROM      hrc_tab
    WHERE  hrc_code = 1;
    dbms_output.put_line('An example record:');
    dbms_output.new_line;
    dbms_output.put_line(to_char(hrc_rec.hrc_code)||' '||hrc_rec.hrc_descr);
END;
/
```

Here's the output of this program:

```
An example record:
1 CEO/COO

PL/SQL procedure successfully completed.
```

The following points are worth noting:

- The fields in the table-oriented record hrc_rec are same as the corresponding column names in the hrc_tab table.

- All the columns in the hrc_tab table are included as fields in the table-oriented record hrc_rec.

TIP   *You can populate a table-oriented record using explicit assignment, a SELECT INTO, a FETCH INTO, or aggregate assignment. However, when you use aggregate assignment, the source and target should both be table-oriented records based on the same table.*

Cursor-Oriented Records

A *cursor-oriented record* is a record that resembles the structure of a PL/SQL cursor. In this case, the individual fields are composed of the columns of the PL/SQL cursor SELECT. The fields in this record correspond one-to-one in name and structure to the columns of the PL/SQL cursor on which the record is based.

You create a cursor-oriented record with the %ROWTYPE operator. Here's the syntax:

```
record_var_name cursor_name%ROWTYPE;
```

where record_var_name is the record variable that has the same record structure as a row in the cursor identified by cursor_name. As with table-oriented records, you directly declare cursor-oriented records without having to define the record type. The record type is inherited from the cursor row structure.

You still access the individual fields in a cursor-oriented record using the dot notation.

Here's a complete example of defining and using a cursor-oriented record:

```
DECLARE
     CURSOR csr_hrc IS
            SELECT * FROM hrc_tab ORDER BY 1;
     hrc_rec csr_hrc%ROWTYPE;
BEGIN
     OPEN csr_hrc;
     dbms_output.put_line('Hierarchy records: ');
     dbms_output.new_line;
     LOOP
         FETCH csr_hrc INTO hrc_rec;
         EXIT WHEN csr_hrc%NOTFOUND;
         dbms_output.put_line(to_char(hrc_rec.hrc_code)|| ' '||hrc_rec.hrc_descr);
     END LOOP;
     CLOSE csr_hrc;
END;
/
```

Here's the output of this program:

```
Hierarchy records:
1 CEO/COO
2 VP
3 Director
4 Manager
5 Analyst

PL/SQL procedure successfully completed.
```

TIP *A cursor-oriented record's structure can resemble multiple columns from multiple tables as the underlying cursor is defined. This gives more flexibility to the programmer.*

TIP *You should define aliases for calculated or derived columns in a cursor SELECT column list.*

TIP *You can base cursor-oriented records only on explicit cursors.*

DML Operations (Specifically, INSERT, UPDATE, and SELECT) Involving Entire PL/SQL Records

PL/SQL 9*i* Release 2 allows INSERT and UPDATE operations involving entire PL/SQL records. Instead of specifying a list of individual record attributes, you can insert records into the database using a single variable of type RECORD or %ROWTYPE. The same is allowed for the UPDATE operation. Also, you can do bulk-binding operations involving SELECT, FETCH, INSERT, UPDATE, and RETURNING INTO using a single variable of type as that of a PL/SQL table of records, instead of specifying individual PL/SQL tables for each SQL column.

The INSERT and UPDATE statements are extended in PL/SQL to enable INSERT and UPDATE operations involving entire records. Here's the syntax for the INSERT statement:

```
INSERT INTO table_name VALUES record_variable;
```

where table_name is the database table into which a new record is inserted and record_variable is the name of the variable of type RECORD or %ROWTYPE that holds the data to be inserted. The number of fields in the record must be same as the number of columns in the table, and the corresponding record fields and table columns must have data types that match one-to-one. Here's an example to illustrate this:

```
DECLARE
     TYPE hrc_rec IS RECORD
              (hrc_code NUMBER,
               hrc_descr VARCHAR2(20));
     v_example_rec hrc_rec;
BEGIN
     v_example_rec.hrc_code := 99;
     v_example_rec.hrc_descr := ' Web Analyst';
     INSERT INTO hrc_tab VALUES v_example_rec;
     COMMIT;
END;
/
```

Here's how the output of preceding example can be verified:

```
SQL> select * from hrc_tab where hrc_code = 99;
  HRC_CODE HRC_DESCR
---------- --------------------
        99  Web Analyst
```

Here's the syntax for the UPDATE statement involving entire records:

```
UPDATE table_name SET ROW = record_variable [WHERE ... ]
```

where table_name is the database table into which a new record is inserted,
record_variable is the name of the variable of type RECORD or %ROWTYPE that
holds the data, and the keyword ROW represents an entire row of the table being
updated. As in the case of the INSERT statement, the number of fields in the
record must be the same as the number of columns in the table, and the corresponding record fields and table columns must have data types that match
one-to-one. Here's an example to illustrate this:

```
DECLARE
     TYPE hrc_rec IS RECORD
              (hrc_code NUMBER,
               hrc_descr VARCHAR2(20));
     v_example_rec hrc_rec;
BEGIN
     v_example_rec.hrc_code := 99;
     v_example_rec.hrc_descr := ' Web Analyst Sr.';
     UPDATE hrc_tab SET ROW = v_example_rec WHERE hrc_code = 99;
     COMMIT;
END;
/
```

Here's how the output of the preceding example can be verified:

```
SQL> select * from hrc_tab where hrc_code = 99;

 HRC_CODE HRC_DESCR
---------- --------------------
       99  Web Analyst Sr.
```

Using entire records in INSERT and UPDATE statements provides ease of use and the code becomes easily maintainable. However, there are some restrictions for using entire records. Those restrictions are as follows:

- In the case of INSERT statement, you can use a record variable only in the VALUES clause. Also, if the VALUE clause contains a record variable, it's the only variable allowed and you shouldn't give any other variable or value in the VALUES clause.

- In the case of UPDATE statement, a record variable is allowed only on the right side of the SET clause. Also, the keyword ROW is allowed only on the left side of the SET clause, and you can't use it with a subquery. You should specify only one SET clause if you use ROW.

- The record variable you use must not be a nested record type or a return value of a function returning a record type.

Index-by Tables

An *index-by table* is a composite data structure composed of a collection of homogenous elements similar to an array. The elements in this collection are unbounded, sparsely distributed, and indexed by integers (hence the name "index-by" table). Prior to Oracle8, these were called "PL/SQL tables." They became available in PL/SQL 2.0 and later versions.

The individual elements in the index-by tables are elements of a scalar data type or a PL/SQL record. These are indexed by BINARY_INTEGER. Since the lower and upper limits of BINARY_INTEGER are $-2**31 -1$ and $2**31 -1$, an index-by table can have these many elements. Although index-by tables are similar to 3GL arrays in that they have homogeneous elements, there are subtle differences in the implementation of index-by tables and arrays. Table 3-2 summarizes these differences.

Table 3-2. Comparison of Index-by Tables and 3GL Arrays

PROPERTY	INDEX-BY TABLE	3GL ARRAYS (C ARRAYS)
Ease of use	Fairly easy.	Fairly easy.
Structure	A two-column structure with a key and a value.	A single-element structure with an index and a value.
Lower and upper bounds	Unbounded.	Have a lower and upper bound.
Sequential	Sparsely distributed.	Sequentially distributed.
Index	Nonsequential and can be negative.	Sequential and has to be zero or positive.
Creation of elements	An element or row is created only when a value is assigned.	Elements are created when defined memory is set aside at declaration time for all the cells in the array.

Defining an Index-by Table

As with PL/SQL records, you define an index-by table variable by first defining a table type and then declaring a variable of that type. The following sections outline these steps.

Defining the Table Type

You define a table type using the TYPE statement. Here's the syntax:

```
TYPE table_type_name IS TABLE OF type [NOT NULL] INDEX BY BINARY_INTEGER;
```

where table_type_name is a name that identifies the structure of the new index-by table containing individual elements of the data type. Notice that each element has an index associated with it and a value. The data type of the element can be any PL/SQL scalar type such as VARCHAR2, NUMBER, DATE, BOOLEAN, and so forth, or it can be a reference to a scalar type using %TYPE or a record type (as of PL/SQL 2.3 and higher). You can specify an optional NOT NULL constraint to indicate that every element created in the index-by table should be a non-null value.

Here's an example of a table declaration:

```
TYPE num_tab IS TABLE OF NUMBER INDEX BY BINARY_INTEGER;
```

Here, num_tab is an index-by table with numbers as its elements.

Declaring a Variable of the Table Type

Once you've defined a table type, you need to declare the actual index-by table of that type. Here's the syntax:

```
<table_var_name> <table_type_name>;
```

where table_type_name is the table type defined using the TYPE . . . TABLE specification and table_var_name is an arbitrary variable name with a data type of this table type. Here's an example:

```
v_example_tab num_tab;
```

> **TIP**   *A TYPE . . . TABLE definition is only abstract, and as such, you can't use it by itself.*

A complete example combining the preceding two steps is as follows:

```
DECLARE
    TYPE num_tab IS TABLE OF NUMBER INDEX BY BINARY_INTEGER;
     v_example_tab num_tab;
BEGIN
    /* Do some processing */
    null;
END;
/
```

> **TIP**   *Defining a TYPE . . . TABLE declaration doesn't occupy any memory until variables of that type are declared and elements are created in the index-by table. An index-by table grows as elements are created by assigning values.*

> **TIP**   *An index-by table declared as NOT NULL must have a value specified for each element.*

Using an Index-by Table

Once you've defined an index-by table and declared variables of that type, the next step is to use the table for processing data. This usually consists of accessing the individual table elements, populating the table with elements (rows and so forth), and performing operations in the index-by table.

Accessing an Index-by Table

The elements in an index-by table are called *rows*, as they have a two-column structure consisting of the index as the first column and the corresponding value as the second column. I use the terms "rows" and "elements" when referring to an index-by table.

You access the individual elements of an index-by table using the name of the table variable and the index. Here's the syntax:

```
<table_var_name>(<index_value>)
```

The parentheses in the preceding code are necessary. Note that the actual table variable name is used and not the table type name.

TIP *When you access the elements of an index-by table, use the table variable name and not the table type name.*

TIP *Index-by types are PL/SQL specific, and as such, they aren't available in SQL. In addition, you can't store them in a database. As a result, you can't perform the SQL DML operations of SELECT, INSERT, UPDATE, and DELETE on index-by tables. Also, there's nothing like COMMIT or ROLLBACK with regard to an index-by table.*

Here's an example for the num_tab table defined previously:

```
DECLARE
    TYPE num_tab IS TABLE OF NUMBER INDEX BY BINARY_INTEGER;
    v_example_tab num_tab;
    v_num NUMBER := 13;
```

```
BEGIN
    v_example_tab(1) := 1001;
    v_example_tab(10) := 1002;
    v_example_tab(-10) := 1003;
    v_example_tab(v_num) := 1004;
    dbms_output.put_line('An example array:');
    dbms_output.new_line;
    dbms_output.put_line(to_char(v_example_tab(1))||' '||
                                    to_char(v_example_tab(10))||' '||
                                    to_char(v_example_tab(-10))||' '||
                                    to_char(v_example_tab(v_num)) );
END;
/
```

Here's the output of this program:

```
An example array:
1001 1002 1003 1004

PL/SQL procedure successfully completed.
```

In this example, an index-by table of four rows is created by explicitly specifying the index and value to each row. Next, these rows or elements are accessed
to display these values. Notice how the table elements are referenced both when
populating the table variable and when accessing the elements in the index-by
table. Also notice how a variable name is used as the index for the fourth row of
the index-by table.

TIP   *You can use any BINARY_INTEGER-compatible literal, variable, or expression as the index of an index-by
table.*

TIP   *An index-by table variable is a read-write variable.
You can use it on both sides of an assignment operator.*

In addition to being able to access individual rows of an index-by table, you
can access the entire table itself in some cases. For example, you can do this
when you initialize a table with another table or when you pass an index-by table
as a parameter to a subprogram. Here's an example to illustrate this:

```
DECLARE
     TYPE num_tab IS TABLE OF NUMBER INDEX BY BINARY_INTEGER;
     v_example_tab1 num_tab;
     v_example_tab2 num_tab;
     v_num NUMBER := 13;
BEGIN
     v_example_tab1(1) := 1001;
     v_example_tab1(10) := 1002;
     v_example_tab1(-10) := 1003;
     v_example_tab1(v_num) := 1004;
     v_example_tab2 := v_example_tab1;
     dbms_output.put_line('An example array:');
     dbms_output.new_line;
     dbms_output.put_line(to_char(v_example_tab2(1))||' '||
                        to_char(v_example_tab2(10))||' '||
                        to_char(v_example_tab2(-10))||' '||
                        to_char(v_example_tab2(v_num)) );
END;
/
```

Here's the output of this program:

```
An example array:
1001 1002 1003 1004

PL/SQL procedure successfully completed.
```

Notice the assignment statement

```
v_example_tab2 := v_example_tab1;
```

Here, the first table as a whole is referenced using the table name, and it's used as
the input to a second table, which is also referenced using the full name.

Accessing an Undefined Row

With index-by tables, a row is created only when a value is assigned. So before this happens, the row doesn't exist. This is because index-by tables have no lower or upper bound for the values. Accessing an undefined row raises a PL/SQL error called a NO_DATA_FOUND exception. In the previous example, rows with indices 2, 10, –10, and 13 have been created. If any row other than these four is referenced, the aforementioned exception is raised. Here's an example to illustrate this concept:

```
DECLARE
    TYPE num_tab IS TABLE OF NUMBER INDEX BY BINARY_INTEGER;
    v_example_tab num_tab;
    v_num NUMBER := 13;
BEGIN
    v_example_tab(1) := 1001;
    v_example_tab(10) := 1002;
    v_example_tab(-10) := 1003;
    v_example_tab(v_num) := 1004;
    dbms_output.put_line(to_char(v_example_tab(100)));
END;
/
```

Here's the output of this program:

```
DECLARE
*
ERROR at line 1:
ORA-01403: no data found
ORA-06512: at line 10
```

To handle this error, you need to use an exception handling block and trap the error. It's up to you how you handle the exception once it's trapped. Here's some sample code for this:

```
DECLARE
    TYPE num_tab IS TABLE OF NUMBER INDEX BY BINARY_INTEGER;
    v_example_tab num_tab;
    v_num NUMBER := 13;
BEGIN
    v_example_tab(1) := 1001;
    v_example_tab(10) := 1002;
```

```
    v_example_tab(-10) := 1003;
    v_example_tab(v_num) := 1004;
    dbms_output.put_line(to_char(v_example_tab(100)));
EXCEPTION WHEN NO_DATA_FOUND THEN
    dbms_output.put_line ('Invalid array element');
END;
/
```

Populating an Index-by Table

The simplest way to populate an index-by table is to explicitly assign values to each row by choosing arbitrary indices. However, you have other ways to create an index-by table. PL/SQL 9*i* allows three ways to assign a record with values:

1. Individual row creation by assignment

2. Assigning rows by means of a LOOP

3. Assigning a table using a second table (aggregate assignment)

I discuss each of the methods in the sections that follow.

Individual Row Creation by Assignment

This method consists of creating each row in the index-by table by choosing a random index and assigning a value to the corresponding element. Each row is referenced using the table_var_name(index) notation on the left side of the assignment operator and assigned with values. In the num_tab table example presented in the section "Accessing an Index-by Table," you learned how to assign the rows with values. Here's the same example reproduced for illustration:

```
DECLARE
    TYPE num_tab IS TABLE OF NUMBER INDEX BY BINARY_INTEGER;
    v_example_tab num_tab;
    v_num NUMBER := 13;
BEGIN
    v_example_tab(1) := 1001;
    v_example_tab(10) := 1002;
    v_example_tab(-10) := 1003;
    v_example_tab(v_num) := 1004;
    dbms_output.put_line('An example array:');
```

```
        dbms_output.new_line;
        dbms_output.put_line(to_char(v_example_tab(1))||' '||
                                            to_char(v_example_tab(10))||' '||
                                            to_char(v_example_tab(-10))||' '||
                                            to_char(v_example_tab(v_num)) );
END;
/
```

Here's the output of the previous code:

```
An example array:
1001 1002 1003 1004

PL/SQL procedure successfully completed.
```

Assigning Rows by Means of a LOOP

Individual row creation by assignment is useful when you want to populate an index-by table nonsequentially. However, you may have a need to populate an index-by table sequentially using already available data—for example, to store the student ID information of a particular class. In this case, the table needs to be filled with a whole set of rows in one shot. You can do this using explicit assignment inside a loop. The difference is that you use a loop and the loop counter is used to set the value of index of each row in the index-by table. Here's an example to illustrate this concept:

```
DECLARE
        TYPE num_tab IS TABLE OF NUMBER INDEX BY BINARY_INTEGER;
        v_example_tab num_tab;
BEGIN
        FOR idx IN 1..10 LOOP
                v_example_tab(idx) := (2**idx)+1;
        END LOOP;
        dbms_output.put_line('An example array:');
        dbms_output.new_line;
        FOR idx IN 1..10 LOOP
                dbms_output.put_line(to_char(v_example_tab(idx)));
        END LOOP;
END;
/
```

Here's the output of this program:

```
An example array:
3
5
9
17
33
65
129
257
513
1025

PL/SQL procedure successfully completed.
```

The following points are worth noting:

- The index for each row in the index-by table is set by the FOR LOOP counter.

- The rows are created sequentially with consecutive indices.

TIP   *You can fill the rows in an index-by table sequentially or nonsequentially. In the former case, it's wise to keep track of the minimum and maximum indices of the rows in the index-by table.*

TIP   *Use a LOOP to populate an index-by table when the rows in the index-by table are to be created sequentially.*

Assigning a Table Using a Second Table (Aggregate Assignment)

This method consists of assigning the entire table with a second table, otherwise known as aggregate assignment. In this case, you don't assign the individual elements of the destination table one by one. Instead, you use type-compatible tables on both sides of the assignment operator. The source table should be populated beforehand. In the num_tab index-by table example presented in the section "Accessing an Index-by Table," you learned how to perform an aggregate assignment. Here's the same example reproduced for illustration:

```
DECLARE
    TYPE num_tab IS TABLE OF NUMBER INDEX BY BINARY_INTEGER;
    v_example_tab1 num_tab;
    v_example_tab2 num_tab;
    v_num NUMBER := 13;
BEGIN
    v_example_tab1(1) := 1001;
    v_example_tab1(10) := 1002;
    v_example_tab1(-10) := 1003;
    v_example_tab1(v_num) := 1004;
    v_example_tab2 := v_example_tab1;
    dbms_output.put_line('An example array:');
    dbms_output.new_line;
    dbms_output.put_line(to_char(v_example_tab2(1))||' '||
                         to_char(v_example_tab2(10))||' '||
                         to_char(v_example_tab2(-10))||' '||
                         to_char(v_example_tab2(v_num)) );
END;
/
```

Here's the output of the previous code:

```
An example array:

1001 1002 1003 1004

PL/SQL procedure successfully completed.
```

In this case, the index and value of each row in the target table is set to the values of the corresponding row in the source table. This is pretty neat, involves less code, and is less error-prone than individual assignment or assignment in a loop.

 TIP *To populate the source table, you can use either explicit assignment or assignment using a LOOP. Aggregate assignment of tables is only possible with tables of the same table type and structure. It isn't enough for the source and target tables to have the same type elements. Use aggregate assignment wherever possible instead of individual field assignment.*

Deleting an Index-by Table

As I mentioned earlier, with index-by tables, a row is created only when a value is assigned; before this point, the row doesn't exist. So when an index-by table is declared a given table type, the index-by table is empty and has no rows defined yet. After you assign rows either by explicit assignment, using a loop, or aggregate assignment, the index-by table is filled with rows.

Is there any way to delete an index-by table or empty it? Yes. PL/SQL offers two ways to delete an index-by table:

1. Define an empty index-by table of the same type as the filled index-by table and perform an aggregate assignment with this empty table. Here's an example that illustrates this:

```
DECLARE
    TYPE num_tab IS TABLE OF NUMBER INDEX BY BINARY_INTEGER;
    v_example_tab1 num_tab;
    v_example_tab2 num_tab;
    v_num NUMBER := 13;
BEGIN
    v_example_tab1(1) := 1001;
    v_example_tab1(10) := 1002;
    v_example_tab1(-10) := 1003;
    v_example_tab1(v_num) := 1004;
    v_example_tab1:= v_example_tab2;
END;
/
```

This deletes the all the rows from v_example_tab1 and removes it from memory.

2. Use the DELETE method on the index-by table. This is available in PL/SQL version 2.3 and higher. This method is illustrated in the next section.

You can't delete an index-by table by setting each row in the index-by table to null. Also, you can't perform the SQL DELETE operation or the DROP operation on index-by tables.

Methods on Index-by Tables

As of PL/SQL 2.3, there are methods defined that you can invoke on an index-by table. A *method* is a PL/SQL procedure or function that you can invoke on an index-by table to perform a certain task involving its elements or the index-by table as a whole. Methods enable you to more easily code operations on an index-by table, such as counting the number of elements, deleting some or all rows, or testing for existence of a particular row. Table 3-3 summarizes these methods.

Table 3-3. Index-by Table Methods

METHOD	USE	SYNTAX
EXISTS	A function that checks for the existence of a particular row. ReturnsTRUE if the row is defined and FALSE otherwise.	table_name.EXISTS(index)
COUNT	A function that returns the number of elements defined.	table_name.COUNT
DELETE	A procedure that deletes some of the elements (i.e., undefines them) or deletes all of the elements, thus emptying the table between the start and end indices.	table_name.DELETE to remove all the rows table_name.DELETE(index) to remove a particular row with the specified index table_name.DELETE(start_index, end_index) to remove all rows defined
FIRST	A function that returns the index of the first row in a table (i.e., the row with the lowest index). It returns NULL if the table is empty.	table_name.FIRST
LAST	A function that returns the index of the last row in a table (i.e., the row with the highest index). It returns NULL if the table is empty.	table_name.LAST
NEXT	A function that returns the index of the row in a table that is next to the row indicated by the specified index. It returns NULL if such a row doesn't exist.	table_name.NEXT(index)
PRIOR	A function that returns the index of the row in a table that is before the row indicated by the specified index. It returns NULL if such a row doesn't exist.	table_name.PRIOR(index)

The following sections present examples to illustrate the use of the methods in Table 3-3.

Example for the EXISTS Method

To demonstrate the use of the EXISTS method, I'll rewrite the example presented
in the section "Accessing an Undefined Row." Here's the code:

```
DECLARE
    TYPE num_tab IS TABLE OF NUMBER INDEX BY BINARY_INTEGER;
     v_example_tab num_tab;
     v_num NUMBER := 13;
BEGIN
    v_example_tab(1) := 1001;
    v_example_tab(10) := 1002;
    v_example_tab(-10) := 1003;
    v_example_tab(v_num) := 1004;
   IF v_example_tab.EXISTS(100) THEN
      dbms_output.put_line(to_char(v_example_tab(100)));
   END IF;
END;
/
```

Without the use of the EXISTS function, the preceding code results in ORA-
01403 error.

Example for the COUNT and DELETE Methods

Consider the example presented in the section "Assigning Rows by Means of
a LOOP." Here it is again:

```
DECLARE
    TYPE num_tab IS TABLE OF NUMBER INDEX BY BINARY_INTEGER;
     v_example_tab num_tab;
BEGIN
    FOR idx IN 1..10 LOOP
        v_example_tab(idx) := (2**idx)+1;
    END LOOP;
    dbms_output.put_line('An example array:');
    dbms_output.new_line;
    FOR idx IN 1..10 LOOP
        dbms_output.put_line(to_char(v_example_tab(idx)));
    END LOOP;
END;
/
```

Notice the second FOR LOOP. How is it possible to know what the indices of the rows in the v_example_tab table are? Of course, here it's evident from the first FOR LOOP. Only a programmer who has defined and populated the index-by table can determine the lower and upper bounds. However, sometimes this is hard to figure out. One way to determine the bounds is to use the COUNT method to determine the upper bound of the index. If you know that rows were populated sequentially starting at a particular index, you can use the COUNT method to figure out the upper bound. Here's the preceding example rewritten using COUNT:

```
DECLARE
    TYPE num_tab IS TABLE OF NUMBER INDEX BY BINARY_INTEGER;
    v_example_tab num_tab;
BEGIN
    FOR idx IN 1..10 LOOP
        v_example_tab(idx) := (2**idx)+1;
    END LOOP;
    dbms_output.put_line('An example array:');
    dbms_output.new_line;
    FOR idx IN 1..v_example_tab.COUNT LOOP
        dbms_output.put_line(to_char(v_example_tab(idx)));
    END LOOP;
END;
/
```

The output of this code is same as that of the previous code.

Next, I present an example for the DELETE method. Here's the code:

```
DECLARE
    TYPE num_tab IS TABLE OF NUMBER INDEX BY BINARY_INTEGER;
    v_example_tab num_tab;
BEGIN
    FOR idx IN 1..10 LOOP
        v_example_tab(idx) := (2**idx)+1;
    END LOOP;
    v_example_tab.DELETE(1);
    v_example_tab.DELETE(2, 5);
    v_example_tab.DELETE;
END;
/
```

One important point to note here is that, after the first row is deleted, the index of the second through tenth rows remains the same. The second row does not get index 1.

Example for the FIRST, LAST, and NEXT Methods

In the last section's example, I used the COUNT method to figure out the upper bound index in an index-by table. Here I make the following two assumptions:

1. The lower bound is fixed at a particular value.

2. The rows are populated sequentially.

Now a more general question arises: How do you access the rows of an index-by table populated in any fashion? You don't know whether the rows are sequential or not, and you don't know what the indices of the rows are. In this case, there's an elegant way to display the rows using the FIRST, LAST, and NEXT methods. Here are the steps involved:

1. Use the FIRST method to get the index of the first element.

2. Loop through the index-by table until you encounter the last element by traversing from one element to the next. You can obtain the index of the last element by using the LAST method. You can navigate to the next element using the NEXT method.

Here's the preceding example rewritten using these three methods:

```
DECLARE
    TYPE num_tab IS TABLE OF NUMBER INDEX BY BINARY_INTEGER;
    v_example_tab num_tab;
    idx BINARY_INTEGER;
BEGIN
    FOR idx IN 1..10 LOOP
        v_example_tab(idx) := (2**idx)+1;
    END LOOP;
    dbms_output.put_line('An example array:');
    dbms_output.new_line;
    idx := v_example_tab.FIRST;
    LOOP
```

```
            dbms_output.put_line(to_char(v_example_tab(idx)));
            EXIT WHEN idx = v_example_tab.LAST;
            idx := v_example_tab.NEXT(idx);
        END LOOP;
END;
/
```

The output of this program is the same as the output of the earlier program. The following points are worth noting:

- The first row in the table is tracked by using v_example_tab.FIRST.

- The last row in the table is defined by using v_example_tab.LAST.

- The values are accessed in the loop starting from the first row and retrieving the next (defined row) using v_example_tab.NEXT(idx) until the last row is encountered and accessed.

TIP   *You can simulate multidimensional arrays using multiple index-by tables.*

TIP   *Use the COUNT function to obtain the number of rows in an index-by table. Without this function, the only way to obtain the count of rows is to keep a row counter while populating the table.*

TIP   *The best way to access the elements in an index-by table is by using the FIRST, LAST, and NEXT methods.*

Index-by Table of Records

The index-by tables that you've seen so far have been tables whose elements were scalar types. However, as I mentioned earlier, an index-by table can have a PL/SQL record as the data type of its elements. This gives rise to index-by tables of records, and this feature is available as of PL/SQL 2.3.

Here are the steps for defining an index-by table of records:

1. Define a record type.

2. Define a table type of the record type.

3. Define a variable of the table type.

Here's an example that illustrates this:

```
DECLARE
   TYPE hrc_org_rec IS RECORD
                  (hrc_org_id NUMBER,
                   hrc_descr VARCHAR2(20),
                   org_short_name VARCHAR2(30));
      TYPE hrc_org_tab IS TABLE OF hrc_org_rec INDEX BY BINARY_INTEGER;
      v_example_tab hrc_org_tab;
BEGIN
      /* Do some processing */
      null;
END;
/
```

Once you've defined an index-by table of records, you can create and then access rows. Here's the syntax for referencing a row in an index-by table of records:

```
table_var_name(index_value).record_field_name
```

Here, table_var_name is index-by table of a record variable, index_value is the index of a particular row being referenced, and record_field_name is the actual field name in the record type that each element of the table is made of.

 TIP *An index-by table of records enables database table data to be transformed into PL/SQL structures. One way to do this is to define the index-by table of records in a package and access it from anywhere, including a client program.*

The following example illustrates this:

```
DECLARE
   TYPE hrc_org_rec IS RECORD
                  (hrc_org_id NUMBER,
             hrc_descr VARCHAR2(20),
             org_short_name VARCHAR2(30));
       TYPE hrc_org_tab IS TABLE OF hrc_org_rec INDEX BY BINARY_INTEGER;
       v_example_tab hrc_org_tab;
       CURSOR csr_hrc_org IS
           SELECT hrc_org_seq.nextval hrc_org_id, h.hrc_descr, o.org_short_name
           FROM   org_tab o, hrc_tab h
           WHERE o.hrc_code = h.hrc_code
                 AND h.hrc_code = 1;
        i BINARY_INTEGER := 1;
BEGIN
     FOR idx IN csr_hrc_org LOOP
         v_example_tab(i).hrc_org_id := idx.hrc_org_id;
         v_example_tab(i).hrc_descr := idx.hrc_descr;
         v_example_tab(i).org_short_name := idx.org_short_name;
         i := i + 1;
     END LOOP;
     dbms_output.put_line('An example output: ');
     dbms_output.new_line;
     FOR j IN 1..v_example_tab.COUNT LOOP
         dbms_output.put_line(to_char(v_example_tab(j).hrc_org_id)||' '||
                                        v_example_tab(j).hrc_descr||' '||
                                        v_example_tab(j).org_short_name);
     END LOOP;
END;
/
```

Here's the output of this program:

```
An example output:
1 CEO/COO Office of CEO ABC Inc.
2 CEO/COO Office of CEO XYZ Inc.
3 CEO/COO Office of CEO DataPro Inc.

PL/SQL procedure successfully completed.
```

The following two points are worth noting:

1. Each field of the record is explicitly assigned. However, since each element in v_example_tab is a record, you can define a second record of the same record type and you can perform an aggregate assignment. Here's the code for the cursor FOR LOOP:

```
FOR idx IN csr_hrc_org LOOP
     v_example_tab(i) := idx;
     i := i + 1;
END LOOP;
```

2. The rows in the v_example_tab table are consecutive, as evident from the population using a cursor FOR LOOP, and so you could use the COUNT method here.

Associative Arrays

In line with index-by tables, Oracle9*i* Release 2 enables you to define index-by tables that are indexed by VARCHAR2 values instead of BINARY_INTEGER. The VARCHAR2 index serves as a primary key of a database table and improves performance, enabling fast lookup of individual array elements, eliminating the need to know the position of the individual element, and helping you avoid looping through all array elements.

TIP *The key used in associative arrays can be an integer or a string. However, the key should be unique.*

TIP *First-time assignment of a value using a key creates an element in the associative array with the corresponding key-value pair. Subsequent assignments using the same key update the corresponding element value.*

Similar to index-by tables, you declare associative arrays by first declaring a type followed by a variable of that type. Here's the syntax:

```
TYPE array_type_name IS TABLE OF type INDEX BY VARCHAR2(size);
```

where array_type_name is a name that identifies the structure of the new associative array containing individual elements of the data type type and indexed by
VARCHAR2 values of a maximum length specified by size. Notice that each element has an index associated with it and a value. The data type of the element
can be any PL/SQL scalar type.

Here's an example:

```
DECLARE
    TYPE site_array IS TABLE OF NUMBER INDEX BY VARCHAR2(20);
    v_example_array site_array;
BEGIN
    v_example_array('Edison') := 10;
    v_example_array('Bloomington') := 11;
    v_example_array('Sunnyvale') := 12;
    dbms_output.put_line(v_example_array.FIRST);
    dbms_output.put_line(v_example_array.LAST);
    dbms_output.put_line(TO_CHAR(v_example_array(v_example_array.FIRST)));
END;
/
```

Here's the output of this code:

```
Bloomington
Sunnyvale
11

PL/SQL procedure successfully completed.
```

The following points are worth noting:

- The key-value pair "Edison 10" was input first. However,
  v_example_array.FIRST returns "Bloomington," as that comes first alpha-
  betically. This is a key feature of associative arrays that isn't found in
  index-by tables.

- You can use the index-by table methods FIRST, LAST, NEXT, and PRIOR
  with associative arrays.

TIP *Associative arrays can't be stored in the database and therefore are temporary. However, you can make them persistent for a database session by specifying the type in a package and creating the corresponding elements in the package body.*

TIP *Associative arrays are efficient when you use them to store data representing small lookup tables because they can be materialized in memory without the use of disk space.*

TIP *Associative array subscripts can be negative, nonsequential, and strings or numbers.*

Summary

This chapter thoroughly covered two PL/SQL composite data types: records and index-by tables. In this chapter, I discussed the various methods of using populating records and index-by tables in a PL/SQL environment. I also provided tips on how to use these two data types in coding PL/SQL applications.

The next chapter describes the method of exception handling in PL/SQL with regard to tracking error messages, both predefined and user-defined.

CHAPTER 4

Error Message Handling

THE THREE MAIN FUNCTIONS of writing programs using any programming language are writing the program, compiling the program, and executing the program. Of these, the compilation and execution stages often result in errors that need to be corrected. Error message handling is part and parcel of any programming language, and PL/SQL is no exception.

There are two stages of error message handling: raising the error and handling the error. Compilation errors are raised by the PL/SQL compiler and should be handled by the programmer interactively before executing the program. A greater responsibility of the programmer is when raising and/or handling execution errors (i.e., errors that are raised at runtime). A foolproof approach is required for this. These types of errors are taken care of either by using the default error-messaging capabilities or by augmenting the default error-messaging capabilities with customized code.

This chapter explores the basics of runtime PL/SQL error handling along with the types of errors and the methods of handling each of them. I illustrate the concept of exceptions by taking into account the organizational hierarchy system presented in Chapter 2. Appendix A lists the schema objects to be created.

PL/SQL Exceptions: Types and Definition

In PL/SQL, a runtime error is called an *exception*. In its simplest definition, an exception is an error raised at runtime either by Oracle or by the programmer. Once raised, an exception has to be properly handled.

Here are the three basic steps in dealing with exceptions:

1. Declare an exception (implicitly or explicitly).

2. Raise the exception (implicitly or explicitly).

3. Handle the exception (necessary).

Before I deal with the techniques of the performing these steps, I'll cover some basic concepts related to PL/SQL error messaging.

All PL/SQL exceptions are characterized by

- *Error type:* This indicates whether the error is an ORA error or a PLS error.

- *Error code:* This is a number indicating the error number.

- *Error text:* This is the text of the error message, including the error code.

Both compilation and runtime errors have an error type, an error code, and error text. All compilation errors have the error type as PLS and runtime errors have the error type as ORA. Sometimes a PLS error is embedded in an outer ORA error. This occurs when you compile anonymous PL/SQL blocks or execute dynamic PL/SQL blocks of code. In the following section, I describe each of these error types.

Error Type

PL/SQL raises two types of errors: ORA errors and PLS errors. ORA errors are mostly runtime errors and should be handled by the program. PLS errors are mostly compile time errors and should be corrected before you execute the program.

Error Code

This is a negative number indicating the error code of the particular error.

Error Text

Error text is an error message specifying the text of the particular error that occurred. The maximum length of an Oracle error message is 512 bytes.

I give examples of both compilation and runtime errors in the following sections, and I also present an example in which a PLS error is embedded within an ORA error.

Compilation Error Example

Here's an example of a compilation error. Consider the following PL/SQL procedure:

```
SQL> create or replace procedure
  2    p1 is
```

```
3  begin
4    null
5  end;
6  /
```

Here's the output of this code:

```
Warning: Procedure created with compilation errors.
```

To see the actual error, use the SQL*Plus command show errors at the SQL prompt. Here are the results:

```
SQL> show errors
Errors for PROCEDURE P1:
LINE/COL ERROR
-------- ----------------------------------------------------------------
5/1      PLS-00103: Encountered the symbol "END" when expecting one of the
         following:
         ;
         The symbol ";" was substituted for "END" to continue.
Here the compilation error is:
PLS-00103: Encountered the symbol "END" when expecting one of the following:
;
The symbol ";" was substituted for "END" to continue.
```

The error type is PLS, the error code is –00103, and the error text is the entire message. This error occurred because a semicolon (;) was missing after the null statement in line 4 of the procedure code.

Runtime Error Example

In this section I present an example of a runtime error. Consider the following procedure:

```
SQL> create or replace procedure p2
  2  is
  3    v_descr VARCHAR2(20);
  4  begin
  5    SELECT hrc_descr
  6    INTO   v_descr
  7    FROM   hrc_tab
```

```
  8     WHERE  hrc_code = 10;
  9     dbms_output.put_line(v_descr);
 10   end;
 11   /
```

Procedure created.

Here's the output of executing the procedure:

```
SQL> exec p2
BEGIN p1; END;

*
ERROR at line 1:
ORA-01403: no data found
ORA-06512: at "PLSQL9I.P2", line 5
ORA-06512: at line 1
```

The runtime error is

```
ORA-01403: no data found
```

The error type is ORA, the error code is –1403, and the error text is the entire message:

```
ORA-01403: no data found
```

PLS Error Within an ORA Error Example

Finally, I show an example of a PLS error embedded within an ORA error. Consider the code of procedure p1. When I convert it into an anonymous PL/SQL block, I get the following:

```
SQL> begin
  2     null
  3   end;
  4   /
end;
```

```
*
ERROR at line 3:
ORA-06550: line 3, column 1:
PLS-00103: Encountered the symbol "END" when expecting one of the following:
;
The symbol ";" was substituted for "END" to continue.
```

This is still a compilation error because the PL/SQL compiler first compiles and then executes an anonymous PL/SQL block. However, the corresponding PLS error is embedded within the ORA error –06550.

PL/SQL Error Built-Ins

PL/SQL has a set of built-in declarations/statements, functions, and procedures to raise and/or handle exceptions. The functions and procedures are similar to the built-in functions such as TO_CHAR, SUBSTR. Each of these is described in the sections that follow.

Declarations/Statements

The following is a list of declarations/statements used in exception handling:

- *EXCEPTION declaration:* You use this declaration when you declare a user-defined exception.

- *RAISE statement:* You use this statement to raise an exception.

- *PRAGMA EXCEPTION_INIT directive:* You use this directive to associate an Oracle error with a user-defined exception.

- *SAVE EXCEPTIONS clause:* This is new in Oracle9*i* and is used to continue processing after a row-wise failure during bulk binding.

CROSS-REFERENCE   *I discuss the SAVE EXCEPTIONS clause further in Chapter 9.*

Functions

You use the following two functions to capture information about Oracle errors occurring in PL/SQL:

- *SQLCODE:* This function returns the Oracle error code of the error in question.

- *SQLERRM:* This function returns the Oracle error message text of the error in question.

Procedure

You use the following procedure to define custom error messages in PL/SQL:

- *RAISE_APPLICATION_ERROR:* You use this procedure to define custom error messages and halt program execution at the point it is used.

Exception Handlers

As Chapter 1 outlined, a PL/SQL block is composed of three sections: a declaration section, an executable section, and an exception handling section. The exception handling section is where runtime errors raised implicitly or explicitly are handled. It's also called an *exception handler.*

TIP   *Although an exception handling section isn't a mandatory requirement to code a PL/SQL block, it's necessary for any PL/SQL program, and it's highly recommended that you code an exception handling section in each PL/SQL program.*

An exception handler is specified by the EXCEPTION WHEN . . . clause. Here's the syntax:

```
EXCEPTION WHEN exception_name THEN
    ... /* code to handle the error */
```

You can specify multiple exceptions as follows:

```
EXCEPTION
     WHEN exception_name1 THEN
         ... /* code to handle the error */
     WHEN exception_name2 THEN
         ... /* code to handle the error */
 ... ...
WHEN OTHERS THEN
         ... /* code to handle the error */
```

Although it's not required, it's sound programming practice to handle all errors in the block in which they occur. To do this, each block should have its own exception handler. When an Oracle error occurs, control is transferred to the immediate exception handler, if there is one. If there isn't an immediate exception handler, control is transferred to the next available exception handler. If no exception handler exists, program execution is terminated with an unhandled exception. The advantages of each block having its own exception handler are that errors don't get propagated and errors specific to the block get handled in that block only.

Types of PL/SQL Exceptions

Basically, exceptions in PL/SQL are classified into the following broad categories:

- Predefined exceptions
- Nonpredefined Oracle errors
- User-defined exceptions
- User-defined PL/SQL error messages

You can track all these types of exceptions either by using the default PL/SQL error-messaging capabilities or by augmenting the default PL/SQL error-messaging capabilities with customized code.

Handling PL/SQL Exceptions

Recall the three steps you need to perform in exception processing:

1. Define the exception.

2. Raise the exception.

3. Handle the exception.

All types of PL/SQL exceptions, whether predefined or not, are handled by means of exception handlers.

I defined exception handlers in the previous section. I repeat the definition here for clarity. Here's the syntax:

```
EXCEPTION WHEN exception_name THEN
    ... /* code to handle the error */
```

You can specify multiple exceptions as follows:

```
EXCEPTION
    WHEN exception_name1 THEN
        ... /* code to handle the error */
    WHEN exception_name2 THEN
        ... /* code to handle the error */
. . . . . .
WHEN OTHERS THEN
        ... /* code to handle the error */
```

The WHEN OTHERS clause acts like a bucket, catching any error not explicitly handled. It specifies to handle all other exceptions that are raised whose names aren't listed (above it) in the EXCEPTION handling section. This means it can detect any unhandled errors in the PL/SQL program. If only WHEN OTHERS is specified, it will trap any raised exception.

You have two ways to handle an exception:

*   Continue program execution after handling the error

*   Stop program execution after handling the error

You can do both using exception handlers. Here's the sequence of steps in the case of an exception occurrence:

1. The exception is raised either implicitly or explicitly.

2. Control transfers to the defined exception handler for the raised exception in the current block. If no exception handler is defined in the current block, control transfers to the exception handler in an outer block defined for the raised exception. In case there is no exception handler defined for the particular exception raised, control transfers to the WHEN OTHERS part of the exception handler either in the current block or in an outer (enclosing) block.

3. The code in the exception handler is executed and program execution resumes or terminates accordingly.

4. If no exception handler has been defined in the entire program, program execution terminates at the point the exception was raised and no code is executed after that point.

Handling Predefined Exceptions

PL/SQL has defined certain commonly occurring Oracle errors as exceptions. These are called *predefined exceptions,* and each such predefined exception has a unique name associated with it. Every Oracle error has an error type, an error number, and error message text, and these predefined exceptions are no exception. Table 4-1 lists the predefined PL/SQL exceptions along with their error codes and descriptions.

Table 4-1. Predefined PL/SQL Exceptions

EXCEPTION	ORACLE ERROR CODE/SQL CODE	DESCRIPTION
ACCESS_INTO_NULL	ORA-06530 –6530	Occurs when populating attributes of an uninitialized (atomically null) object.
CASE_NOT_FOUND	ORA-06592 –6592	Occurs in case of a CASE statement defined without an ELSE clause when the selector doesn't match any of the values specified in the WHEN clauses.
COLLECTION_IS_NULL	ORA-06531 –6531	Occurs when populating elements of an uninitialized PL/SQL collection or invoking methods on an uninitialized PL/SQL collection.

(continued)

Table 4-1. Predefined PL/SQL Exceptions (continued)

EXCEPTION	ORACLE ERROR CODE/SQL CODE	DESCRIPTION
CURSOR_ALREADY_OPEN	ORA-06511 –6511	Occurs when trying to open an already opened PL/SQL cursor.
DUP_VAL_ON_INDEX	ORA-00001 –1	Occurs when inserting a record that violates a primary key or unique key, or a unique index.
INVALID_CURSOR	ORA-01001 –1001	Occurs when referencing an unopened cursor.
INVALID_NUMBER	ORA-01722 –1722	Occurs in a SQL statement when the conversion of a character string into a number fails or when the LIMIT clause expression in a bulk FETCH doesn't result in a positive value. In PL/SQL, VALUE_ERROR is raised.
LOGIN_DENIED	ORA-01017 –1017	Occurs when an invalid username/password is specified while logging in.
NO_DATA_FOUND	ORA-01403 +100	Occurs in three cases: first, when a SELECT. . . INTO implicit cursor returns more than one row; second, when an undefined element is referenced in an index-by table or a deleted element is referenced in a nested table; and third when accessing beyond an EOF while performing PL/SQL file I/O.
NOT_LOGGED_ON	ORA-01012 –1012	Occurs when accessing an Oracle database without logging in.
PROGRAM_ERROR	ORA-06501 –6501	This refers to an internal PL/SQL error.
ROWTYPE_MISMATCH	ORA-06504 –6504	Occurs when the types of a host cursor variable and PL/SQL cursor variable don't match, like a mismatch of the actual and formal parameters of a procedure or function.
SELF_IS_NULL	ORA-30625 –30625	Occurs when a MEMBER method is invoked on a null instance of an object.

(continued)

Table 4-1. Predefined PL/SQL Exceptions (continued)

EXCEPTION	ORACLE ERROR CODE/SQL CODE	DESCRIPTION
STORAGE_ERROR	ORA-06500 –6500	Occurs when there's insufficient memory for processing or there's a memory corruption.
SUBSCRIPT_BEYOND_COUNT	ORA-06533 –6533	Occurs when referencing an element of a PL/SQL collection with an index greater than the largest existing index.
SUBSCRIPT_OUTSIDE_LIMIT	ORA-06532 –6532	Occurs when referencing an element of a PL/SQL collection with an index outside the valid range.
SYS_INVALID_ROWID	ORA-01410 –1410	Occurs when the conversion of a character string into a ROWID fails.
TIMEOUT_ON_RESOURCE	ORA-00051 –51	Occurs when a time-out happens when Oracle is waiting for a resource.
TOO_MANY_ROWS	ORA-01422 –1422	Occurs when a SELECT . . . INTO implicit query returns multiple rows.
VALUE_ERROR	ORA-06502 –6502	Occurs when an arithmetic, conversion, truncation, or size-constraint error occurs in PL/SQL statements.
ZERO_DIVIDE	ORA-01476 –1476	Occurs when an attempt is made to divide by zero.

PL/SQL defines these exceptions in a package called STANDARD that's available to all schemas.

In the case of predefined exceptions, the process of exception handling boils down to one step: handling the exception. There's no need to define and raise the predefined exception. PL/SQL automatically does these steps for you.

TIP *There's no need to declare and raise a predefined PL/SQL exception. It's implicitly raised by PL/SQL. However, this isn't a restriction: You can raise it if needed explicitly using the RAISE statement.*

As mentioned earlier, predefined exceptions are handled using exception handlers. Here's an example to illustrate handling of predefined exceptions:

```
DECLARE
     v_descr VARCHAR2(20);
BEGIN
     SELECT hrc_descr
     INTO      v_descr
     FROM     hrc_tab
     WHERE   hrc_code = 10;
     dbms_output.put_line(' The hierarchy description for code 10 is: '||v_descr);
EXCEPTION WHEN NO_DATA_FOUND THEN
     dbms_output.put_line('ERR: Invalid Hierarchy Code 10');
END;
/
```

Here's the output of this program:

```
ERR: Invalid Hierarchy Code 10

PL/SQL procedure successfully completed.
```

The following points are worth noting:

- The SELECT . . . INTO doesn't return any row for hrc_code 10, and as a result the NO_DATA_FOUND predefined exception is raised implicitly.

- Control transfers to the exception handler specified by

  ```
  EXCEPTION WHEN NO_DATA_FOUND THEN
  ```

  The code in this exception handler is executed.

- The code following the SELECT statement isn't executed at all.

You can write the same program using WHEN OTHERS. Here's the code:

```
DECLARE
    v_descr VARCHAR2(20);
BEGIN
    SELECT hrc_descr
    INTO      v_descr
    FROM    hrc_tab
    WHERE  hrc_code = 10;
    dbms_output.put_line(' The hierarchy description for code 10 is: '||v_descr);
EXCEPTION WHEN OTHERS THEN
    dbms_output.put_line('ERR: Invalid Hierarchy Code 10');
END;
/
```

The output of this example is the same as the output of the previous example.
The following points are worth noting:

- The SELECT . . . INTO raises the predefined exception NO_DATA_FOUND, which is caught by the exception handler WHEN OTHERS. However, in this case, it can't be known that the NO_DATA_FOUND exception was raised.

- Even if NO_DATA_FOUND wasn't raised and any other exception was raised, the output would have been the same. This is because WHEN OTHERS traps all possible exceptions occurring in the program.

 TIP *WHEN OTHERS traps all possible exceptions occurring in a PL/SQL program.*

To better improve the error-processing capabilities, it's recommended that you include a WHEN OTHERS handler in addition to the handlers for any specific exceptions that might possibly be raised, such as NO_DATA_FOUND.

Here's the code for the previous program rewritten as shown here. This program traps the NO_DATA_FOUND exception. Any exception other than NO_DATA_FOUND is trapped by the WHEN OTHERS exception handler.

```
DECLARE
     v_descr VARCHAR2(20);
BEGIN
     SELECT hrc_descr
     INTO       v_descr
     FROM     hrc_tab
     WHERE   hrc_code = 10;
     dbms_output.put_line(' The hierarchy description for code 10 is: '||v_descr);
EXCEPTION
     WHEN NO_DATA_FOUND THEN
            dbms_output.put_line('ERR: Invalid Hierarchy Code 10');
     WHEN OTHERS THEN
            dbms_output.put_line('ERR: An error occurred');
END;
/
```

Now, how do you know what Oracle error occurred in case WHEN OTHERS got executed? You get this information by means of two built-in functions, SQLCODE and SQLERRM, that PL/SQL provides.

SQLCODE and SQLERRM

SQLCODE returns the error code of the Oracle error that most recently occurred, and SQLERRM returns the corresponding error message text. Every Oracle error, whether it's a predefined exception or not, has a SQLCODE and a SQLERRM associated with it. Also, SQLERRM always begins with the error type ORA followed by the error code and the error message text. SQLCODE need not necessarily be the error code. A distinctive example of this is the error code –1403, which corresponds to the predefined exception NO_DATA_FOUND. The SQLCODE for this is +100, and it's the only positive SQLCODE. The corresponding SQLERRM returns the message

```
ORA-1403: no data found
```

For all other Oracle errors, the SQLCODE is negative. If no exception has been raised, SQLCODE returns zero and SQLERRM returns the message

```
ORA-0000: normal, successful completion
```

An error number can be passed as an argument to SQLERRM. However, passing a positive number other than 100 always returns the message

```
non-ORACLE exception
```

prefixed with the number passed.

The best use of these two functions would be in the WHEN OTHERS handler. This information helps in logging the particular error.

Here's the previous program written in a more meaningful way using SQLCODE and SQLERRM:

```
DECLARE
    v_descr VARCHAR2(20);
BEGIN
    SELECT hrc_descr
    INTO    v_descr
    FROM    hrc_tab
    WHERE   hrc_code = 10;
    dbms_output.put_line(' The hierarchy description for code 10 is: '||v_descr);
EXCEPTION
    WHEN NO_DATA_FOUND THEN
        dbms_output.put_line('ERR: Invalid Hierarchy Code 10');
    WHEN OTHERS THEN
        dbms_output.put_line('ERR: An error occurred with info :'||
                                    TO_CHAR(SQLCODE)||' '||SQLERRM);
END;
/
```

Here's the output of this code:

```
The hierarchy description for code 10 is: Assistant

PL/SQL procedure successfully completed.
```

TIP *Always include a WHEN OTHERS handler in addition to the handlers for any specific exceptions that might be raised, such as NO_DATA_FOUND. In this case, it traps the Oracle error raised using SQLCODE and SQLERRM.*

TIP   *In the case of nested blocks, always include a WHEN OTHERS handler in the topmost level of every PL/SQL program.*

Continuing with Program Execution After Handling the Exception

The previous programs illustrate cases in which the program execution terminates after an exception occurs. However, there may be requirements when the program needs to resume execution after handling an exception. To resume execution after handling an exception, place the particular PL/SQL statement in a nested block with its own exception handlers. Here's an example to illustrate this:

```
DECLARE
    v_descr VARCHAR2(20);
BEGIN
    BEGIN
        SELECT hrc_descr
        INTO      v_descr
        FROM     hrc_tab
       WHERE   hrc_code = 10;
  dbms_output.put_line(' The lowest hierarchy available is: Code 10  '||v_descr);
    EXCEPTION WHEN NO_DATA_FOUND THEN
        INSERT INTO hrc_tab VALUES (10, 'Assistant');
        COMMIT;
    END;
    BEGIN
        SELECT hrc_descr
        INTO      v_descr
        FROM     hrc_tab
      WHERE   hrc_code = 1;
      dbms_output.put_line(' The highest hierarchy available is: Code 1  '||
                                        v_descr);
    EXCEPTION WHEN NO_DATA_FOUND THEN
        dbms_output.put_line('ERR: Invalid Data for Hierarchy');
    END;
EXCEPTION
```

```
   WHEN OTHERS THEN
        dbms_output.put_line('ERR: An error occurred with info :'||
                                   TO_CHAR(SQLCODE)||' '||SQLERRM);
END;
/
```

Here's the output of this program:

```
The highest hierarchy available is: Code 1  CEO/COO

PL/SQL procedure successfully completed.
```

The following points are worth noting:

- The first SELECT . . . INTO raises NO_DATA_FOUND and the corresponding handler executes the INSERT statement. This is because this SELECT statement is included in a nested block with its own exception handler.

- Execution resumes after processing the previous exception and the output of the second SELECT . . . INTO is displayed. Note that this too is included in its own nested block.

- The WHEN OTHERS handler in the outermost block handles any other exceptions occurring in any of the two nested blocks and the ones in the outer block. This is shown in the following code. Any other exceptions in the nested blocks between the lines 4 and 15, and between the lines 16 and 26, is handled by the exception handler in lines 27 through 30.

```
SQL> DECLARE
  2      v_descr VARCHAR2(20);
  3   BEGIN
  4     BEGIN
  5       SELECT hrc_descr
  6       INTO   v_descr
  7       FROM   hrc_tab
  8       WHERE  hrc_code = 10;
  9       dbms_output.put_line(
 10            ' The lowest hierarchy available is: Code 10  '||
 11              v_descr);
```

```
12    EXCEPTION WHEN NO_DATA_FOUND THEN
13      INSERT INTO hrc_tab VALUES (10, 'Assistant');
14      COMMIT;
15    END;
16    BEGIN
17      SELECT hrc_descr
18      INTO   v_descr
19      FROM   hrc_tab
20      WHERE  hrc_code = 1;
21      dbms_output.put_line(
22          ' The highest hierarchy available is: Code 1  '||
23          v_descr);
24    EXCEPTION WHEN NO_DATA_FOUND THEN
25      dbms_output.put_line('ERR: Invalid Data for Hierarchy');
26    END;
27  EXCEPTION
28    WHEN OTHERS THEN
29      dbms_output.put_line('ERR: An error occurred with info :'||
30                           TO_CHAR(SQLCODE)||' '||SQLERRM);
31  END;
/
The highest hierarchy available is: Code 1   CEO/COO

PL/SQL procedure successfully completed.
```

Handling User-Defined Exceptions

User-defined exceptions are exceptions defined in a PL/SQL program that are specific to the application program being coded. These aren't part of the exceptions defined by PL/SQL in the STANDARD package, nor are they ORACLE errors occurring in program execution. These exceptions are identified by name.

Declaring User-Defined Exceptions

In addition to the preceding errors, PL/SQL allows you to define your own predefined exceptions. You declare user-defined exceptions explicitly in the declaration section of a PL/SQL block just like other PL/SQL declarations. You specify the data type of these exceptions with the keyword EXCEPTION. Here's the syntax:

```
exception_name EXCEPTION;
```

where exception_name is the name of the defined exception and is of type
EXCEPTION.

Here's an example to illustrate this:

```
DECLARE
    sites_undefined_for_org EXCEPTION;
BEGIN
    . . . . .
END;
```

The following points are worth noting:

- You must define user-defined exceptions using the EXCEPTION keyword.

- User-defined exceptions aren't associated with any error number or error
  message text.

 TIP *It's a recommended practice to define user-defined
exceptions for trapping and handling application-specific
errors.*

Raising User-Defined Exceptions with the RAISE Statement

Once you've declared a user-defined exception, you have to raise it explicitly
using the RAISE statement. Here's the syntax:

```
RAISE exception_name;
```

where exception_name is the name of the user-defined exception that's declared
in the declaration section.

Here's an example to illustrate this:

```
DECLARE
    sites_undefined_for_org EXCEPTION;
BEGIN
    . . . . .
    IF (condition) THEN
        RAISE sites_undefined_for_org;
    END IF;
EXCEPTION WHEN sites_undefined_for_org THEN
    . . . . .
END;
```

In this code, condition is a PL/SQL condition for which the user-defined exception sites_undefined_for_org is RAISEd.

Handling User-Defined Exceptions with a WHEN Clause

Like predefined exceptions, user-defined exceptions are handled using exception handlers. For each user-defined exception, you have to specify a WHEN clause in the exception handler. To illustrate this, I first insert a record into org_tab as follows:

```
BEGIN
    insert into org_tab values
    (3, 1007, 'Office of Dir Tech ABC Inc.','Office of Director Tech ABC Inc.');
COMMIT;
END;
/
```

Here's the complete code illustrating user-defined exceptions:

```
DECLARE
    sites_undefined_for_org EXCEPTION; -- a user-defined exception
    v_cnt NUMBER;
BEGIN
    SELECT COUNT(*)
    INTO     v_cnt
    FROM    org_site_tab
    WHERE org_id = 1007;
    IF (v_cnt=0) THEN
        -- explicitly raising the user-defined exception
        RAISE sites_undefined_for_org;
    END IF;
EXCEPTION
    -- handling the raised user-defined exception
    WHEN sites_undefined_for_org THEN
        dbms_output.put_line('There are no sites defined for organization 1007');
    WHEN OTHERS THEN
        dbms_output.put_line('ERR: An error occurred with info :'||
                                TO_CHAR(SQLCODE)||' '||SQLERRM);
END;
/
```

Here's the output of this program:

```
There are no sites defined for organization 1007

PL/SQL procedure successfully completed.
```

 TIP *Unless raised explicitly using a RAISE statement, a user-defined exception is never raised.*

 TIP *Once RAISEd, a user-defined exception has to be handled using an exception handler.*

Defining User-Defined Exceptions with the Same Names As Predefined Exceptions

PL/SQL provides several predefined exceptions, each with a particular name. These exceptions are defined in the STANDARD PL/SQL package provided by Oracle. To override these definitions, user-defined exceptions defined of type EXCEPTION can have the same name as the predefined exceptions. Now the question arises, how do you handle a user-defined exception defined with the same name as a predefined exception, and distinguish between the two? To handle predefined and user-defined exceptions in the same block separately, prefix the predefined exception with the word STANDARD followed by a dot (.). However, it's not a good idea to override predefined exceptions—you should define user-defined exceptions instead. Here's an example to illustrate this:

```
DECLARE
      DUP_VAL_ON_INDEX EXCEPTION;
BEGIN
    . . . . . .
EXCEPTION WHEN DUP_VAL_ON_INDEX or STANDARD.DUP_VAL_ON_INDEX THEN
    . . . . . .
END;
```

TIP *A user-defined exception with the same name as a predefined PL/SQL exception overrides the predefined PL/SQL exception. To handle both of these exceptions, reference the predefined exception using the dot notation by prefixing the STANDARD name to the predefined exception name.*

Handling Nonpredefined Oracle Errors

Nonpredefined errors are Oracle errors raised by the PL/SQL or SQL engine that don't have a predefined exception name associated with them. You have two ways to handle such errors:

1. Use an exception handler with a WHEN OTHERS clause and capture the error using SQLCODE and SQLERRM.

2. Associate a user-defined exception with the corresponding error code and the trap, and handle the error using the user-defined exception.

The first method was described in the section "Handling Predefined Exceptions" under SQLCODE and SQLERRM.

The second method is illustrated here. It's quite meaningful to associate a nonpredefined Oracle error with a user-defined exception when you know the Oracle error that's likely to be raised when you code the program. Examples of such errors are as follows:

- A primary or unique key constraint violation while inserting records

- An integrity constraint violation, such as a missing primary key value for a foreign key when inserting into the child table, or existing child records when deleting a parent record in the parent table

- A check constraint violation on a particular column value while inserting or updating records

In these cases, it's quite meaningful to associate the Oracle error with a user-defined exception and then use an exception handler to handle this exception. For example, a check constraint failure on a column value makes more sense when it's associated with a user-defined exception than when it's trapped in the WHEN OTHERS handler.

PRAGMA_EXCEPTION_INIT

PL/SQL provides a compiler directive, or *pragma,* named EXCEPTION_INIT to associate a user-defined exception with a nonpredefined Oracle error number. It's like giving a name for such an Oracle error. Here are the steps to perform to use this compiler directive:

1. Declare a user-defined exception.

2. Use PRAGMA EXCEPTION_INIT to associate the user-defined exception with an Oracle error.

Here's the syntax for this directive:

```
DECLARE
     exception_name EXCEPTION;
     PRAGMA(exception_name, oracle_error_number);
BEGIN
    .. .. ...
 EXCEPTION WHEN exception_name THEN
     .. .. ... /* Handle the error */
END;
```

where exception_name is the name of the user-defined exception and oracle_error_number is the Oracle error number including the minus sign if the error number is negative (as is most often the case).

 TIP *You must specify PRAGMA EXCEPTION_INIT in the declaration section after the user-defined exception declaration. It's better to specify it immediately following the user-defined exception declaration.*

Here's an example to illustrate this:

```
DECLARE
     invalid_org_level EXCEPTION;
     PRAGMA EXCEPTION_INIT(invalid_org_level, -2290);
BEGIN
    .. .. ...
EXCEPTION WHEN invalid_org_level THEN
    .. .. ...
END;
```

Here's a complete example:

```
DECLARE
     invalid_org_level EXCEPTION;
     PRAGMA EXCEPTION_INIT(invalid_org_level, -2290);
BEGIN
     INSERT INTO org_level VALUES (1001, 'P');
     COMMIT;
EXCEPTION WHEN invalid_org_level THEN
     dbms_output.put_line(
'Organization Level can be only one of '||
'C - Corporate, E - Executive, M - Mid-level, L - Lower Level');
END;
/
```

Here's the output of this program:

```
Organization Level can be only one of C - Corporate, E - Executive, M -
Mid-level, L - Lower Level

PL/SQL procedure successfully completed.
```

The following points are worth noting:

- A user-defined exception invalid_org_level is defined.

- The Oracle error "ORA-02290: check constraint (OWNER.CONSTRAINT_NAME) violated" is associated with the invalid_org_level exception defined in this way.

- The user-defined exception is and has to be handled using an exception handler specified by EXCEPTION WHEN invalid_org_level.

- There's no need to raise the user-defined exception. It's automatically raised by PL/SQL. This is what is meant by associating the user-defined exception with the Oracle error.

TIP *There's no need to raise the user-defined exception after you associate it with a nonpredefined Oracle error. It's raised automatically by PL/SQL. However, this isn't a restriction; it can be raised explicitly as well.*

TIP *You can associate more than one user-defined exception with the same error number.*

TIP *You normally use PRAGMA EXCEPTION_INIT to associate a nonpredefined Oracle error with a user-defined exception. However, you can also use it to associate user-defined error messages with user-defined exceptions.*

Handling Exceptions Raised in Declaration and Exception Handling Sections

Exceptions can be raised not only in the executable section between BEGIN and END but also in the declaration and the exception handling sections of a PL/SQL block. I discuss the methods to handle these kinds of exceptions in the sections that follow.

Exceptions Raised in the Declaration Section

Exceptions raised in the declaration section are handled in the corresponding handler in the immediate enclosing block. If no such handler exists in the immediate enclosing block, control transfers to the first enclosing block having such a handler. Otherwise, the program terminates with an unhandled exception. Here's an example to illustrate this:

```
DECLARE
    v_num NUMBER(2) := 100;
BEGIN
    /* .. .. ... Do some processing */
    null;
EXCEPTION
    WHEN VALUE_ERROR THEN
            /* .. .. ... Handle the error */
        NULL;
    WHEN OTHERS THEN
```

```
                    dbms_output.put_line('ERR: An error occurred with info :'||
                                              TO_CHAR(SQLCODE)||' '||SQLERRM);
END;
/
```

Here's the output of this program:

```
DECLARE
*
ERROR at line 1:
ORA-06502: PL/SQL: numeric or value error: number precision too large
ORA-06512: at line 2
```

The declaration initializes a NUMBER variable of length 2 to a value of length 3. This raises the VALUE_ERROR exception. However, this exception, which is raised in the declaration section, doesn't get handled either by the WHEN VALUE_ERROR or by the WHEN OTHERS handler given. This is because these handlers are for exceptions raised in the current block between BEGIN and END, excluding the exception handling block. To circumvent this problem, you have to define an enclosing block to handle the exception raised in the declaration section of the enclosed block. Here's the code for this:

```
BEGIN
DECLARE
    v_num NUMBER(2) := 100;
BEGIN
    /* .. .. ... Do some processing */
    null;
EXCEPTION
    WHEN VALUE_ERROR THEN
          /* .. .. ... Handle the error */
       NULL;
    WHEN OTHERS THEN
          dbms_output.put_line('ERR: An error occurred with info :'||
                                      TO_CHAR(SQLCODE)||' '||SQLERRM);
END;
EXCEPTION
    WHEN VALUE_ERROR THEN
          /* .. .. ... Handle the error */
       dbms_output.put_line('Value error occurred');
    WHEN OTHERS THEN
          dbms_output.put_line('ERR: An error occurred with info :'||
```

```
                         TO_CHAR(SQLCODE)||' '||SQLERRM);
END;
/
```

Here's the output of this program:

```
Value error occurred

PL/SQL procedure successfully completed.
```

This enables the raised exception to propagate to the enclosing block and eventually be handled by its exception handler.

Exceptions Raised in the Exception Handling Section

Similar to exceptions raised in the declaration section of a block, exceptions (either predefined or user-defined) that are raised in the exception section of the current block are handled in the enclosing block. Exceptions raised in this way are immediately propagated to the enclosing block because only one exception can be "active" at any point in time in the exception handler. Here's an example to illustrate this:

```
DECLARE
     excep1 EXCEPTION;
     excep2 EXCEPTION;
BEGIN
     . . . . . .
   IF (condition) THEN
      RAISE excep1;
   END IF;
EXCEPTION
     WHEN excep1 THEN
             log_error( . . . . . . );
           RAISE excep2;
     WHEN excep2 THEN
             NULL;
     WHEN OTHERS THEN
         dbms_output.put_line('ERR: An error occurred with info :'||
                         TO_CHAR(SQLCODE)||' '||SQLERRM);
END;
```

The excep2 exception raised in the exception section is not handled by the WHEN excep2 handler in the same block. To circumvent this problem, you need to define an enclosing block with a similar exception handler. Here's the code for this:

```
DECLARE
    excep1 EXCEPTION;
    excep2 EXCEPTION;
BEGIN
    BEGIN
        . . . . . .
        IF (condition) THEN
            RAISE excep1;
        END IF;
    EXCEPTION
        WHEN excep1 THEN
            log_error( . . . ... );
            RAISE excep2;
    END;
EXCEPTION WHEN excep2 THEN
            NULL;
WHEN OTHERS THEN
            dbms_output.put_line('ERR: An error occurred with info :'||
                            TO_CHAR(SQLCODE)||' '||SQLERRM);
END;
```

TIP   *Control can't branch out from an exception handler to the current block. Also, control can't branch out from the current block to an exception handler in the current or enclosing blocks. However, control can branch from an exception handler to an enclosing block.*

Reraising an Exception

Reraising an exception is common when it's needed to handle an exception locally and then propagate it to the enclosing block so that it can be handled differently there. You do this by simply specifying the keyword RAISE without any exception name following it in the exception handler. Here's the previous example rewritten to illustrate this:

```
DECLARE
     excep1 EXCEPTION;
BEGIN
   BEGIN
        . . . . . .
        IF (condition) THEN
             RAISE excep1;
        END IF;
      EXCEPTION
         WHEN excep1 THEN
              log_error( . . . . . . );
              RAISE;
      END;
EXCEPTION WHEN excep1 THEN
             NULL;
WHEN OTHERS THEN
             dbms_output.put_line('ERR: An error occurred with info :'||
                            TO_CHAR(SQLCODE)||' '||SQLERRM);
END;
```

The following points are worth noting:

- The exception excep1 is raised first in the nested block. It's then handled in the nested block itself. However, in the exception handler for excep1 in the nested block, you log the error and then re-RAISE this exception. This is specified by the keyword RAISE following the call to log_error procedure.

- The reraised exception automatically propagates to the enclosing block where it's handled differently.

Scope of PL/SQL Exceptions

A PL/SQL block consists of a declaration section followed by an executable section, specified by a BEGIN . . . END. It also contains an exception handling section. An exception can be raised in the declaration section, in the executable BEGIN . . . END section, or in the exception handling section. The scope of a user-defined exception is the block in which it's defined or any nested blocks within its current block. It can be referenced by name and handled in the exception handler within this block.

Predefined exceptions are automatically propagated out of the current block if no exception handler exists in the current block. They're caught in the immediate enclosing block that has an exception handler defined. Nonpredefined Oracle errors are available to any WHEN OTHERS handler in the current block or enclosing blocks. However, if such an error is associated with a user-defined exception, its scope is once again the same as the scope of the user-defined exception.

If you want to reference a user-defined exception outside of a PL/SQL block, it's best to define the exception in a package so that it can be referenced by name in any block, outer or inner. Like packaged variables, packaged exceptions have global scope and visibility.

TIP   *A user-defined exception is available in its current blocks or any of its nested blocks.*

TIP   *You can't declare more than one user-defined exception with the same name in the same block. However, you can do this in any of its nested blocks. In this case, the exception local to the block overrides all the others. However, this local exception can only be handled either by an exception handler with the same name in the local block or by a WHEN OTHERS handler in any of the outer blocks.*

User-Defined PL/SQL Error Messages

So far you've dealt with errors that were defined by Oracle SQL and/or PL/SQL and user-defined exceptions. In the former case, the error code and error message text were defined by Oracle and these errors were handled by exception handlers using the predefined exceptions or a WHEN OTHERS exception handler, or by associating user-defined exceptions with Oracle errors. In the latter case, exceptions were defined by the programmer, raised explicitly, and handled using the corresponding exception names.

In addition to Oracle SQL and/or PL/SQL errors and user-defined exceptions, PL/SQL provides you with the flexibility to define your own error messages customized toward the specific application you're coding. This section highlights the methods for defining user-defined error messages and handling them.

Defining User-Defined Error Messages in PL/SQL

To define customized error messages, PL/SQL provides the procedure RAISE_APPLICATION_ERROR. Here's the signature of this procedure:

```
RAISE_APPLICATION_ERROR(error_no IN NUMBER, error_message IN VARCHAR2,
[keep_errors IN BOOLEAN]);
```

where error_no is any number between –20000 and –20999, error_message is the customized error message of the error being raised of a length that doesn't exceed 512 bytes, and keep_errors is a boolean flag. Here's an example of using this procedure:

```
RAISE_APPLICATION_ERROR(-20000, 'Organization 1010 does not exist.', FALSE);
```

The preceding statement means that the customized error message is specific to a particular application and has the error number –20000 and the error message text

```
Organization 1010 does not exist.
```

The keep_errors boolean flag is optional. It has a default value of FALSE. If a value of TRUE is passed for this flag, the new error defined in this way is added to the list of already raised errors (if one exists). A value of FALSE will replace the current list of errors with the new error defined in this way.

Note that in all the earlier cases, when trapping errors, messages were given using DBMS_OUTPUT.PUT_LINE, and as such, these messages were being displayed to the screen output in tools such as SQL*Plus. But PL/SQL is a procedural language widely used in many kinds of development and execution environments—for example, client-server environments such as Oracle Developer, embedded SQL and PL/SQL applications, and so forth. Also, PL/SQL, being the major procedural language for Oracle, is used to code subprograms and database triggers that encapsulate business logic in the database. Imagine an error-definition and handling mechanism in such situations. This is where RAISE APPLICATION_ERROR comes in as a handy mechanism to raise customized server-side errors and propagate them to the client side.

Handling User-Defined Error Messages in PL/SQL

Whenever a user-defined error message is defined with a call to RAISE_APPLICATION_ERROR, it behaves as if an exception has been raised. Execution of the PL/SQL program stops at this point and the program either terminates with the defined error or returns the customized error number and message text to the calling environment.

The procedure RAISE_APPLICATION_ERROR can perform two functions:

- Define customized error messages.

- Propagate a server-side customized error number and message to a client program in a client-server environment that can be then detected by exception handlers such as WHEN_OTHERS.

I describe the method of handling such errors in each case in the sections that follow.

Defining Customized Error Messages

Here's a complete example to demonstrate the use of RAISE_APPLICATION_ERROR:

```
CREATE OR REPLACE PROCEDURE org_proc
                        (p_flag_in VARCHAR2,
                         p_hrc_code NUMBER,
                         p_org_id NUMBER,
                         p_org_short_name VARCHAR2,
                         p_org_long_name VARCHAR2)
IS
    v_error_code NUMBER;
BEGIN
        IF (p_flag_in = 'I') THEN
            BEGIN
                INSERT INTO org_tab VALUES
                        (p_hrc_code, p_org_id, p_org_short_name, p_org_long_name);
            EXCEPTION WHEN OTHERS THEN
                v_error_code := SQLCODE;
                IF v_error_code = -1 THEN
                    RAISE_APPLICATION_ERROR(-20000, 'Organization '||
                                            TO_CHAR(p_org_id)||
            ' already exists. Cannot create a duplicate with the same id.');
                ELSIF v_error_code = -2291 THEN
RAISE_APPLICATION_ERROR(-20001, 'Invalid Hierarchy Code '||
                                            TO_CHAR(p_hrc_code)||
                                    ' specified. Cannot create organization.');
                END IF;
            END;
```

```
ELSIF (p_flag_in = 'C') THEN
          BEGIN
               UPDATE org_tab
                    set org_short_name = p_org_short_name,
                        org_long_name = p_org_long_name
               WHERE hrc_code = p_hrc_code
                    AND org_id = p_org_id;
               IF SQL%NOTFOUND THEN
                    RAISE_APPLICATION_ERROR(-20002, 'Organization '||
                                                    TO_CHAR(p_org_id)||
                         ' does not  exist. Cannot change info for the same.');
               END IF;
          END;
ELSIF (p_flag_in = 'D') THEN
          BEGIN
               DELETE org_tab
               WHERE hrc_code = p_hrc_code
                    AND org_id = p_org_id;
               IF SQL%NOTFOUND THEN
                    RAISE_APPLICATION_ERROR(-20003, 'Organization '||
                                                    TO_CHAR(p_org_id)||
                         ' does not  exist. Cannot delete info for the same.');
               END IF;
          EXCEPTION WHEN OTHERS THEN
               v_error_code := SQLCODE;
               IF v_error_code = -2292 THEN
                    RAISE_APPLICATION_ERROR(-20004, 'Organization '||
                                                    TO_CHAR(p_org_id)||
               'has site details defined for it. Cannot perform delete
operation.');
               END IF;
          END;
END IF;
END;
/
```

The following points are worth noting:

- This procedure calls the RAISE_APPLICATION_ERROR in several places with different error numbers and error messages that are customized. These aren't part of the ORA errors defined by Oracle.

- At each execution of RAISE_APPLICATION_ERROR, processing stops and the program is terminated with the customized error message as output.

Here's the output of several instances of executing this procedure:

```
SQL> exec org_proc('I',1,1001,'Office of CEO ABC Inc.','Office of CEO ABC
Inc.');
BEGIN org_proc('I',1,1001,'Office of CEO ABC Inc.','Office of CEO ABC Inc.');
END;
*
ERROR at line 1:
ORA-20000: Organization 1001 already exists. Cannot create a duplicate with the
same id.
ORA-06512: at "PLSQL9I.ORG_PROC", line 16
ORA-06512: at line 1

SQL> exec org_proc('I',6,1011,'Office of Mgr ABC Inc.','Office of Mgr ABC
Inc.');
BEGIN org_proc('I',6,1011,'Office of Mgr ABC Inc.','Office of Mgr ABC Inc.');
END;
*
ERROR at line 1:
ORA-20001: Invalid Hierarchy Code 6 specified. Cannot create organization.
ORA-06512: at "PLSQL9I.ORG_PROC", line 18
ORA-06512: at line 1

SQL> exec org_proc('D',1, 1001, null, null);
BEGIN org_proc('D',1, 1001, null, null); END;
*
ERROR at line 1:
ORA-20004: Organization 1001 has site details defined for it. Cannot perform
delete
operation.
ORA-06512: at "PLSQL9I.ORG_PROC", line 41
ORA-06512: at line 1
```

Propagating a Server-Side Customized Error Number and Message to a Client Program

Consider the preceding procedure being called from a client program. You can trap and handle the error returned by RAISE_APPLICATION_ERROR in the client program in two ways.

First, you can use a WHEN OTHERS handler and track the SQLCODE. Here's code that illustrates this:

```
DECLARE
    v_hrc_code NUMBER := 6;
    v_org_id NUMBER := 1011;
    v_org_short_name VARCHAR2(30) := 'Office of  Mgr. ABC Inc.';
```

```
    v_org_long_name VARCHAR2(60) := 'Office of Mgr. ABC Inc.';
BEGIN
    org_proc('I', v_hrc_code, v_org_id, v_org_short_name, v_org_long_name);
EXCEPTION WHEN OTHERS THEN
    DBMS_OUTPUT.PUT_LINE(TO_CHAR(SQLCODE)|| ' '||SQLERRM);
END;
/
```

Here's the output of this program:

```
-20001 ORA-20001: Invalid Hierarchy Code 6 specified. Cannot create
organization.

PL/SQL procedure successfully completed.
```

SQLCODE and SQLERRM will return the customized error number and error message text passed to RAISE_APPLICATION_ERROR in each case.

TIP   *The benefit of using RAISE_APPLICATION_ERROR is twofold. It not only raises the customized error and stops further execution, but it also returns the customized error number and error message as the SQLCODE and SQLERRM to the calling environment.*

Second, you can use a PRAGMA EXCEPTION_INIT to associate the particular error code with a user-defined exception and then handle it explicitly by using this exception name in the exception handler. Here's the previous program rewritten this way:

```
DECLARE
    v_hrc_code NUMBER := 6;
    v_org_id NUMBER := 1010;
    v_org_short_name VARCHAR2(30) := 'Office of  Mgr. ABC Inc.';
    v_org_long_name VARCHAR2(60) := 'Office of Mgr. ABC Inc.';
    excep1 EXCEPTION;
    PRAGMA EXCEPTION_INIT(excep1, -20000);
    excep2 EXCEPTION;
    PRAGMA EXCEPTION_INIT(excep2, -20001);
BEGIN
    org_proc('I', v_hrc_code, v_org_id, v_org_short_name, v_org_long_name);
EXCEPTION
```

```
        WHEN excep1 or excep2 THEN
              DBMS_OUTPUT.PUT_LINE(SQLERRM);
        WHEN OTHERS THEN
              DBMS_OUTPUT.PUT_LINE(TO_CHAR(SQLCODE)||SQLERRM);
END;
/
```

Here's the output of this program:

```
ORA-20001: Invalid Hierarchy Code 6 specified. Cannot create organization.

PL/SQL procedure successfully completed.
```

I conclude this chapter with a section full of tips for error message and exception handling in PL/SQL.

Tips for PL/SQL Error Message and Exception Handling

The following is a short list of some of the recommended practices in error message handling.

 CROSS-REFERENCE *For a detailed list of recommended practices, refer to Chapter 16.*

- Always use a WHEN OTHERS handler in the outermost level of the PL/SQL program to handle previously unhandled error messages.

- Log an error in an error table with information such as the error code and error message text.

- Use customized error messages tailored to the specific application and categorize these messages based on their severity level.

- Don't override predefined exception names when defining user-defined exceptions.

- Don't define duplicate user-defined exceptions when dealing with nested blocks.

- Write error-handling routines that separate error processing from business logic processing.

Summary

This chapter dealt with error message and exception handling in PL/SQL. I discussed the types of exceptions and the various methods of handling them, and I presented the method of creating customized error messages and handling them.

The next chapter deals with defining and using stored subprograms in PL/SQL.

Stored Subprograms (Procedures, Functions, and Packages)

THE UNIVERSAL CONCEPT OF A PL/SQL program is that the PL/SQL block could be one of three types: an anonymous block, a labeled block, or a named block. The PL/SQL block is quite handy in coding PL/SQL programs tailored toward a specific function and employing other PL/SQL programming constructs. However, it has a disadvantage: You can't store it in the database like you can a table. If you need to share a block within another application, then you must rewrite it for that specific application. How easy and efficient would it be if the code were shareable? PL/SQL provides you with a mechanism, the *stored subprogram*, that permits you to share code between applications. A stored subprogram has the major advantage of being stored in the database and it's therefore shareable.

A stored subprogram is a named PL/SQL block that's stored in the database. PL/SQL 9*i* supports three types of stored subprograms:

- Procedures

- Functions

- Packages

This brings up the concept of procedures and functions in 3GL languages such as Pascal, C, C++, and Java. PL/SQL extends the 3GL capabilities by providing the stored subprograms feature.

A stored subprogram in PL/SQL has the following features:

- It's uniquely named.

- It's stored in the database.

- It's available as metadata in the data dictionary.

- Parameters can be passed to it, and values (one value or multiple values) can be returned from it.

- It can be executed at the top level or called from other PL/SQL programs by using its name.

In addition to the stored subprograms' capability to be stored in the database, procedures, functions, and packages offer many advantages. Their primary benefits are as follows:

- *Modularity:* Stored subprograms introduce the concept of *modular programming,* with a single, large program being broken down into logically independent modules and each module coded separately. The main program can then be written by calling these individual procedures with any additional code that's required. This enables you to write APIs tailored toward a specific application.

- *Encapsulation:* Stored subprograms enable the encapsulation of business logic, such as business rules and application logic, into the database.

- *Centralization of code:* Because the stored subprograms are stored in the database and run on the server side, they're easy to maintain. The code is available in a single location and multiple applications can use it.

- *Reusability:* As mentioned previously, multiple programs can reuse the same subprogram, and, when necessary, with different sets of data.

- *Better performance:* A subprogram allows you to group together sets of SQL statements, which results in better performance with fewer database calls and reduced network traffic in two-tier and three-tier application environments. Also, as of PL/SQL 9*i,* stored subprograms can make use of native compilation, subsequent conversion to C code, and then storage in machine code as opposed to interpreted code. This enables faster execution.

This chapter begins with the definition and use of procedures and functions, and then it goes on to highlight the concept of PL/SQL packages. I detail the ins and outs of using these three types of subprograms. I also present additional topics, such as returning resultsets from subprograms and using certain new features with regard to procedures, functions, and packages.

I illustrate the concept of stored subprograms by taking into account the organizational hierarchy system presented in Chapter 2. Also, I define an order entry system with tables that are dynamically created. Appendix A presents the schema objects to be created.

Creating and Using Procedures and Functions

Procedures and functions are two of the ways in which the 3GL modular programming capabilities are implemented in PL/SQL in the form of stored objects. This section discusses the method of creating and executing procedures and functions. It also outlines the method of defining parameters to procedures and functions. The concept of native compilation of stored subprograms is highlighted.

A procedure or function consists of four parts:

- A signature or header

- The keyword IS or AS

- Local declarations (optional)

- The body of the procedure (including exception handlers) between BEGIN and END

Creating and Using a Procedure

You create a procedure with the CREATE OR REPLACE PROCEDURE statement. Here's the syntax:

```
CREATE [OR REPLACE] PROCEDURE procedure_name
[(parameter_name1 parameter_mode datatype,
  . . . . . .
parameter_nameN parameter_mode datatype)]
[AUTHID {DEFINER | CURRENT_USER}]
{IS | AS}
   [PRAGMA AUTONOMOUS_TRANSACTION;]
   [local declaration section]
BEGIN
   executable section
[EXCEPTION
   exception handling section]
END [procedure_name];
```

where procedure_name is the name of the procedure being created, parameter1 through parameterN are the names of the procedure parameters, parameter_mode is one of [{IN | OUT [NOCOPY] | IN OUT [NOCOPY]}], and datatype is the data type of the associated parameter. The local declaration section is specified without the DECLARE keyword and the BEGIN . . . END section resembles that of a regular PL/SQL block. The AUTHID clause specifies the execution privileges of the procedure and is explained in the section "Definer and Invoker Rights" later in this chapter. The PRAGMA refers to autonomous transactions and is explained in Chapter 8. For the purposes of this section, I ignore the AUTHID clause and the PRAGMA while defining procedures or functions.

Here's an example of a simple procedure:

```
CREATE OR REPLACE PROCEDURE show_line
                    (ip_line_length IN NUMBER,
                     ip_separator   IN VARCHAR2)
IS
  actual_line VARCHAR2(150);
BEGIN
    FOR idx in 1..ip_line_length LOOP
       actual_line := actual_line || ip_separator;
    END LOOP;
    DBMS_OUTPUT.PUT_LINE(actual_line);
EXCEPTION WHEN OTHERS THEN
    dbms_output.put_line(SQLERRM);
END;
/
```

 TIP *The semicolon (;) at the end of the END statement and the forward slash (/) after it are necessary. This follows from the syntax of a PL/SQL block.*

Once you've created the show_line procedure, you can call it from a PL/SQL block as follows:

```
BEGIN
    show_line(50, '=');
END;
/
```

Here's the output of the preceding program:

```
SQL> BEGIN
  2       show_line(50, '=');
  3  END;
  4  /
==================================================

PL/SQL procedure successfully completed.
```

The following points are worth noting:

- The signature or the header of the procedure is

```
show_line (ip_line_length IN NUMBER, ip_separator  IN VARCHAR2).
```

   This item is called a signature or header because it identifies the procedure
   uniquely and is used to execute the procedure or call it from another procedure or a PL/SQL block, or from the client side. Here, the name of the
   procedure is show_line and it takes two input parameters named
   ip_line_length and ip_separator. The ip_line_length parameter is
   a numeric parameter and is of IN mode. The ip_separator parameter is of
   type VARCHAR2 and is also of IN mode. Note that the length of the parameters isn't specified. This length is determined when the actual data values
   are passed when the procedure is executed or called.

- The keyword IS follows the signature.

- The local declaration section is

```
actual_line VARCHAR2(150);
```

- The procedure body is the code between BEGIN and END.

- The procedure is called as an executable statement in the PL/SQL block.

In the case of compilation errors, you'll see the message

```
Warning: Procedure created with compilation errors.
```

You can see the corresponding errors by using the command

```
SQL> show errors
```

in interactive tools such as SQL*Plus.

Creating and Using a Function

A *function* is a stored subprogram that returns a value. You create a function with the CREATE OR REPLACE FUNCTION statement. Here's the syntax:

```
CREATE [OR REPLACE] FUNCTION function_name
[(parameter_name1 parameter_mode datatype,
  . . . . . .
parameter_nameN parameter_mode datatype)]
RETURN datatype
[AUTHID {DEFINER | CURRENT_USER}]
{IS | AS}
   [PRAGMA AUTONOMOUS_TRANSACTION;]
   [local declaration section]
BEGIN
   executable section
[EXCEPTION
   exception handling section]
END [function_name];
```

where function_name is the name of the function being created, parameter1 through parameterN are the names of the function parameters, parameter_mode is one of [{IN | OUT [NOCOPY] | IN OUT [NOCOPY]}], and datatype is the data type of the associated parameter. As in the case of procedures, the local declaration section is specified without the DECLARE keyword, and the BEGIN . . . END section resembles that of a regular PL/SQL block. Also, the AUTHID clause specifies the execution privileges of the function and the PRAGMA refers to autonomous transactions.

The definition of a function differs from that of a procedure in the signature. The signature of a function has an additional RETURN clause that specifies the data type of the return value of the function. It's mandatory that you specify the RETURN clause while defining a function.

Here's an example of a simple function:

```
CREATE OR REPLACE FUNCTION f_line
                      (ip_line_length IN NUMBER,
                       ip_separator   IN VARCHAR2)
RETURN VARCHAR2
IS
  actual_line VARCHAR2(150);
BEGIN
     FOR idx in 1..ip_line_length LOOP
        actual_line := actual_line || ip_separator;
     END LOOP;
     RETURN (actual_line);
EXCEPTION WHEN OTHERS THEN
     dbms_output.put_line(SQLERRM);
     RETURN (null);
END;
/
```

TIP   *The semicolon (;) at the end of the END statement and the forward slash (/) after it are necessary.*

Once you've created the f_line function, you can call it from a PL/SQL block as follows:

```
DECLARE
     v_line VARCHAR2(150);
BEGIN
     v_line := f_line(50, '=');
     DBMS_OUTPUT.PUT_LINE(v_line);
END;
/
```

The output of the preceding program is the same as the output of the procedure show_line.

The following points are worth noting:

- The signature or header of the function is

```
f_line (ip_line_length IN NUMBER, ip_separator  IN VARCHAR2) RETURN VARCHAR2.
```

- The keyword IS follows the signature.

- The local declaration section is

```
actual_line VARCHAR2(150);
```

- The procedure body is the code between BEGIN and END.

Calling a Function and the RETURN Statement

Unlike a procedure, a function is called as a part of an expression that evaluates to a value whose data type matches the return type of the function. Also, functions can be called from DML statements such as SELECT, INSERT, and so forth. I discuss this in the next section.

Notice the RETURN statement inside the body of the function. It's necessary to specify this. It returns a value to the calling environment. The RETURN statement can return a value in three ways: a hard-coded value, a single variable holding a value, or an expression that evaluates to a value whose data type matches that of the RETURN clause specified in the signature of the function. You can specify more than one RETURN statement in the body of the function. As soon as the RETURN statement is encountered, the function execution stops and the control returns to the calling environment.

The RETURN statement has two general forms:

```
RETURN;
RETURN expression;
```

You can use the first form of the RETURN statement in procedures. It stops the execution of the procedure at that point and transfers control to the calling program. It *can't* return a value.

The second form of the RETURN statement is and must be used in functions. It not only transfers control to the calling program, but it also returns a value.

 TIP *Once created, the procedure or function is stored in compiled form in the database. Also, the source code of the procedure or function is stored in the data dictionary.*

TIP *Once created, the procedure or function should normally be dropped and re-created if the code for the procedure or function changes. To avoid two operations of dropping and re-creating, you can specify the OR REPLACE clause when you create the procedure or function, so that the old version of the procedure is overwritten with the new version each time it is created.*

TIP *Creating a procedure or function is a DDL command, and an implicit COMMIT is performed both before and after the command is executed.*

Executing a Procedure or a Function

The owner of a procedure or a function can execute it, or else the EXECUTE privilege should be granted to a user other than the owner. You can do this with the GRANT statement. Here's the syntax:

```
GRANT EXECUTE ON sub_program_name to user_name;
```

where sub_program_name is the name of the procedure or function and user_name is the schema name executing the procedure.

In addition to this, you should create a synonym in the user schema executing the procedure. If you don't, the procedure or function name must be preceded by its owner schema name in the corresponding procedure or function call.

By default, a stored subprogram is executed under the privileges of its owner. This means all object references are resolved as per the owner's privilege set. Also, the output of the stored subprogram is reflected in the owner schema. This behavior can be changed from Oracle8*i* onward using a feature called invoker rights, which I cover in the section "Definer and Invoker Rights."

TIP *The privileges for the dependent objects of a stored subprogram must be granted explicitly and not via a role.*

You can execute a procedure or function in one of three ways:

- As an executable statement or as part of an expression from a PL/SQL block. The PL/SQL block can be an anonymous PL/SQL block, a body of another procedure or function, or a block in a client program. I demonstrated this method of executing a procedure or function in the previous two sections.

- Using the EXECUTE command in interactive environments such as SQL*Plus.

- Using the CALL statement.

The EXECUTE command enables you to execute a procedure or function in SQL*Plus. Here's the syntax for executing procedures:

```
EXECUTE procedure_name(arg1, . . . , argN)
```

where procedure_name is the name of the procedure being executed and arg1, ..., argN are the arguments with a one-to-one correspondence to the parameters defined in the signature of the procedure.

Here's the show_line procedure being executed in this way:

```
SQL> set serverout on;
SQL> exec show_line(50, '=')
```

The EXECUTE command for function takes a different form. Here's the syntax:

```
EXECUTE :var := function_name(arg1, . . . , argN)
```

where var is a SQL*Plus variable with the same data type as the return type of the function and is defined using the VARIABLE command in SQL*Plus; function_name is the name of the function being executed; and arg1, ..., argN are the arguments with a one-to-one correspondence to the parameters defined in the signature of the function. You can see the value of the var variable using the PRINT command in SQL*Plus.

Here's the f_line function executed in this way:

```
SQL> VARIABLE var VARCHAR2(150)
SQL> EXECUTE :var := f_line(50,'=')
SQL> PRINT var
```

The third way of calling procedures and functions is using the CALL statement. This is a new SQL statement introduced in Oracle8*i*. Here's the syntax:

```
CALL proc_or_func_name([arg1, ... , argN]) [INTO host_variable];
```

where proc_or_func_name is the name of the procedure or function being executed; arg1, ..., argN are the arguments with a one-to-one correspondence to the parameters defined in the signature of the procedure or function; and host_variable is a host variable to store the return value of functions. The INTO clause is used only for functions.

Here are the show_line procedure and the f_line function executed using the CALL statement:

```
SQL> CALL show_line(50, '=');
SQL> VARIABLE v_line VARCHAR2(150);
SQL> CALL f_line(50, '=') INTO :v_line;
SQL> PRINT v_line
```

The parentheses are necessary even when no arguments are specified. Here's an example:

```
CREATE OR REPLACE PROCEDURE p1
IS
BEGIN
     dbms_output.put_line('Welcome!!! ');
END;
/
```

Here's the output of executing this procedure using the CALL statement:

```
SQL> CALL p1();
Welcome!!!

Call completed.
```

Omitting the parentheses results in this error:

```
SQL> CALL p1;
CALL p1
     *
ERROR at line 1:
ORA-06576: not a valid function or procedure name
```

TIP   *The CALL statement is a SQL statement and isn't valid in PL/SQL blocks except in PL/SQL blocks executing dynamic SQL.*

Specifying Procedure or Function Parameters

I discuss the following methods of specifying parameters in the following sections:

- Naming parameters

- Specifying parameter modes

- Specifying the type for parameters

- Specifying default values for parameters

Naming Parameters

Naming parameters consists of distinguishing between actual parameters and formal parameters. As you learned in the earlier sections, when a procedure or function is defined with parameters, the signature consists of parameter names and their corresponding data types. These are called *formal parameters,* and the procedure or function body references them using these names. When the sub-program is executed, the actual values corresponding to the formal parameters are passed. These are termed *actual parameters* and can be in the form of literals or constants, or as variables holding values.

As an example, consider the procedure show_line. The signature of the procedure is

```
show_line (ip_line_length IN NUMBER, ip_separator  IN VARCHAR2)
```

The two parameters, ip_line_length and ip_separator, are the formal parameters of the procedure. These parameters are referenced inside the body of the procedure.

Now the question arises, from where does the procedure derive the values of these two parameters? It's from the values of the actual parameters passed while calling the procedure. Recall the call to the show_line procedure. Here's the code again:

```
BEGIN
    show_line(50, '=');
END;
/
```

Here, the constant 50 and the literal '=' are the actual parameters to the procedure. They can be variables too. For example, you can modify the preceding call as follows:

```
DECLARE
    v_length NUMBER := 50;
    v_separator VARCHAR2(1) := '=';
BEGIN
    show_line(v_length, v_separator);
END;
/
```

TIP   *When a procedure or function is called, the actual parameters are evaluated and their values are assigned to the corresponding formal parameters in case of input parameter mode.*

TIP   *The data types of the actual and formal parameters must be compatible on a one-to-one basis.*

You can pass the actual parameters to a procedure or function in three ways: positional notation, named notation, and mixed notation.

The way the show_line procedure is called in the previous example illustrates *positional notation*. In positional notation, you specify the actual parameters in the same order as the formal parameters with data types corresponding one-to-one. In this case, the v_length actual parameter is associated with the ip_line_length formal parameter, and the v_separator actual parameter is associated with the ip_separator formal parameter.

Named notation uses the name of the formal parameter followed by an arrow and then the actual parameter name in the call of the procedure. Here's the show_line procedure called in this way:

```
DECLARE
    v_length NUMBER := 50;
    v_separator VARCHAR2(1) := '=';
BEGIN
    show_line(ip_line_length=>v_length, ip_separator=>v_separator);
END;
/
```

The arrow serves as the association operator between the actual and formal parameters. The formal parameter is specified to the left of the arrow and the actual parameter is specified to the right of the arrow. In named notation, you can specify the parameters in any order. Thus, the following call statement is also valid:

```
DECLARE
    v_length NUMBER := 50;
    v_separator VARCHAR2(1) := '=';
BEGIN
    show_line(ip_separator=>v_separator, ip_line_length=>v_length);
END;
/
```

The third notation is *mixed notation,* in which you can mix positional and named notation. In this case, positional notation must precede named notation. Here's an example:

```
DECLARE
    v_length NUMBER := 50;
    v_separator VARCHAR2(1) := '=';
BEGIN
    show_line(v_length, ip_separator=>v_separator);
END;
/
```

Specifying Parameter Modes

As I mentioned earlier, a procedure can take parameters and perform an action, whereas a function can take parameters and return a single value to the calling environment. Now, two questions arise:

1. Can a procedure return a value to the calling environment?

2. Can a procedure or function return multiple values to the calling environment?

The answer to both of these questions is yes, and returning values to the calling environment is made possible by specifying the parameter modes while defining the signature of the stored subprogram. PL/SQL provides three parameter modes for formal parameters: IN, OUT, and IN OUT.

The IN mode acts as a read-only specifier so that the value of the called formal parameter can't be changed inside the value of the subprogram. The show_line procedure has both the parameters specified as IN. The actual parameter corresponding to an IN formal parameter can be a constant, a literal, an expression, or a variable. If you omit the mode while you define the signature, IN mode is assumed by default.

The OUT mode acts as a write specifier and allows a value to be assigned to it inside the body of the subprogram. Thus, an OUT parameter acts like an uninitialized variable that can be read from and written into. Moreover, the OUT mode enables you to return a value to the calling environment using the actual parameter. Therefore, the actual parameter corresponding to an OUT formal parameter must be a variable. The contents of the formal parameter are assigned to the actual parameter in this case, and the modified value is available to the calling environment by means of the actual parameter, provided the subprogram call ends successfully.

Here's the show_line procedure modified to include an OUT parameter:

```
CREATE OR REPLACE PROCEDURE show_line2
                    (ip_line_length IN NUMBER,
                     ip_separator   IN VARCHAR2,
                     op_line OUT VARCHAR2)
IS
  actual_line VARCHAR2(150);
BEGIN
    FOR idx in 1..ip_line_length LOOP
       actual_line := actual_line || ip_separator;
    END LOOP;
    op_line := actual_line;
```

```
EXCEPTION WHEN OTHERS THEN
    dbms_output.put_line(SQLERRM);
    op_line := null;
END;
/
```

You can then call this procedure as follows:

```
DECLARE
    v_length NUMBER := 50;
    v_separator VARCHAR2(1) := '=';
    v_line VARCHAR2(150);
BEGIN
    show_line2(v_length, v_separator, v_line);
    dbms_output.put_line(v_line);
END;
/
```

The following points are worth noting:

- The actual parameter v_line corresponds to the OUT formal parameter op_line and is defined as an uninitialized variable.

- The value of the v_line actual parameter is available to the calling program, after the call to show_line2. This is what I mean when I say the procedure returns a value.

 TIP   *The actual parameter corresponding to an OUT formal parameter can hold a value prior to the subprogram call. However, when the procedure or function is called, this value is lost unless the OUT parameter is passed by reference using NOCOPY. NOCOPY is discussed in the section "Parameter Passing by Reference."*

TIP   *You should explicitly assign values to OUT formal parameters. These values are returned to the calling environment by means of the actual parameters except when the subprogram exits abnormally by means of an exception, in which case the OUT parameters return null values.*

The IN OUT mode acts as a read-write specifier and allows a value to be read from the actual parameter and a modified value to be returned to the calling program. Thus, an IN OUT parameter acts as an initialized variable inside the body of the subprogram. You must explicitly assign a value to the formal parameter in IN OUT mode. Also, the actual parameter corresponding to an IN OUT formal parameter must be a variable.

TIP   *In IN mode, the parameter is passed by reference (i.e., a pointer to the value is passed), and in OUT and IN OUT modes, the parameter is passed by value (i.e., a copy of the value is passed out or in and out). This is the default behavior. You can change this behavior by using the NOCOPY compiler hint.*

Multiple values can be returned by a procedure using multiple OUT parameters. Functions can also be defined using OUT or IN OUT parameters. In this case, the function returns values in addition to the function return value.

TIP   *It's recommended that you use functions without OUT or IN OUT parameters. Use a procedure instead.*

Specifying the Type for Parameters

The data type of the formal parameters can be any valid PL/SQL type. However, the data type shouldn't specify any length or precision for the formal parameter. This is because the length or precision is determined by the value of the actual parameter corresponding to the formal parameter.

Now what about data types such as SUBTYPE, %TYPE, and %ROWTYPE? You can define data types such as SUBTYPE as subtypes of the primary types. In this case, you must define the actual parameter as having a data type as the subtype and not the primary type. Here's an example to illustrate this:

```
declare
    subtype st1 is number not null;
  v_value NUMBER;
    procedure p1(ip_1 st1)
    is
    begin
      dbms_output.put_line(to_char(ip_1));
    end;
 begin
          p1(v_value);
end;
/
```

This raises the following error:

```
declare
*
ERROR at line 1:
ORA-06502: PL/SQL: numeric or value error
ORA-06512: at line 10
```

You can define subtypes with constraints such as NOT NULL as shown in the previous code. In this case, the value of the actual parameter being passed should be non-null. Here's an example to illustrate this:

```
declare
    subtype st1 is number not null;
    procedure p1(ip_1 st1)
    is
    begin
      dbms_output.put_line(to_char(ip_1));
    end;
 begin
          p1(null);
end;
/
```

Here's the output of the preceding code:

```
p1(null);
         *

ERROR at line 9:
ORA-06550: line 9, column 14:
PLS-00567: cannot pass NULL to a NOT NULL constrained formal parameter
ORA-06550: line 9, column 11:
PL/SQL: Statement ignored
```

TIP   *The data type of OUT parameters can't be a subtype defined as NOT NULL, as they initially evaluate to null inside the body of the subprogram.*

Also, data types such as %TYPE and %ROWTYPE have length or precision limitations depending on the underlying column. This means that declaring a formal parameter as type %TYPE or %ROWTYPE restricts its length or precision to a certain value. If the actual parameter value has a length or precision greater than that of the formal parameter subtype as NOT NULL, you get the ORA-06502 error.

The data type of the formal parameter can also be a composite PL/SQL data type such as an index-by table or a record (either user-defined or %ROWTYPE). An index-by table of records is also allowed. In addition, the data type of a formal parameter can be a REF CURSOR (strong or weak). I discuss this in the section "Subprograms Returning Resultsets" later in this chapter. Finally, the data type of a formal parameter can be a user-defined object type or collection.

Specifying Default Values for Parameters

A stored subprogram once defined with formal parameters can be called with actual parameters. However, the number of actual parameters passed should be equal to the number of formal parameters defined. Until now this was the case. Now the following question arises: Can some of the actual parameters be omitted by providing default values for the formal parameters?

The answer to this question is yes. You can specify default values for the formal parameters while you define the procedure or function, and you need not pass an actual parameter to the subprogram call, provided you follow certain rules. Here's the syntax for providing default values for a formal parameter:

```
parameter_name [parameter_mode] data_type [:= | DEFAULT] default_value
```

where parameter_name is the name of the formal parameter; parameter_mode is either IN, OUT, or IN OUT; data_type is a predefined or user_defined data type of said parameter; and default_value is the type-compatible value of the parameter assigned by default.

Here's an example of the show_line procedure with a default value for one parameter:

```
CREATE OR REPLACE PROCEDURE show_line
                        (ip_line_length IN NUMBER,
                         ip_separator   IN VARCHAR2 DEFAULT '=')
IS
  actual_line VARCHAR2(150);
BEGIN
     FOR idx in 1..ip_line_length LOOP
         actual_line := actual_line || ip_separator;
     END LOOP;
     DBMS_OUTPUT.PUT_LINE(actual_line);
EXCEPTION WHEN OTHERS THEN
     dbms_output.put_line(SQLERRM);
END;
/
```

The call to this procedure can be as follows:

```
BEGIN
     show_line(50);
END;
/
```

The following points are worth noting:

- The show_line procedure is called by passing only one actual parameter. The value for the second parameter is derived from the default value of its formal parameter.

- If the first formal parameter also has a default value, then the show_line procedure can be called with no arguments at all. However, to omit the value for the first parameter and provide an actual parameter for the second, you must use named notation.

Here's an example to illustrate the second point:

```
CREATE OR REPLACE PROCEDURE show_line
                    (ip_line_length IN NUMBER DEFAULT 50,
                     ip_separator   IN VARCHAR2 DEFAULT '=')
IS
  actual_line VARCHAR2(150);
BEGIN
     FOR idx in 1..ip_line_length LOOP
         actual_line := actual_line || ip_separator;
     END LOOP;
     DBMS_OUTPUT.PUT_LINE(actual_line);
EXCEPTION WHEN OTHERS THEN
     dbms_output.put_line(SQLERRM);
END;
/
```

The call to this procedure can be as follows:

```
BEGIN
     show_line;
END;
/
```

However, the following call results in an error:

```
BEGIN
    show_line('_');
END;
/
```

Although the ip_line_length formal parameter has a default value, PL/SQL interprets the previous call as though '_' is being passed for the ip_line_length parameter, and hence gives a value error as shown here:

```
SQL> BEGIN
  2      show_line('_');
  3   END;
  4  /
BEGIN
*
ERROR at line 1:
ORA-06502: PL/SQL: numeric or value error: character to number conversion error
     ORA-06512: at line 2
```

To avoid this, you should use named notation as follows:

```
BEGIN
  show_line(ip_separator=>'_');
END;
/
```

Here's the output of the preceding call:

```
PL/SQL procedure successfully completed.
```

Stored Subprogram Metadata

As mentioned earlier, stored procedures and functions are stored in the database in compiled form. This compiled code is termed *p-code* and is in an interpreted form that is readable by the PL/SQL engine. Now, what about the source code of the procedure or function? It's also stored in the database as metadata in the data dictionary views.

When it's created, the procedure or function is recorded as a database object in two data dictionary views: USER_OBJECTS and ALL_OBJECTS. The source code itself is stored in two other data dictionary views: USER_SOURCE and ALL_SOURCE. These views are like SQL VIEWS but they store metadata about the procedure or function. The views beginning with "USER_" store information about objects in the current user schema, and those beginning with "ALL_" store information about objects in all schemas so far defined. In the latter case, the OWNER column identifies each schema name. USER_OBJECTS and ALL_OBJECTS store the procedure or function name, its status, and other information. Here's the structure of these two views:

```
SQL> desc user_objects
 Name                                      Null?    Type
 ----------------------------------------------------------------------
 OBJECT_NAME                                        VARCHAR2(128)
 SUBOBJECT_NAME                                     VARCHAR2(30)
 OBJECT_ID                                          NUMBER
 DATA_OBJECT_ID                                     NUMBER
 OBJECT_TYPE                                        VARCHAR2(18)
 CREATED                                            DATE
 LAST_DDL_TIME                                      DATE
 TIMESTAMP                                          VARCHAR2(19)
 STATUS                                             VARCHAR2(7)
```

```
TEMPORARY                                      VARCHAR2(1)
GENERATED                                      VARCHAR2(1)
SECONDARY                                      VARCHAR2(1)


SQL> desc all_objects
Name                            Null?    Type
------------------------------------------------------------------
OWNER                           NOT NULL VARCHAR2(30)
OBJECT_NAME                     NOT NULL VARCHAR2(30)
SUBOBJECT_NAME                           VARCHAR2(30)
OBJECT_ID                       NOT NULL NUMBER
DATA_OBJECT_ID                           NUMBER
OBJECT_TYPE                              VARCHAR2(18)
CREATED                         NOT NULL DATE
LAST_DDL_TIME                   NOT NULL DATE
TIMESTAMP                                VARCHAR2(19)
STATUS                                   VARCHAR2(7)
TEMPORARY                                VARCHAR2(1)
GENERATED                                VARCHAR2(1)
SECONDARY                                VARCHAR2(1)
```

Of all the rows, OBJECT_NAME, OBJECT_TYPE, and STATUS are of specific importance. OBJECT_NAME stores the name of the procedure or function, OBJECT_TYPE is either PROCEDURE or FUNCTION and STATUS is either VALID or INVALID. Querying these two views reveals the metadata (i.e., data about the procedure or function). Here's an example for the show_line procedure created earlier:

```
SQL> select * from user_objects where object_name = 'SHOW_LINE';

OBJECT_NAME
-----------------------------------------------------------
SUBOBJECT_NAME              OBJECT_ID DATA_OBJECT_ID OBJECT_TYPE
-----------------------------------------------------------
CREATED   LAST_DDL_ TIMESTAMP          STATUS  T G S
----- ------ --------- ----- - - -
SHOW_LINE
                            32317                   PROCEDURE
14-APR-02 14-APR-02 2002-04-14:13:52:16 VALID    N N N
```

Also, the source for the show_line procedure is stored in USER_SOURCE and ALL_SOURCE. Here's the structure of these two views:

197

```
SQL> desc user_source
 Name                                              Null?     Type
 ---------------------- ---- ----------------
  NAME                                                       VARCHAR2(30)
  TYPE                                                       VARCHAR2(12)
  LINE                                                       NUMBER
  TEXT                                                       VARCHAR2(4000)

SQL> desc all_source
 Name                                              Null?     Type
 ---------------------- ---- ----------------
  OWNER                                                      VARCHAR2(30)
  NAME                                                       VARCHAR2(30)
  TYPE                                                       VARCHAR2(12)
  LINE                                                       NUMBER
  TEXT                                                       VARCHAR2(4000)
```

You can obtain the source of the procedure or function by querying the TEXT column of these views. Here's an example for the show_line procedure created earlier:

```
SQL> select text from user_source where name = 'SHOW_LINE';

TEXT
---------------------------------------
PROCEDURE show_line
                                (ip_line_length IN NUMBER DEFAULT 50,
                                 ip_separator   IN VARCHAR2 DEFAULT '=')
IS
  actual_line VARCHAR2(150);
BEGIN
     FOR idx in 1..ip_line_length LOOP
        actual_line := actual_line || ip_separator;
     END LOOP;
     DBMS_OUTPUT.PUT_LINE(actual_line);
EXCEPTION WHEN OTHERS THEN
    dbms_output.put_line(SQLERRM);
END;

13 rows selected.
```

Native Compilation of PL/SQL Code

PL/SQL 9*i* allows native compilation of PL/SQL packages, procedures, and functions; subsequent conversion to native C code; and then storage in machine code. The PL/SQL is translated into C code rather than p-code, which is in interpreted mode, and compiled using the C compiler on the given platform and then linked directly into Oracle processes. When the particular stored subprogram is invoked, the natively compiled program is mapped to the PGA. This native compilation of PL/SQL code is most effective when you're writing compute-intensive PL/SQL subprograms that perform database-independent tasks. In this case, native compilation results in faster execution of PL/SQL. Here are the steps involved:

1. Translate into C code from PL/SQL.

2. Write this C code to the file system.

3. Invoke and run the C compiler.

4. Link the resulting object code into Oracle.

To compile a stored subprogram natively, you must set the initialization parameter PLSQL_COMPILER_FLAGS to NATIVE. By default its value is INTERPRETED. You can set this parameter in one of three ways:

-   In the init.ora file (this affects any stored parameter file settings, or spfile settings)

-   Using the ALTER SYSTEM command

-   Using the ALTER SESSION command

Here's an example:

```
ALTER SESSION SET PLSQL_COMPILER_FLAGS = 'NATIVE';
```

All subsequent recompilations of PL/SQL stored subprograms result in native compilation. The mode is stored within the subprogram metadata in the data dictionary view USER_STORED_SETTINGS. If the subprogram is automatically recompiled as a result of dependency checking, the setting in this view is used. Here's an example of determining the current setting of native compilation of stored subprograms:

```
select uo.object_name, uo.object_type, uss.param_value
from user_stored_settings uss, user_objects uo
```

```
where uss.object_id = uo.object_id
and uss.param_name = 'plsql_compiler_flags'
and uo.object_type in ('PROCEDURE', 'FUNCTION' );
```

Here's the output of this SELECT statement:

```
SQL> column object_name format a30;
SQL> column object_type format a15;
SQL> column param_value format a30;
SQL> set pages 100
SQL> select uo.object_name, uo.object_type, uss.param_value
  2    from user_stored_settings uss, user_objects uo
  3    where uss.object_id = uo.object_id
  4    and uss.param_name = 'plsql_compiler_flags'
  5    and uo.object_type in ('PROCEDURE', 'FUNCTION' );

OBJECT_NAME                    OBJECT_TYPE      PARAM_VALUE
------------------------ ---- ---------------  ---------------
CREATE_DYN_TABLE               PROCEDURE        INTERPRETED,NON_DEBUG
CREATE_ORDER                   PROCEDURE        INTERPRETED,NON_DEBUG
F1                             FUNCTION         INTERPRETED,NON_DEBUG
FLUSH                          PROCEDURE        INTERPRETED,NON_DEBUG
F_CURSOR                       FUNCTION         INTERPRETED,NON_DEBUG
F_CURSOR_EXP                   FUNCTION         INTERPRETED,NON_DEBUG
F_CURSOR_EXP_COMPLEX           FUNCTION         INTERPRETED,NON_DEBUG
F_GET_FORMATTED_ORG_NAME       FUNCTION         INTERPRETED,NON_DEBUG
F_LINE                         FUNCTION         INTERPRETED,NON_DEBUG
F_REPORT                       FUNCTION         INTERPRETED,NON_DEBUG
GETALLHIERARCHIES              FUNCTION         INTERPRETED,NON_DEBUG
LOG_ERROR                      PROCEDURE        INTERPRETED,NON_DEBUG
ORG_PROC                       PROCEDURE        INTERPRETED,NON_DEBUG
P1                             PROCEDURE        INTERPRETED,NON_DEBUG
P_NOCOPY                       PROCEDURE        INTERPRETED,NON_DEBUG
P_PRINT_REPORT                 PROCEDURE        INTERPRETED,NON_DEBUG
SHOW_LINE                      PROCEDURE        INTERPRETED,NON_DEBUG
SHOW_LINE2                     PROCEDURE        INTERPRETED,NON_DEBUG
```

Note that the param_value is INTERPRETED, meaning the procedure or function is stored as p_code. If it's natively compiled, it will be NATIVE.

Also, a C compiler must be installed on the system as the translated C code is compiled and linked into a shared library and then executed natively. In addition, the following settings come into the picture:

- *PLSQL_NATIVE_C_COMPILER:* Full path name of the C compiler. This setting is optional.

- *PLSQL_NATIVE_LIBRARY_DIR:* Directory where the shared objects as a result of native compilation are stored.

- *PL/SQL_NATIVE_LIBRARY_SUBDIR_COUNT:* The number of subdirectories created under the previously specified directory. This setting is recommended if the number of subprograms to be natively compiled exceeds 10,000.

- *PLSQL_NATIVE_LINKER:* The full path name of a linker used to link the object file into a shared object or DLL. This is optional.

- *PLSQL_NATIVE_MAKE_FILE_NAME:* The full name of the make file used by the make utility to generate shared objects.

- *PLSQL_NATIVE_MAKE_UTILITY:* The full path name of a make utility used to generate the shared object from the C source.

 TIP   *Only stored subprograms can be natively compiled. Anonymous and labeled PL/SQL blocks are still executed as p-code.*

PL/SQL Packages

A *package* is a stored program unit that groups logically related PL/SQL objects and stores them in the database as a single object. The related PL/SQL objects can be constants, variables, cursors, exceptions, procedures, and/or functions. A PL/SQL package has two parts: the package specification and the package body. The *package specification* consists of the declarations of the related objects to be included in the package. In the case of procedures and functions, only the signature or the header of the procedure or function is included in the package specification. The actual implementation of these procedures and functions is given in the *package body.* In addition, the package body may contain other declarations such as variables, constants, cursors, and even procedures and functions not defined in the package specification.

The declarations in the package specification are called *public declarations,* as their scope is the entire database session, and all application programs having access to said package can reference them. The declarations and additional procedures and functions defined in the package body are termed *private* because they're accessible only to the creator of the package. In this way, you can reference them only in the code contained in the package body and not by other PL/SQL applications.

Now the question arises, why is there a need for two separate objects, a package specification and a package body? The answer is twofold: information hiding and easy maintenance. By separating the implementation details from the definition, you don't need to recompile or change application programs when the implementation changes. If the business logic of a packaged procedure or function changes, the change can be applied only to the package body. In this way, referencing programs remain unaffected. Also, in this way, the package is more secure because the package header remains the same. And, by defining private objects inside the package body, there's information hiding from other users of the package. These objects remain private to the particular package.

Other advantages of packages include encapsulation, modularity, and better performance. By defining a package specification and package body, related objects can be encapsulated inside the database as a single unit consisting of the application logic, which also leads to modularity. Also, when a packaged subprogram is referenced for the first time, the entire package is loaded into memory. This improves performance by reducing disk I/O for subsequent calls. Also, it checks dependencies because the package body can be changed and recompiled independent of the package specification. When the definition of the public objects change, only the package specification needs to be changed and recompiled.

Creating and Using a Package

Creating a package involves creating a specification and a body separately. Both are stored separately in the database. You create a package specification with the CREATE OR REPLACE PACKAGE statement. Here's the syntax:

```
CREATE [OR REPLACE] PACKAGE package_name
[AUTHID {CURRENT_USER | DEFINER}]
    {IS | AS}
    [PRAGMA SERIALLY_REUSABLE;]
[type_definition ... ]
[constant_declaration ... ]
[variable_declaration ... ]
[exception_declaration ... ]
[cursor_declaration ... ]
[procedure_header ... ]
[function_header ... ]
END [package_name];
```

where package_name is the name of the package being created and the definitions correspond to type definitions, constants, variables, exceptions, cursors, procedure signatures, and/or function signatures. The AUTHID clause specifies the execution privileges of the package and is explained in the section "Definer and Invoker Rights" later in this chapter. PRAGMA SERIALLY_REUSABLE refers to serially reusable packages and is explained in the section "Additional Package Features" of this chapter. Here's an example of a simple package:

```
CREATE OR REPLACE PACKAGE orgMaster
IS
   max_sites_for_an_org NUMBER;
   TYPE rc IS REF CURSOR;
   PROCEDURE createOrg (ip_hrc_code NUMBER,
                                        ip_org_id NUMBER,
                                        ip_org_short_name VARCHAR2,
                                        ip_org_long_name VARCHAR2,
                                        op_retcd OUT NUMBER,
                                        op_err_msg OUT VARCHAR2);
   PROCEDURE updateOrg(ip_org_id NUMBER,
                                        ip_org_short_name VARCHAR2,
                                        ip_org_long_name VARCHAR2,
                                        op_retcd OUT NUMBER,
                                        op_err_msg OUT VARCHAR2);
   PROCEDURE removeOrg(ip_org_id NUMBER,
                                        op_retcd OUT NUMBER,
                                        op_err_msg OUT VARCHAR2);
   FUNCTION getOrgInfo(ip_org_id NUMBER) RETURN rc;
   FUNCTION getAllOrgs(ip_hrc_code NUMBER) RETURN rc;
   PROCEDURE assignSiteToOrg(ip_org_id NUMBER,
                             ip_site_no NUMBER,
                             op_retcd OUT NUMBER,
                             op_err_msg OUT VARCHAR2);
 END orgMaster;
/
```

This code creates a package named org_master with one variable named max_sites_for_an_org, one type definition of type REF CURSOR, four procedures, and two functions.

Once you've created the package specification, you should create a corresponding package body. Here's the syntax:

```
[CREATE [OR REPLACE] PACKAGE BODY package_name
{IS | AS}
   [PRAGMA SERIALLY_REUSABLE;]
```

```
[private_declarations]
[cursor_body ... ]
[public_procedure_implementation ... ]
[public_function_implementation ... ]
 [BEGIN
    sequence_of_statements]
END [package_name];]
```

where package_name is the name of the package as specified in the package specification, private_declarations corresponds to declarations being included only in the package body, cursor_body is the definition of the cursor along with the associated SELECT statement, and public_procedure_implementation and public_function_implementation are the procedure and function bodies corresponding to the signatures defined in the package specification. Also,

```
[BEGIN
    sequence_of_statements]
```

is an initialization section of the package and is explained later in this section.

Here's an example of a package body for the package org_master defined previously:

```
CREATE OR REPLACE PACKAGE BODY orgMaster
IS
-- Procedure to create a new Org record in org_tab
    PROCEDURE createOrg (ip_hrc_code NUMBER,
                                        ip_org_id NUMBER,
                                        ip_org_short_name VARCHAR2,
                                        ip_org_long_name VARCHAR2,
                                        op_retcd OUT NUMBER,
                                        op_err_msg OUT VARCHAR2)
    IS
        BEGIN
        INSERT INTO org_tab VALUES
        (ip_hrc_code, ip_org_id, ip_org_short_name, ip_org_long_name);
        op_retcd := 0;
    EXCEPTION WHEN DUP_VAL_ON_INDEX THEN
            op_retcd := -1;
            op_err_msg := 'Organization with Id '||TO_CHAR(ip_org_id)||
                                    ' already exists.';
        WHEN OTHERS THEN
                op_retcd := SQLCODE;
                op_err_msg := SQLERRM;
    END createOrg;
```

```
-- Procedure to update the short and long names of an Org in org_tab
-- based on input org_id
   PROCEDURE updateOrg(ip_org_id NUMBER,
                                       ip_org_short_name VARCHAR2,
                                       ip_org_long_name VARCHAR2,
                                       op_retcd OUT NUMBER,
                                       op_err_msg OUT VARCHAR2)

     IS
     BEGIN
         UPDATE org_tab
         SET org_short_name = ip_org_short_name,
                 org_long_name = ip_org_long_name
         WHERE org_id = ip_org_id;
         IF (SQL%NOTFOUND) THEN
            op_retcd := -1;
            op_err_msg := 'Organization with Id '||TO_CHAR(ip_org_id)||
                                  ' does not exist.';

            RETURN;
            END IF;
            op_retcd := 0;
   EXCEPTION WHEN OTHERS THEN
            op_retcd := SQLCODE;
            op_err_msg := SQLERRM;
   END updateOrg;
-- Procedure to delete a record in org_tab
   PROCEDURE removeOrg(ip_org_id NUMBER,

                                       op_retcd OUT NUMBER,
                                       op_err_msg OUT VARCHAR2)

     IS
     BEGIN
         DELETE org_tab WHERE org_id = ip_org_id;
         IF (SQL%NOTFOUND) THEN
               op_retcd := -1;
               op_err_msg := 'Organization with Id '||TO_CHAR(ip_org_id)||
                                    ' does not exist.';

               RETURN;
            END IF;
            op_retcd := 0;
     EXCEPTION WHEN OTHERS THEN
            op_retcd := SQLCODE;
            op_err_msg := SQLERRM;
   END removeOrg;
-- Function to return a row in org_tab for a given org_id.
-- It returns a resultset of type REF CURSOR defined in the package specification
```

```
        FUNCTION getOrgInfo(ip_org_id NUMBER) RETURN rc
        IS
            v_rc rc;
        BEGIN
                OPEN v_rc FOR SELECT * FROM org_tab WHERE org_id = ip_org_id;
            RETURN (v_rc);
    EXCEPTION WHEN OTHERS THEN
            RAISE_APPLICATION_ERROR(-20001, SQLERRM);
END getOrgInfo;
-- Function to return all rows in org_tab.
-- It returns a resultset of type REF CURSOR defined in the package specification
        FUNCTION getAllOrgs(ip_hrc_code NUMBER) RETURN rc
      IS
            v_rc rc;
        BEGIN
                OPEN v_rc FOR SELECT * FROM org_tab WHERE hrc_code = ip_hrc_code;
            RETURN (v_rc);
    EXCEPTION WHEN OTHERS THEN
            RAISE_APPLICATION_ERROR(-20002, SQLERRM);
END getAllOrgs;
- Procedure to insert a row into org_site_tab based on
- input org_id and site_no
    PROCEDURE assignSiteToOrg(ip_org_id NUMBER,
                            ip_site_no NUMBER,
                            op_retcd OUT NUMBER,
                            op_err_msg OUT VARCHAR2)
IS
    v_num NUMBER;
BEGIN
    BEGIN
            SELECT 1
            INTO        v_num
            FROM      org_site_tab
            WHERE    org_id = ip_org_id
                    AND   site_no = ip_site_no;
            IF (v_num = 1) THEN
                op_retcd := 0;
                RETURN;
            END IF;
        EXCEPTION WHEN NO_DATA_FOUND THEN
                INSERT INTO org_site_tab VALUES (ip_org_id, ip_site_no);
        END;
    op_retcd := 0;
```

```
   EXCEPTION WHEN OTHERS THEN
       op_retcd := SQLCODE;
       op_err_msg := SQLERRM;
  END assignSiteToOrg;
 END orgMaster;
/
```

The following points are worth noting:

- The package specification and the package body have the same name. This is mandatory.

- There is no BEGIN statement at the beginning of the package. Don't confuse this with the BEGIN sequence_of_statements section included at the end. This is an initialization section and doesn't act as a BEGIN for the package.

- The DECLARE keyword isn't used while declaring constants, variables, type definitions, exceptions, and/or cursors.

- The CREATE OR REPLACE clause isn't used while defining procedures and/or functions.

- The public declarations can appear in any order as long they're declared before they're referenced. Also, these shouldn't be repeated in the package body.

- In the case of cursors, the specification can contain the cursor name with its return type. In this case, the cursor is to be defined completely in the package body. If it isn't specified with a return type, the entire cursor along with its associated SELECT statement should be specified in the specification and this doesn't need to be repeated in the package body.

- The procedure and/or function signatures must be repeated in the package body, while giving the corresponding implementation details.

TIP *Each of the public procedures and/or functions defined in the package header must have a corresponding implementation in the package body. Also, the signature of each procedure or function in the specification should match word-for-word with the signature in the package body.*

TIP   *Compile the package specification first and then the body.*

TIP   *A package specification can exist without a package body but not vice versa. In this case, the package can't include any procedures and/or functions in its specification.*

Referencing Package Objects

The individual objects defined in a package specification are global in scope in that they're available for the entire session and accessible by all application programs having the required privileges. Hence, they're termed *public objects*. You can reference public objects in application programs (i.e., outside of the package body) with the following syntax:

```
package_name.object_name
```

Here's an example:

```
DECLARE
    v_retcd NUMBER;
    v_err_msg VARCHAR2(1000);
BEGIN
    orgMaster.createOrg(3, 1011,'Office of Dir. SSL','Office of Dir. SSL',
                                    v_retcd, v_err_msg);
    IF (v_retcd <> 0) THEN
      DBMS_OUTPUT.PUT_LINE('ERR: '||v_err_msg);
    END IF;
END;
/
```

The output of this program can be verified as follows:

```
SQL> select * from org_tab where org_id = 1011;

  HRC_CODE     ORG_ID ORG_SHORT_NAME
  ----- ----- ------------------
ORG_LONG_NAME
------------------------------
          3      1011 Office of Dir. SSL
Office of Dir. SSL
```

The following points are worth noting:

- The packaged procedure createOrg is called like a stand-alone stored procedure but it's prefixed with the package name and a dot.

- The procedure is executed and control is transferred to the calling PL/SQL block just like a stand-alone procedure.

However, inside a package body, you can reference the objects defined in its specification without the dot notation.

Private Objects

What about *private objects* defined inside of the package body? These objects are accessible only to the particular package body and you can also reference them without the dot notation.

Consider the org_master package defined previously. The procedure removeOrg removes an organization based on the input org_id. Now, what about the org site details existing for said organization? These first have to be removed, otherwise the deletion of records in the org_tab table will fail. Also, this deletion is transparent to other applications accessing the removeOrg procedure. Hence, you can code a separate procedure inside the package body for deleting the org site details before you delete the org itself. I'll call this procedure removeOrgSites. With this change in place, the package body for org_master looks like this:

```
CREATE OR REPLACE PACKAGE BODY orgMaster
IS
-- Procedure to remove rows from org_site_tab table for a given org_id
-- This is necessary before deleting rows from org_tab.
-- This procedure is called from removeOrg procedure
PROCEDURE removeOrgSites(ip_org_id NUMBER,

                                    op_retcd OUT NUMBER,
                                    op_err_msg OUT VARCHAR2)
```

```
        IS
        BEGIN
            DELETE org_site_tab WHERE org_id = ip_org_id;
            op_retcd := 0;
        EXCEPTION WHEN OTHERS THEN
                op_retcd := SQLCODE;
                op_err_msg := SQLERRM;
        END removeOrgSites;
-- Procedure to create a new Org record in org_tab
    PROCEDURE createOrg (ip_hrc_code NUMBER,
                        ip_org_id NUMBER,
                        ip_org_short_name VARCHAR2,
                        ip_org_long_name VARCHAR2,
                        op_retcd OUT NUMBER,
                        op_err_msg OUT VARCHAR2)
        IS
            BEGIN
            INSERT INTO org_tab VALUES
            (ip_hrc_code, ip_org_id, ip_org_short_name, ip_org_long_name);
            op_retcd := 0;
        EXCEPTION WHEN DUP_VAL_ON_INDEX THEN
                op_retcd := -1;
                op_err_msg := 'Organization with Id '||TO_CHAR(ip_org_id)||
                                    ' already exists.';
            WHEN OTHERS THEN
                op_retcd := SQLCODE;
                op_err_msg := SQLERRM;
    END createOrg;
-- Procedure to update the short and long names of an Org in org_tab
-- based on input org_id
    PROCEDURE updateOrg(ip_org_id NUMBER,
                        ip_org_short_name VARCHAR2,
                        ip_org_long_name VARCHAR2,
                        op_retcd OUT NUMBER,
                        op_err_msg OUT VARCHAR2)
        IS
        BEGIN
            UPDATE org_tab
            SET org_short_name = ip_org_short_name,
                    org_long_name = ip_org_long_name
            WHERE org_id = ip_org_id;
            IF (SQL%NOTFOUND) THEN
                op_retcd := -1;
```

```
                op_err_msg := 'Organization with Id '||TO_CHAR(ip_org_id)||
                                        ' does not exist.';
            RETURN;
            END IF;
            op_retcd := 0;
    EXCEPTION WHEN OTHERS THEN
            op_retcd := SQLCODE;
            op_err_msg := SQLERRM;
    END updateOrg;
-- Procedure to delete a record in org_tab
  PROCEDURE removeOrg(ip_org_id NUMBER,
                      op_retcd OUT NUMBER,
                      op_err_msg OUT VARCHAR2)
    IS
    BEGIN
        removeOrgSites(ip_org_id, op_retcd, op_err_msg);
        IF (op_retcd <> 0) then
          RETURN;
        END IF;
        DELETE org_tab WHERE org_id = ip_org_id;
        IF (SQL%NOTFOUND) THEN
            op_retcd := -1;
            op_err_msg := 'Organization with Id '||TO_CHAR(ip_org_id)||
                                        ' does not exist.';
            RETURN;
          END IF;
          op_retcd := 0;
      EXCEPTION WHEN OTHERS THEN
            op_retcd := SQLCODE;
            op_err_msg := SQLERRM;
    END removeOrg;
-- Function to return a row in org_tab for a given org_id.
-- It returns a resultset of type REF CURSOR defined in the package specification
  FUNCTION getOrgInfo(ip_org_id NUMBER) RETURN rc
    IS
        v_rc rc;
    BEGIN
            OPEN v_rc FOR SELECT * FROM org_tab WHERE org_id = ip_org_id;
        RETURN (v_rc);
  EXCEPTION WHEN OTHERS THEN
        RAISE_APPLICATION_ERROR(-20001, SQLERRM);
END getOrgInfo;
-- Function to return all rows in org_tab.
```

```
-- It returns a resultset of type REF CURSOR defined in the package specification
  FUNCTION getAllOrgs(ip_hrc_code NUMBER) RETURN rc
  IS
     v_rc rc;
  BEGIN
          OPEN v_rc FOR SELECT * FROM org_tab WHERE hrc_code = ip_hrc_code;
       RETURN (v_rc);
 EXCEPTION WHEN OTHERS THEN
        RAISE_APPLICATION_ERROR(-20002, SQLERRM);
END getAllOrgs;
-- Procedure to insert a row into org_site_tab based  on
-- input org_id and site_no
  PROCEDURE assignSiteToOrg(ip_org_id NUMBER,
                            ip_site_no NUMBER,
                            op_retcd OUT NUMBER,
                            op_err_msg OUT VARCHAR2)
IS
    v_num NUMBER;
BEGIN
    BEGIN
          SELECT 1
          INTO      v_num
          FROM      org_site_tab
          WHERE   org_id = ip_org_id
                AND  site_no = ip_site_no;
        IF (v_num = 1) THEN
            op_retcd := 0;
            RETURN;
        END IF;
      EXCEPTION WHEN NO_DATA_FOUND THEN
            INSERT INTO org_site_tab VALUES (ip_org_id, ip_site_no);
    END;
    op_retcd := 0;
  EXCEPTION WHEN OTHERS THEN
      op_retcd := SQLCODE;
      op_err_msg := SQLERRM;
  END assignSiteToOrg;
 END orgMaster;
 /
```

The following points are worth noting:

- The private procedure removeOrgSites is available only inside the package body of orgMaster.

- The private procedure removeOrgSites is called from the removeOrg procedure. In fact, the only place it can be called from is the package body of orgMaster.

Package Instantiation and Initialization

The very first time a packaged variable is referenced, or a packaged procedure or function is called, the package is loaded into memory (shared pool) from the disk and remains there for the duration of the session. This process is called *package instantiation*. For each user, a memory location is assigned in the shared pool for the package, a copy of the packaged variables is made in the session memory, and the packaged variables persist for the duration of the session. These variables constitute the package runtime state. Also, any initialization of variables or code to be executed one time is done at this time. You can specify this initialization process by means of an initialization section in the package body after the implementation details of the package. Here's the syntax:

```
[BEGIN
  sequence_of_statements ... ]
```

Here's the orgMaster package body with an initialization section included:

```
CREATE OR REPLACE PACKAGE BODY orgMaster
IS
-- Procedure to remove rows from org_site_tab table for a given org_id
-- This is necessary before deleting rows from org_tab.
-- This procedure is called from removeOrg procedure
PROCEDURE removeOrgSites(ip_org_id NUMBER,
                         op_retcd OUT NUMBER,
                         op_err_msg OUT VARCHAR2)
  IS
  BEGIN
      DELETE org_site_tab WHERE org_id = ip_org_id;
      op_retcd := 0;
  EXCEPTION WHEN OTHERS THEN
          op_retcd := SQLCODE;
          op_err_msg := SQLERRM;
```

213

```
                END removeOrgSites;
-- Procedure to create a new Org record in org_tab
     PROCEDURE createOrg (ip_hrc_code NUMBER,
                          ip_org_id NUMBER,
                          ip_org_short_name VARCHAR2,
                          ip_org_long_name VARCHAR2,
                          op_retcd OUT NUMBER,
                          op_err_msg OUT VARCHAR2)
     IS
           BEGIN
           INSERT INTO org_tab VALUES
           (ip_hrc_code, ip_org_id, ip_org_short_name, ip_org_long_name);
           op_retcd := 0;
     EXCEPTION WHEN DUP_VAL_ON_INDEX THEN
           op_retcd := -1;
           op_err_msg := 'Organization with Id '||TO_CHAR(ip_org_id)||
                                    ' already exists.';
        WHEN OTHERS THEN
              op_retcd := SQLCODE;
              op_err_msg := SQLERRM;
     END createOrg;
-- Procedure to update the short and long names of an Org in org_tab
-- based on input org_id
     PROCEDURE updateOrg(ip_org_id NUMBER,
                         ip_org_short_name VARCHAR2,
                         ip_org_long_name VARCHAR2,
                         op_retcd OUT NUMBER,
                         op_err_msg OUT VARCHAR2)
     IS
     BEGIN
           UPDATE org_tab
           SET org_short_name = ip_org_short_name,
                 org_long_name = ip_org_long_name
           WHERE org_id = ip_org_id;
           IF (SQL%NOTFOUND) THEN
              op_retcd := -1;
              op_err_msg := 'Organization with Id '||TO_CHAR(ip_org_id)||
                                      ' does not exist.';
              RETURN;
           END IF;
           op_retcd := 0;
     EXCEPTION WHEN OTHERS THEN
```

```
              op_retcd := SQLCODE;
              op_err_msg := SQLERRM;
      END updateOrg;
-- Procedure to delete a record in org_tab
   PROCEDURE removeOrg(ip_org_id NUMBER,
                       op_retcd OUT NUMBER,
                       op_err_msg OUT VARCHAR2)
     IS
     BEGIN
          removeOrgSites(ip_org_id, op_retcd, op_err_msg);
          IF (op_retcd <> 0) then
             RETURN;
          END IF;
          DELETE org_tab WHERE org_id = ip_org_id;
          IF (SQL%NOTFOUND) THEN
               op_retcd := -1;
               op_err_msg := 'Organization with Id '||TO_CHAR(ip_org_id)||
                                       ' does not exist.';
                RETURN;
            END IF;
            op_retcd := 0;
       EXCEPTION WHEN OTHERS THEN
               op_retcd := SQLCODE;
               op_err_msg := SQLERRM;
      END removeOrg;
-- Function to return a row in org_tab for a given org_id.
-- It returns a resultset of type REF CURSOR defined in the package specification
   FUNCTION getOrgInfo(ip_org_id NUMBER) RETURN rc
     IS
        v_rc rc;
     BEGIN
             OPEN v_rc FOR SELECT * FROM org_tab WHERE org_id = ip_org_id;
         RETURN (v_rc);
   EXCEPTION WHEN OTHERS THEN
         RAISE_APPLICATION_ERROR(-20001, SQLERRM);
END getOrgInfo;
-- Function to return all rows in org_tab.
-- It returns a resultset of type REF CURSOR defined in the package specification
   FUNCTION getAllOrgs(ip_hrc_code NUMBER) RETURN rc
     IS
        v_rc rc;
     BEGIN
```

```
                OPEN v_rc FOR SELECT * FROM org_tab WHERE hrc_code = ip_hrc_code;
        RETURN (v_rc);
    EXCEPTION WHEN OTHERS THEN
            RAISE_APPLICATION_ERROR(-20002, SQLERRM);
END getAllOrgs;
-- Procedure to insert a row into org_site_tab based  on
-- input org_id and site_no
    PROCEDURE assignSiteToOrg(ip_org_id NUMBER,
                              ip_site_no NUMBER,
                              op_retcd OUT NUMBER,
                              op_err_msg OUT VARCHAR2)
IS
    v_num NUMBER;
BEGIN
    BEGIN
            SELECT 1
            INTO        v_num
            FROM        org_site_tab
            WHERE   org_id = ip_org_id
                    AND   site_no = ip_site_no;
            IF (v_num = 1) THEN
                op_retcd := 0;
                RETURN;
            END IF;
        EXCEPTION WHEN NO_DATA_FOUND THEN
                INSERT INTO org_site_tab VALUES (ip_org_id, ip_site_no);
        END;
        op_retcd := 0;
    EXCEPTION WHEN OTHERS THEN
        op_retcd := SQLCODE;
        op_err_msg := SQLERRM;
    END assignSiteToOrg;
-- This is the initialization section that is executed
-- the first time a package sub-program is invoked
-- or a packaged variable is referenced
BEGIN
        max_sites_for_an_org := 4;
    END orgMaster;
    /
```

The following points are worth noting:

- The initialization section is specified as the last part of the package body.

- There's no separate END for this BEGIN.

- The initialization section is executed only once at the time of package instantiation.

TIP   *To execute a packaged procedure or function, or to reference a packaged public variable, the schema executing the package must own the package or have the EXECUTE privilege on the package granted to it.*

TIP   *Like procedures and functions, packages (both package specification and package body) are recorded in the data dictionary views USER_OBJECTS and ALL_OBJECTS, and their source code is stored in USER_SOURCE and ALL_SOURCE. In this case, the object_type is either PACKAGE for package specification or PACKAGE BODY for the package body.*

TIP   *Like stored procedures and functions, a PL/SQL package can also be natively compiled and executed.*

Subprograms Returning Resultsets

Stored subprograms, such as stand-alone functions or packaged functions, return a single value that can be used in the calling environment. Even stored procedures can return a value to the calling environment by means of OUT parameters. You can specify multiple OUT parameters to return multiple values. However, it may sometimes be necessary to have subprograms return resultsets or rows of data instead of scalar values. PL/SQL is a flexible language and provides this capability. In PL/SQL, subprograms can return resultsets in two ways: using REF cursors and table functions. I describe the first method in this section.

CROSS-REFERENCE   *Chapter 11 describes the use of table functions to return resultsets.*

A function can return a resultset by specifying a return type of REF CURSOR. A procedure can do this by specifying an OUT parameter of type REF CURSOR. There are two ways to define the REF cursor type:

1. Use the generic (weak) REF CURSOR type SYS_REFCURSOR available in Oracle9*i*. In this case, specify the return type of the function or the data type of the OUT parameter of the procedure as of type SYS_REFCURSOR. The advantage of specifying a weak REF cursor is that you don't need to bother about the number of columns selected.

2. Define a REF CURSOR type in a package specification and use this as the return type or the data type of the OUT parameter.

TIP   *You can declare only the type definition of a REF CURSOR type in a package specification. You can't declare cursor variables of this type in the package specification because they don't have a persistent state.*

Here's an example function that returns a resultset using the SYS_REFCURSOR type:

```
CREATE OR REPLACE FUNCTION getAllHierarchies
RETURN SYS_REFCURSOR
IS
   v_rc SYS_REFCURSOR;
BEGIN
    OPEN v_rc FOR SELECT * FROM hrc_tab;
```

```
        RETURN (v_rc);
EXCEPTION WHEN OTHERS THEN
        RAISE_APPLICATION_ERROR(-20002, SQLERRM);
END;
/
```

You can call this function from a PL/SQL block as follows:

```
DECLARE
        v_rc SYS_REFCURSOR;
        hrc_rec hrc_tab%ROWTYPE;
BEGIN
        v_rc := getAllHierarchies;
        LOOP
                FETCH v_rc INTO hrc_rec;
                EXIT WHEN v_rc%NOTFOUND;
                dbms_output.put_line(TO_CHAR(hrc_rec.hrc_code)||' '||hrc_rec.hrc_descr);
        END LOOP;
EXCEPTION WHEN OTHERS THEN
        dbms_output.put_line(TO_CHAR(SQLCODE)||' '||SQLERRM);
END;
/
```

Here's the output of this program:

```
1 CEO/COO
2 VP
3 Director
4 Manager
5 Analyst
10 Assistant

PL/SQL procedure successfully completed.
```

The following points are worth noting:

- The function getAllHierarchies has a return type of SYS_REFCURSOR. Also, a local cursor variable is defined inside the function. This cursor variable is OPENed for a query. The set of rows returned by this query is identified by the cursor variable. In fact, a pointer to this resultset is stored.

- Outside the function, in the calling environment, the function is called and assigned to a second cursor variable of compatible type. This second cursor variable isn't opened for query. In fact, it shouldn't be. The FETCH operation takes place outside of the function. This is the power of a function returning resultsets. The second cursor variable now points to the resultset returned by the function.

The method of using a REF CURSOR type in a package and using this as a function return type was illustrated in the orgMaster package previously defined. The functions getOrgInfo and getAllOrgs both return resultsets based on a REF CURSOR type defined in this package.

Using Stored Functions in SQL Statements

As mentioned earlier, stored functions are invoked as part of a PL/SQL expression, or they can be called from procedural statements such as the IF statement. Now the question is, can they be called from SQL statements? The answer is yes. Just like built-in SQL functions, stored functions (either stand-alone or packaged) can be called from SQL statements provided they meet certain criteria. PL/SQL 2.1 and above offer this flexibility. Specifically, a stored function can be called from the following SQL statements:

- SELECT statement (SELECT column list, and WHERE, HAVING, GROUP BY, CONNECT BY, START WITH, and ORDER BY clauses)

- INSERT statement (VALUES clause)

- UPDATE statement (SET clause)

TIP *Only functions (not procedures) are directly callable from SQL statements. However, these functions can call PL/SQL procedures inside their bodies.*

TIP *A stored function can't be called from a CHECK CONSTRAINT clause of a CREATE TABLE or ALTER TABLE statement or be used to specify a default value for a column.*

Here's the syntax for calling a stored function from SQL:

```
[[schema_name.]package_name.]function_name[(arg1, ... , argN) ]
```

where schema_name is the schema in which the stored function is created,
package_name is the PL/SQL package in which the function is defined (in the
case of packaged functions), and arg1, . . ., argN are the arguments corresponding to the formal parameters of the function. The schema_name is optional
as is the package_name in the case of a stand-alone function.

Here's an example of calling a stored function from a SELECT statement:

```
CREATE OR REPLACE FUNCTION f_get_formatted_org_name
                          (ip_hrc_code NUMBER,
                           ip_org_id NUMBER)
RETURN VARCHAR2
IS
    v_name VARCHAR2(120);
BEGIN
    SELECT 'Org Name: (Short) '||org_short_name||' (Long) '||org_long_name
    INTO       v_name
    FROM   org_tab
    WHERE hrc_code = ip_hrc_code
           AND org_id = ip_org_id;
    RETURN (v_name);
END f_get_formatted_org_name;
/
SELECT f_get_formatted_org_name(hrc_code, org_id) "Formatted Org Name"
FROM   org_tab
ORDER BY hrc_code, org_id;
```

Here's the output of this SELECT:

```
SQL> SELECT f_get_formatted_org_name(hrc_code, org_id) "Formatted Org Name"
  2  FROM   org_tab
  3  ORDER BY hrc_code, org_id;

Formatted Org Name
----------------------------------------

Org Name: (Short) Office of CEO ABC Inc. (Long) Office of CEO ABC Inc.
Org Name: (Short) Office of CEO XYZ Inc. (Long) Office of CEO XYZ Inc.
Org Name: (Short) Office of CEO DataPro Inc. (Long) Office of CEO DataPro Inc.
Org Name: (Short) Office of VP Sales ABC Inc. (Long) Office of VP Sales ABC Inc.
```

```
Org Name: (Short) Office of VP Mktg ABC Inc. (Long) Office of VP Mktg ABC Inc.
Org Name: (Short) Office of VP Tech ABC Inc. (Long) Office of VP Tech ABC Inc.
Org Name: (Short) Office of Dir Tech ABC Inc. (Long) Office of Director Tech ABC
 Inc.

Org Name: (Short) Office of Dir. SSL (Long) Office of Dir. SSL

8 rows selected.
```

TIP   *The caller of the stored PL/SQL function must either own the function or have the EXECUTE privilege granted on the function. In case the function is part of a view definition, the caller must have SELECT privileges on the view. No separate EXECUTE privilege is necessary in this case.*

TIP   *You can use a synonym for the function instead of the actual function name, but only if the function is a stand-alone function.*

TIP   *If a column name in a database table has the same name as a function without parameters, the column name takes precedence over the function name. To access the function, prefix the function name with the schema name. However, it's recommended that you code the function name with a unique name different from any other database object or column name.*

Criteria for Calling Stored Functions from SQL

As mentioned earlier in this section, a PL/SQL function must meet the following criteria to be able to be called from a SQL statement:

- The function must be a stored function, either stand-alone or part of a package.

- When you specify actual parameters to functions called from SQL, only positional notation is allowed. Also, you should specify all parameters, even if default values exist for the formal parameters. This rule doesn't apply to functions called from procedural statements.

- The function must be a row function and not a column group function.

- All the function's formal parameters must be of IN mode.

- The data type of all the function's formal parameters are valid SQL types and not PL/SQL types such as BOOLEAN RECORD, TABLE, REF CURSOR, and so forth.

- The return type of the function is a valid SQL type.

Purity of a Function Called from SQL

A function called from SQL can have certain side effects on database tables and packaged variables that it reads or writes. These side effects are specified using *purity levels.* You can specify four purity levels for a function: WNDS, RNDS, WNPS, and RNPS. These are explained in the following code:

- *WNDS—Writes no database state:* The function does not modify database tables.

- *RNDS—Reads no database state:* The function does not query database tables.

- *WNPS—Writes no package state:* The function does not change the values of packaged variables.

- *RNPS—Reads no package state:* The function does not reference the values of packaged variables.

- *TRUST:* Allows easy calling from functions that do have RESTRICT_REFERENCES declarations to those that do not.

In general, any function callable from SQL must be *pure*—that is, it must meet the following requirements in terms of purity levels:

- It must obey WNDS (i.e., it can't modify database tables). This assertion is relaxed in Oracle8*i*.

- If the function is executed in parallel or remotely, it must obey WNPS and RNPS.

- If the function is called from WHERE, HAVING, GROUP BY, CONNECT BY, START WITH, and ORDER BY clauses, it must obey WNPS.

- If the function calls any subprograms inside it, those subprograms must obey the preceding purity rules. In other words, a function is only as pure as the procedures or functions it calls.

For stored stand-alone functions, the purity levels are checked at runtime.
Starting from Oracle8*i*, the purity level of a stored function, either stand-alone or packaged, is checked at runtime when the function is called from a SQL statement. Any violations thereof result in an error. However, PL/SQL provides a way of checking the purity level of packaged functions at compile time using a PRAGMA. The purity level of a packaged function can be asserted by using a PL/SQL PRAGMA called PRAGMA RESTRICT_REFERENCES. Here's the syntax:

```
PRAGMA RESTRICT_REFERENCES ( DEFAULT|function_name, WNDS [, WNPS] [, RNDS]
[, RNPS] [, TRUST] );
```

where function_name is the name of the packaged function, and WNDS, WNPS, RNDS, and RNPS refer to the four purity levels. The DEFAULT and TRUST keywords are explained later in this section.

Prior to Oracle8*i*, packaged functions must be defined with the PRAGMA specified to be callable from SQL. Here's an example of using this PRAGMA:

```
CREATE OR REPLACE PACKAGE rfPkg
IS
  FUNCTION f_get_formatted_org_name
                  (ip_hrc_code NUMBER,
                   ip_org_id NUMBER)
  RETURN VARCHAR2;
  PRAGMA RESTRICT_REFERENCES(f_get_formatted_org_name, WNDS, WNPS);
END rfPkg;
/
```

Here's the corresponding package body:

```
CREATE OR REPLACE PACKAGE BODY rfPkg
IS
  FUNCTION f_get_formatted_org_name
                              (ip_hrc_code NUMBER,
                               ip_org_id NUMBER)
  RETURN VARCHAR2
  IS
     v_name VARCHAR2(120);
  BEGIN
     SELECT 'Org Name: (Short) '||org_short_name||' (Long) '||org_long_name
     INTO      v_name
     FROM   org_tab
     WHERE hrc_code = ip_hrc_code
            AND org_id = ip_org_id;
     RETURN (v_name);
  END f_get_formatted_org_name;
END rfPkg;
 /
```

Here's the SELECT statement calling the packaged function:

```
SELECT rfPkg.f_get_formatted_org_name(hrc_code, org_id) "Formatted Org Name"
FROM   org_tab
ORDER BY hrc_code, org_id;
```

Here's the output of this SELECT:

```
SQL> SELECT rfPkg.f_get_formatted_org_name(hrc_code, org_id) "Formatted Org
Name"
  2  FROM  org_tab
  3  ORDER BY hrc_code, org_id;

Formatted Org Name
-------------------- ---- ---------------
 Org Name: (Short) Office of CEO ABC Inc. (Long) Office of CEO ABC Inc.
 Org Name: (Short) Office of CEO XYZ Inc. (Long) Office of CEO XYZ Inc.
 Org Name: (Short) Office of CEO DataPro Inc. (Long) Office of CEO DataPro Inc.
 Org Name: (Short) Office of VP Sales ABC Inc. (Long) Office of VP Sales ABC Inc.
 Org Name: (Short) Office of VP Mktg ABC Inc. (Long) Office of VP Mktg ABC Inc.
 Org Name: (Short) Office of VP Tech ABC Inc. (Long) Office of VP Tech ABC Inc.
 Org Name: (Short) Office of Dir Tech ABC Inc. (Long) Office of Director Tech ABC
  Inc.
```

Org Name: (Short) Office of Dir. SSL (Long) Office of Dir. SSL

8 rows selected.[I only got 7 rows back
Org Name: (Short) Office of CEO ABC Inc. (Long) Office of CEO ABC Inc.
Org Name: (Short) Office of CEO XYZ Inc. (Long) Office of CEO XYZ Inc.
Org Name: (Short) Office of CEO DataPro Inc. (Long) Office of CEO DataPro Inc.
Org Name: (Short) Office of VP Sales ABC Inc. (Long) Office of VP Sales ABC Inc.
Org Name: (Short) Office of VP Mktg ABC Inc. (Long) Office of VP Mktg ABC Inc.
Org Name: (Short) Office of VP Tech ABC Inc. (Long) Office of VP Tech ABC Inc.
Org Name: (Short) Office of Dir. SSL (Long) Office of Dir. SSL - TE]

Any function violating the PRAGMA will result in a compilation error at the time of parsing. Here's an example to illustrate this:

```
CREATE OR REPLACE PACKAGE rfPkg2
IS
  FUNCTION f_get_formatted_org_name
                    (ip_hrc_code NUMBER,
                     ip_org_id NUMBER)
  RETURN VARCHAR2;
  PRAGMA RESTRICT_REFERENCES(f_get_formatted_org_name, WNDS, WNPS);
END rfPkg2;
/
CREATE OR REPLACE PACKAGE BODY rfPkg2
IS
  FUNCTION f_get_formatted_org_name
                    (ip_hrc_code NUMBER,
                     ip_org_id NUMBER)
  RETURN VARCHAR2
  IS
    v_name VARCHAR2(120);
    v_hrc_descr VARCHAR2(20);
    v_org_short_name VARCHAR2(30);
    v_org_long_name VARCHAR2(60);
  BEGIN
    SELECT 'Org Name: (Short) '||org_short_name||' (Long) '||org_long_name
    INTO    v_name
    FROM  org_tab
    WHERE hrc_code = ip_hrc_code
          AND org_id = ip_org_id;
    SELECT hrc_descr
```

```
        INTO    v_hrc_descr
        FROM    hrc_tab
        WHERE   hrc_code = ip_hrc_code;
        SELECT org_short_name, org_long_name
        INTO     v_org_short_name, v_org_long_name
        FROM   org_tab
        WHERE hrc_code = ip_hrc_code
               AND org_id = ip_org_id;
        INSERT INTO sec_hrc_org_tab VALUES
        (ip_hrc_code, v_hrc_descr, ip_org_id,
         v_org_short_name, v_org_long_name);
        RETURN (v_name);
   END f_get_formatted_org_name;
END rfPkg2;
/
```

Compiling the preceding package results in the following error:

```
PLS-00452: Subprogram 'F_GET_FORMATTED_ORG_NAME' violates its
  associated pragma
```

This error happens because the function body writes to the database (the INSERT INTO sec_hrc_org_tab . . . statement) as opposed to its associated PRAGMA declaration of WNDS.

TIP *You should specify the PRAGMA RESTRICT_REFERENCES only in the package specification following the function signature. You shouldn't specify it in the package body.*

TIP *You can also specify the PRAGMA RESTRICT_REFERENCES in the initialization section of the package using the package name to replace the function name in the PRAGMA syntax. In this case, a package function is only as pure as the initialization section of the package.*

Specifying the Default Behavior of the PRAGMA

You can specify the PRAGMA RESTRICT_REFERENCES without the function name. You can use the DEFAULT keyword instead of the function name to override the purity level of each individual function. Here's the syntax:

```
PRAGMA RESTRICT_REFERENCES ( DEFAULT, WNDS [, WNPS] [, RNDS] [, RNPS] [, TRUST] );
```

In this case, purity level gets asserted for all functions following this specification in the entire package.

TIP *If specified, make sure the PRAGMA is defined for each function in the package. However, you can override this need to define the PRAGMA for each function by specifying the DEFAULT keyword instead of the function name as explained previously.*

Specifying the TRUST Keyword

The TRUST keyword allows calling of functions coded without the PRAGMA RESTRICT_REFERENCES from functions that have the PRAGMA specified. This means the second function is declared pure. A good example of this is when calling Java routines published in PL/SQL from PL/SQL functions. Both the published function and the PL/SQL function reside inside a package. In this case, you can use the TRUST keyword. When TRUST is present, the restrictions listed in the PRAGMA aren't actually enforced, but they're trusted to be true.

There are two ways to do this:

1. Code the PRAGMA with the TRUST keyword on the published PL/SQL function. Then PL/SQL functions calling this published function can determine the purity level of the published function and respond with errors in case of the PRAGMA violations. Here's an example to illustrate this:

```
CREATE OR REPLACE PACKAGE dirPkg IS
    FUNCTION FileType(ip_file_name VARCHAR2)
    RETURN VARCHAR2
    IS
    LANGUAGE JAVA
```

```
      NAME 'dirClass.fileType(java.lang.String) return java.lang.String';
          PRAGMA RESTRICT_REFERENCES(FileType,WNDS,TRUST);


   FUNCTION displayFileType(ip_file_name VARCHAR2)
    RETURN VARCHAR2;
          PRAGMA RESTRICT_REFERENCES(displayFileType,WNDS);
    END dirPkg;
/
CREATE OR REPLACE PACKAGE BODY dirPkg IS
    FUNCTION displayFileType(ip_file_name VARCHAR2)
    RETURN VARCHAR2
   IS
       v_descr VARCHAR2(100);
   BEGIN
       v_descr := ip_file_name||' '||' is a '||FileType(ip_file_name);
       RETURN (v_descr);
   END displayFileType;
END dirPkg;
/
```

2. Code the PRAGMA with the TRUST keyword on the calling PL/SQL
    function and the published function with no PRAGMA specified. Then
    the calling PL/SQL function can call any other function without any
    restrictions. Here's an example to illustrate this:

```
CREATE OR REPLACE PACKAGE dirPkg2 IS
    FUNCTION FileType(ip_file_name VARCHAR2)
    RETURN VARCHAR2
    IS
    LANGUAGE JAVA
    NAME 'dirClass.fileType(java.lang.String) return java.lang.String';
    FUNCTION displayFileType(ip_file_name VARCHAR2)
    RETURN VARCHAR2;
          PRAGMA RESTRICT_REFERENCES(displayFileType,WNDS, TRUST);
    END dirPkg2;
/
CREATE OR REPLACE PACKAGE BODY dirPkg2 IS
    FUNCTION displayFileType(ip_file_name VARCHAR2)
    RETURN VARCHAR2
   IS
       v_descr VARCHAR2(100);
   BEGIN
```

```
        v_descr := ip_file_name||' '||' is a '||FileType(ip_file_name);
        RETURN (v_descr);
    END displayFileType;
END dirPkg2;
/
```

In this case, displayFileType is trusted to be pure. Hence, it isn't checked, whether it complies with the WNDS restriction or not. As a result, it can call FileType. Note that FileType is not coded with the RESTRICT_REFERENCES PRAGMA.

> **TIP** *The purity of all functions, either stand-alone or packaged, is verified at runtime. Packaged functions as of Oracle8i and higher don't need the PRAGMA RESTRICT_REFERENCES.*

> **TIP** *Specifying the PRAGMA for packaged functions improves the execution performance, as the purity level is checked at compile time.*

Now that the purity levels are in place, the following restrictions apply to calling stored functions from SQL:

- A function called from a query or DML statement must not end the current transaction with a COMMIT or ROLLBACK.

- If it's called from a SELECT statement, the function must not execute a DML statement or otherwise modify the database. Doing so results in the following error:

```
ORA-14551: Cannot perform a DML operation inside a query
```

- A function called from a DML statement must not read or modify the table currently being modified by that DML statement. Doing so results in the following error:

```
ORA-06571: Function <function_name> does not guarantee not to update
database.
```

- If it's called from a parallelized DML statement, the function must not execute a DML statement or otherwise modify the database.

Parameter Passing by Reference

Parameters to stored subprograms are of two types: actual parameters and formal parameters. You can define formal parameters with three modes: IN, OUT, and IN OUT. Actual parameters come into the picture when you call the stored subprogram, and they have a one-to-one correspondence with the formal parameters. Generally, there are two distinct ways of passing actual parameters: call by value and call by reference.

In the case of *call by value*, the value of the actual parameter is copied into the formal parameter. That is, a copy of the actual parameter is made. In the case of *call by reference*, a pointer to the actual parameter is passed to the corresponding formal parameter. Thus, no copy is made and both actual and formal parameters refer to the same memory location. Call by reference is faster because it avoids the copy. This is illustrated in a later section, "Performance Improvement of NOCOPY."

PL/SQL uses call by reference for IN mode and call by value for OUT and IN OUT modes. This preserves the exception semantics while passing OUT and IN OUT parameters. By default, if a subprogram exits normally, the values assigned to the OUT and IN OUT formal parameters inside the body of the subprogram are copied into the corresponding actual parameters. However, if the subprogram terminates with an unhandled exception, this copying isn't done. Also, call by value can impact performance with reduced execution time and excess memory consumption when large data structures are passed as OUT or IN OUT parameters. This is especially true when passing resultsets, collections, an index-by table of records, or objects.

PL/SQL 8*i* onward define a compiler hint called NOCOPY that you can specify for OUT and IN OUT parameters. Specifying NOCOPY overrides the default call by value behavior for OUT and IN OUT modes and enables parameters in these modes to be passed by reference. This eliminates the performance bottleneck mentioned earlier. However, NOCOPY is a compiler hint and not a directive, so it may not apply always—that is, even if it's specified, the parameter may still be passed by value.

Here's the syntax of using NOCOPY:

```
parameter_name [OUT| IN OUT] NOCOPY datatype
```

where parameter_name is the name of the parameter and datatype represents the data type of said parameter. You can use either the OUT or IN OUT parameter mode with NOCOPY. Here's an example:

```
CREATE OR REPLACE PROCEDURE p_nocopy
                    (ip_1 IN NUMBER,
                      op_2 OUT NOCOPY VARCHAR2)
IS
BEGIN
     NULL;
END;
/
```

Table 5-1 describes the behavior of specifying IN, INOUT, OUT, and NOCOPY.

Table 5-1. Behavior of Various Parameter Modes

IN	IN OUT	OUT	IN OUT NOCOPY, OUT NOCOPY
Actual parameter is passed by reference.	The actual parameter is passed by value.	The actual parameter is passed by value.	The actual parameter is passed by reference.
A pointer (address) to the value is passed.	A copy of the value is passed out.	A copy of the value is passed in and out.	The address of the value is passed.
N/A	The OUT value is rolled back in case of an unhandled. exception	The OUT value is rolled back in case of an unhandled exception.	You can't predict the correctness of the OUT value always, as no rollback occurs in the case of an unhandled exception.

TIP   *You can use NOCOPY only for parameters in OUT or IN OUT mode. NOCOPY is a compiler hint and not a directive, and hence it may be ignored sometimes. With NOCOPY, changes to formal parameter values affect the values of the actual parameters also, so if a subprogram exits with an unhandled exception, the unfinished changes are not rolled back. That is, the actual parameters may still return modified values.*

NOCOPY and Exception Handling

Of interest in exception handling is the role played by NOCOPY, because, in most cases, the values are passed by reference. In the case of abnormal termination of a subprogram due to an unhandled exception, the values of the NOCOPY actual parameters aren't reliable.

In the case of an unhandled exception, no copying of the actual parameters into the formal parameters is done by default, and changes are rolled back. In the case of NOCOPY, addresses of the actual and formal parameters are the same and so these changes might not be rolled back.

Performance Improvement of NOCOPY

NOCOPY improves performance when passing large data structures. It's significantly faster than passing by value. To illustrate the performance benefit of NOCOPY, consider the following small package consisting of two procedures and a function. Here, I declare a collection of type VARRAY containing 100,000 elements:

```
CREATE OR REPLACE PACKAGE NoCopyPkg
is
   type arr is varray(100000) of hrc_tab%ROWTYPE;
   procedure p1(ip1 IN OUT arr);
   procedure p2(ip1 IN OUT NOCOPY arr);
   FUNCTION get_time RETURN NUMBER;
END NoCopyPkg;
/
```

The corresponding package body is defined as follows:

```
CREATE OR REPLACE PACKAGE BODY NoCopyPkg
is
 PROCEDURE p1(ip1 IN OUT arr)
 IS
 BEGIN
    NULL;
 END;
 PROCEDURE p2(ip1 IN OUT NOCOPY arr)
 IS
 BEGIN
    NULL;
 END;
```

```
FUNCTION get_time RETURN NUMBER
IS
BEGIN
     RETURN (dbms_utility.get_time);
EXCEPTION WHEN OTHERS THEN
     RAISE_APPLICATION_ERROR(-20010, SQLERRM);
END get_time;


END NoCopyPkg;
/
```

This package defines a collection type called VARRAY, or variable array, having a maximum of 100,000 elements. It also defines two procedures that each pass an array of 100,000 elements in the IN OUT mode, one without NOCOPY and the other with NOCOPY specified. The function get_time retrieves the current time in one-hundredth of a second.

Now, I can use the packaged procedures and functions by defining the following PL/SQL block:

```
declare
  arr1 NoCopyPkg.arr   := NoCopyPkg.arr(null);
   cur_t1 number;
     cur_t2 number;
     cur_t3 number;
 begin
 select * into arr1(1) from hrc_tab where hrc_code = 1;
/* Create 99999 new elements in the variable array
and populate each with the value in the 1st element */
arr1.extend(99999, 1);
cur_t1 := NoCopyPkg.get_time;
NoCopyPkg.p1(arr1);
cur_t2 := NoCopyPkg.get_time;
NoCopyPkg.p2(arr1);
   cur_t3 := NoCopyPkg.get_time;
   dbms_output.put_line(' Without NOCOPY '||to_char((cur_t2-cur_t1)/100));
   dbms_output.put_line(' With NOCOPY '||to_char((cur_t3-cur_t2)/100));
 end;
 /
```

Here's the output of the preceding program:

```
Without NOCOPY .67
With NOCOPY 0

PL/SQL procedure successfully completed.
```

The output of the preceding program may vary depending on the hardware and software configuration, but you should note the difference in speed between using NOCOPY and not using it.

The following points are worth noting:

- The procedures p1 and p2 inside the package do nothing except pass the variable array of 100,000 elements. p1 uses call by value and p2 uses call by reference.

- The SELECT statement at the beginning of the PL/SQL block populates the very first element of the variable array arr1. Note that arr1 is initialized to null, meaning it creates one element that is null.

- The EXTEND method is used on the variable array to create 99,999 copies of the first element.

- The time taken to pass by value is significantly more than that taken to pass by reference.

Restrictions on NOCOPY

As mentioned earlier, NOCOPY is only a compiler hint and not a directive. So in some cases it may be ignored and the parameter passed by value. Certain restrictions apply to NOCOPY. For NOCOPY to take effect

- The actual parameter can't be an element of an index-by table, but it can be an entire index-by table.

- The actual parameter can't be constrained by precision, scale, or NOT NULL. However, this restriction doesn't apply to constrained elements or attributes, or length-constrained character strings.

- The actual and formal parameters can't be explicitly defined records with either one or both records defined using %ROWTYPE or %TYPE, and constraints on corresponding fields in the records differ. This restriction also applies if the actual parameter is defined by means of an implicit record such as the index of a cursor FOR LOOP.

- Passing the actual parameter requires an implicit data type conversion.

- The subprogram containing the NOCOPY parameters can't be involved in an external or remote procedure call.

Definer and Invoker Rights

PL/SQL subprograms, by default, were executed in the schema of the owner of these objects prior to Oracle8*i*. This is referred to as *definer rights*, meaning these programs were executed in and according to the authorization and authentication of the schema defining these programs. Also, any underlying objects to be created, altered, or dropped in the process of execution were in the definer schema. This approach has a disadvantage, however.

The output of these subprograms became available as kind of centralized in the definer schema. That is, even executed by different schemas, the output becomes available in the tables in the owner schema. This centralization of data is unsuitable if each user requires a local disparate copy of the output in his or her own schema.

Invoker Rights Model

Oracle8*i* introduced the concept of *invoker rights*, which enables subprograms to be executed in and according to the authorization and authentication of the schema invoking (i.e., executing) the subprogram. Invoker rights are specified by the AUTHID clause. The syntax for this clause is as follows:

```
AUTHID CURRENT_USER | DEFINER
```

You can specify the AUTHID clause for a procedure, function, package, or object type only. Here, CURRENT_USER is the schema name of the user executing the subprogram or object type, and DEFINER is the schema name of the user owning the subprogram or object type. DEFINER is the default.

One Application Program, Multiple Schemas

Consider an order entry application that processes orders for different regions. Each region should operate its own separate schema, so there are tables such as ORDERS and ORDER_ITEMS. It isn't so simple, however. These tables have to be created having the region_name as part of the table name and in the schema of each individual region. This means that the table names have to be dynamically generated. Not only this—the DML operations should be performed on these tables in the schema of the individual region. To dynamically generate the table names, the immediate solution seems to be using DBMS_SQL. What about creating the tables and performing the DML on these tables in the schema of the individual region? AUTHID does the job.

For simplicity, let's assume that there are two regions: region1 and region2. The corresponding schema names are region1 and region2. Also, there is a third user, which is the common user whose schema owns the common code. Let's signify this common user with the username "name" and the password "plsql9i/plsql9i."

Here's the code to create the schemas region1 and region2:

```
connect system/manager;
create user region1 identified by region1;
grant connect, resource to region1;

create user region2 identified by region2;
grant connect, resource to region2;
```

The following code illustrates a sample procedure implementing both of the preceding requirements:

```
Create or replace Procedure create_dyn_table
                        (i_region_name VARCHAR2,
                         retcd OUT NUMBER,
                         errmsg OUT VARCHAR2)
authid current_user
Is
   cur_id INTEGER;
   ret_code INTEGER;
  Dyn_string VARCHAR2(1000);
  Dyn_Table_name VARCHAR2(21);
Begin
  dyn_table_name := 'ORDERS_FOR_'||i_region_name;
  dyn_string := ' CREATE TABLE ' ||dyn_table_name||
' (order_id NUMBER(10) PRIMARY KEY,
```

```
    order_date DATE     NOT NULL,
    total_qty  NUMBER,
    total_price NUMBER(15,2))';
  cur_id := DBMS_SQL.OPEN_CURSOR;
  DBMS_SQL.PARSE(cur_id, dyn_string, DBMS_SQL.V7);
  ret_code := DBMS_SQL.EXECUTE(cur_id);
  DBMS_SQL.CLOSE_CURSOR(cur_id);
  retcd := 0;
EXCEPTION WHEN OTHERS THEN
  retcd := SQLCODE;
  errmsg := 'ERR: Creating table '||dyn_table_name ||' - '||SQLERRM;
End;
/
```

Now this procedure is created in the schema plsql9i/plsql9i, and the individual users region1 and region2 can execute this procedure in their own schemas. The following script does the job:

```
/* File name authid.sql */
connect plsql9i/plsql9i;
Create or replace Procedure create_dyn_table
                          (i_region_name VARCHAR2,
                           retcd OUT NUMBER,
                           errmsg OUT VARCHAR2)
authid current_user
is
    cur_id INTEGER;
    ret_code INTEGER;
  dyn_string VARCHAR2(1000);
  dyn_Table_name VARCHAR2(21);
Begin
  dyn_table_name := 'ORDERS_FOR_'||i_region_name;
  dyn_string := ' CREATE TABLE ' ||dyn_table_name||
' (order_id NUMBER(10) PRIMARY KEY,
    order_date DATE     NOT NULL,
    total_qty  NUMBER,
    total_price NUMBER(15,2))';
  cur_id := DBMS_SQL.OPEN_CURSOR;
  DBMS_SQL.PARSE(cur_id, dyn_string, DBMS_SQL.V7);
  ret_code := DBMS_SQL.EXECUTE(cur_id);
  DBMS_SQL.CLOSE_CURSOR(cur_id);
  retcd := 0;
```

```
EXCEPTION WHEN OTHERS THEN
   retcd := SQLCODE;
   errmsg := 'ERR: Creating table '||dyn_table_name ||' - '||SQLERRM;
End;
/
grant execute on create_dyn_table to public;
connect region1/region1;
create synonym create_dyn_table for plsql9i.create_dyn_table;
declare
   retcd NUMBER;
   errmsg VARCHAR2(100);
begin
   create_dyn_table('REGION1',retcd, errmsg);
end;
/
select table_name from user_tables where table_name like '%REGION1';
connect region2/region2;
create synonym create_dyn_table for plsql9i.create_dyn_table;
declare
   retcd NUMBER;
   errmsg VARCHAR2(100);
begin
   create_dyn_table('REGION2',retcd, errmsg);
end;
/
select table_name from user_tables where table_name like '%REGION2';
```

Here's the output of the preceding script:

```
Connected.
Procedure created.
Grant succeeded.
Connected.
Synonym created.
PL/SQL procedure successfully completed.
TABLE_NAME
------------------
ORDERS_FOR_REGION1
Connected.
Synonym created.
PL/SQL procedure successfully completed.
TABLE_NAME
------------------
ORDERS_FOR_REGION2
```

Thus, you can see that the invoker rights model provides centralization of code (application programs) and decentralization (in fact, localization) of data. Semantic external references in the code are resolved in the schema of the invoker of the code.

Subprograms That Can Include AUTHID Clause

Only the following stored subprograms can include the AUTHID clause in their respective headers: procedure, function, package specification, and object type. This means the AUTHID clause is valid only in the following PL/SQL statements:

```
CREATE [OR REPLACE] PROCEDURE [schema_name.]procedure_name
[(parameter_list)]
[AUTHID {CURRENT_USER|DEFINER}] {IS/AS}
CREATE [OR REPLACE] FUNCTION [schema_name.]function_name
[(parameter_list)]
      RETURN datatype
[AUTHID {CURRENT_USER|DEFINER}] {IS/AS}
CREATE [OR REPLACE] PACKAGE [schema_name.]package_name
 [AUTHID {CURRENT_USER|DEFINER}] {IS/AS}
```

Not all SQL and PL/SQL statements can be used using the AUTHID CURRENT_USER clause. Semantic references are resolved only for the following types of statements:

- DML: Only SELECT, INSERT, UPDATE, and DELETE statements

- Cursors: Only OPEN and OPEN-FOR statements

- Dynamic SQL: EXECUTE IMMEDIATE and OPEN-FOR-USING statements

- DBMS_SQL: SQL statements that are parsed with the DBMS_SQL.PARSE procedure.

- Transaction control: Only LOCK TABLE statement.

TIP   *When no AUTHID clause is specified, the default is AUTHID DEFINER.*

TIP   *Invoker rights checks for privileges at program execution time. This is in contrast to definer rights, where external references are resolved at compile time. Also, only data element references (of tables and views) can be resolved, not those of program elements.*

TIP   *When you use invoker rights, external references in SQL statements are resolved with the privileges of the invoker. References in PL/SQL statements are still resolved with the privileges of the owner. Granting via roles is allowed as long as it doesn't affect the compile time resolution of the invoker rights routine.*

Invoker Rights and Dynamic SQL

The create_dyn_table used the AUTHID clause to take advantage of invoker rights. This procedure made use of dynamic SQL using DBMS_SQL to explain invoker rights. Once dynamic SQL comes into the picture, many issues are involved, such as

- Which user is the owner of the program?

- Which user is executing the program?

- Under which schema is the application output being created?

As the example in the preceding section illustrates, invoker rights provide the answer to all these questions. As a rule of the thumb, follow the next Tip when you use dynamic SQL, either native dynamic SQL or DBMS_SQL.

TIP *When you use dynamic SQL and/or dynamic PL/SQL, either using native dynamic SQL or DBMS_SQL, always specify AUTHID CURRENT_USER for all stored subprograms.*

Additional Package Features

This section highlights two important features of packages: overloading of packaged subprograms and serially reusable packages.

Overloading Packaged Procedures and Functions

Overloading refers to defining more than one packaged procedure or function with the same name and with a different set of parameters. It's one of the ways to implement *polymorphism,* an object-oriented concept of using an object method in more than one way. More specifically, different objects respond to the same method in different ways. When it comes to packaged procedures and functions, the same subprogram is used in more than one way to achieve different results.

TIP *Only packaged procedures and functions can be overloaded. Stand-alone or top-level procedures and functions can't be overloaded.*

Consider the orgMaster package defined previously. It defined two functions, getOrgInfo and getAllOrgs, for retrieving the information about one particular organization or all organizations for a particular hierarchy, respectively. Using overloading, you can code these two procedures with a single name but with different parameters. Here's the code for this:

```
CREATE OR REPLACE PACKAGE orgMaster2
IS
    max_sites_for_an_org NUMBER;
    TYPE rc IS REF CURSOR;
    PROCEDURE createOrg (ip_hrc_code NUMBER,
```

```
                        ip_org_id NUMBER,
                        ip_org_short_name VARCHAR2,
                        ip_org_long_name VARCHAR2,
                        op_retcd OUT NUMBER,
                        op_err_msg OUT VARCHAR2);
   PROCEDURE updateOrg(ip_org_id NUMBER,
                        ip_org_short_name VARCHAR2,
                        ip_org_long_name VARCHAR2,
                        op_retcd OUT NUMBER,
                        op_err_msg OUT VARCHAR2);
   PROCEDURE removeOrg(ip_org_id NUMBER,
                        op_retcd OUT NUMBER,
                        op_err_msg OUT VARCHAR2);
   FUNCTION getOrgDetails(ip_hrc_code NUMBER) RETURN rc;
   FUNCTION getOrgDetails(ip_hrc_code NUMBER, ip_org_id NUMBER) RETURN rc;
   PROCEDURE assignSiteToOrg(ip_org_id NUMBER,
                        ip_site_no NUMBER,
                        op_retcd OUT NUMBER,
                        op_err_msg OUT VARCHAR2);
 END orgMaster2;
/
CREATE OR REPLACE PACKAGE BODY orgMaster2
IS
-- Procedure to delete records from the org_site_tab table
-- before deleting from org_table. This procedure is called
-- from the removeOrg procedure
PROCEDURE removeOrgSites(ip_org_id NUMBER,
                        op_retcd OUT NUMBER,
                        op_err_msg OUT VARCHAR2)

  IS
  BEGIN
      DELETE org_site_tab WHERE org_id = ip_org_id;
      op_retcd := 0;
  EXCEPTION WHEN OTHERS THEN
          op_retcd := SQLCODE;
          op_err_msg := SQLERRM;
  END removeOrgSites;
-- Procedure to create a record in the org_tab table
   PROCEDURE createOrg (ip_hrc_code NUMBER,
                        ip_org_id NUMBER,
                        ip_org_short_name VARCHAR2,
                        ip_org_long_name VARCHAR2,
                        op_retcd OUT NUMBER,
                        op_err_msg OUT VARCHAR2)
```

```
IS
        BEGIN
        INSERT INTO org_tab VALUES
       (ip_hrc_code, ip_org_id, ip_org_short_name, ip_org_long_name);
       op_retcd := 0;
EXCEPTION WHEN DUP_VAL_ON_INDEX THEN
       op_retcd := -1;
       op_err_msg := 'Organization with Id '||TO_CHAR(ip_org_id)||
                               ' already exists.';
     WHEN OTHERS THEN
            op_retcd := SQLCODE;
            op_err_msg := SQLERRM;
   END createOrg;
-- Procedure to update the long and short names for a
-- given org_id in the org_tab table
   PROCEDURE updateOrg(ip_org_id NUMBER,
                       ip_org_short_name VARCHAR2,
                       ip_org_long_name VARCHAR2,
                       op_retcd OUT NUMBER,
                       op_err_msg OUT VARCHAR2)
    IS
    BEGIN
         UPDATE org_tab
         SET org_short_name = ip_org_short_name,
                 org_long_name = ip_org_long_name
         WHERE org_id = ip_org_id;
         IF (SQL%NOTFOUND) THEN
             op_retcd := -1;
             op_err_msg := 'Organization with Id '||TO_CHAR(ip_org_id)||
                                   ' does not exist.';
             RETURN;
             END IF;
             op_retcd := 0;
   EXCEPTION WHEN OTHERS THEN
             op_retcd := SQLCODE;
             op_err_msg := SQLERRM;
    END updateOrg;
-- Procedure to remove a record from the org_tab table
   PROCEDURE removeOrg(ip_org_id NUMBER,
                       op_retcd OUT NUMBER,
                       op_err_msg OUT VARCHAR2)
    IS
    BEGIN
```

```
              removeOrgSites(ip_org_id, op_retcd, op_err_msg);
           IF (op_retcd <> 0) then
              RETURN;
          END IF;
           DELETE org_tab WHERE org_id = ip_org_id;
          IF (SQL%NOTFOUND) THEN
                 op_retcd := -1;
                 op_err_msg := 'Organization with Id '||TO_CHAR(ip_org_id)||
                                        ' does not exist.';
                  RETURN;
             END IF;
             op_retcd := 0;
      EXCEPTION WHEN OTHERS THEN
                 op_retcd := SQLCODE;
                 op_err_msg := SQLERRM;
     END removeOrg;
-- Over-loaded  function that returns a row from the org_tab table
-- based on input hrc_code and org_id
   FUNCTION getOrgDetails(ip_hrc_code NUMBER, ip_org_id NUMBER) RETURN rc
   IS
       v_rc rc;
   BEGIN
            OPEN v_rc FOR SELECT * FROM org_tab
                                  WHERE hrc_code = ip_hrc_code
                                     AND org_id = ip_org_id;

       RETURN (v_rc);
 EXCEPTION WHEN OTHERS THEN
        RAISE_APPLICATION_ERROR(-20001, SQLERRM);
END getOrgDetails;
-- Over-loaded  function that returns all rows from the org_tab table
-- for an input hrc_code. This function has the same name as the function
-- above, but the number of parameters is different in each case.
   FUNCTION getOrgDetails(ip_hrc_code NUMBER) RETURN rc
   IS
       v_rc rc;
   BEGIN
            OPEN v_rc FOR SELECT * FROM org_tab WHERE hrc_code = ip_hrc_code;
       RETURN (v_rc);
 EXCEPTION WHEN OTHERS THEN
        RAISE_APPLICATION_ERROR(-20002, SQLERRM);
END getOrgDetails;
-- Procedure to create a row in the org_site_tab table
-- based on input org_id and  site_no
```

```
PROCEDURE assignSiteToOrg(ip_org_id NUMBER,
                          ip_site_no NUMBER,
                          op_retcd OUT NUMBER,
                          op_err_msg OUT VARCHAR2)
IS
   v_num NUMBER;
BEGIN
   BEGIN
        SELECT 1
        INTO       v_num
        FROM       org_site_tab
        WHERE    org_id = ip_org_id
               AND   site_no = ip_site_no;
        IF (v_num = 1) THEN
            op_retcd := 0;
            RETURN;
        END IF;
     EXCEPTION WHEN NO_DATA_FOUND THEN
            INSERT INTO org_site_tab VALUES (ip_org_id, ip_site_no);
     END;
    op_retcd := 0;
   EXCEPTION WHEN OTHERS THEN
       op_retcd := SQLCODE;
       op_err_msg := SQLERRM;
 END assignSiteToOrg;
-- Initialization section for the package
BEGIN
     max_sites_for_an_org := 4;
END orgMaster2;
/
```

The following points are worth noting:

- Two functions are defined with the same name, getOrgDetails, one with
  one parameter and the other with two parameters. Thus the function
  getOrgDetails is overloaded.

- These two functions differ primarily in the number of parameters defined
  for them. Their return types are the same.

Now you can call these overloaded functions from a PL/SQL program as
follows :

```
DECLARE
     v_rc orgMaster2.rc;
     org_rec org_tab%ROWTYPE;
BEGIN
    DBMS_OUTPUT.PUT_LINE('Org Details for Org 1001');
    DBMS_OUTPUT.PUT_LINE('------------------');
    v_rc := orgMaster2.getOrgDetails(1, 1001);
    FETCH v_rc INTO org_rec;
    DBMS_OUTPUT.PUT_LINE(TO_CHAR(org_rec.hrc_code)||' '||
                         TO_CHAR(org_rec.org_id)||' '||
                         org_rec.org_short_name||' '||
                         org_rec.org_long_name);
    DBMS_OUTPUT.PUT_LINE('Org Details for Hierarchy 1');
    DBMS_OUTPUT.PUT_LINE('------------------');
    v_rc := orgMaster2.getOrgDetails(1);
    LOOP
        FETCH v_rc INTO org_rec;
        EXIT WHEN v_rc%NOTFOUND;
        DBMS_OUTPUT.PUT_LINE(TO_CHAR(org_rec.hrc_code)||' '||
                                 TO_CHAR(org_rec.org_id)||' '||
                                 org_rec.org_short_name||' '||
                             org_rec.org_long_name);

    END LOOP;
    CLOSE v_rc;
END;
/
```

Here's the output of the preceding program:

```
Org Details for Org 1001
------------------
1 1001 Office of CEO ABC Inc. Office of CEO ABC Inc.
Org Details for Hierarchy 1
------------------
1 1001 Office of CEO ABC Inc. Office of CEO ABC Inc.
1 1002 Office of CEO XYZ Inc. Office of CEO XYZ Inc.
1 1003 Office of CEO DataPro Inc. Office of CEO DataPro Inc.

PL/SQL procedure successfully completed.
```

Conditions for Overloading

You can overload procedures or functions only if they satisfy at least one of these conditions:

- Their signatures differ in the number of parameters. For example, you can overload the following two procedures:

```
procedure p_proc(ip_1 NUMBER);
procedure p_proc(ip_1 NUMBER, ip_2 NUMBER);
```

- The data types of their parameters are of different data types and the data types aren't in the same family. For example, you can overload the following two functions:

```
function f_diff(ip_1 NUMBER, ip_2 NUMBER) RETURN NUMBER;
function f_diff(ip_1 DATE ip_2 DATE) RETURN NUMBER;
```

These are the only two conditions for overloading, and you can't overload procedures or functions in any other situation. So you can't overload two or more procedures or functions if

- Their signatures differ only in parameter name or mode.

- Their signatures differ only in return type (in the case of functions).

- Their parameters differ in data types but are in the same family, such as INTEGER and NUMBER.

 TIP *To specify purity levels for overloaded functions, specify the PRAGMA RESTRICT_REFERENCES for each overloaded definition of the function.*

Serially Reusable Packages

As mentioned earlier, the runtime state of a package is kept in session memory and persists for the duration of the session. This session memory is nothing but the user global area (UGA), and as the number of users increases, so does the consumption of session memory. To prevent this, you can mark a package as SERIALLY_REUSABLE so that

- The runtime state of the package persists only for the duration of the database call. That is, the state of the package is reset at the end of each database call. This resets the value of all package global variables and any open global cursors are closed automatically.

- The runtime state of the package is allocated a small pool instead of the UGA, and this memory is reused after the database call is completed.

The primary advantage of serially reusable packages is better memory management for scalability.

You mark a package as serially reusable by using a PRAGMA. Here's the syntax:

```
PRAGMA SERIALLY_REUSABLE;
```

A package specification has the preceding PRAGMA specified. If the package also has a package body, it must too have the PRAGMA specified.

TIP *You can't specify the PRAGMA SERIALLY_REUSABLE for a package body only. You have to specify it for the package specification and body.*

TIP *A package marked as serially reusable can't have its public declarations or procedures and/or functions accessed from a database trigger. Doing so results in the following error:*

```
cannot access Serially Reusable package <package_name> in
the context of a trigger.
```

A good example of testing serially reusable packages is by testing

- The state of packages variables across database calls

- The state of package cursors across database calls

Here's an example to illustrate the state of package variables across database calls:

```
CREATE OR REPLACE PACKAGE srPkg1
IS
    PRAGMA SERIALLY_REUSABLE;
    num_var NUMBER;
   char_var VARCHAR2(20);
   PROCEDURE initialize;
   FUNCTION display_num RETURN NUMBER;
   FUNCTION display_char RETURN VARCHAR2;
END srPkg1;
/
```

Here's the corresponding package body:

```
CREATE OR REPLACE PACKAGE BODY srPkg1
IS
    PRAGMA SERIALLY_REUSABLE;
    PROCEDURE initialize
    IS
    BEGIN
        num_var := 100;
        char_var := 'Test String1';
    END;
    FUNCTION display_num RETURN NUMBER
    IS
    BEGIN
       RETURN (num_var);
    END;
    FUNCTION display_char RETURN VARCHAR2
    IS
    BEGIN
        RETURN (char_var);
    END;
END srPkg1;
/
```

Now the following PL/SQL block makes a database call to the packaged procedure and functions:

```
DECLARE
    v_num NUMBER;
    v_char VARCHAR2(20);
BEGIN
    srPkg1.initialize;
    v_num := srPkg1.display_num;
    v_char := srPkg1.display_char;
    dbms_output.put_line(TO_CHAR(v_num)|| ' '||v_char);
END;
/
```

Here's the output of the preceding program:

```
100 Test String1

PL/SQL procedure successfully completed.d
```

Next, a second database call to the display functions yields the following results:

```
DECLARE
    v_num NUMBER;
    v_char VARCHAR2(20);
BEGIN
    v_num := srPkg1.display_num;
    v_char := srPkg1.display_char;
    dbms_output.put_line(TO_CHAR(v_num)|| ' '||v_char);
END;
/
SQL> DECLARE
  2      v_num NUMBER;
  3      v_char VARCHAR2(20);
  4  BEGIN
  5      v_num := srPkg1.display_num;
  6      v_char := srPkg1.display_char;
  7      dbms_output.put_line(TO_CHAR(v_num)|| ' '||v_char);
  8  END;
  9  /

PL/SQL procedure successfully completed.
```

The following points are worth noting:

- The results after the first database call and the second database call are different even though num_var and char_var are package global variables.

- If the package wasn't defined as serially reusable, the second database call would yield the same result as the first one.

Here's an example to illustrate the state of package cursors at the end of each database call:

```
CREATE OR REPLACE PACKAGE srPkg2
IS
    PRAGMA SERIALLY_REUSABLE;
  CURSOR csr_sites IS
        SELECT * from site_tab ORDER BY site_no;
    PROCEDURE displaySites;
END srPkg2;
/
```

Here's the corresponding package body:

```
CREATE OR REPLACE PACKAGE BODY srPkg2
IS
    PRAGMA SERIALLY_REUSABLE;
    PROCEDURE displaySites
    IS
      site_rec site_tab%ROWTYPE;
    BEGIN
        OPEN csr_sites;
        FETCH csr_sites INTO site_rec;
         dbms_output.put_line(TO_CHAR(site_rec.site_no)||' '||
                                            site_rec.site_descr);
        FETCH csr_sites INTO site_rec;
        dbms_output.put_line(TO_CHAR(site_rec.site_no)||' '||
                                            site_rec.site_descr);
    END displaySites;
END srPkg2;
/
```

Now the following PL/SQL block makes a database call to the packaged procedure displaySites:

```
BEGIN
     srPkg2.displaySites;
END;
/
```

Here's the output of the preceding program:

```
1 New York
2 Washington

PL/SQL procedure successfully completed.
```

Then a second database call to the display functions yields the same results.

```
BEGIN
     srPkg2.displaySites;
END;
/
```

The following points are worth noting:

- The results after the first database call and the second database call are the same even though csr_sites is a global cursor. This is because the cursor is automatically closed after each database call to displaySites.

- If the package wasn't defined as serially reusable, the second database call would have yielded the third and fourth rows in the site_tab table instead of the first and second as shown by the first call.

Summary

This chapter covered the ins and outs of stored subprograms. Specifically, I discussed stored procedures, functions, and packages with respect to their method of creation and use. I highlighted special features of these items, such as subprograms returning resultsets, calling stored functions from SQL statements, definer and invoker rights, and parameter passing by reference. Finally, I described additional package features, such as overloading of packaged subprograms and serially reusable packages. The next chapter discusses database triggers and their details.

CHAPTER 6

Database Triggers

IN CHAPTER 5, I described three types of stored subprograms: procedures, functions, and packages. In addition to these subprogram types, PL/SQL enables a fourth type of stored subprogram called a *database trigger*. A database trigger is a stored subprogram that's stored in the database and executed implicitly on the occurrence of an event. The event can be a DDL operation, such as an object creation, alteration, or dropping; a DML operation, such an INSERT, an UPDATE, or a DELETE on a table or view; a system event, such as database startup and shutdown, logon, and logoff; or a user event, such as schema logon and logoff.

Database triggers enable you to perform various functions that would otherwise be tedious for you to code. The most common uses of database triggers are as follows:

- For DDL and DML auditing

- For enforcing complex validation rules to prevent inappropriate and inconsistent data from being input into the database

- For performing related actions when a particular action occurs

- For enforcing complex data-integrity relationships that you can't otherwise specify declaratively, such as a cascading update operation on a child table whenever a parent row is updated

- For automatically generating derived values

- For system event handling

After defining triggers, I go on to highlight the various types of triggers. I describe the implications of creating triggers and the concepts involved therein. I then explain the concept of creating triggers on views. Finally, I present descriptions of the new triggers introduced in Oracle8*i*.

I illustrate the concept of triggers by taking into account the organizational hierarchy system presented in Chapter 2. In addition, I use the table DDL_AUDIT to test user-event triggers. Appendix A lists the schema objects to be created.

PL/SQL Triggers: Types and Definition

A database trigger is a stored program executed in response to a database event. This event is called the *triggering event,* and it can be one of the following:

- A DDL operation such as CREATE, ALTER, or DROP

- A DML operation such as INSERT, UPDATE, or DELETE

- A system event such as database STARTUP, SHUTDOWN, or SERVERERROR

- A user event such as LOGON or LOGOFF

A triggering event is initiated on the execution of a triggering statement such as an INSERT, UPDATE, or DELETE statement, or a CREATE, ALTER, or DROP statement. A triggering event is also initiated on database startup and shutdown or user logon and logoff.

Types of Triggers

Triggers are classified according to the event that causes them to fire and the time of that event. You can set them to fire either before or after the particular event. Triggers fall into three main categories: DML triggers, INSTEAD-OF triggers, and triggers on system and user events.

DML Triggers

DML triggers fire when an INSERT, UPDATE, or DELETE statement is executed on a database table. They can be further classified as ROW or STATEMENT triggers. ROW and STATEMENT triggers specify how many times the trigger body should be executed.

INSTEAD-OF Triggers

INSTEAD-OF triggers fire on DML statements issued against either a relational view or an object view. I discuss these triggers further in the section "Read-Only Views, Updateable Views, and INSTEAD-OF Triggers."

Triggers on System and User Events

Triggers on system events and user events fire on the occurrence of system events such as database startup and shutdown, whenever a server error occurs, or when a user event such as user logon and logoff occurs or a DDL command is executed. I discuss these types of triggers further in the section "New Database Triggers."

A second classification of triggers is based on the time the event occurred. These are BEFORE and AFTER triggers. The trigger should fire before or after the occurrence of the triggering event. These triggers can pertain to DML triggers or triggers on system and user events.

Defining Triggers

A database trigger is defined using the CREATE OR REPLACE TRIGGER statement. Here's the general syntax:

```
CREATE [OR REPLACE] TRIGGER trigger_name
[BEFORE|AFTER|INSTEAD OF] triggering_event
[referencing_clause]
[WHEN trigger_restriction]
[FOR EACH ROW]
trigger_body ;
```

where trigger_name is the name of the trigger being created, triggering_event specifies a particular event that fires the trigger, and trigger_body is a PL/SQL block specifying the action the trigger performs when fired. Instead of a PL/SQL block, the trigger body can be a CALL statement invoking a PL/SQL procedure or function or a Java stored procedure published in PL/SQL. REFERENCING clause, WHEN trigger_restriction, and FOR EACH ROW are explained in the sections "REFERENCING Clause," "WHEN Clause," and "ROW and STATEMENT Triggers," respectively.

Here's an example:

```
CREATE OR REPLACE TRIGGER ai_org_trig
AFTER INSERT ON org_tab
FOR EACH ROW
BEGIN
        UPDATE sec_hrc_audit
          SET num_rows = num_rows+1
          WHERE hrc_code = :NEW.hrc_code;
```

```
        IF (SQL%NOTFOUND) THEN
           INSERT INTO sec_hrc_audit VALUES (:NEW.hrc_code, 1);
        END IF;
END;
/
```

As you can see from the CREATE OR REPLACE TRIGGER statement, a trigger has three distinct parts: the triggering event, the triggering restriction, and the trigger body. Depending on the type of trigger, the *triggering event* can be a DML event, a system event, or a user event that causes the trigger to fire. In the example trigger, the triggering event is the statement

```
AFTER INSERT ON org_tab
```

In this case, the event is the INSERT operation on the org_tab table, and this trigger fires whenever an INSERT operation is done on the org_tab table and after the new row is written to the org_tab table. The INSERT statement that causes the INSERT trigger event to fire is termed the *triggering statement.* The *triggering restriction* is an optional condition specified as a WHEN clause that causes the trigger body to be executed only when the condition is TRUE. The *trigger body* specifies the code to be executed (i.e., the sequence of actions to be performed) when the trigger fires. In the example trigger, the trigger body is the following:

```
BEGIN
        UPDATE sec_hrc_audit
          SET num_rows = num_rows+1
          WHERE hrc_code = :NEW.hrc_code;     .
        IF (SQL%NOTFOUND) THEN
           INSERT INTO sec_hrc_audit VALUES (:NEW.hrc_code, 1);
        END IF;
END;
```

In this case, the trigger updates the num_rows column by incrementing it by 1 in the sec_hrc_audit table for the newly inserted hrc_code if it exists; otherwise, it inserts a row into the sec_hrc_audit table with a count of 1.

A trigger doesn't accept parameters, includes an executable section with BEGIN and END, and can include an optional declaration section and an exception handling section. The BEGIN . . . END section can include SQL and/or PL/SQL statements, and calls to PL/SQL procedures and functions (either stand-alone or packaged). Also, the trigger body can be a single CALL statement invoking a PL/SQL procedure or function, or a Java stored procedure published in PL/SQL.

TIP   *Triggers exist in a separate namespace from database tables, so it's possible to create a database trigger with the same name as a database table. However, this isn't recommended.*

Next, I discuss DML triggers. I discuss INSTEAD-OF triggers in after that, and I explain system and user event triggers in the section "New Database Triggers."

Defining DML Triggers

You define DML triggers on a particular database table and they fire during the execution of an INSERT, an UPDATE, or a DELETE.

You define DML triggers with the CREATE OR REPLACE TRIGGER statement. Here's the syntax:

```
CREATE [OR REPLACE] TRIGGER trigger_name
[BEFORE|AFTER] triggering_event [OF column_name] ON table_name
[referencing_clause]
[WHEN trigger_restriction]
[FOR EACH ROW]
trigger_body ;
```

where trigger_name is the name of the DML trigger being created; triggering_event is one or a combination of INSERT, UPDATE, and/or DELETE; and table_name is the table on which the INSERT, UPDATE, and/or DELETE is being executed. The [OF column_name] clause specifies the column_name being updated in the case of an UPDATE operation as the triggering event. BEFORE or AFTER specifies the time the trigger should fire (i.e., before or after the DML statement is executed). trigger_body is the sequence of actions to be performed when the trigger is fired, and the [WHEN condition] clause specifies any condition that when evaluated to TRUE causes the trigger body to execute. I explain the REFERENCING clause later.

TIP   *You can specify multiple DML operations for the triggering event by separating them with the OR keyword.*

The example trigger specified is an example of a DML trigger. Here's the same trigger repeated for your reference:

```
CREATE OR REPLACE TRIGGER ai_org_trig
AFTER INSERT ON org_tab
FOR EACH ROW
BEGIN
        UPDATE sec_hrc_audit
          SET num_rows = num_rows+1
          WHERE hrc_code = :NEW.hrc_code;
       IF (SQL%NOTFOUND) THEN
          INSERT INTO sec_hrc_audit VALUES (:NEW.hrc_code, 1);
       END IF;
END;
/
```

The following points are worth noting:

- The triggering event is an INSERT operation and the trigger fires after inserting into the org_tab table.

- The trigger body contains the code to be executed when this trigger fires. Here, a record in the sec_hrc_audit table is updated for the inserted hrc_code if it exists; otherwise, a new row is inserted into the sec_hrc_audit table.

ROW and STATEMENT Triggers

DML triggers can be of two types: ROW level and STATEMENT level. A ROW-level DML trigger fires once for each row of the DML operation affecting the table. You specify it with the FOR EACH ROW clause. The example trigger ai_org_trig is a ROW-level trigger. Its trigger body is executed once for each row inserted into the org_tab table. A STATEMENT-level trigger fires once for the triggering statement affecting the table. This means that if a single UPDATE statement affects ten rows, a ROW-level trigger is fired ten times, whereas a STATEMENT-level trigger is fired only once.

Table 6-1 presents a comparison between ROW-level triggers and STATE-MENT-level triggers.

Table 6-1. Comparison Between ROW-Level and STATEMENT-Level Triggers

ROW LEVEL	STATEMENT LEVEL
Fired for each row affected by the triggering statement.	Fired once for the triggering statement.
Not fired if the triggering event affects no rows.	Fired even if the triggering event doesn't affect any rows.
Both BEFORE and AFTER can be specified.	Both BEFORE and AFTER can be specified.
Trigger body has access to the row data.	Trigger body doesn't have access to the row data.
Currently affected by the triggering event.	Currently affected by the triggering event.
AFTER ROW triggers lock the data rows.	Doesn't lock rows.

In the example of the ai_org_trig trigger, the new value of the hrc_code being inserted is referenced in the trigger body as :NEW.hrc_code. This is possible as it is a ROW-level trigger.

The example of the ai_org_trig trigger can be changed to a STATEMENT trigger as follows:

```
CREATE OR REPLACE TRIGGER ai_org_trig_statement
AFTER INSERT ON org_tab
BEGIN
    FOR idx IN (SELECT hrc_code, COUNT(*) cnt
                        FROM    org_tab
                        GROUP BY hrc_code) LOOP
        UPDATE sec_hrc_audit
        SET num_rows = idx.cnt
        WHERE hrc_code = idx.hrc_code;
      IF (SQL%NOTFOUND) THEN
        INSERT INTO sec_hrc_audit VALUES (idx.hrc_code, idx.cnt);
      END IF;
    END LOOP;
END;
/
```

The following points are worth noting:

- The triggering event is an INSERT operation, and the trigger fires after inserting into the org_tab table.

- The trigger body accesses the org_tab table each time an INSERT statement is issued on the org_tab table. Even if an INSERT SELECT . . . is issued on the org_tab table and this results in multiple rows being inserted into the org_tab table, the ai_org_trig_statement is fired only once. The STATEMENT trigger is appropriate when an action is to be taken only once after the triggering statement is executed multiple times, whereas a ROW-level trigger is useful when the action is to be performed for each row of the triggering statement.

REFERENCING Clause

This clause specifies how the data being currently modified by the triggering event should be referenced inside the trigger body. By default, currently modified data is available inside the trigger body in the case of a ROW trigger and is referenced by two correlation identifiers, :NEW and :OLD. These correlation identifiers act as bind variables and hold the data of the current row as a record of type table_name%ROWTYPE, where table_name is the name of the database table on which the DML trigger is defined. However, :NEW and :OLD are only pseudo-records—they aren't actual records. They just simulate the record concept. Inside the body of the trigger, the column values can be referenced as :NEW.column_name or :OLD.column_name, where column_name is a valid column in the table on which the ROW trigger is fired.

In the example of the ai_org_trig trigger, the new value of the hrc_code column being inserted is referenced in its trigger body as :NEW.hrc_code.

The REFERENCING clause allows you to reference the columns in row currently being modified by using custom names instead of :NEW and :OLD. Here's the syntax:

```
[REFERENCING [OLD AS custom_name_for_old] [NEW AS custom_name_for_new]]
```

where custom_name_for_old and custom_name_for_new are the custom defined names for :OLD and :NEW, respectively.

TIP *You should reference NEW and OLD with a colon (:) inside the trigger body. Even if you use custom names, you should still reference them with the colon.*

TIP *You can use NEW and OLD in both BEFORE and AFTER ROW triggers.*

TIP *You can use the REFERENCING clause only for ROW-level triggers. If you use the REFERENCING clause in STATEMENT-level triggers, a compilation error occurs.*

Here's the example of the ai_org_trig ROW-level trigger with a REFERENCING clause added to it:

```
CREATE OR REPLACE TRIGGER ai_org_trig
AFTER INSERT ON org_tab
REFERENCING NEW AS new_org
FOR EACH ROW
BEGIN
        UPDATE sec_hrc_audit
          SET num_rows = num_rows+1
          WHERE hrc_code = :new_org.hrc_code;
        IF (SQL%NOTFOUND) THEN
          INSERT INTO sec_hrc_audit VALUES (:new_org.hrc_code, 1);
        END IF;
END;
/
```

Notice that :new_org is used instead of :NEW.

The values of :OLD and :NEW are different for INSERT, UPDATE, and DELETE triggering events. In the case of the INSERT statement, only :NEW is defined. For UPDATE, both :OLD and :NEW are available. And in the case of

DELETE, only :OLD is defined. Referencing values with :OLD.column_name
or :NEW.column_name in cases where :OLD and :NEW are undefined results in
null values.

WHEN Clause

The WHEN clause specifies any WHERE condition to be specified for the execution of the trigger body. This WHERE condition applies to the rows currently
being affected by the triggering event. If the condition evaluates to TRUE for
a row, the trigger body is executed. Here's the syntax:

```
WHEN trigger_restriction
```

where trigger_restriction is a condition that evaluates to a BOOLEAN value,
either TRUE or FALSE.

Here's an example of a trigger defined with a WHEN clause:

```
CREATE OR REPLACE TRIGGER ai_org_trig
AFTER INSERT ON org_tab
REFERENCING NEW AS new_org
FOR EACH ROW
WHEN (new_org.hrc_code <> 1)
BEGIN
        UPDATE sec_hrc_audit
          SET num_rows = num_rows+1
          WHERE hrc_code = :new_org.hrc_code;
        IF (SQL%NOTFOUND) THEN
          INSERT INTO sec_hrc_audit VALUES (:new_org.hrc_code, 1);
        END IF;
END;
/
```

The following points are worth noting:

- The WHEN clause follows the FOR EACH ROW clause.

- The colon (:) isn't used when referencing OLD and NEW in the WHEN
  clause.

- This trigger doesn't fire while inserting an org record with hrc_code
  equal to 1.

TIP *The WHEN clause is only valid for ROW-level triggers.*

TIP *The triggering statement isn't rolled back if the condition in the WHEN clause evaluates to FALSE.*

Multiple Triggering Events in a Single DML Trigger

As mentioned earlier, you can specify multiple DML operations for the triggering event by separating them with the OR keyword. To distinguish between the three operations, PL/SQL provides trigger predicates. PL/SQL defines three predicates called INSERTING, UPDATING, and DELETING to account for INSERT, UPDATE, and DELETE operations, respectively. You use these predicates like BOOLEAN conditions in an IF statement in the trigger body. Here's an example:

```
IF INSERTING THEN
  . . .
ELSIF UPDATING THEN
  . . .
ELSIF DELETING THEN
  . . .
END IF;
```

Consider the ai_org_trig trigger mentioned previously. This trigger updates the sec_hrc_audit table whenever a new row is inserted into the org_tab table. But what about when a row is deleted from the orc_tab table? The num_rows column in the sec_hrc_audit table should be decremented in this case. It suffices to write a new trigger with DELETE as the triggering event. However, with the use of trigger predicates, a single trigger can achieve the same functionality for both the INSERT and DELETE operations. Here's the example of ai_org_trig modified in this way:

```
CREATE OR REPLACE TRIGGER ai_org_trig
AFTER INSERT OR DELETE ON org_tab
FOR EACH ROW
BEGIN
```

```
    IF INSERTING THEN
        UPDATE sec_hrc_audit
          SET num_rows = num_rows+1
          WHERE hrc_code = :NEW.hrc_code;
      IF (SQL%NOTFOUND) THEN
          INSERT INTO sec_hrc_audit VALUES (:NEW.hrc_code, 1);
        END IF;
    ELSIF DELETING THEN
        UPDATE sec_hrc_audit
          SET num_rows = num_rows-1
          WHERE hrc_code = :OLD.hrc_code;
    END IF;
END;
/
```

The following points are worth noting:

- A single trigger is defined for two triggering events, INSERT and DELETE.

- Conditional predicates are used to distinguish between INSERT and DELETE operations and separate code is executed for each.

Number and Type of DML Triggers You Can Define on a Single Table

As mentioned earlier, DML triggers can be BEFORE or AFTER and can be at ROW or STATEMENT level. Taking into account these two factors, you can define a total of four DML triggers on a table: Before Statement, Before Row, After Row, and After Statement.

Also, DML triggers can fire when an INSERT, UPDATE, or DELETE statement is issued on the table on which the trigger is defined. Taking this into consideration, a total of 12 possible trigger combinations is available. Table 6-2 summarizes the possible trigger combinations.

Table 6-2. Trigger Combinations

TRIGGER TYPE	DESCRIPTION
BEFORE INSERT (STATEMENT level)	Before writing new rows to the database as a result of an INSERT
BEFORE INSERT (ROW level)	Before writing each row affected by an INSERT, firing once per row
AFTER INSERT (ROW level)	After writing each row affected by an INSERT, firing once per row
AFTER INSERT (STATEMENT level)	After inserting all rows as a result of an INSERT
BEFORE UPDATE (STATEMENT level)	Before modifying rows as a result of an UPDATE
BEFORE UPDATE (ROW level)	Before modifying each row affected by an UPDATE, firing once per row
AFTER UPDATE (ROW level)	After writing each change affected by an UPDATE, firing once per row
AFTER UPDATE (STATEMENT level)	After modifying all rows as a result of an UPDATE
BEFORE DELETE (STATEMENT level)	Before deleting rows as a result of an INSERT
BEFORE DELETE (ROW level)	Before deleting each row affected by a DELETE, firing once per row
AFTER DELETE (ROW level)	After deleting each row affected by a DELETE, firing once per row
AFTER DELETE (STATEMENT level)	After deleting all rows as a result of a DELETE

Although there are 12 possible combinations, you can define multiple triggers of the same type on the same table. (This is possible as of PL/SQL 2.1 onward.) Another important consideration is the order in which triggers fire. The firing order is as follows:

1. Before Statement (fires once per DML statement, no matter how many rows it affects).

2. Before Row (fires once per each row affected by the DML statement).

3. Execute the triggering statement itself.

4. After Row (fires once per each row affected by the DML statement).

5. After Statement (fires once per DML statement, no matter how many rows it affects).

Triggers and Metadata

Like stored subprograms, database triggers are stored in the database in compiled form as p-code. The trigger is stored in two data dictionary views, USER_OBJECTS and ALL_OBJECTS. The source code is stored in USER_TRIGGERS and ALL_TRIGGERS along with the related trigger information such as trigger type, triggering event, table name on which the trigger is defined, referencing names, and status (either enabled or disabled). These views are like SQL VIEWS, but they store metadata about the trigger. The USER_TRIGGERS view stores information about triggers in the current user schema, and the ALL_TRIGGERS view stores information about objects in all schemas so far defined. In the latter case, the OWNER column identifies each schema name. USER_OBJECTS and ALL_OBJECTS store the trigger name, its status, and other information. Here's the structure of these views:

```
SQL> desc user_objects
 Name                                      Null?    Type
 ----------------------------------------- -------- ----------------
 OBJECT_NAME                                        VARCHAR2(128)
 SUBOBJECT_NAME                                     VARCHAR2(30)
 OBJECT_ID                                          NUMBER
 DATA_OBJECT_ID                                     NUMBER
 OBJECT_TYPE                                        VARCHAR2(18)
 CREATED                                            DATE
 LAST_DDL_TIME                                      DATE
 TIMESTAMP                                          VARCHAR2(19)
 STATUS                                             VARCHAR2(7)
 TEMPORARY                                          VARCHAR2(1)
 GENERATED                                          VARCHAR2(1)
 SECONDARY                                          VARCHAR2(1)
SQL> desc all_objects
```

Name	Null?	Type
OWNER	NOT NULL	VARCHAR2(30)
OBJECT_NAME	NOT NULL	VARCHAR2(30)
SUBOBJECT_NAME		VARCHAR2(30)
OBJECT_ID	NOT NULL	NUMBER
DATA_OBJECT_ID		NUMBER
OBJECT_TYPE		VARCHAR2(18)
CREATED	NOT NULL	DATE
LAST_DDL_TIME	NOT NULL	DATE
TIMESTAMP		VARCHAR2(19)
STATUS		VARCHAR2(7)
TEMPORARY		VARCHAR2(1)
GENERATED		VARCHAR2(1)
SECONDARY		VARCHAR2(1)

Of all the columns, OBJECT_NAME, OBJECT_TYPE, and STATUS are of specific importance. OBJECT_NAME stores the name of the trigger, OBJECT_TYPE is TRIGGER, and STATUS is either VALID or INVALID. Querying these two views reveals the metadata (i.e., data about the trigger). Here's an example for the ai_org_trig trigger created earlier:

```
SQL> select * from user_objects where object_name = 'AI_ORG_TRIG';

OBJECT_NAME
------------------------------------------
SUBOBJECT_NAME                OBJECT_ID DATA_OBJECT_ID OBJECT_TYPE
-------------- ---- -------- ---------
CREATED    LAST_DDL_ TIMESTAMP            STATUS  T G S
----- ---- --------- ----- - - -
AI_ORG_TRIG
                              32367                       TRIGGER
21-APR-02 21-APR-02 2002-04-21:21:29:25 VALID    N N N
```

Also, the source along with related trigger information is stored in USER_TRIGGERS and ALL_TRIGGERS. Here's the structure of these two views:

```
SQL> desc user_triggers
```

Name	Null?	Type
TRIGGER_NAME		VARCHAR2(30)
TRIGGER_TYPE		VARCHAR2(16)
TRIGGERING_EVENT		VARCHAR2(227)

```
TABLE_OWNER                                 VARCHAR2(30)
BASE_OBJECT_TYPE                            VARCHAR2(16)
TABLE_NAME                                  VARCHAR2(30)
COLUMN_NAME                                 VARCHAR2(4000)
REFERENCING_NAMES                           VARCHAR2(128)
WHEN_CLAUSE                                 VARCHAR2(4000)
STATUS                                      VARCHAR2(8)
DESCRIPTION                                 VARCHAR2(4000)
ACTION_TYPE                                 VARCHAR2(11)
TRIGGER_BODY                                LONG
```

```
SQL> desc all_triggers
 Name                                    Null?    Type
 --------------------------------------- -------- ----------------
 OWNER                                             VARCHAR2(30)
 TRIGGER_NAME                                      VARCHAR2(30)
 TRIGGER_TYPE                                      VARCHAR2(16)
 TRIGGERING_EVENT                                  VARCHAR2(227)
 TABLE_OWNER                                       VARCHAR2(30)
 BASE_OBJECT_TYPE                                  VARCHAR2(16)
 TABLE_NAME                                        VARCHAR2(30)
 COLUMN_NAME                                       VARCHAR2(4000)
 REFERENCING_NAMES                                 VARCHAR2(128)
 WHEN_CLAUSE                                       VARCHAR2(4000)
 STATUS                                            VARCHAR2(8)
 DESCRIPTION                                       VARCHAR2(4000)
 ACTION_TYPE                                       VARCHAR2(11)
 TRIGGER_BODY                                      LONG
```

Here's a query to obtain all trigger information for triggers defined on the org_tab table:

```
select trigger_name, trigger_type, triggering_event,
          table_name, referencing_names, status
from user_triggers
where table_name = 'ORG_TAB'
```

Here's the output of this query:

```
TRIGGER_NAME                          TRIGGER_TYPE
----------------------------------- ----------------
TRIGGERING_EVENT
-------------------------------------------------
```

```
TABLE_NAME
----------------
REFERENCING_NAMES
--------------------------------------------------
STATUS
-----
AI_ORG_TRIG                   AFTER EACH ROW
INSERT OR DELETE
ORG_TAB
REFERENCING NEW AS NEW OLD AS OLD
ENABLED

AI_ORG_TRIG_STATEMENT         AFTER STATEMENT
INSERT
ORG_TAB
REFERENCING NEW AS NEW OLD AS OLD
ENABLED
```

You can obtain the trigger body of ai_org_trig by querying the
TRIGGER_BODY column of these views. It's a long column, and in environments
such as SQL*Plus, you should set the length of a long column using a command
as follows:

```
SQL> set long 20000;
```

Here's an example for the ai_org_trig trigger created earlier:

```
SQL> select trigger_body from user_triggers where trigger_name = 'AI_ORG_TRIG';

TRIGGER_BODY
-------------------------------------------------------
BEGIN
    IF INSERTING THEN
        UPDATE sec_hrc_audit
          SET num_rows = num_rows+1
          WHERE hrc_code = :NEW.hrc_code;
      IF (SQL%NOTFOUND) THEN
          INSERT INTO sec_hrc_audit VALUES (:NEW.hrc_code, 1);
        END IF;
    ELSIF DELETING THEN
        UPDATE sec_hrc_audit
          SET num_rows = num_rows-1
          WHERE hrc_code = :OLD.hrc_code;
    END IF;
END;
```

Other Trigger Concepts

In this section, I discuss the features to enable and disable triggers, the privileges required to create triggers, the method of compiling triggers, and the restrictions on creating triggers.

Enabling and Disabling Triggers

A trigger is enabled by default, provided any condition specified in the trigger is met. A disabled trigger, however, doesn't fire on the execution of the triggering statement even if the trigger condition evaluates to TRUE. One example of disabling a trigger is when you're loading large amounts of data from external sources. You disable the triggers on a particular table, and after the data loading you enable them again.

You enable or disable triggers using the ALTER TRIGGER statement. Here's the syntax:

```
ALTER TRIGGER trigger_name ENABLE|DISABLE|COMPILE;
```

where trigger_name is the name of the trigger being enabled or disabled. I explain the COMPILE option in the section "Method of Compiling Triggers" later in this chapter. Here's an example:

```
ALTER TRIGGER ai_org_trig DISABLE;
```

It's also possible to enable or disable all triggers on a particular table. You do this with the ALTER TABLE statement. Here's the syntax:

```
ALTER TABLE table_name ENABLE| DISABLE ALL TRIGGERS;
```

Here's an example:

```
ALTER TABLE org_tab DISABLE ALL TRIGGERS;
```

The STATUS column in the USER_TRIGGERS and ALL_TRIGGERS views indicates whether a trigger is enabled or disabled.

In addition to enabling and disabling triggers, you can drop a trigger on a particular table. This is similar to dropping subprograms. When a trigger is dropped, it no longer exists and its references are removed from the corresponding data dictionary views. Here's the syntax:

```
DROP TRIGGER trigger_name;
```

Privileges Required to Create Triggers

To create a trigger in the current schema, you should grant the CREATE TRIGGER privilege to the owner. To create a trigger in any schema, you should grant the CREATE ANY TRIGGER privilege. This enables creation of a trigger in any schema and on any table in that schema. To alter a trigger in any schema for enabling, disabling, or compiling triggers, you should grant the ALTER ANY TRIGGER privilege. To drop a trigger in any schema, you should grant the DROP ANY TRIGGER privilege. For creating system triggers at the database level, in addition to the CREATE TRIGGER or CREATE ANY TRIGGER privilege, you must grant the ADMINISTER DATABASE TRIGGER privilege.

You must grant all trigger privileges explicitly and not via a role. CREATE ANY TRIGGER, ALTER ANY TRIGGER, and DROP ANY TRIGGER work on schemas other than SYS. You must grant all referenced objects the appropriate privileges. The statements in the trigger body are executed under the privileges of the trigger's owner, not under the privileges of the user issuing the triggering statement.

Method of Compiling Triggers

A trigger is compiled when it's first created. Compiling a trigger involves resolving syntax and semantic references and p-code generation. A trigger with compilation errors is still created, but at runtime the triggering statement fails. However, its state may be invalidated if any of its dependent objects is altered. In this case, it's necessary to recompile the trigger. You can recompile a trigger in two ways:

1. *Automatically:* You do this when a trigger that's invalidated due to dependencies is invoked the next time.

2. *Declaratively:* You do this using the ALTER TRIGGER statement. Here's the syntax:

```
ALTER TRIGGER trigger_name COMPILE;
```

Restrictions on Using Triggers

You have several restrictions on using triggers, such as the maximum size of the trigger body and the type of DML and DCL statements you can use. You also have restrictions relating to mutating and constraining tables. Here's the list of restrictions:

- A trigger can't exceed 32KB in size.

- You can't use DDL statements. In the case of DML, you can use only INSERT, UPDATE, DELETE, and SELECT . . . INTO or a cursor SELECT. You can't use COMMIT, ROLLBACK, and SAVEPOINT.

- You can't declare variables of LONG and LONG RAW. Also, you can't use :NEW and :OLD on LONG or LONG RAW columns of the triggering table.

- LOB columns can be read only inside the body of a trigger. This means you can't assign the :NEW.lob_column a value inside the trigger body.

Mutating table restrictions pertain to what tables and columns a trigger body can access. A table is called *mutating* if it's currently being modified by a trigger or an INSERT, UPDATE, or DELETE statement. Also, a table that gets modified as a result of a DELETE CASCADE referential integrity constraint is also considered mutating. A *constraining* table is a table that's specified in the REFERENCES clause of the foreign key constraint definition. The concept of mutating tables applies to ROW-level triggers, with the exception that a STATEMENT trigger fired as a result of the DELETE CASCADE effect is considered mutating. There are two restrictions on mutating and constraint tables of a trigger: The trigger body can't read from (query) or modify a mutating table of the triggering statement and the trigger body can't read from or modify the primary, unique, or foreign key columns of a constraint table of the triggering table. Other columns may be modified.

In the case of mutating tables, the trigger does fire, but the trigger body isn't executed and control transfers out of the trigger with the following error:

```
ORA-04901: table schema_name.table_name is mutating, trigger/function
                    may not see it
```

This error is raised during trigger execution and not during trigger creation and compilation.

- The only case in which a ROW-level trigger can read from or modify the triggering table is when the triggering statement is an INSERT statement that affects only one row. INSERT . . . SELECT is not allowed, even if it affects only one row.

To avoid mutating errors, create a ROW-level trigger that reads the new values of the current row and then a STATEMENT trigger that queries or modifies the mutating table based on the new row value read. This requires a PL/SQL package to store the new values read from the ROW trigger. This is one way to handle mutating errors. An alternative method to handling mutating tables involves errors using autonomous transactions. However, you should use this method carefully. The perfect scenario for using autonomous transactions to avoid mutating table errors is when the logic of the trigger is not affected by the fact that changes made to the triggering table (i.e., the main transaction) aren't visible to the autonomous transaction until the main transaction is committed. Mutating table errors are very unlikely in normal situations, but you should take care to avoid them if possible.

 CROSS-REFERENCE *Chapter 8 covers autonomous transactions in detail.*

Read-Only Views, Updateable Views, and INSTEAD-OF Triggers

Views are logical windows of tables, either relational or object. A *relational view* can be based on a single base table or it can involve multiple tables. An *object view* is based on one or more object tables or tables having object columns, and it involves the use of object types. The primary purpose of a view is to SELECT information, hence it's read-only. Here are the conditions under which a view is updateable:

- No joins

- No SET operators

- No aggregate functions

- No GROUP BY, CONNECT BY, or START WITH clauses

- No DISTINCT operator

- No pseudo-columns or expressions

If the view meets these conditions, Oracle DML statements can be issued on the view and modifications are done to the underlying base tables of the view. Now what about DML operations on views that aren't directly modifiable? The answer is INSTEAD-OF triggers.

Even if a view satisfies the conditions in the preceding list and hence is directly modifiable, you can define INSTEAD-OF triggers on it to specify additional modification criteria such as validations on values being inserted, updated, or deleted. In this case, the trigger body validates the rows being modified and reflects the changes in the underlying tables.

Defining INSTEAD-OF Triggers

An INSTEAD-OF trigger is a trigger defined on a view (relational or object) that allows DML operations on the underlying base tables. A triggering statement on a view executes the code of the corresponding INSTEAD-OF trigger instead of the triggering statement. What the code does is trigger-specific depending on the application and the behavior of the INSERT, UPDATE, and DELETE operations defined in the INSTEAD-OF trigger body.

You can also define INSTEAD-OF triggers using the CREATE OR REPLACE TRIGGER statement. Here's the syntax:

```
CREATE [OR REPLACE] TRIGGER trigger_name
INSTEAD OF triggering_event [OF column_name] ON view_name
[referencing_clause]
[FOR EACH ROW]
trigger_body ;
```

where trigger_name is the name of the INSTEAD-OF trigger being created; triggering_event is one or a combination of INSERT, UPDATE, and/or DELETE; and view_name is the view on which the INSERT, UPDATE, and/or DELETE is being executed. The [OF column_name] clause is to specify the column_name being updated in the case of an UPDATE operation as the triggering event. INSTEAD-OF specifies that the trigger body should be executed instead of the DML statement corresponding to the triggering event. trigger_body is the sequence of actions to be performed when the INSTEAD-OF trigger is fired. referencing_clause specifies how the correlation identifiers OLD and NEW should be referenced inside the trigger body.

First, create the view hrc_org_site as follows:

```
CREATE VIEW hrc_org_site
AS
SELECT h.hrc_code, hrc_descr,
```

```
                o.org_id, org_short_name, org_long_name,
                    os.site_no, site_descr
FROM      org_site_tab os, org_tab o, hrc_tab h, site_tab s
WHERE   os.org_id = o.org_id
        AND o.hrc_code = h.hrc_code
        AND os.site_no = s.site_no;
```

Next, create an INSTEAD-OF trigger on this view. Here's the code:

```
CREATE OR REPLACE TRIGGER hrc_org_site_trig
INSTEAD OF INSERT OR UPDATE OR DELETE on hrc_org_site
FOR EACH ROW
BEGIN
    IF INSERTING THEN
        INSERT INTO hrc_tab VALUES (:NEW.hrc_code, :NEW.hrc_descr);
        INSERT INTO org_tab VALUES (:NEW.hrc_code, :NEW.org_id,
                                    :NEW.org_short_name,
                                    :NEW.org_long_name);
        INSERT INTO org_site_tab VALUES (:NEW.org_id, :NEW.site_no);
    ELSIF UPDATING THEN
      IF (:NEW.hrc_descr != :OLD.hrc_descr) THEN
        UPDATE hrc_tab
        SET          hrc_descr = :NEW.hrc_descr
        WHERE   hrc_code =  :OLD.hrc_code;
      END IF;
IF (:NEW.org_short_name != :OLD.org_short_name) THEN
        UPDATE org_tab
        SET           org_short_name = :NEW.org_short_name
        WHERE   hrc_code =  :OLD.hrc_code
                AND org_id = :OLD.org_id;
ELSIF (:NEW.org_long_name != :OLD.org_long_name) THEN
        UPDATE org_tab
        SET           org_long_name = :NEW.org_long_name
        WHERE   hrc_code =  :OLD.hrc_code
                AND org_id = :OLD.org_id;
      END IF;
      UPDATE org_site_tab
      SET        site_no = :NEW.site_no
      WHERE org_id = :NEW.org_id;
      IF (SQL%NOTFOUND) THEN
          INSERT INTO org_site_tab VALUES (:NEW.org_id, :NEW.site_no);
      END IF;
```

```
    ELSIF DELETING THEN
        DELETE org_site_tab WHERE org_id = :OLD.org_id;
        DELETE org_level WHERE org_id = :OLD.org_id;
        DELETE org_tab WHERE hrc_code = :OLD.hrc_code
                        AND org_id = :OLD.org_id;
    END IF;
    EXCEPTION WHEN OTHERS THEN
        RAISE_APPLICATION_ERROR(-20010, 'ERR occurred in trigger hrc_org_site_trig '||
                                SQLERRM);
    END;
    /
```

The following points are worth noting:

- This trigger defines the behavior of INSERT, UPDATE, and DELETE operations on the join view hrc_org_site.

- An INSERT on the view inserts into hrc_tab, org_tab, and org_site_tab in this order.

- An UPDATE on the view updates the hrc_descr column of the hrc_tab table or the org_short_name and org_long_name columns of the org_tab table. However, it updates the site_no column of the org_site_tab table if a row already exists for the org_id; otherwise, it inserts a new row into the org_site_tab table.

- A DELETE on the view deletes the corresponding rows from the org_site_tab, org_level, and org_tab tables. It leaves the hrc_tab table unchanged.

To test this trigger, issue INSERT, UPDATE, and DELETE statements against the view hrc_org_site. Here's the code:

```
INSERT INTO hrc_org_site VALUES (11, 'ANALYST',1012, 'Office of Analyst',
'Office of Analyst', 4, null);

UPDATE hrc_org_site SET org_short_name = 'Office of Analyst ABC Inc.',
org_long_name = 'Office of Analyst ABC Inc.', site_no = 4
WHERE hrc_code = 11
      AND org_id = 1012;

DELETE hrc_org_site WHERE org_id = 1012;
```

Here's how you can test the output of this code:

```
SQL> SELECT * FROM hrc_tab WHERE hrc_code = 11;

no rows selected

SQL> SELECT * FROM org_tab WHERE org_id = 1012;

no rows selected

SQL> SELECT * FROM org_site_tab WHERE org_id = 1012;

no rows selected

SQL> INSERT INTO hrc_org_site VALUES (11, 'ANALYST',1012, 'Office of Analyst',
  2  'Office of Analyst', 4, null);

1 row created.

SQL> SELECT * FROM hrc_tab WHERE hrc_code = 11;

  HRC_CODE HRC_DESCR
----------- -----------------------
        11 ANALYST

SQL> SELECT * FROM org_tab WHERE org_id = 1012;

  HRC_CODE     ORG_ID ORG_SHORT_NAME
---------- ---------- ----------------------
ORG_LONG_NAME
--------------------------------------
        11       1012 Office of Analyst
Office of Analyst


SQL> SELECT * FROM org_site_tab WHERE org_id = 1012;

    ORG_ID    SITE_NO
--------- -----------
1012            4
```

You can test the code for the UPDATE statement as follows:

```
SQL> UPDATE hrc_org_site SET org_short_name = 'Office of Analyst ABC Inc.',
  2  org_long_name = 'Office of Analyst ABC Inc.', site_no = 4
  3  WHERE hrc_code = 11
  4      AND org_id = 1012;

1 row updated.

SQL> select * from hrc_tab where hrc_code = 11;

  HRC_CODE HRC_DESCR
---------- ----------------------
        11 ANALYST

SQL> select * from org_tab where org_id = 1012;

  HRC_CODE     ORG_ID ORG_SHORT_NAME
---------- ---------- ----------------------
ORG_LONG_NAME
--------------------------------------
        11       1012 Office of Analyst ABC Inc.
Office of Analyst ABC Inc.


SQL> select * from org_site_tab where org_id = 1012;

    ORG_ID    SITE_NO
--------- -----------
      1012          4
```

You can test the output of the DELETE statement as follows:

```
SQL> DELETE hrc_org_site WHERE org_id = 1012;

1 row deleted.

SQL> select * from hrc_tab where hrc_code = 11;

  HRC_CODE HRC_DESCR
--------- -----------
        11 ANALYST
```

```
SQL> select * from org_tab where org_id = 1012;


no rows selected


SQL> select * from org_site_tab where org_id = 1012;


no rows selected
SQL> select * from org_level where org_id = 1012;


no rows selected
```

You can't define the BEFORE and AFTER triggers on views. You can reference :OLD and :NEW only in the body of an INSTEAD-OF trigger. INSTEAD-OF triggers are by default ROW level, and the FOR EACH ROW clause is optional. That is, even if this clause isn't specified, an INSTEAD-OF trigger is ROW level. The DML trigger predicates are still available in INSTEAD-OF triggers. You can't specify the WHEN clause for INSTEAD-OF triggers. If the view is defined with the WITH CHECK option, it isn't enforced when INSTEAD-OF triggers are fired during INSERT or UPDATE. You have to write code inside the trigger body to take care of this. Any triggers defined on the base tables of a view are fired when an INSERT, UPDATE, or DELETE operation is done on the view.

Uses of INSTEAD-OF Triggers

You can use INSTEAD-OF triggers for performing DML in views or nested tables. Here are some of their more common uses:

- To perform DML on views that aren't directly modifiable by INSERT, UPDATE, or DELETE.

- To alter the behavior of INSERT, UPDATE, or DELETE on directly modifiable views.

- To perform data validation on views that are directly modifiable by INSERT, UPDATE, or DELETE.

- To modify nested table columns of a view. Nested tables are a type of collection.

CROSS-REFERENCE   *I discuss nested tables further in*
Chapter 11.

New Database Triggers

Until Oracle 8.0.*x*, the definition of database triggers was limited to only database tables and DML such as INSERT, UPDATE, and DELETE operations. Oracle8*i* has extended the scope of database triggers by lifting these restrictions. Now you can define database triggers independent of tables and independent of DML.

In addition to these triggers, PL/SQL 8*i* onward enables you to create database triggers during system events such as the following:

- Database startup and shutdown

- Logon and logoff from the database

- Server-side error occurrence

It also enables you to create database triggers during user events such as these:

- Session logon and logout

- User events such as DDL execution (i.e., database object creation, alteration, and dropping)

Here's the syntax for creating triggers on system events and user events:

```
CREATE [OR REPLACE] TRIGGER trigger_name
[BEFORE|AFTER] {triggering_event} ON [DATABASE|[schema.]SCHEMA]
[WHEN trigger_restriction]
trigger_body ;
```

where trigger_name is the name of the trigger being created; triggering_event is one or a valid combination of the system_ events STARTUP, SHUTDOWN, SERVERERROR, LOGON, and/or LOGOFF, or one or a valid combination of the user events LOGON and LOGOFF, CREATE, ALTER, and/or DROP. BEFORE or AFTER specifies the time the trigger should fire (i.e., before or after the event occurs). trigger_body is the sequence of actions to be performed when the trigger is fired, and the [WHEN condition] clause specifies any condition that when evaluated to TRUE causes the trigger body to execute. DATABASE or SCHEMA specifies the scope of the trigger (i.e., at the database level) for all schemas or for a specific schema.

System Event and User Event Triggers

Corresponding to each of the previously discussed system events and user events, you can define new database triggers as shown in Tables 6-3 and 6-4.

Table 6-3. System Event Triggers

EVENT NAME	TIMING	DESCRIPTION
STARTUP	AFTER	During database startup. Can only be created at the database level.
SHUTDOWN	BEFORE	During database shutdown (i.e., just before start of an instance shutdown). Can only be created at the database level.
SERVERERROR	AFTER	Once an exception occurs. Can be at the database or schema level.
LOGON	AFTER	After a client application logs onto a database successfully. Can be at the database or schema level.
LOGOFF	BEFORE	Before logging out of a client application, just before start of logoff. Can be at the database or schema level.

Table 6-4. User Event Triggers

EVENT NAME	TIMING	DESCRIPTION
LOGON	AFTER	After logging into a session. Can be at the database or schema level.
LOGOFF	BEFORE	Before logging out of a session, just before the start of user logoff. Can be at the database or schema level.
SERVERERROR	AFTER	In response to a server error. Can be at the database or schema level.
CREATE	BEFORE AND AFTER	Whenever a new database object is created. It can be created at the schema level or for an entire database.
ALTER	BEFORE and AFTER	Before or after a database object is altered. It can be created at the schema or database level.
DROP	BEFORE and AFTER	Before or after a database object is dropped. It can be created at the schema level or for an entire database.

TIP   *There's no concept of ROW level or STATEMENT level for these triggers. However, you can define the CREATE, ALTER, and DROP triggers either at the schema level or for an entire database.*

Trigger Attributes

Like the :NEW and :OLD attributes available on DML BEFORE and AFTER ROW triggers, there are attributes associated with the previously described system and user events. You can use these attributes in the previously mentioned SYSTEM or USER EVENT INITIATED triggers.

TIP *Use these trigger attributes by prefixing them with "SYS." just like user-defined functions. These attributes are available as functions.*

TIP *Run the CATPROC.SQL script to make these attributes available.*

Attributes for Database-Level Events

Table 6-5 summarizes the event attributes for use with system and user event triggers.

Table 6-5. Attributes for Database-Level Events

ATTRIBUTE	TYPE	DESCRIPTION
Sys.sysevent	VARCHAR2(20)	System event firing the trigger. The event name refers to one of the system events.
Sys.instance_num	NUMBER	Instance number.
Sys.database_name	VARCHAR2(50)	Database name.
Sys.server_error	NUMBER	Returns the error number at a given position on error stack:@@@1 – Top of the stack.
Sys.is_servererror	BOOLEAN	Returns TRUE if given error is on error stack; otherwise, it returns FALSE.
Sys.login_user	VARCHAR2(30)	Login user name.

Attributes for User-Level Events

Attributes for schema-level or user-level events include those listed in Table 6-5 in addition to those listed in Table 6-6.

Table 6-6. Attributes for User-Level Events

ATTRIBUTE	TYPE	DESCRIPTION
Sys.dictionary_obj_Type	. VARCHAR(20)	Type of the dictionary object on which the DDL operation occurred
Sys.dictionary_obj_Name	VARCHAR(30)	Name of the dictionary object on which the DDL operation occurred
Sys.dictionary_obj_Owner	VARCHAR(30)	Owner of the dictionary object on which the DDL operation occurred
Sys.des_encrypted_Password	VARCHAR(2)	The DES encrypted password of the user being created or altered

List of Events

Events can be either system events or user events. In this section, I first discuss system events and then I cover user events.

System Events

System events are related to instance startup and shutdown and server-error message events. Table 6-7 summarizes the various system events and the attributes you can specify for each.

Table 6-7. System Events and Their Attributes

EVENT	ATTRIBUTES
STARTUP	Sys.Sysevent Sys.login_user Sys.Instance_num Sys.Database_name
SHUTDOWN	Sys.sysevent Sys.login_user Sys.instance_num Sys.database_name
SERVERERROR	Sys.sysevent Sys.login_user Sys.instance_num Sys.database_name Sys.server_error Sys.is_servererror

Here's an example of a SHUTDOWN system event trigger. As an illustration of a system event trigger, create a BEFORE SHUTDOWN trigger to alert all logged-on users:

```
CREATE OR REPLACE TRIGGER ON_SHUTDOWN
BEFORE SHUTDOWN
ON DATABASE
```

```
BEGIN
   <Send a database alert to all logged on users using Advanced Queuing>
END;
/
```

You can implement the preceding method using Event Publishing to all subscribed users. You do this using Advanced Queuing.

TIP *Triggers created on the system events STARTUP and SHUTDOWN should be ON DATABASE level.*

TIP *When you define LOGON, STARTUP, and SERVERERROR triggers, you can specify only AFTER context.*

TIP *When you define LOGOFF and SHUTDOWN triggers, you can specify only BEFORE context.*

TIP *Database-level event triggers trigger an autonomous transaction, committing any DML in the trigger logic independent of the current main transaction.*

User Events

User events are the events associated with user or session logon and logoff, response to a server error, and DDL and DML operations.

Table 6-8 summarizes the various user events and the attributes that you can specify for each.

Table 6-8. User Events and Their Attributes

EVENT	ATTRIBUTES
LOGON	Sys.sysevent Sys.login_user Sys.instance_num Sys.database_name
LOGOFF	Sys.sysevent Sys.login_user Sys.instance_num Sys.database_name
BEFORE CREATE AFTER CREATE	Sys.sysevent Sys.login_user Sys.instance_num Sys.Database_name Sys.Dictionary_obj_type Sys.Dictionary_obj_name Sys.Dictionary_obj_owner
BEFORE ALTER AFTER ALTER	Sys.Sysevent Sys.Login_user Sys.Instance_num Sys.database_name Sys.dictionary_obj_type Sys.dictionary_obj_name Sys.dictionary_obj_owner
BEFORE DROP AFTER DROP	Sys.Sysevent Sys.Login_user Sys.Instance_num Sys.Database_name Sys.dictionary_obj_type Sys.Dictionary_obj_name Sys.Dictionary_obj_owner

Here's an example of a LOGON user event trigger. You can use an AFTER LOGON trigger to analyze all objects in the logged-on schema for estimating statistics.

```
CREATE OR REPLACE TRIGGER On_Logon
AFTER LOGON
ON SCHEMA
BEGIN
  DBMS_UTILITY.ANALYZE_SCHEMA(sys.login_user, 'ESTIMATE');
END;
/
```

You can do DDL auditing using AFTER CREATE, ALTER, and DROP triggers, in the same way as you did DML auditing in the AFTER ROW INSERT, UPDATE, and DELETE triggers. Assume a DDL_audit table as follows:

```
CREATE TABLE DDL_AUDIT
(object_name VARCHAR2(30) NOT NULL,
 Object_type VARCHAR2(30) NOT NULL,
 WHEN_CREATED DATE NOT NULL,
 WHO_CREATED VARCHAR2(30) NOT  NULL,
 WHEN_UPDATED DATE,
 WHO_UPDATED VARCHAR2(30) );
```

You can create an AFTER CREATE trigger as follows and populate this audit table whenever a database object is created in the current schema the user has logged into. Here's the code:

```
CREATE OR REPLACE TRIGGER after_ddl_creation
AFTER CREATE ON SCHEMA
BEGIN
  INSERT INTO ddl_audit VALUES
  (SYS.DICTIONARY_OBJ_NAME, SYS.DICTIONARY_OBJ_TYPE, SYSDATE, USER, NULL, NULL);
END;
/
```

Next, create a dummy procedure to test the automatic execution of this trigger. Here's the code for the procedure:

```
CREATE OR REPLACE PROCEDURE p_dummy
IS
BEGIN
  NULL;
END;
/
```

To test the results, query the ddl_audit table as follows:

```
SELECT * FROM ddl_audit;
```

Here's the output of this query:

```
SQL> SELECT * FROM ddl_audit;

OBJECT_NAME                      OBJECT_TYPE                      WHEN_CREA
-------------------------------- -------------------------------- ----------
WHO_CREATED                      WHEN_UPDA WHO_UPDATED
-------------------------------- -------------------------------- ----------
P_DUMMY                          PROCEDURE                        21-APR-02
PLSQL9I
```

TIP *When the trigger is defined at the database and schema levels, such as SERVERERROR, the schema-level trigger will fire before the database-level trigger, but both will fire.*

TIP   *All of the DLL triggers operate in the context of the current transaction.*

TIP   *When you define BEFORE and/or AFTER CREATE and ALTER triggers, you can't drop the object you're creating inside the body of the trigger. In the case of the corresponding DROP triggers, the object you're dropping can't be altered inside the body of the trigger.*

Summary

In this chapter, I discussed database triggers. I started with the definition and types of triggers, and moved on to deal with the inherent concepts involved in each type of trigger along with the trigger restrictions. In the next chapter I discuss native dynamic SQL and dynamic PL/SQL.

Native Dynamic SQL and Dynamic PL/SQL

ORACLE SUPPORTS TWO types of SQL: static SQL and dynamic SQL. In *static SQL*, the
_____own at compile time and syntax and semantic refer-
_____npile time. In *dynamic SQL*, the SQL statements are
_____d executed dynamically at runtime. This is true for
_____*amic SQL* is an implementation of dynamic SQL and
_____ntegrated into PL/SQL.
_____mic SQL and dynamic PL/SQL using DBMS_SQL was a lot
_____a lot of code and effort. Oracle8*i* introduced native
_____, which provides the following advantages over

_____oding.

_____er in terms of efficiency and execution.

_____r objects.

_____d the native dynamic SQL features by adding the following:

_____for bulk dynamic SQL, the ability to process multiple rows
_____le DML statement. Prior to Oracle9*i*, native dynamic SQL
_____SQL indirectly, if the bulk SQL statement was enclosed
_____ . . . END.

- Multirow updates and deletes with a RETURNING clause using dynamic
SQL. Prior to Oracle9*i*, native dynamic SQL supported a RETURNING
clause only in the case of a single-row output.

This chapter explores the capabilities of PL/SQL in the area of native dynamic SQL and provides techniques for performing the following:

- Dynamic DDL

- Dynamic SELECTS

- Dynamic INSERT, UPDATE, and DELETE

- Dynamic PL/SQL

- Exception handling

- DDL and DML with objects

Chapter 9 covers the new features introduced in Oracle9*i*. This chapter starts by explaining the benefits of native dynamic SQL over DBMS_SQL.

I shall use the tables region_tab, supplier_tab, order_tab, and order_items tab for demonstrating native dynamic SQL. Also, I create individual tables with dynamically constructed names such as ORDERS_FOR_<region_name> and ORDER_ITEMS_FOR_<region_name> based on the structure of the ORDER_TAB and ORDER_ITEMS tables.

DBMS_SQL vs. Native Dynamic SQL

Although you can use DBMS_SQL to perform dynamic SQL and dynamic PL/SQL, native dynamic SQL is better suited to performing DML, DDL, PL/SQL, and transaction and session control statements for the following reasons:

- Native dynamic SQL enables you to place dynamic SQL statements and dynamic PL/SQL blocks directly into PL/SQL code, without the use of an API. This is similar to static SQL, and it's much easier in native dynamic SQL than in DBMS_SQL in terms of coding.

- The "native" in native dynamic SQL refers to the built-in support for dynamic SQL inside the PL/SQL interpreter. Native dynamic SQL is also integrated with SQL, so its performance is on par with static SQL's. There is no API involved, thus the high costs involved in procedure call and data copying when using DBMS_SQL are minimized.

- Native dynamic SQL supports the full range of object extensibility features, such as user-defined types and objects including collections and REFs, within PL/SQL. These features aren't supported by the DBMS_SQL package.

- Native dynamic SQL, like static SQL, supports fetching into records of type %ROWTYPE or as defined by the TYPE . . . IS RECORD . . . statement.

So what use is DBMS_SQL then?

- DBMS_SQL is well suited to performing dynamic SQL and PL/SQL from client-side applications such as Oracle Developer.

- The maximum length of the dynamic SQL statement is limited to 32KB. Statements larger than this can be handled only by the DBMS_SQL package.

- DBMS_SQL is good when the same SQL statement is executed multiple times in the same session as it reuses the parsed SQL statement. Native dynamic SQL prepares the SQL statement each time it is processed.

Here's an example of the code involved in creating a table whose name is dynamically constructed using native dynamic SQL and DBMS_SQL:

```
/* Native Dynamic SQL */
DECLARE
  dyn_tab_name VARCHAR2(30) := 'temp';
  dyn_string VARCHAR2(150);
BEGIN
 dyn_string := 'create table '||dyn_tab_name||' ( col1 NUMBER NOT NULL) ';
 EXECUTE IMMEDIATE dyn_string;
END;
/
```

You can verify the output of this PL/SQL block as follows:

```
SQL> desc temp
 Name                                      Null?    Type
 ----------------------------------------- -------- ----------------------
 COL1                                      NOT NULL NUMBER
```

Using native dynamic SQL involves just two steps:

1. Construct the dynamic SQL statement in the form of string.

2. Execute the SQL statement.

```
drop table temp;
-- DBMS_SQL
DECLARE
  dyn_tab_name VARCHAR2(30) := 'temp';
  dyn_string VARCHAR2(150);
  c INTEGER;
  ret_code INTEGER;
BEGIN
 dyn_string := 'create table '||dyn_tab_name||
                                    ' ( col1 NUMBER NOT NULL) ';
 c := DBMS_SQL.OPEN_CURSOR;
 DBMS_SQL.PARSE(c, dyn_string, DBMS_SQL.V7);
 ret_code := DBMS_SQL.EXECUTE(c);
  DBMS_SQL.CLOSE_CURSOR(c);
END;
/
```

Using DBMS_SQL involves five steps:

1. Construct the dynamic SQL statement in the form of string.

2. Declare a cursor handle and open a cursor for the handle.

3. Parse the dynamically constructed SQL statement and associate the SQL statement with the cursor handle.

4. Execute the SQL statement.

5. Close the cursor handle.

As you can see, it's much easier to code with native dynamic SQL than with DBMS_SQL. Also, depending on the type of SQL statement, DBMS_SQL involves more steps than native dynamic SQL. For example, to use bind variables, an extra step of explicitly binding the variables to the values is required in DBMS_SQL.

Also, in the case of SELECT statements with DBMS_SQL, two extra steps of defining the columns in the SELECT and retrieving values from the dynamic SQL into local PL/SQL variables are required in addition to the execute and FETCH steps.

Native Dynamic SQL Statements

The native dynamic SQL statements pertaining to dynamic DDL, DML, and session control are as follows:

1. EXECUTE IMMEDIATE <dyn_string>;
2. EXECUTE IMMEDIATE <dyn_string> USING <plsql_variables_list_comma_separated>;
3. EXECUTE IMMEDIATE <dyn_string> INTO <plsql_variables_list_comma_separated>
        USING <bind_variables_list_comma_separated>;
4. OPEN <cursor> FOR <dyn_query_string>;
5. OPEN <cursor> FOR <dyn_query_string>
USING <plsql_variables_list_comma_separated>;
6. FETCH <cursor> INTO <plsql_variables_list_comma_separated_or_PL/SQL_record>;
7. CLOSE <cursor>;
8. EXECUTE IMMEDIATE 'BEGIN. . . . END;' USING <plsql_variables_list_comma_separated>;

The first two statements are used for dynamic DDL. The third statement is used for single-row dynamic SELECTS. The fourth through seventh statements are used for multirow dynamic SELECTS. The last statement is used for dynamic PL/SQL.

The whole string including BEGIN and END is constructed dynamically by concatenation. The EXECUTE IMMEDIATE statement prepares, executes, and deallocates a dynamic SQL statement. The OPEN statement extends the OPEN cursor statements for opening cursors based on a dynamic SQL query constructed as a string. The FETCH and CLOSE statements extend the FETCH and CLOSE cursor statements to support dynamic queries. The last statement enables dynamic PL/SQL (i.e., executing procedures and functions whose names are constructed at runtime or anonymous PL/SQL blocks involving runtime variables).

Native dynamic SQL supports SQL-specific data types. However, it doesn't support PL/SQL-specific data types such as BOOLEAN, index-by tables, and user-defined records. The only exception to this rule is fetching into user-defined records while executing dynamic single-row and multirow queries.

Dynamic DDL

Dynamic DDL involves using any of the DDL statements with values for database objects provided at runtime. This eliminates the need for compile time semantics. A typical usage of dynamic DDL might be to create a table where the table and/or column names are available at runtime.

The statements

```
EXECUTE IMMEDIATE <dyn_string>;
EXECUTE IMMEDIATE <dyn_string> USING <plsql_variables_list_comma_separated>;
```

are used to execute dynamic DLL statements.

The requirement is to create one orders_for_<region> table for each region that stores the order information for that region. This is done in three steps:

1. The procedure create_dyn_table creates the individual orders_for_<region> table using native dynamic SQL.

2. The procedure create_dyn_table2 creates the individual order_items_for_<region> table using native dynamic SQL.

3. The procedure create_dyn_for_all calls these two procedures for each region in region_tab.

Here's the code for these procedures:

```
Create or replace Procedure create_dyn_table
                          (i_region_name VARCHAR2,
                           retcd OUT NUMBER,
                           errmsg OUT VARCHAR2)
authid current_user
Is
  Dyn_string VARCHAR2(1000);
  Dyn_Table_name VARCHAR2(30);
Begin
  Dyn_table_name := 'ORDERS_FOR_'||replace(trim(i_region_name),' ','_');
  Dyn_string := ' CREATE TABLE ' ||dyn_table_name||
' (order_id NUMBER(10) PRIMARY KEY,
   order_date DATE     NOT NULL,
   total_qty  NUMBER,
   total_price NUMBER(15,2) ,
   supp_id  NUMBER(6) REFERENCES supplier_tab(supp_id)) ';
```

```
    EXECUTE IMMEDIATE dyn_string ;

    retcd := 0;

EXCEPTION WHEN OTHERS THEN
    retcd := SQLCODE;
    errmsg := 'ERR: Creating table '||dyn_table_name ||' - '||SQLERRM;
End;
/
```

This procedure does the following:

- Creates a dynamic table name concatenating the input region name with the constant ORDERS_FOR_ and places it in a PL/SQL variable named dyn_table_name. This is for the orders table for each region.

- Creates a dynamically generated CREATE TABLE statement using the dyn_table_name variable and places it in a PL/SQL variable named dyn_string. The table structure is the same as that of the ORDER_TAB table.

- Executes this dynamic string using the EXECUTE IMMEDIATE statement.

- Outputs a return code of 0 on success in the form of an OUT parameter named retcd. On error it outputs the corresponding SQLCODE and SQLERRM in the form of two OUT parameters, retcd and errmsg.

Next, here's the code for the create_dyn_table2 procedure:

```
Create or replace Procedure create_dyn_table2
                          (i_region_name VARCHAR2,
                           retcd OUT NUMBER,
                           errmsg OUT VARCHAR2)
authid current_user
Is
    Dyn_string VARCHAR2(1000);
    Dyn_Table_name VARCHAR2(30);
Begin
    Dyn_table_name := 'ORDER_ITEMS_FOR_'|| replace(trim(i_region_name),' ','_');
    Dyn_string := ' CREATE TABLE ' ||dyn_table_name||
' (order_id NUMBER(10) NOT NULL,
  item_id  VARCHAR2(10) NOT NULL,
  unit_price NUMBER(11,2) NOT NULL,
  quantity    NUMBER) ';
```

```
        EXECUTE IMMEDIATE dyn_string ;

    dyn_string :=
            ' alter table ORDER_ITEMS_FOR_'||i_region_name||' add constraint '||
            'fk_oifor'||i_region_name||' foreign key (order_id) references '||
                ' orders_for_'||i_region_name||'(order_id) ';
    EXECUTE IMMEDIATE dyn_string ;
    retcd := 0;
EXCEPTION WHEN OTHERS THEN
  retcd := SQLCODE;
  errmsg := 'ERR: Creating/Altering table '||dyn_table_name ||' - '||SQLERRM;
End;
/
```

This procedure does the following:

- Creates a dynamic table name concatenating the input region name with the constant ORDER_ITEMS_FOR_ and places it in a PL/SQL variable named dyn_table_name. This process is for the order items table for each region.

- Creates a dynamically generated CREATE TABLE statement using the dyn_table_name variable and places it in a PL/SQL variable named dyn_string. The table structure is the same as that of the ORDER_ITEMS table.

- Executes this dynamic string using the EXECUTE IMMEDIATE statement.

- Creates a second dynamically generated ALTER TABLE statement using the dyn_table_name variable and places it in the same variable dyn_string. This process is for specifying foreign key constraints on the corresponding ORDER_ITEMS_FOR_ table.

- Executes this dynamic string using the EXECUTE IMMEDIATE statement.

- Outputs a return code of 0 on success in the form of an OUT parameter named retcd. On error it outputs the corresponding SQLCODE and SQLERRM in the form of two OUT parameters, retcd and errmsg.

Next, here's the code for the create dyn_for_all procedure:

```
Create or replace Procedure create_dyn_for_all
                               (retcd OUT NUMBER, errmsg OUT VARCHAR2)
Authid current_user
Is
  CURSOR csr_region IS
    SELECT region_name
    FROM   region_tab;
BEGIN
  FOR idx IN csr_region LOOP
    create_dyn_table(idx.region_name, retcd, errmsg);
    IF retcd <> 0 THEN
      EXIT;
    END IF;
    create_dyn_table2(idx.region_name, retcd, errmsg);
    IF retcd <> 0 THEN
      EXIT;
    END IF;
  END LOOP;
EXCEPTION WHEN OTHERS THEN
  Retcd := SQLCODE;
  Errmsg := SQLERRM;
END;
/
```

This procedure does the following:

- Declares a cursor for all the region names in the region_tab table.

- For each row in the cursor, it invokes the create_dyn_table and
  create_dyn_table2 procedures, passing the region name as an IN parameter to both. This creates the ORDERS_FOR_<region> and
  ORDER_ITEMS_FOR_<region> tables, where <region> stands for each
  region name in the region_tab table.

- Outputs a return code of 0 on success in the form of an OUT parameter
  named retcd. On error it outputs the corresponding SQLCODE and
  SQLERRM in the form of two OUT parameters, retcd and errmsg.

Here's the code for executing this procedure:

```
DECLARE
   Retcd NUMBER;
   Errmsg VARCHAR2(32767);
BEGIN
   Create_dyn_for_all(retcd, errmsg);
   IF (retcd <> 0) THEN
      RAISE_APPLICATION_ERROR(-20102, errmsg);
   END IF;
EXCEPTION WHEN OTHERS THEN
   RAISE_APPLICATION_ERROR(-20103, SQLERRM);
END;
/
```

Here's how you verify the output of this PL/SQL block:

```
SQL> column object_name format a30;
SQL> select object_name, object_type from user_objects
  2  where object_name like 'ORDER%FOR%';

OBJECT_NAME                    OBJECT_TYPE
------------------------------ -------------------
ORDERS_FOR_REGION1             TABLE
ORDERS_FOR_REGION2             TABLE
ORDERS_FOR_REGION3             TABLE
ORDERS_FOR_REGION4             TABLE
ORDER_ITEMS_FOR_REGION1        TABLE
ORDER_ITEMS_FOR_REGION2        TABLE
ORDER_ITEMS_FOR_REGION3        TABLE
ORDER_ITEMS_FOR_REGION4        TABLE

8 rows selected.
```

Dynamic SELECTS

Queries may return a single row or multiple rows. In this section, I discuss the techniques for performing single-row and multirow SELECTS with dynamic SQL using the tables previously created.

Single-Row SELECTS

The statement

```
EXECUTE IMMEDIATE <dyn_string> INTO <plsql_variables_list_comma_separated>
USING <bind_variables_list_comma_separated>;
```

is used to execute dynamic single-row SELECTS.

Suppose you want to update the order_tab information with the latest total quantity and total price for a given order for all possible regions. In this case, you require a dynamic SELECT that returns a single row, the summation of quantity and price for an input order_id.

The procedure update_dyn_table uses a dynamic SELECT that returns a single row. Here's the code for this procedure:

```
Create or replace Procedure update_dyn_table
                                        (i_region_name VARCHAR2,
                                         i_order_id NUMBER,
                                         retcd OUT NUMBER,
                                         errmsg OUT VARCHAR2)
authid current_user
Is
  Dyn_upd_string1 VARCHAR2(1000);
  Dyn_query_string VARCHAR2(1000);
  Dyn_Table_name1 VARCHAR2(30);
  Dyn_Table_name2 VARCHAR2(30);
  V_total_price NUMBER;
  V_total_quantity NUMBER;
Begin
  Dyn_table_name1 := 'ORDER_ITEMS_FOR_'||replace(trim(i_region_name),' ','_');
  Dyn_table_name2 := 'ORDERS_FOR_'||i_region_name;
  Dyn_query_string := ' SELECT SUM(quantity), SUM(unit_price*quantity) FROM '||
                                  dyn_table_name1||
                                  ' WHERE order_id = :input_order_id ';
  Dyn_upd_string1 :=   ' UPDATE '||dyn_table_name2||
              ' SET total_qty = :total_qty, total_price = :total_price WHERE '||
                      ' order_id = :input_order_id ';
```

```
        EXECUTE IMMEDIATE dyn_query_string INTO v_total_price, v_total_quantity
        USING i_order_id;
        EXECUTE IMMEDIATE dyn_upd_string1
          USING v_total_quantity, v_total_price, i_order_id;
      retcd := 0;
EXCEPTION WHEN OTHERS THEN
  retcd := SQLCODE;
  errmsg :='ERR:'||SQLERRM;
End;
/
```

This procedure does the following:

- Creates two dynamic table names concatenating the input region name with the constants ORDER_ITEMS_FOR_ and ORDERS_FOR_ and places them in two PL/SQL variables named dyn_table_name1 and dyn_table_name2. This process is for the order items table and the orders table for each region, respectively.

- Creates a dynamically generated SELECT statement using the dyn_table_name1 variable and places it in a PL/SQL variable named dyn_query_string. This process is for selecting the total quantity and total price from the ORDER_ITEMS_FOR_<region> table for each input order_id. It uses a bind variable called :input_order_id for the input order_id. Each SELECT returns only one row corresponding to the input order_id.

- Creates a dynamically generated UPDATE statement using the dyn_table_name2 variable and places it in a PL/SQL variable named dyn_upd_string1. This process is for updating the total_qty and total_price columns in the ORDERS_FOR_<region> table for each order_id. It uses a bind variable called :input_order_id for the input order_id. It also uses two more bind variables named :total_qty and :total_price for setting the values of the total quantity and total price for each order.

- Executes these two dynamic strings using the EXECUTE IMMEDIATE statement. This statement retrieves the total quantity and total price for each order_id from the ORDER_ITEMS_FOR_<region> table and updates the corresponding record in the ORDERS_FOR_<region> table.

- Outputs a return code of 0 on success in the form of an OUT parameter named retcd. On error it outputs the corresponding SQLCODE and SQLERRM in the form of two OUT parameters, retcd and errmsg.

Multirow SELECTS

Multirow SELECTS are handled in a separate manner from single-row SELECTS. With static SQL, multirow SELECTS were handled either by declaring explicit cursors or using cursor variables. Also, the cursor variables used could be instances of strong or weak REF CURSORs. With native dynamic SQL, you don't need to use a cursor variable with hard-coded queries. Prior to Oracle8*i*, cursor variables were restricted in that they could only be opened for static queries. For example, the following declaration was allowed:

```
DECLARE
    TYPE dynamic_rc IS REF CURSOR;
    v_rc dynamic_rc;
BEGIN
  OPEN v_rc FOR SELECT order_id FROM order_items_for_region1;
  . . .
  OPEN v_rc FOR SELECT order_id FROM order_items_for_region2;
  . . .
END;
```

This way of using OPEN has the disadvantage of opening the cursor variable multiple times for each region involved if all the regions have to be processed. As you can see from the previous example, this involves writing and maintaining a lot of code. With native dynamic SQL, the cursor variable has to be opened once only. Here's what a portion of this code looks like:

```
DECLARE
    TYPE dynamic_rc IS REF CURSOR;
    v_rc dynamic_rc;
    Dyn_table_name  VARCHAR2(100);
    Dyn_query_string VARCHAR2(1000);
BEGIN
  Dyn_table_name := 'ORDER_ITEMS_FOR_'||i_region_name;
  Dyn_query_string := 'SELECT order_id FROM '||dyn_table_name;
  OPEN v_rc FOR dyn_query_string;

  . . .
END;
```

Here, i_region_name is assumed to be a variable that's assigned dynamically with a region name.

The way to handle multirow queries with native dynamic SQL is to use a weak REF CURSOR. A weak REF CURSOR points to a work area in the System Global Area (SGA) for holding a resultset. A weak type REF CURSOR is declared and OPENed for the dynamic query string. The normal FETCHing in a LOOP and the CLOSE operation follow the opening of the cursor. Here are the steps:

1. Declare a weak REF CURSOR type.

2. Declare a cursor variable of this type.

3. Construct the dynamic query string.

4. Open the cursor variable for this dynamic query string. Any values for bind variables specified in the USING clause are evaluated in this step.

5. FETCH in a loop the rows one by one and process them. Fetching into records of type %ROWTYPE or user-defined records is allowed.

6. Close the cursor variable.

The statements

```
OPEN <cursor_var> FOR <dyn_query_string>;
OPEN <cursor_var> FOR <dyn_query_string>
USING <plsql_variables_list_comma_separated>;
FETCH <cursor_var> INTO <plsql_variables_list_comma_separated_or_plsql_record>;
CLOSE <cursor_var>;
```

are used to execute dynamic multirow SELECTS.

As an example, consider the procedure update_dyn_table created earlier, which accepts a particular region_name and order_id. You can extend this procedure to be processed for all orders and in a particular region. Here's the code:

```
Create or replace Procedure update_dyn_for_all_orders
                        (i_region_name VARCHAR2,
                         retcd OUT NUMBER,
                         errmsg OUT VARCHAR2)
Is
    Dyn_table_name  VARCHAR2(100);
    Dyn_query_string VARCHAR2(1000);
    Type csr_dyn IS REF CURSOR;
     csr_dyn1 csr_dyn;
    v_order_id NUMBER;
```

```
BEGIN
   Dyn_table_name := 'ORDER_ITEMS_FOR_'||replace(trim(i_region_name),' ','_');
   Dyn_query_string := 'SELECT order_id FROM '||dyn_table_name;
   OPEN csr_dyn1 FOR dyn_query_string;
   LOOP
     FETCH csr_dyn1 INTO v_order_id;
     EXIT WHEN csr_dyn1%NOTFOUND;
     update_dyn_table(i_region_name, v_order_id, retcd, errmsg);
     IF retcd <> 0 THEN
        EXIT;
     END IF;
   END LOOP;
EXCEPTION WHEN OTHERS THEN
  Retcd := SQLCODE;
  Errmsg := SQLERRM;
END;
/
```

This procedure does the following:

- Declares a type definition of type REF CURSOR named csr_dyn and a cursor variable named csr_dyn1 as an instance of the csr_dyn type. This section of the code is for processing a multirow query and is later opened for a query.

- Creates a dynamic table name by concatenating the input region name with the constant ORDER_ITEMS_FOR_ and places it in a PL/SQL variable named dyn_table_name. This process is for the order items table for each region.

- Creates a dynamically generated SELECT statement using the dyn_table_name variable and places it in a PL/SQL variable named dyn_query_string. This process is for selecting all order_id column values from the ORDER_ITEMS_FOR_<region> table. This SELECT returns multiple rows from each ORDER_ITEMS_FOR_<region> table.

- Executes this dynamic string using the OPEN-FOR and FETCH . . . INTO statements. First the REF CURSOR variable is opened for the dynamic SELECT. Next, the cursor variable is fetched into a local variable named v_order_id. Then, for each row returned by the query, update_dyn_table is executed, passing the input region name and the fetched order_id as inputs. This procedure retrieves the total quantity and total price for each order_id from the ORDER_ITEMS_FOR_<region> table and updates the corresponding record in the ORDERS_FOR_<region> table.

- Outputs a return code of 0 on success in the form of an OUT parameter named retcd. On error it outputs the corresponding SQLCODE and SQLERRM in the form of two OUT parameters, retcd and errmsg.

You can further extend this procedure to encompass all orders in all regions. I call this procedure update_dyn_global. The logic for this procedure doesn't require dynamic SQL. For all regions in the region_tab, it loops through to execute update_dyn_for_all_orders listed previously with the region_name pointing to the current cursor row as the first input parameter. Here's the code:

```
Create or replace Procedure update_dyn_global
                        (retcd OUT NUMBER,
                          errmsg OUT VARCHAR2)
Is
  CURSOR csr_region IS
      SELECT region_name FROM region_tab;
BEGIN
    FOR idx IN csr_region LOOP
    update_dyn_for_all_orders(idx.region_name, retcd, errmsg);
    IF retcd <> 0 THEN
       EXIT;
    END IF;
  END LOOP;
EXCEPTION WHEN OTHERS THEN
  Retcd := SQLCODE;
  Errmsg := SQLERRM;
END;
/
```

This procedure does the following:

- Declares a cursor for all the region names in the region_tab table.

- For each row in the cursor, it invokes the update_dyn_for_all_orders procedure, passing the region name as an IN parameter to both.

- Outputs a return code of 0 on success in the form of an OUT parameter named retcd. On error it outputs the corresponding SQLCODE and SQLERRM in the form of two OUT parameters, retcd and errmsg.

TIP *Only weak REF CURSORS are allowed for processing multirow queries using native dynamic SQL. If you use strong REF CURSORS, the following error is obtained: PLS-00455: cursor '<cursor_variable_name>' cannot be used in a dynamic SQL OPEN statement.*

TIP *When you use bind variables in the dynamic query string, the corresponding USING clause can contain only bind arguments of the IN type.*

Dynamic INSERT, UPDATE, and DELETE

In addition to DDL statements and DML single-row SELECT statements, you can construct INSERT, UPDATE, and DELETE statements dynamically and execute them at runtime.

You use the statements

```
EXECUTE IMMEDIATE <dyn_string>;
EXECUTE IMMEDIATE <dyn_string> INTO <plsql_variables_list_comma_separated>
USING <bind_variables_list_comma_separated>;
```

to execute dynamic INSERT, UPDATE, and DELETE statements. The dynamic SQL string can also have a RETURNING clause if needed. As an example, the update_dyn_table procedure created earlier used an UPDATE statement using native dynamic SQL. Here's the code for your reference:

```
Create or replace Procedure update_dyn_table
                              (i_region_name VARCHAR2, i_order_id NUMBER,
                               retcd OUT NUMBER, errmsg OUT VARCHAR2)
authid current_user
Is
  Dyn_upd_string1 VARCHAR2(1000);
  Dyn_query_string VARCHAR2(1000);
  Dyn_Table_name1 VARCHAR2(30);
  Dyn_Table_name2 VARCHAR2(30);
  V_total_price NUMBER;
  V_total_quantity NUMBER;
Begin
```

```
Dyn_table_name1 := 'ORDER_ITEMS_FOR_'||replace(trim(i_region_name),' ','_');
Dyn_table_name2 := 'ORDERS_FOR_'||i_region_name;
Dyn_query_string := ' SELECT SUM(quantity), SUM(unit_price*quantity) FROM '||
                                dyn_table_name1||
                                    ' WHERE order_id = :input_order_id ';
Dyn_upd_string1 :=   ' UPDATE '||dyn_table_name2||
            ' SET total_qty = :total_qty, total_price = :total_price WHERE '||
                        ' order_id = :input_order_id ';

  EXECUTE IMMEDIATE dyn_query_string INTO v_total_price, v_total_quantity
  USING i_order_id;
  EXECUTE IMMEDIATE dyn_upd_string1
    USING v_total_quantity, v_total_price, i_order_id;
  retcd := 0;
EXCEPTION WHEN OTHERS THEN
  retcd := SQLCODE;
  errmsg := 'ERR: '||SQLERRM';
End;
/
```

Also, you can insert data into the ORDERS_FOR_<region_name> and ORDER_ITEMS_FOR_<region_name> tables using dynamic INSERT statements.

In the case of dynamic INSERT, UPDATE, and DELETE statements executed using EXECUTE IMMEDIATE, the implicit cursor attribute SQL%ROWCOUNT is available and returns the number of rows processed by the INSERT, UPDATE, or DELETE.

Using Bind Variables

Binding refers to the linking of program values to variables at runtime. This is done by means of bind variables. Using bind variables in native dynamic SQL makes the code execute faster and makes it easier to maintain. It's faster because the same SQL statement is executed with different values of the bind variables, so that a single cursor is shareable by multiple SQL statements. Also, binding takes care of data type conversion implicitly since native data types are involved. Otherwise, you should use the conversion functions such as TO_DATE, TO_CHAR. You specify bind variables using a colon (:) followed by the variable name, and you specify the actual values using the USING clause. Note that the actual values can also be held in PL/SQL variables, but these variables are not prefixed with a colon.

Here are the steps involved:

1. Specify the bind variables while constructing the SQL statement dynamically. It's here that you prefix the bind variable names with the colon.

2. Specify the actual values for the bind variables using the USING clause of the EXECUTE IMMEDIATE statement or OPEN-FOR statement. These are called *bind arguments*.

Here's an example of using bind variables:

```
Dyn_upd_string1 :=  ' UPDATE '||dyn_table_name2||
               ' SET total_qty = :total_qty, total_price = :total_price WHERE '||
                    ' order_id = :input_order_id ';

 EXECUTE IMMEDIATE dyn_upd_string1
    USING v_total_quantity, v_total_price, i_order_id;
```

where :total_qty, :total_price, and :input_order_id are three bind variables. The actual values are held in the PL/SQL variables v_total_quantity, v_total_price, and i_order_id.

The following points are worth noting:

- The bind variables aren't declared.

- The bind variables are prefixed with a colon.

TIP   *Don't explicitly declare a bind variable.*

TIP   *Only use bind variables for data values and not for values that hold metadata values such as table names, column names, and SQL statement clauses. Use PL/SQL variables to hold the latter type of values. Using bind variables to specify schema object names can result in errors that can cause confusion. For example, an error such as "ORA-00903: invalid table name" can occur even when the specified table exists.*

Binding works as follows: The dynamic string specified in the EXECUTE IMMEDIATE statement is first parsed at runtime. Next, syntax and semantic references are resolved. This is why you can't specify schema object names by means of bind variables. The runtime PL/SQL engine can't determine such names correctly. At the time of execution, the PL/SQL engine replaces the bind variable with the value in the corresponding variable specified in the USING clause.

TIP *The data types of the variables in the USING clause must be valid SQL types and not PL/SQL types.*

Bind arguments can be of three types: IN, OUT, and IN OUT. These are like the IN, OUT, and IN OUT parameter modes for subprograms. For dynamic queries, native dynamic SQL supports only IN bind arguments. However, for dynamic DML statements using a RETURNING clause, OUT bind arguments are allowed.

Bind variables are permitted in dynamic PL/SQL blocks and can be supplied in place of actual parameters of a subprogram that's being executed as dynamic PL/SQL. However, the type of each bind argument must be the same as the corresponding parameter mode.

Dynamic PL/SQL

Native dynamic SQL supports the execution of PL/SQL blocks dynamically—that is, executing anonymous PL/SQL blocks supplied as strings enclosed within BEGIN . . . END depending on runtime variable values. Also, subprograms whose names are dynamically constructed can be executed using dynamic PL/SQL. A third use of dynamic PL/SQL is executing bulk dynamic SQL statements by enclosing them within BEGIN . . . END.

The statement

```
EXECUTE IMMEDIATE 'BEGIN . . . END;' USING <plsql_variables_list_comma_separated>;
```

is used for dynamic PL/SQL. Note that the enclosing BEGIN . . . END is necessary.

Here are the rules for executing dynamic PL/SQL:

- The dynamic PL/SQL block must start with a DECLARE or BEGIN and end with an END followed by a semicolon (;). If the dynamic SQL string ends with a semicolon, it's treated as a PL/SQL block.

- Dynamic PL/SQL blocks do not have access to local variables defined within the block. Hence, only PL/SQL global variables defined in a package and stand-alone subprogram names can be referenced inside the dynamic PL/SQL block.

The procedure update_dyn_for_all_orders listed previously accepted region_name as an input parameter and the procedure update_dyn_global executed this procedure for all regions in a loop. Instead, you could write individual procedures for each region with their names dynamically constructed by suffixing them with each region name. Again, you can use a cursor loop to obtain the individual region names. I call the procedure that does this update_dyn_global2. Here's the code for this procedure:

```
Create or replace Procedure update_dyn_global2
                                        (retcd OUT NUMBER,
                                        errmsg OUT VARCHAR2)
Is
  CURSOR csr_region IS
      SELECT region_name FROM region_tab;
Dyn_proc_name VARCHAR2(100);
Dyn_plsql_string VARCHAR2(1000);
BEGIN
    FOR idx IN csr_region LOOP
    EXECUTE IMMEDIATE ' BEGIN update_dyn_'||replace(trim(idx.region_name),' ','_')||' (:1, :2) ; END;'
      USING OUT retcd, OUT errmsg;
    IF retcd <> 0 THEN
       EXIT;
    END IF;
  END LOOP;
EXCEPTION WHEN OTHERS THEN
  Retcd := SQLCODE;
  Errmsg := SQLERRM;
END;
/
```

This procedure does the following:

- Declares a cursor for all the region names in the region_tab table.

- For each row in the cursor, it dynamically constructs a procedure name by concatenating the region name to the constant update_dyn_ and then dynamically executes this procedure. This process uses two bind parameters corresponding to the OUT parameters for each procedure.

- Outputs a return code of 0 on success in the form of an OUT parameter named retcd. On error it outputs the corresponding SQLCODE and SQLERRM in the form of two OUT parameters, retcd and errmsg.

Here, the individual procedures generated dynamically should have already been created by a similar procedure called create_proc_dyn_global.

Exception Handling in Native Dynamic SQL

I should note two points about exception handling when using native dynamic SQL:

- An exception handler in an enclosing block can catch exceptions in native dynamic SQL statements enclosed within it.

- Always define an exception handling section by specifying it an enclosing PL/SQL block.

As an example, consider the procedure update_dyn_global. The exception handler

```
EXCEPTION WHEN OTHERS THEN
  Retcd := SQLCODE;
  Errmsg := SQLERRM;
```

between the enclosing BEGIN . . . END will trap any exceptions that arise due to the failure of the dynamic PL/SQL statement or normal PL/SQL failure. To trap each of these exceptions separately, you can define individual exception handlers by specifying a nested block in the outer BEGIN . . . END as follows:

```
BEGIN
  EXECUTE IMMEDIATE ' BEGIN '||dyn_plsql_string ||' END; '
    USING OUT retcd, OUT errmsg;
    IF (retcd <> 0) THEN
      EXIT;
    END IF;
EXCEPTION WHEN OTHERS THEN
  Retcd := SQLCODE;
  Errmsg := 'ERR: '||dyn_plsql_string||' - '||SQLERRM;
END;
```

You may not need to do this in the case of more generic exception handlers, because irrespective of where the exception was raised, control branches to the exception handling section. However, this code helps to track each exception individually and improves block structuring.

Native Dynamic SQL and Objects

There's no difference in the structure of code written when you use objects for native dynamic SQL. Instead of relational tables, you use object tables and/or tables with objects as columns.

 CROSS-REFERENCE   *I discuss native dynamic SQL and objects further in Chapter 10.*

Summary

In this chapter, I provided an in-depth analysis of native dynamic SQL. I started with a comparison of native dynamic SQL and DBMS_SQL, and then I moved on to present the methods of executing various SQL statements such as DDL, DML, and PL/SQL blocks. Finally, I highlighted exception handling in the case of native dynamic SQL. The next chapter outlines the concept of autonomous transactions in PL/SQL.

Autonomous Transactions

THIS CHAPTER FOCUSES on the concept of autonomous transactions, which were first introduced in Oracle 8i. Here, I briefly explain transaction management prior to autonomous transactions and go on to outline how this feature enables developers to execute and then commit or roll back part of a transaction without affecting the overall session's transaction. Finally, I present some key points regarding autonomous transactions.

I illustrate the concept of autonomous transactions by taking into account an order entry application with the facility for error logging. This uses the tables supplier_tab, order_tab, order_tran_coming_in, and error_log, whose definitions I provide in Appendix A. The supplier_tab and order_tab tables store information about suppliers and the orders taken by each supplier. The error_log table stores Oracle errors encountered in the process of performing DML operations on the order_tab table. The individual records in this table are tied to order_id. The order_tran_coming_in table tracks the information about incoming order transactions, which I describe later in this chapter, in the section "Autonomous Triggers". This case study also uses two stored procedures called log_error and create_order to enable inputting of records to the error_log table and creating an order respectively. These two procedures are defined in the section "Specifying a Transaction as Autonomous." Two database triggers, named bi_order_tab and ai_order_tab, record information about incoming order transactions, and you can read more about these triggers in the section "Autonomous Triggers" later in this chapter.

Transaction Management Prior to Autonomous Transactions

Database operations such as DML are executed within the context of a transaction. A *transaction* is sequence of one or more SQL statements that performs a logical unit of work. Transactions, session specific by definition, are controlled by the COMMIT and ROLLBACK operations. Whenever a COMMIT or ROLLBACK occurs, the locks held on resources are released.

Before the release of PL/SQL 8.1, only one transaction could be active at any given point of time. This was on a per-session basis. Thus, in effect, a COMMIT or ROLLBACK forced the entire transaction to be saved or rolled back. This proved to be a drawback when it came to PL/SQL; the capability to save or roll back only a part of the transaction was a desired functionality. PL/SQL 8.1 removed this bottleneck by introducing something called *autonomous trans-actions*. I describe this feature in more detail in the next section.

Autonomous Transactions: Definition and Use

An autonomous transaction partitions a single, entire transaction into subtransactions. Control shifts from the main transaction (MT) to the autonomous transaction (AT). Once the latter transaction executes, the main transaction resumes. The important point to note here is that the autonomous transaction executes independent of the main transaction, and the scope of COMMIT or ROLLBACK is limited to the context of this autonomous transaction only.

To illustrate this, consider an error-logging application in which a main transaction raises an error. The application needs to roll back the main transaction and also save the corresponding error information to the database. Prior to Oracle 8i, this process was possible by means of DBMS_PIPE or DBMS_AQ. Now autonomous transactions simplify the process, which involves the following steps:

1. The main transaction traps the error in the application and issues a ROLLBACK.

2. A subtransaction defined as autonomous captures this error and issues a COMMIT to save only the error information, and not the main transaction.

This simplifies the code to be written and its maintenance, by eliminating the need to do these steps:

1. Open a second session and pass the error info from the main session to this second session using DBMS_PIPE or DBMS_AQ.

2. Roll back the transaction in the main session and commit the error info in the second session.

Advantages of Autonomous Transactions

Autonomous transactions offer several advantages over traditional transaction processing. These are

- *Modularization and simplification of code:* As independent units of work, autonomous transactions don't affect the main transaction. This allows you to write separate routines for logging, auditing, and the like and thus modularize the code for these type of applications.

- *Performing COMMIT operations in triggers:* Autonomous transactions can help you to perform COMMIT operations from inside database triggers, as detailed later in the section "Autonomous Triggers."

- *Calling user-defined functions from SQL that perform DML:* You can use autonomous transactions to call user-defined functions from SQL that write to the database, which I show you how to do later in the section "Key Points Regarding Autonomous Transactions."

The following sections discuss the method of specifying autonomous transactions and the processing involved in them, along with an outline of autonomous triggers and some key points regarding autonomous transactions.

Specifying a Transaction as Autonomous

You define an autonomous transaction in a PL/SQL block by specifying the following statement in the declaration section of that block:

```
PRAGMA AUTONOMOUS_TRANSACTION
```

This PRAGMA directs the PL/SQL compiler to partition a PL/SQL block in which it's declared as an autonomous or independent transaction.

The following rules apply to define a block as an autonomous transaction:

- The PL/SQL block should be a top-level block and not a nested block, if it's an anonymous block.

- If the PL/SQL block isn't anonymous, it should be a procedure or a function, either as part of a package or as a stored program unit. When defining autonomous transactions in a package, only individual procedures or functions in the package can be designated as autonomous. The entire package itself can't be declared as autonomous.

- The PL/SQL block can also be a method of a stored object type.

- The PL/SQL block can also be a database trigger.

- Nested blocks can't be autonomous.

I illustrate the concept of autonomous transactions by taking into account the order entry application described earlier. Consider the tables supplier_tab and order_tab with inputted data. Also consider the error_log table.

The procedure log_error shown next inputs records to the error_log table:

```
CREATE OR REPLACE PROCEDURE  log_error
                    (p_order_id NUMBER,
                     p_error_code NUMBER,
                     p_error_text VARCHAR2)
IS
  PRAGMA AUTONOMOUS_TRANSACTION;
BEGIN
  INSERT INTO error_log VALUES
  (p_order_id, p_error_code, p_error_text, USER, SYSDATE);
  COMMIT;
END;
/
```

Consider the following procedure to create an order:

```
CREATE OR REPLACE PROCEDURE  create_order(p_order_id NUMBER)
IS
BEGIN
  INSERT INTO order_tab VALUES(p_order_id, SYSDATE, NULL, NULL, 1001);
  COMMIT;
EXCEPTION WHEN OTHERS THEN
  log_error(p_order_id, SQLCODE, SQLERRM);
  ROLLBACK;
END;
/
```

To test the preceding code, start with the following two SELECT statements:

```
SQL> select * from order_tab;

ORDER_ID ORDER_DAT  TOTAL_QTY TOTAL_PRICE    SUPP_ID
------- -------- --------- -------- ----------
     101 26-DEC-01        100         750 1001
SQL> select * from error_log;
no rows selected
```

Now insert a new record with a duplicate order_id. To do this, you use the create_order procedure described previously. Here are the sequence of steps you follow:

```
SQL> exec create_order(101)
PL/SQL procedure successfully completed.
SQL> select * from order_tab;
ORDER_ID ORDER_DAT  TOTAL_QTY TOTAL_PRICE    SUPP_ID
-------- --------- ---------- --------- ----------
     101 26-DEC-01        100       750 1001
SQL> column error_text format a70;
SQL> select * from error_log;
  ORDER_ID ERROR_CODE
  ------     ------

ERROR_TEXT
--------------------------------------------------

LOGGED_USER          LOGGED_DA
---------------      --------
       101        -1
ORA-00001: unique constraint (PLSQL9I.SYS_C002737) violated
PLSQL9I                      26-DEC-01

SQL> rollback;
Rollback complete.
ORDER_ID ORDER_DAT  TOTAL_QTY TOTAL_PRICE    SUPP_ID
-------- --------- ---------- --------- ----------
     101 26-DEC-01        100       750 1001
SQL> select * from error_log;

ORDER_ID ERROR_CODE
  ------  ------
ERROR_TEXT
-------------------------------------------------

LOGGED_USER          LOGGED_DA
---------------      --------
    101     -1
ORA-00001: unique constraint (PLSQL9I.SYS_C002737) violated
PLSQL9I              26-DEC-01
```

I include the ROLLBACK statement to highlight the point that the row inserted into the error_log table is committed independently of the ROLLBACK issued in the create_order procedure. So the subsequent SELECT from the error_log table yields the same row as the one obtained prior to the ROLLBACK.

An autonomous transaction begins with a BEGIN and ends at the END in a BEGIN . . . END block or in an autonomous routine. Any DECLARE block appearing before this BEGIN isn't considered part of the autonomous transaction even if it contains the PRAGMA AUTONOMOUS_TRANSACTION declaration. Also, this PRAGMA can appear in any order in the declaration section. As an example, consider the following PL/SQL block:

```
DECLARE
  PRAGMA AUTONOMOUS_TRANSACTION;
  FUNCTION dummy_log_error RETURN NUMBER;
  v_num NUMBER(1) := 0;
  retcd NUMBER := dummy_log_error;
  FUNCTION dummy_log_error RETURN NUMBER
  IS
  BEGIN
    INSERT INTO error_log VALUES ( -99,-99,'Dummy Error!',USER, SYSDATE);
    RETURN (-99);
  END;
BEGIN
    INSERT INTO error_log VALUES (v_num, v_num, 'No Error!',USER, SYSDATE);
    COMMIT;
END;
/
```

When this PL/SQL block is executed, you get the following output:

```
ORDER_ID ERROR_CODE
-------- ----------
ERROR_TEXT
--------------------------------------------------
LOGGED_USER                     LOGGED_DA
------------------------------  ----------
     101          -1
ORA-00001: unique constraint (PLSQL9I.SYS_C002737) violated
PLSQL9I                         26-DEC-01

      -99         -99
Dummy Error!
PLSQL9I                         30-DEC-01

        0           0
No Error!
PLSQL9I                         30-DEC-01
```

Next you perform a ROLLBACK, resulting in the following output:

```
SQL> rollback;
Rollback complete.
SQL> select * from error_log;
  ORDER_ID ERROR_CODE
-------- --------

ERROR_TEXT
---------------------------------------------------
LOGGED_USER                   LOGGED_DA
---------------------------   ----------
       101          -1
ORA-00001: unique constraint (PLSQL9I.SYS_C002737) violated
PLSQL9I                           26-DEC-01


         0          0
No Error!
PLSQL9I                           30-DEC-01
```

Note that the dummy row doesn't appear after the rollback. This shows that the INSERT performed by the function dummy_log_error is ignored by the autonomous transaction and is considered part of the main transaction.

Processing of Autonomous Transactions

The following describes the steps involved in the execution of an autonomous transaction:

1. The main transaction (MT) begins.

2. The MT encounters a call to an autonomous routine. The MT pauses, and control transfers to the autonomous routine.

3. The autonomous transaction (AT) begins. The AT begins when it encounters a BEGIN after the PRAGMA in the autonomous routine. It begins with the first executable section and ignores any declarations appearing before. The AT then performs SQL operations in the autonomous scope. The AT is in effect as long as the BEGIN block is active. Any DECLARE block appearing before the BEGIN block isn't considered part of AT.

4. The AT performs COMMIT or ROLLBACK operations. This ends the current AT, but doesn't exit the autonomous routine. Now there are two possibilities: Either a second autonomous transaction is started or the autonomous transaction terminates normally. In the first case, the second AT executes in a manner similar to the first. In the second case, control returns to the MT.

5. The MT resumes.

6. The MT ends.

Figure 8-1 depicts the processing involved in autonomous transactions.

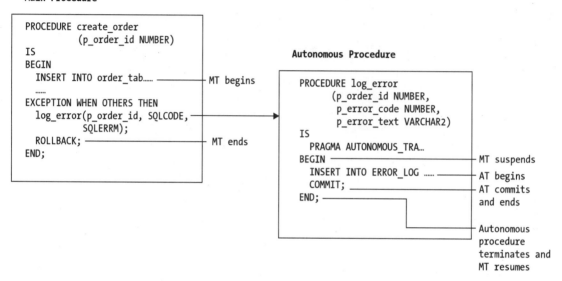

Figure 8-1. Processing of autonomous transactions

Autonomous transactions are completely independent of main transactions. As such, the behavior of COMMIT, ROLLBACK, and SAVEPOINT in an autonomous transaction is completely independent of the main transaction (see Table 8-1).

Table 8-1. Behavior of COMMIT, ROLLBACK, and SAVEPOINT in ATs and MTs

AUTONOMOUS TRANSACTION	MAIN TRANSACTION
Commits	Commits
Commits	Rolls back
Rolls back	Commits
Rolls back	Rolls back
SAVEPOINT A (Can and should roll back to A)	SAVEPOINT B(Can and should roll back to B)IF B is defined before A, ROLLBACK to B does not roll back the AT.

Here A is a savepoint defined in the AT and B is a savepoint defined in the MT. An autonomous transaction must define its own savepoints. Even if B is defined "before" A, ROLLBACK to B doesn't roll back the AT.

Autonomous Triggers

You can issue COMMIT and ROLLBACK inside the body of database triggers using autonomous transactions. The main transaction that the database trigger has to fire remains unaffected. Only the DML inside the trigger body is committed or rolled back.

To illustrate this, consider the scenario in which order transactions coming in are recorded. For this purpose, consider the order_tran_coming_in table described in the case study.

Whenever a new order record is inserted into the order table, a new record is inserted into the order_tran_coming_in table. Two database triggers, one before insert and another, after insert are created to function as follows:

    i. The before insert trigger logs the input order transaction coming in and commits it in the order_tran_coming_in table.

    ii. The after insert trigger updates the successful flag to 'Y' for the particular order that most recently came in, using the order id.

The code for these two triggers is given below:

```
create or replace trigger bi_order_tab
before insert on order_tab for each row
declare
   pragma autonomous_transaction;
begin
   insert into order_tran_coming_in values (:NEW.order_id,

:NEW.order_date,

                                              SYSDATE,
                                              'N');

   commit;
end;
/


create or replace trigger ai_order_tab
after insert on order_tab for each row
declare
```

```
  pragma autonomous_transaction;
begin
  update order_tran_coming_in
  set    success_flag = 'Y'
  where  order_id = :NEW.order_id;
  commit;
end;
/
```

To test this, use the following PL/SQL block:

```
BEGIN
 INSERT INTO order_tab VALUES(102, SYSDATE, NULL, NULL, 1001);
 INSERT INTO order_tab VALUES(103, SYSDATE, NULL, NULL, 1001);
 INSERT INTO order_tab VALUES(103, SYSDATE, NULL, NULL, 1001);
EXCEPTION WHEN DUP_VAL_ON_INDEX THEN
   ROLLBACK;
END;
```

The following results indicate the effect of autonomous transactions in the database triggers on order_tab table:

```
SQL> select * from order_tab;
ORDER_ID ORDER_DAT  TOTAL_QTY TOTAL_PRICE    SUPP_ID
------- -------- --------- -------- ----------
    101 26-DEC-01        100        750 1001
SQL> select * from order_tran_coming_in;
no rows selected
SQL> BEGIN
  2    INSERT INTO order_tab VALUES(102, SYSDATE, NULL, NULL, 1001);
  3    INSERT INTO order_tab VALUES(103, SYSDATE, NULL, NULL, 1001);
  4    INSERT INTO order_tab VALUES(103, SYSDATE, NULL, NULL, 1001);
  5  EXCEPTION WHEN DUP_VAL_ON_INDEX THEN
  6     ROLLBACK;
  7  END;
  8  /
PL/SQL procedure successfully completed.
SQL> select * from order_tab;
ORDER_ID ORDER_DAT  TOTAL_QTY TOTAL_PRICE    SUPP_ID
------- -------- --------- -------- ----------
    101 26-DEC-01        100        750 1001

SQL> select order_id, order_date,
  2     to_char(tran_coming_in_date, 'MM/DD/YYYY HH24:MI:SS') tran_coming_in_date,
  3  success_flag
  4  from order_tran_coming_in;
```

```
ORDER_ID ORDER_DAT TRAN_COMING_IN_DATE S
---------- ---------- ------------------------
       103   26-DEC-01   12/26/2001 23:42:50      Y
       103   26-DEC-01   12/26/2001 23:42:50      N
       102   26-DEC-01   12/26/2001 23:42:50      Y
```

Key Points About Autonomous Transactions

In this section, I outline some key points that you should know about autonomous transactions. Specifically, the following text outlines, with relation to autonomous transactions, the behavior of ALTER SESSION, dealing with deadlocks, COMMIT or ROLLBACK behavior, conditions for defining autonomous transactions, dealing with exceptions, multiple autonomous transactions, dealing with concurrency, calling user-defined functions from SQL, and isolation level.

Autonomous Transactions with ALTER SESSION

Autonomous transactions share the same session as the main transaction, so any changes made to the session by means of ALTER SESSION statements are visible in both the autonomous transaction and the main transaction. However, autonomous transactions execute in a different transaction context than the main transaction. Also, any nonautonomous subprogram calls originating from the autonomous block share the same transaction context as the autonomous transaction. However, a second autonomous routine called from the first autonomous transaction executes in a different transaction context.

Autonomous Transactions and Deadlocks

You must define autonomous transactions in such a manner that you aren't creating deadlocks with the main transaction for resources and locks. A *deadlock* occurs when an autonomous transaction tries to access a resource held by the main transaction, which is suspended until the autonomous transaction ends. The autonomous transaction ends up waiting for the main transaction to release the locks, resulting in a deadlock.

Conditions for Defining Autonomous Transactions

Only top-level anonymous blocks can include the PRAGMA AUTONOMOUS_TRANSACTION declaration. Compiling the following code results in the error

```
PLS-00710: PRAGMA AUTONOMOUS_TRANSACTION cannot be declared here
```

as evident from the following code:

```
SQL> create or replace procedure log_error(p_order_id NUMBER,
  2                                          p_error_code NUMBER,
  3                                          p_error_text VARCHAR2)
  4  IS
  5  BEGIN
  6    DECLARE
  7      PRAGMA AUTONOMOUS_TRANSACTION;
  8    BEGIN
  9        INSERT INTO error_log VALUES
 10  (p_order_id, p_error_code, p_error_text, USER, SYSDATE);
 11      COMMIT;
 12    END;
 13  END;
 14  /
Warning: Procedure created with compilation errors.

SQL> sho errors
Errors for PROCEDURE LOG_ERROR:
LINE/COL ERROR
---------- -------------------------------------------------- ----------------
7/12       PLS-00710: PRAGMA AUTONOMOUS_TRANSACTION cannot be declared here
```

When using the PRAGMA AUTONOMOUS_TRANSACTION in a package, a single PRAGMA declaration can't be used to make all the subprograms autonomous. Each subprogram must have the PRAGMA declaration explicitly declared in it. Thus the package specification alone isn't enough to determine which subprograms are defined as autonomous.

Autonomous transactions can be defined in PL/SQL only. Other languages such as C, C++, or Java can be used only to call routines in these languages from a PL/SQL routine that is defined as autonomous.

COMMIT or ROLLBACK Behavior and Autonomous Transactions

An autonomous transaction ends with a COMMIT or ROLLBACK statement. Therefore, you should include an explicit COMMIT or ROLLBACK in an autonomous transaction program. If you don't, any pending transactions are rolled back automatically. This is a transaction-level rollback and not a statement-level rollback, which means all uncommitted changes in the autonomous transaction are rolled back. Consider the log-error procedure described previously. Removing the COMMIT statement, re-creating this procedure and then executing the create_order procedure causes the following error:

```
ORA-06519: active autonomous transaction detected and rolled back
```

This is evident from the following:

```
SQL> CREATE OR REPLACE PROCEDURE  log_error(p_order_id NUMBER,
  2                                          p_error_code NUMBER,
  3                                          p_error_text VARCHAR2)
  4  IS
  5    PRAGMA AUTONOMOUS_TRANSACTION;
  6  BEGIN
  7  INSERT INTO error_log VALUES
  8    (p_order_id, p_error_code, p_error_text, USER, SYSDATE);
  9  END;
 10  /

Procedure created.
SQL> select * from order_tab;

ORDER_ID ORDER_DAT  TOTAL_QTY TOTAL_PRICE    SUPP_ID
--------- ------------- ------------- --------------

    101 26-DEC-01        100       750  1001

SQL> exec create_order(101);
BEGIN create_order(101); END;
*
ERROR at line 1:
ORA-06519: active autonomous transaction detected and rolled back
ORA-06512: at "PLSQL9I.LOG_ERROR", line 7
ORA-06512: at "PLSQL9I.CREATE_ORDER", line 6
ORA-00001: unique constraint (PLSQL9I.SYS_C002737) violated
ORA-06512: at line 1
```

Exceptions and Autonomous Transactions

When an autonomous transaction exits with an exception (i.e., not normally),
a transaction-level rollback occurs and all pending changes in the autonomous
transaction are rolled back. This is in contrast with nonautonomous routines,
where uncommitted changes aren't rolled back if the exception is caught and
handled.

Multiple Autonomous Transactions

You can initiate multiple autonomous transactions in one autonomous transaction context. You do so by defining more than one COMMIT and/or ROLLBACK
statement inside an autonomous block. When you include a ROLLBACK, it pertains to the current transaction and not the main transaction. So you can roll
back to a savepoint in the current transaction and not in the main transaction.
An example of multiple autonomous transactions is shown in Figure 8-2.

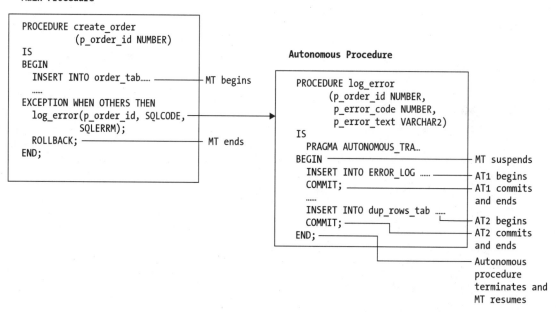

Figure 8-2. Multiple autonomous transactions in an autonomous block

Concurrency with Autonomous Transactions

Autonomous transactions run concurrently with the main transaction. The TRANSACTIONS parameter in the initialization file INIT.ORA determines the number of concurrent transactions per session. The default value in Oracle 9i for the TRANSACTIONS parameter is derived from the value of the SESSIONS parameter using the following formula: 1.1×SESSIONS. Here SESSIONS specifies the maximum number of sessions that can be created in the system (which effectively determines the maximum number of concurrent users in a system) and is dependent on the maximum number of user processes that can simultaneously connect to Oracle. If the value of TRANSACTIONS is exceeded, Oracle raises the exception

```
ORA-01574: maximum number of concurrent transactions exceeded
```

Autonomous Transactions and Calling User-Defined Functions from SQL

With autonomous transactions, you can call user-defined functions performing DML from SQL. Just define the user-defined function as an autonomous transaction, and the function becomes callable from SQL (e.g., in a SELECT statement). You can use this capability because autonomous transactions always imply the rule "read no database state" (RNDS) and "write no database state" (WNDS) even if an INSERT, UPDATE, or DELETE operation is executed within them.

Autonomous Transactions and Isolation Level

A COMMIT or ROLLBACK should be given in an autonomous transaction. Once a COMMIT or ROLLBACK executes within an autonomous transaction, those changes are visible to the main transaction. However, Oracle allows hiding of those changes from the main transaction by setting the isolation level of main transactions to SERIALIZABLE instead of going with the default value, READ COMMITTED. This is done using the SET TRANSACTION statement, which follows this syntax:

```
SET TRANSACTION ISOLATION LEVEL SERIALIZABLE;
```

Two points in regard to the isolation level are worth noting:

- The changes made by an autonomous transaction are visible to transactions other than the main transaction (i.e., the transaction that initiated the autonomous transaction) when the autonomous transaction ends by either a COMMIT or ROLLBACK.

- Setting the isolation level to SERIALIZABLE only hides the changes of the autonomous transaction from the main transaction until the main transaction is committed. Once the main transaction is committed, those changes from the autonomous transaction become visible to the main transaction.

What Is Isolation Level?

Isolation level specifies the way to handle transactions that modify the database. It also affects the visibility of changes in one transaction to other transactions. The SQL92 standard defines four isolation levels, namely, READ UNCOMMITTED, REPEATABLE READ, READ COMMITTED, and SERIALIZABLE. Out of these, Oracle 9i supports only READ COMMITTED and SERIALIZABLE isolation levels:

- *READ COMMITTED:* This setting, the default for all Oracle transactions, enables an Oracle query to see the data that was committed before the query started. Changes made by other transactions to tables accessed by the query during the time of this query's execution aren't visible to the query. In other words, transactions executing in this mode are transaction-set consistent on a per-statement basis.

- *SERIALIZABLE:* This setting implies that all statements in a transaction operate on an image of the database as of the beginning of that transaction. This means the current transaction can't see the data committed by another transaction unless a COMMIT occurs. These types of transactions are transaction-set consistent on a per-transaction basis.

Summary

This chapter discussed the concept of autonomous transactions. Starting with a brief introduction to default transaction management, I detailed the definition and use of autonomous transactions. I provided a case study to explain the concepts, and highlighted the steps involved in the processing of autonomous transactions. I described the use of autonomous transactions in database triggers. Finally, I presented tips and techniques involved in the use of autonomous transactions. The next chapter discusses native bulk binds in detail.

CHAPTER 9

Native Bulk Binds

You CAN RUN SQL statements from within PL/SQL blocks. You typically execute them as follows:

1. The PL/SQL engine, which is usually located on the server side, does the pure PL/SQL execution. However, client-side programs have their own PL/SQL engine.

2. Any SQL DML statements are forwarded to the SQL engine for execution. The resulting data or DML after-execution results are passed back to the PL/SQL engine.

This is also true for SQL statements being executed within a loop in PL/SQL. As a result, context switching occurs as SQL statements are passed between the PL/SQL and the SQL engines.

iiOne important area when you're executing SQL within PL/SQL (and more specifically, when you're executing within loops) is *optimization*. Because your code contains a mixture of PL/SQL and SQL, two parsing processes are involved.

The PL/SQL is executed by the PL/SQL engine, which is usually located on the server side. Remember, though, that client-side programs can also have their own PL/SQL engine. Any SQL DML statements are forwarded to the SQL engine for execution. The resulting data or DML after-execution results are passed back to the PL/SQL engine. This can lead to a performance overhead, particularly when you're working with looping constructs.

This process of passing statements to different engines is known as *context switching* and can result in less than optimal execution of your code. But as long as execution takes place and the results are correct, who cares? Well, your users will care. You should always be working toward optimal performance. Context switching results in traffic from PL/SQL to SQL and vice versa. Every round-trip involves overhead, and too many round-trips can hinder performance. Now the question is, why are so many round-trips required? One of the causes of such round-trips between engines is iterative execution, as many round trips may be involved.

One solution to this performance problem is provided via the use of bulk binding. *Bulk binding,* which was introduced in Oracle8*i,* improves overall PL/SQL performance and it has been further enhanced in Oracle9*i* by the addition of the following features:

- Support for processing to continue in the case of bulk binds involving DML in case an exception occurs, using the SAVE EXCEPTIONS clause.

- Direct support for *bulk dynamic SQL,* the capability to process multiple rows of data in a single DML statement. Prior to Oracle9*i,* native dynamic SQL supported bulk SQL indirectly if the bulk SQL statement was enclosed within a BEGIN . . . END.

- Multiple row updates and deletes with a RETURNING clause using dynamic SQL. Prior to Oracle9*i,* native dynamic SQL supported a RETURNING clause only in the case of a single-row output.

In this chapter, you'll explore the capabilities of bulk binds in the area of improving performance, and you'll learn techniques for performing

- Bulk DML

- Bulk querying

- Bulk dynamic SQL

I also introduce the new features in Oracle9*i* in this chapter.

I illustrate the concept of native bulk binds using the tables region_tab, region_tab_temp, sec_region_tab, supplier_tab, order_tab, and order_items. I provide the definition of these tables in Appendix A. Also, I create individual tables with dynamically constructed names such as ORDERS_FOR_<region_name> and ORDER_ITEMS_FOR_<region_name> based on the structure of the ORDER_TAB and ORDER_ITEMS tables.

Bulk DML

Bulk DML consists of executing INSERT, UPDATE, or DELETE statements in bulk using PL/SQL index-by tables or collections as the input for the DML statement. You perform bulk DML using the FORALL statement.

Consider the following PL/SQL subprogram:

```
DECLARE
   Type region_rec IS Record
    (region_id NUMBER(4),
      region_name VARCHAR2(10));
   Type region_tbl IS TABLE of region_rec
     INDEX BY BINARY_INTEGER;
  Region_recs region_tbl;
  Ret_code NUMBER;
  Ret_errmsg VARCHAR2(1000);
Procedure load_regions
          (region_recs IN region_tbl,
           retcd OUT NUMBER,
           errmsg OUT VARCHAR2)
Is
BEGIN
 -- Clean up region_tab table initially
 DELETE FROM region_tab;
 FOR i in region_recs.FIRST..region_recs.LAST LOOP
     INSERT INTO region_tab
     values (region_recs(i).region_id, region_recs(i).region_name);
 END LOOP;
COMMIT;
EXCEPTION WHEN OTHERS THEN
  Retcd := SQLCODE;
  Errmsg := SQLERRM;
END;
BEGIN
   FOR i IN 1..5 LOOP
     Region_recs(i).region_id := i;
     Region_recs(i).region_name := 'REGION'||i;
   END LOOP;
   Load_regions(region_recs, ret_code, ret_errmsg);
EXCEPTION WHEN OTHERS THEN
  RAISE_APPLICATION_ERROR(-20111,SQLERRM);
END;
/
```

For each element in the region_recs table, a context switch occurs as the INSERT statement in the FOR LOOP is sent to the SQL engine once for each iteration of the FOR LOOP. This means the traffic is heavy when the number of regions is large. In this case, the INSERT statement affects more database rows, and the use of bulk binds can improve performance considerably.

Binding refers to the assignment of values to PL/SQL variables in SQL statements. The binding of an entire set of values at once is called *bulk binding*. Bulk binds minimize the number of trips and hence the number of context switches between the PL/SQL and SQL engines. This improves performance significantly.

You use the FORALL statement to perform DML bulk binds. Here's the syntax:

```
FORALL index IN lower_bound..upper_bound [SAVE EXCEPTIONS]
    sql_statement;
```

where index is the index of the collection element; lower_bound and upper_bound are the starting and ending values of the index numbers for accessing the elements of the collection; and sql_statement is an INSERT, UPDATE, or DELETE statement. By specifying the lower and upper bounds, you specify a range of collection elements. The SAVE EXCEPTIONS clause is new to Oracle9*i*, and I explain it in the section "SAVE EXCEPTIONS Clause" later in this chapter.

TIP   *The FORALL statement is an implementation of an iteration algorithm; it isn't a FOR LOOP. You can't use the FORALL statement as a cursor FOR LOOP.*

You can do the previous INSERT operation using a bulk bind. Here's the code:

```
DECLARE
    Type region_id_tbl IS TABLE of NUMBER INDEX BY BINARY_INTEGER;
    Type region_name_tbl IS TABLE of VARCHAR2(20) INDEX BY BINARY_INTEGER;
    region_ids region_id_tbl;
    region_names region_name_tbl;
    ret_code NUMBER;
    ret_errmsg VARCHAR2(1000);
Procedure load_regions_bulk_bind
        (region_ids IN region_id_tbl,
         region_names IN region_name_tbl,
         retcd OUT NUMBER,
         errmsg OUT VARCHAR2)
Is
BEGIN
 -- clean up the region_tab table initially.
  DELETE FROM region_tab;
  FORALL i IN region_ids.FIRST..region_ids.LAST
```

```
      INSERT INTO region_tab values (region_ids(i), region_names(i));
  Retcd := 0;
EXCEPTION WHEN OTHERS THEN
  COMMIT;
  Retcd := SQLCODE;
  Errmsg := SQLERRM;
END;
BEGIN
  FOR i IN 1..5 LOOP
    Region_ids(i) := i;
    Region_names(i) := 'REGION'||i;
  END LOOP;
  Load_regions_bulk_bind(region_ids, region_names, ret_code, ret_errmsg);
EXCEPTION WHEN OTHERS THEN
  RAISE_APPLICATION_ERROR(-20112, SQLERRM);
END;
/
```

Here's how you can verify the output of this program:

```
SQL> select * from region_tab;
 REGION_ID REGION_NAM
---------- ----------
         1 REGION1
         2 REGION2
         3 REGION3
         4 REGION4
         5 REGION5
```

This program declares two index-by table types named region_id_tbl and region_name_tbl of the NUMBER and VARCHAR2 types, respectively. Then it declares two index-by tables named region_ids and region_names of these two index-by table types, respectively. It also declares a local procedure named load_regions_bulk_bind that takes as input two index-by tables of type region_id_tbl and region_name_tbl and does the following:

- Cleans up the region_tab table initially.

- INSERTS into the region_tab table using the bulk DML FORALL statement, taking the input for region_id from the region_ids index-by table and the input for region_name from the region_names index-by table. This single statement inserts five rows into the region_tab table in a single database call.

- COMMITS the inserted rows.

- Outputs a return code of 0 on success in the form of an OUT parameter named retcd. On error it outputs the corresponding SQLCODE and SQLERRM in the form of two OUT parameters, retcd and errmsg.

- Finally, the body of the PL/SQL block populates the two index-by tables, region_ids and region_names, with five region IDs and five region names. Then it invokes the load_regions_bulk_bind procedure that performs the bulk bind.

To verify the performance of bulk binds, you can do a massive INSERT once with a normal FOR LOOP and a second time using a FORALL statement. A reduced timing difference in the case of the FORALL statement illustrates the performance improvement. Here's a sample program that shows this:

```
DECLARE
    Type region_id_tbl IS TABLE of NUMBER INDEX BY BINARY_INTEGER;
    Type region_name_tbl IS TABLE of VARCHAR2(20) INDEX BY BINARY_INTEGER;
    region_ids region_id_tbl;
    region_names region_name_tbl;
    Ret_code NUMBER;
    Ret_errmsg VARCHAR2(1000);
    time1 number;
    time2 number;
    time3 number;
Procedure load_regions
            (region_ids IN region_id_tbl,
             region_names IN region_name_tbl,
             retcd OUT NUMBER,
             errmsg OUT VARCHAR2)
    Is
BEGIN
  FOR i in 1..10000 LOOP
     INSERT INTO region_tab_temp
     values (region_ids(i), region_names(i));
  END LOOP;
COMMIT;
EXCEPTION WHEN OTHERS THEN
```

```
    Retcd := SQLCODE;
    Errmsg := SQLERRM;
END;
Procedure load_regions_bulk_bind
          (region_ids IN region_id_tbl,
           region_names IN region_name_tbl,
           retcd OUT NUMBER,
           errmsg OUT VARCHAR2)
Is
BEGIN
  FORALL i IN 1..10000
      INSERT INTO region_tab_temp values (region_ids(i), region_names(i));
  Retcd := 0;
EXCEPTION WHEN OTHERS THEN
  COMMIT;
  Retcd := SQLCODE;
  Errmsg := SQLERRM;
END;
BEGIN
  DELETE region_tab_temp;
  FOR i IN 1..10000 LOOP
    Region_ids(i) := i;
    Region_names(i) := 'REGION'||i;
  END LOOP;
  time1 := dbms_utility.get_time;
  Load_regions(region_ids, region_names, ret_code, ret_errmsg);
  time2 := dbms_utility.get_time;
  Load_regions_bulk_bind(region_ids, region_names, ret_code, ret_errmsg);
  time3 := dbms_utility.get_time;
  dbms_output.put_line('Time without bulk bind is '||to_char(time2-time1)||
                                          ' secs');
  dbms_output.put_line('Time with bulk bind is '||to_char(time3-time2)||' secs');
EXCEPTION WHEN OTHERS THEN
  RAISE_APPLICATION_ERROR(-20111,SQLERRM);
END;
/
```

Here's the output of this program:

```
Time without bulk bind is 339 secs
Time with bulk bind is 19 secs

PL/SQL procedure successfully completed.
```

As you can see, the FORALL statement is significantly faster than that without the bulk bind. Nonexisting intermediate elements raise the following exception:

```
ORA-22160: element at index[i] does not exist
```

With FORALL, multiple INSERT, UPDATE, or DELETE statements are processed in a single call to the database. This improves execution time. Only a single INSERT, UPDATE, or DELETE statement that references collection elements can be executed by FORALL. The SQL statement is executed once for each index of the specified range. The DML must reference collection elements indexed by *index* in the FORALL statement. The collection can be an index-by table, a nested table, a VARRAY, or a host array. Only subscripted collections are bulk bound. The index can be referenced only within the FORALL statement and only as a collection subscript. Also, the collection subscript can't be an expression, and the subscripted index can't be an expression. The bounds must specify a valid range of consecutive index numbers. However, the upper and lower bounds don't need to span the entire range of the collection. The SQL statement can reference more than one collection. You can use FORALL when you perform native dynamic SQL also.

TIP   *As of Oracle9i Release 2, you can bulk bind %ROWTYPE index-by tables for DML. This means you can use record types for bulk DML. However, this isn't supported when you use native dynamic SQL with bulk DML.*

What Happens on SQL Error?

On SQL error, the immediate SQL operation is terminated by means of an automatic rollback. Then the execution stops. Only the immediate SQL statement is rolled back. Once successful, the preceding SQL statements aren't rolled back. A COMMIT as follows:

```
EXCEPTION WHEN OTHERS THEN
   COMMIT;
```

saves the successful SQL statements that precede the failed one.

So all the rows that are meant to be processed by the bulk DML statement aren't processed and it seems there's no way to continue after a row-wise exception. This was the case with PL/SQL prior to Oracle9*i*. Oracle9*i* enhances bulk DML with the capability to handle the error and continue processing after the failed row. I discuss this capability in the next section.

SAVE EXCEPTIONS Clause

Oracle9*i* enhances bulk DML with the capability to handle the error in the case of a row-wise exception and continue processing after the failed row. This is done with the SAVE EXCEPTIONS clause of the FORALL statement. Here's the syntax:

```
FORALL index IN lower_bound..upper_bound SAVE EXCEPTIONS
  sql_statement;
```

where index is the index of collection element; lower_bound and upper_bound are the starting and ending values of the index numbers for accessing the elements of the collection; and sql_statement is an INSERT, UPDATE, or DELETE statement. By specifying the lower and upper bounds, you specify a range of collection elements. The SAVE EXCEPTIONS clause is new to Oracle9*i*, and it saves the error rows in an implicit cursor attribute named SQL%BULK_EXCEPTIONS and allows the FORALL statement to continue processing the remaining rows.

Oracle9*i* also has a new exception with error code –24381. This error is as follows:

```
ORA-24381: error(s) in array DML
```

You can associate this error with a user-defined exception using PRAGMA EXCEPTION_INIT.

The implicit cursor attribute SQL%BULK_EXCEPTIONS is also new to Oracle9*i*. It works as follows:

- It resembles a PL/SQL table of records containing error_index and error_code as the record fields.

- You obtain the number of rows in this PL/SQL table by using the SQL%BULK_EXCEPTIONS.COUNT function.

- Information of any rows rejected from the processing of the DML statement is recorded in this PL/SQL table and the corresponding error_index and error_code are so populated. This has to be done in a FOR LOOP with a lower bound of 1 and an upper bound of the total number of errors in the SQL%BULK_EXCEPTIONS PL/SQL table. The error_index gives the iteration index or the row number of the failed row in the FORALL statement and is referenced by SQL%BULK_EXCEPTIONS(index).error_index. The error_code gives the SQLCODE corresponding to the failed row in the FORALL statement and is referenced by SQL%BULK_EXCEPTIONS(index).error_code. You obtain the corresponding error message by using SQLERRM as follows:

```
SQLERRM(-SQL%BULK_EXCEPTIONS(index).error_code);
```

Here's the code to illustrate this:

```
FOR i in 1..SQL%BULK_EXCEPTIONS.COUNT LOOP
   DBMS_OUTPUT.PUT_LINE('Iteration '||
             SQL%BULK_EXCEPTIONS(i).error_index||' failed with error '||
            ' SQLERRM(-SQL%BULK_EXCEPTIONS(i).error_code));
END LOOP;
```

Here's a complete example using the FORALL statement with the SAVE EXCEPTIONS clause:

```
DECLARE
   Type region_id_tbl IS TABLE of NUMBER INDEX BY BINARY_INTEGER;
   Type region_name_tbl IS TABLE of VARCHAR2(20) INDEX BY BINARY_INTEGER;
   region_ids region_id_tbl;
   region_names region_name_tbl;
   ret_code NUMBER;
   ret_errmsg VARCHAR2(1000);
Procedure load_regions_bulk_bind
          (region_ids IN region_id_tbl,
           region_names IN region_name_tbl,
           retcd OUT NUMBER,
           errmsg OUT VARCHAR2)
Is
   bulk_bind_excep EXCEPTION;
   PRAGMA EXCEPTION_INIT(bulk_bind_excep, -24381);
BEGIN
   -- clean up the region_tab table initially.
   DELETE FROM region_tab;
   FORALL i IN region_ids.FIRST..region_ids.LAST SAVE EXCEPTIONS
       INSERT INTO region_tab values (region_ids(i), region_names(i));
   Retcd := 0;
EXCEPTION WHEN bulk_bind_excep THEN
```

```
    FOR i in 1..SQL%BULK_EXCEPTIONS.COUNT LOOP
        DBMS_OUTPUT.PUT_LINE('Iteration '||
              SQL%BULK_EXCEPTIONS(i).error_index||' failed with error '||
              SQLERRM(-SQL%BULK_EXCEPTIONS(i).error_code));
    END LOOP;
    COMMIT;
    Retcd := SQLCODE;
    Errmsg := 'Bulk DML error(s) ';
  WHEN OTHERS THEN
    Retcd := SQLCODE;
    Errmsg := SQLERRM;
END;
BEGIN
  FOR i IN 1..5 LOOP
    Region_ids(i) := i;
    Region_names(i) := 'REGION'||i;
  END LOOP;
  Region_names(3) := 'REGION WITH NAME3';
  Load_regions_bulk_bind(region_ids, region_names, ret_code, ret_errmsg);
EXCEPTION WHEN OTHERS THEN
  RAISE_APPLICATION_ERROR(-20112, SQLERRM);
END;
/
```

Here's the output of the preceding code:

```
Iteration 3 failed with error ORA-01401: inserted value too large for column

PL/SQL procedure successfully completed.

SQL> select * from region_tab;

 REGION_ID REGION_NAM
---------- ----------
         1 REGION1
         2 REGION2
         4 REGION4
         5 REGION5
```

Note that region 3 isn't inserted.

To restore the row for region 3, you do the following INSERT followed by a COMMIT:

```
BEGIN
   insert into region_tab values (3, 'REGION3');
   commit;
END;
/
```

TIP   *If you don't use the SAVE EXCEPTIONS clause, the behavior of FORALL resembles that of pre-Oracle9i and it will stop execution when an exception occurs.*

TIP   *The SAVE EXCEPTIONS clause is also supported in native dynamic SQL using FORALL.*

FORALL Statement Attributes

Similar to the implicit cursor attributes, the bulk bind operation has the scalar attributes %FOUND, %NOTFOUND, and %ROWCOUNT associated with it. %ROWCOUNT functions on *all* executions of the SQL statement involving the bulk bind. However, %FOUND and %NOTFOUND refer only to the last execution of the SQL statement.

In addition, the implicit cursor (opened by Oracle when the FORALL executes an INSERT, UPDATE, or DELETE statement and identified by the keyword SQL) has one more composite attribute, %BULK_ROWCOUNT, which has the semantics of an index-by table. Its *i*th element stores the number of rows processed by the *i*th execution of a SQL statement. If the *i*th execution affects no rows, %BULK_ROWCOUNT(i) returns 0.

You can rewrite the first example I presented involving bulk binds to use both SQL%BULK_ROWCOUNT and SQL%ROWCOUNT. Here I track all the executions in which the SQL statement affected zero rows. Overall, if no rows were affected at all, SQL%ROWCOUNT returns 0.

```
DECLARE
   Type region_id_tbl IS TABLE of NUMBER INDEX BY BINARY_INTEGER;
   Type region_name_tbl IS TABLE of VARCHAR2(20) INDEX BY BINARY_INTEGER;
   region_ids region_id_tbl;
   region_names region_name_tbl;
```

```
   ret_code NUMBER;
   ret_errmsg VARCHAR2(1000);
   Procedure load_regions_bulk_bind
                  (region_ids IN region_id_tbl,
                   region_names IN region_name_tbl,
                   retcd OUT NUMBER,
                 errmsg OUT VARCHAR2)
  Is
BEGIN
  FORALL i IN region_ids.FIRST..region_ids.LAST
     INSERT INTO region_tab values (region_ids(i), region_names(i));
   FOR i in 1..region_ids.COUNT LOOP
      IF SQL%BULK_ROWCOUNT(i) > 0 THEN
        -- <track this particular execution>
        dbms_output.put_line(to_char(sql%bulk_rowcount(i)));
        NULL;
      END IF;
   END LOOP;
      IF SQL%ROWCOUNT = 0 THEN
        DBMS_OUTPUT.PUT_LINE('No Rows inserted overall');
      ELSE
        COMMIT;
      END IF;
EXCEPTION WHEN OTHERS THEN
  COMMIT;
  Retcd := SQLCODE;
  Errmsg := SQLERRM;
END;
BEGIN
  region_ids(1) := 6;
  region_names(1) := 'region6';
  load_regions_bulk_bind(region_ids, region_names, ret_code, ret_errmsg);
END;
/
```

 TIP *%BULK_ROWCOUNT and the FORALL statement use the same subscripts. You can't use %BULK_ROWCOUNT as an input value in an assignment statement involving another collection. You can't pass %BULK_ROWCOUNT as a parameter to subprograms.*

TIP *Referencing a row in SQL%BULK_ROWCOUNT that's outside the defined subscripts returns a NULL value and won't raise the NO_DATA_FOUND exception. This illustrates the deviation of %BULK_ROWCOUNT from an index-by table, though its semantics are similar to that of an index-by table. Thus, you can't apply the methods for an index-by table to %BULK_ROWCOUNT.*

Bulk Query

You use BULK COLLECT to bulk bind queries. Here's the syntax:

```
... BULK COLLECT INTO collection_name [, collection_name] ...
```

where collection_name is the name of the index-by table, nested table, or VARRAY.

You can use BULK COLLECT in SELECT . . . INTO, FETCH INTO, and RETURNING INTO clauses.

TIP *You can reference multiple collections in the INTO list.*

I first discuss BULK COLLECT using a SELECT . . . INTO statement. I follow this with a discussion of BULK COLLECT in FETCH INTO and RETURNING INTO clauses.

Using BULK COLLECT in SELECT . . . INTO

You can use BULK COLLECT in a SELECT . . . INTO statement. Here's the syntax:

```
SELECT column_name BULK COLLECT INTO collection_name;
```

where column_name is the name of the column being fetched by the SELECT and collection_name is the name of the index-by table, nested table, or VARRAY.

As an example, consider the update_dyn_global procedure presented in Chapter 7. I've reproduced it here for your reference:

```
Create or replace Procedure update_dyn_global
                                    (retcd OUT NUMBER,
                                     errmsg OUT VARCHAR2)
Is
  CURSOR csr_region IS
     SELECT region_name FROM region_tab;
BEGIN
   FOR idx IN csr_region LOOP
    update_dyn_for_all_orders(idx.region_name, retcd, errmsg);
    IF retcd <> 0 THEN
       EXIT;
    END IF;
  END LOOP;
EXCEPTION WHEN OTHERS THEN
  Retcd := SQLCODE;
  Errmsg := SQLERRM;
END;
/
```

You can rewrite this procedure using BULK COLLECT. I call this modified procedure update_dyn_global_bulk. Here's the code:

```
Create or Replace Procedure update_dyn_global_bulk
                                   (retcd OUT NUMBER,
                                    errmsg OUT VARCHAR2)
authid current_user
Is
  TYPE NameTbl IS TABLE OF region_tab.region_name%TYPE;
  Region_names NameTbl;
BEGIN
  SELECT region_name BULK COLLECT INTO region_names
  FROM region_tab ORDER BY region_name;
  FOR i IN region_names.FIRST..region_names.LAST LOOP
    update_dyn_for_all_orders(region_names(i), retcd, errmsg);
    IF retcd <> 0 THEN
       EXIT;
    END IF;
  END LOOP;
EXCEPTION WHEN OTHERS THEN
  Retcd := SQLCODE;
```

```
   Errmsg := SQLERRM;
END;
/
```

This procedure does the following:

- Declares an index-by table type named NameTbl of type region_tab.region_name%TYPE and then declares an index-by table named region_names of this type.

- Bulk queries the column region_name into this region_names index-by table using the SELECT . . . BULK COLLECT INTO statement.

- For each element in the region_names index-by table, it invokes the update_dyn_for_all_orders procedure, passing the region name as an input parameter.

- Outputs a return code of 0 on success in the form of an OUT parameter named retcd. On error it outputs the corresponding SQLCODE and SQLERRM in the form of two OUT parameters, retcd and errmsg.

The primary advantage of using BULK COLLECT is that it maximizes performance by reducing the number of context switches between the SQL and PL/SQL engines.

The SQL engine bulk binds entire database columns. So, column values corresponding to all the rows are loaded into the collection. However, you can restrict the number of rows to be loaded by using ROWNUM while selecting the records. Here's the code to do so:

```
SELECT region_name BULK COLLECT INTO region_names WHERE ROWNUM < 51;
```

 TIP *The SQL engine automatically initializes and extends referenced collections in the BULK COLLECT clause. It starts filling the collections at index 1 and inserts elements consecutively, overwriting any existing values. The resulting collection is a dense collection without any nonexisting intermediate elements.*

Using BULK COLLECT in Fetching

You can also use BULK COLLECT when fetching multiple rows from a cursor. Here's the syntax:

```
FETCH cursor_name BULK COLLECT INTO collection_name;
```

where cursor_name is the name of the cursor being fetched and collection_name is the name of the index-by table, nested table, or VARRAY.

I've altered the procedure update_dyn_global_bulk created earlier as follows to illustrate bulk fetch from a cursor into a collection. I call this modified procedure update_dyn_global_bulk2. Here's the code:

```
Create or Replace Procedure update_dyn_global_bulk2
                           (retcd OUT NUMBER,
                            errmsg OUT VARCHAR2)
authid current_user
Is
  TYPE NameTbl IS TABLE OF region_tab.region_name%TYPE;
  Region_names NameTbl;
CURSOR csr_region_names IS
    SELECT region_name FROM region_tab ORDER BY region_name;
BEGIN
    OPEN csr_region_names;
    FETCH csr_region_names BULK COLLECT INTO region_names;
    FOR i IN region_names.FIRST..region_names.LAST LOOP
     update_dyn_for_all_orders(region_names(i), retcd, errmsg);
     IF retcd <> 0 THEN
       EXIT;
     END IF;
    END LOOP;
  CLOSE csr_region_names;
EXCEPTION WHEN OTHERS THEN
  Retcd := SQLCODE;
  Errmsg := SQLERRM;
END;
/
```

This procedure does the following:

- Declares an index-by table type named NameTbl of type region_tab.region_name%TYPE and then declares an index-by table named region_names of this type.

- Declares a cursor named csr_region_names to SELECT an ordered set of region names from the region_tab table.

- Opens the cursor and bulk fetches the cursor into the region_names index-by table using the FETCH . . . BULK COLLECT INTO statement.

- For each element in the region_names index-by table, it invokes the update_dyn_for_all_orders procedure, passing the region name as an input parameter.

- Outputs a return code of 0 on success in the form of an OUT parameter named retcd. On error it outputs the corresponding SQLCODE and SQLERRM in the form of two OUT parameters, retcd and errmsg.

> **TIP**   *You can bulk fetch into one or more collections. As of Oracle9i Release 2, you can bulk fetch into a collection of records (for example, an index-by table of records). This is also true when you use native dynamic SQL.*

> **TIP**   *You can't use the SELECT . . . BULK COLLECT statement in a FORALL statement.*

Using BULK COLLECT in RETURNING INTO

You can also use BULK COLLECT in a FORALL statement as part of the RETURNING INTO clause. Here's the syntax:

```
FORALL index IN lower_bound..upper_bound [SAVE EXCEPTIONS]
  sql_statement
  RETURNING column_name INTO collection_name;
```

where index is the index of collection element; lower_bound and upper_bound are the starting and ending values of the index numbers for accessing the elements of the collection; and sql_statement is an INSERT, UPDATE, or DELETE statement. Also, column_name is the name of the modified column being returned into a collection named collection_name. Here's an example:

```
DECLARE
   Type region_id_tbl IS TABLE of NUMBER INDEX BY BINARY_INTEGER;
   Type region_name_tbl IS TABLE of VARCHAR2(20) INDEX BY BINARY_INTEGER;
   region_ids region_id_tbl;
   region_names region_name_tbl;
   out_region_names region_name_tbl;
   ret_code NUMBER;
   ret_errmsg VARCHAR2(1000);
Procedure load_regions_bulk_bind
          (region_ids IN region_id_tbl,
           region_names IN region_name_tbl,
           retcd OUT NUMBER,
           errmsg OUT VARCHAR2)
   Is
BEGIN
   -- clean up the sec_region_tab table initially.
   DELETE FROM sec_region_tab;
   FORALL i IN region_ids.FIRST..region_ids.LAST
       INSERT INTO sec_region_tab values (region_ids(i), region_names(i));
   Retcd := 0;
EXCEPTION WHEN OTHERS THEN
   Retcd := SQLCODE;
   Errmsg := SQLERRM;
END;
BEGIN
   FOR i IN 1..5 LOOP
     Region_ids(i) := i;
     Region_names(i) := 'REGION'||i;
   END LOOP;
   Load_regions_bulk_bind(region_ids, region_names, ret_code, ret_errmsg);
   IF (ret_code <> 0) THEN
     RAISE_APPLICATION_ERROR(-20111, SQLERRM);
   END IF;
   FORALL i IN 1..5
     UPDATE sec_region_tab
     SET region_name = 'NEW '||region_name
     WHERE region_id = region_ids(i)
      RETURNING region_name BULK COLLECT INTO out_region_names;
FOR i in out_region_names.FIRST..out_region_names.LAST LOOP
   DBMS_OUTPUT.PUT_LINE(out_region_names(i));
```

```
END LOOP;
EXCEPTION WHEN OTHERS THEN
  RAISE_APPLICATION_ERROR(-20112, SQLERRM);
END;
/
```

Here's the output of the preceding program:

```
NEW REGION1
NEW REGION2
NEW REGION3
NEW REGION4
NEW REGION5

PL/SQL procedure successfully completed.
```

This program declares two index-by table types named region_id_tbl and region_name_tbl of the NUMBER and VARCHAR2 types, respectively. Then it declares two index-by tables named region_ids and region_names of these two index-by table types, respectively. It also declares a second region names index-by table named out_region_names to hold the multiple region names returned by a RETURNING INTO clause, and it declares a local procedure named load_regions_bulk_bind that takes as input two index-by tables of types region_id_tbl and region_name_tbl and does the following:

- Cleans up the sec_region_tab table initially.

- INSERTS into the sec_region_tab table using the bulk DML FORALL statement taking the input for region_id from the region_ids index-by table and the input for region_name from the region_names index-by table. This single statement inserts five rows into the sec_region_tab table in a single database call.

- COMMITS the inserted rows.

- The code outputs a return code of 0 on success in the form of an OUT parameter named retcd. On error it outputs the corresponding SQLCODE and SQLERRM in the form of two OUT parameters, retcd and errmsg. The body of the PL/SQL block populates the two index-by tables region_ids and region_names with five region IDs and five region names. Then it invokes the load_regions_bulk_bind procedure that performs the bulk bind.

This code then updates the region_name column in the sec_region_tab table with a new value for all the rows and uses the RETURNING . . . BULK COLLECT INTO clause to return the updated column values into the out_region_names index-by table. Finally, it prints the values in the out_region_names index-by table.

TIP   *As of Oracle9i Release 2, BULK COLLECT into a PL/SQL table of records in RETURNING INTO is allowed.*

Host Arrays and Bulk DML

The use of host arrays is recommended for client-side programs to exchange data between client-side programs and the database. Anonymous PL/SQL blocks with an enclosing BEGIN . . . END are used to bulk bind input and output host arrays.

Host arrays are arrays declared in a host language such as C or C++. To identify host arrays in a PL/SQL program you specify them by prefixing the array name with a colon (:). Here's an example:

```
EXEC SQL EXECUTE
  BEGIN
    FORALL i IN :lower_bound..:upper_bound
      DELETE FROM region_tab WHERE region_id = :region_ids(i);
  . . . . . .
END;
```

where :region_ids is the host array declared in Pro*C or the host environment.

TIP   *Since host arrays are not PL/SQL arrays, you can't use methods such as FIRST and LAST with host arrays.*

Bulk Dynamic SQL

As I explained in Chapter 7, native dynamic SQL is preferred over static SQL because it's faster. Prior to Oracle9*i*, you could perform bulk dynamic SQL using only DBMS_SQL. Oracle9*i* has enhanced native dynamic SQL to support bulk operations. Primarily, Oracle9*i* supports the following type of bulk operations using dynamic SQL:

- EXECUTE IMMEDIATE with BULK COLLECT using a SELECT . . . INTO statement for bulk querying

- EXECUTE IMMEDIATE with a FORALL statement for bulk DML

- EXECUTE IMMEDIATE with a FORALL . . . RETURNING INTO . . . statement for bulk DML

- FETCH . . . BULK COLLECT INTO . . . for bulk fetch from a cursor variable opened using native dynamic SQL

These statements specify the various ways of using native dynamic SQL with bulk binds. Using bulk binding with dynamic SQL combines the performance advantage of using bulk binds to reduce context switching with the ability to execute quickly using native dynamic SQL statements. The following sections provide further detail.

EXECUTE IMMEDIATE with BULK COLLECT Using a SELECT . . . INTO Statement for Bulk Querying

You use EXECUTE IMMEDIATE with BULK COLLECT using a SELECT . . . INTO statement as follows:

```
EXECUTE IMMEDIATE 'select_statement' BULK COLLECT INTO collection_name;
```

As an example, consider the update_dyn_global_bulk_bind procedure mentioned earlier. You can replace the SELECT . . . BULK COLLECT INTO statement

```
SELECT region_name
BULK COLLECT INTO region_names FROM region_tab ORDER BY region_name;
```

with a dynamic SQL statement as follows:

```
 EXECUTE IMMEDIATE  'SELECT region_name FROM region_tab ORDER BY region_name'
BULK_COLLECT INTO region_names;
```

EXECUTE IMMEDIATE with a FORALL Statement for Bulk DML

You use EXECUTE IMMEDIATE with a FORALL statement for bulk DML as follows:

```
FORALL index IN lower_bound..upper_bound
   EXECUTE_IMMEDIATE 'sql_statement_using_bind_variables'
   USING collection_name;
```

As an example, consider the program presented in the section "Bulk DML." You can replace the FORALL statement

```
FORALL i IN region_ids.FIRST..region_ids.LAST
    INSERT INTO region_tab values (region_ids(i), region_names(i));
```

with a dynamic statement as follows:

```
FORALL i IN region_ids.FIRST..region_ids.LAST
    EXECUTE IMMEDIATE
        'INSERT INTO region_tab values (:ip_region_ids, :ip_region_names)'
    USING region_ids(i), region_names(i);
```

Here, :ip_region_ids and :ip_region_names are two bind variables whose corresponding bind arguments are the index-by tables region_ids and region_names, respectively.

EXECUTE IMMEDIATE with a FORALL . . . RETURNING INTO . . . Statement for Bulk DML

You use EXECUTE IMMEDIATE with a FORALL . . . RETURNING INTO . . . statement for bulk DML as follows:

```
FORALL index IN lower_bound..upper_bound
   EXECUTE_IMMEDIATE 'sql_statement_using_bind_variables_and_returning_clause'
   USING collection_name
   RETURNING BULK COLLECT INTO output_collection_name;
```

As an example, consider the program presented in the section "Using BULK COLLECT with RETURNING INTO." You can replace the FORALL . . . RETURNING INTO . . . statement

```
FORALL i IN 1..5
    UPDATE sec_region_tab
    SET region_name = 'NEW '||region_name
    WHERE region_id = region_ids(i)
      RETURNING region_name BULK COLLECT INTO out_region_names;
```

with a dynamic SQL statement as follows:

```
FORALL i IN 1..5
    'UPDATE sec_region_tab '||
    'SET region_name = :ip_val||'region_name'||
    'WHERE region_id = :in_ids
    'RETURNING  region_name INTO :out_rg_names'
    USING 'NEW ', region_ids(i)
    RETURNING BULK COLLECT INTO out_region_names;
```

Here, :ip_val is an input bind variable and :out_rg_names is an output bind variable whose corresponding bind argument is the index-by table out_region_names.

FETCH . . . BULK COLLECT INTO . . . for Bulk Fetch from a Cursor Variable Opened Using Native Dynamic SQL

Here's the code for bulk fetch from a cursor variable opened using native dynamic SQL:

```
OPEN cursor_variable_name FOR dyn_sql_statement;
. . .
FETCH cursor variable_name BULK COLLECT INTO collection_name;
. . .
```

As an example, consider the update_dyn_global_bulk2 procedure mentioned earlier. You can replace the statements

```
CURSOR csr_region_names IS
    SELECT region_name FROM region_tab ORDER BY region_name;
BEGIN
```

```
    OPEN csr_region_names;
    FETCH csr_region_names BULK COLLECT INTO region_names;
```

with dynamic SQL statements as follows:

```
TYPE rc IS REF CURSOR;
csr_region_names rc;
BEGIN
    OPEN csr_region_names FOR
      'SELECT region_name FROM region_tab ORDER BY region_name';
    FETCH csr_region_names BULK COLLECT INTO region_names;
```

Here, a weak REF CURSOR type is defined and then a cursor variable of this type is defined. A dynamic query is opened for this cursor variable and fetching is done using the FETCH . . . BULK COLLECT INTO statement.

 TIP *When you use bulk dynamic SQL for INSERT, UPDATE, or DELETE operations, you can't use a PL/SQL table of records for bulk binding. That is, you can't use it in FORALL and RETURNING INTO . . . BULK COLLECT statements.*

Summary

This chapter discussed the concept of bulk binding in Oracle9*i*. Starting with a discussion of what a bulk bind is, I then covered bulk DML and bulk querying. I discussed the exception handling mechanism new to bulk DML in Oracle9*i*. Finally, I presented the bulk binding improvements in Oracle9*i*, namely bulk dynamic SQL.

The next chapter presents a discussion of objects in Oracle9*i* and their use in SQL and PL/SQL, along with related features.

Part Three

Object-Oriented Features in PL/SQL 9*i*

The World of Objects

This chapter highlights those features of Oracle9*i* that go beyond the realm of relational structure—namely, in the area of object extensions in Oracle9*i*. The primary object extensions exclusive to Oracle9*i* are mainly the introduction of object type inheritance, dynamic method dispatch, type evolution, and the introduction of SQLJ object types. User-defined constructors were introduced in Oracle9*i* Release 2. User-defined object types, along with methods, object tables, object-relational tables, and object views, were first introduced in Oracle8.

Oracle9*i* has built within it a significant set of features to incorporate objects in the database. The primary object features include:

- Object types and methods that operate on these types as independent objects as well as part of an object table or a relational table with object columns, which I refer to as *object-relational tables*.

- Object REFS and the introduction of REF columns in the database as a better alternative to foreign key relationships. These are basically pointers between objects and/or object-relational tables.

- Object views and their use in SQL and PL/SQL.

- The introduction of collections that include variable arrays (VARRAYS) and nested tables, including multilevel collections. Collections can also be stored in the database.

- Large objects in the form of BLOBS, CLOBS, and BFILES.

- User-defined operators and their use in PL/SQL.

- Object PL/SQL that allows manipulation of object types, object REFS, and collections, as well as large objects in PL/SQL.

- Certain object-oriented features such as the implementation of type inheritance, polymorphism (including dynamic polymorphism or dynamic method dispatch), and type evolution.

- Java object storage in the form of SQLJ object types.

These features serve as object extensions to the relational structure. In this chapter, I focus on object types, object tables, and object-relational tables with respect to their creation, manipulation, and storage in the database, including objects in DML and their use in PL/SQL. I also discuss enhanced object-oriented features such as type inheritance, building of type hierarchies, polymorphism, and type evolution and SQLJ object types. Finally, I outline user-defined operators.

CROSS-REFERENCE   *Chapter 11 covers collections and Chapter 12 covers large objects.*

Object Types and Object Tables

This section discusses the use of object types and object REFS as independent objects in PL/SQL. It also covers using objects in the database, including DML on objects.

Object Types and Their Creation and Use in PL/SQL

An *object type* is an Oracle data structure that's identified by a name and defines a set of *attributes* (data-inherent) and operations on these attributes called *methods*. An *object* is an instance of an object type. An object gets instantiated when a variable of an object type is declared and initialized. Each instance of the object has its own memory and thus its own local copy of the attributes. Objects add several features to application programming, primarily encapsulation, abstraction, inheritance, and polymorphism. The sections that follow provide a brief description of each of these properties.

Encapsulation

Encapsulation ensures that applications using a given object can access the object's data only through that object's methods. In this way, the data and methods are encapsulated into a single object, and accessing applications are ignorant of the actual implementation of the methods.

Abstraction

The attributes and methods of an object exhibit data and procedural abstraction. The attributes of an object can be manipulated only by using the object's methods. Also, the object type represents an abstract data type of the real-world object in question.

Inheritance

Inheritance is the property of a child object to derive the properties of a base (parent) object. For example, a *classic book* can inherit the common properties pertaining to the *book* object. This eliminates the need to redefine these properties in the corresponding *classic book* object type. Object types exhibit inheritance and allow construction of type hierarchies involving supertypes and subtypes.

Polymorphism

Polymorphism is the ability to use multiple methods with the same name with different data. There are two types of polymorphism: static and dynamic. *Static* polymorphism refers to choosing the appropriate method based on the data at compile time and is ideally implemented using method overloading. *Dynamic* polymorphism refers to selecting the appropriate method to be executed depending on the data at runtime. In PL/SQL 9*i*, dynamic polymorphism is implemented using dynamic method dispatch. Figure 10-1 depicts a typical object scenario.

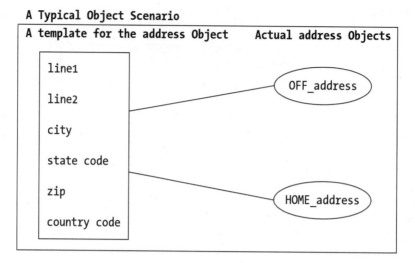

Figure 10-1. A typical object scenario

Defining an Object Type

An object type has a type specification and a type body. The *type specification* contains the attributes of the object type and the signature of the member methods. It's defined with the CREATE OR REPLACE TYPE . . .AS OBJECT statement. Here's the syntax:

```
CREATE OR REPLACE TYPE [schema.]type_name
[AUTHID DEFINER | CURRENT_USER] AS OBJECT | UNDER super_type (
  attribute_name datatype [, attribute_name datatype, ..] |
[{MAP | ORDER} MEMBER function_specification] |
[ [[NOT] INSTANTIABLE| FINAL| OVERRIDING] MEMBER | STATIC
{procedure_specification | function_specification }
[, [[NOT] INSTANTIABLE| FINAL| OVERRIDING] MEMBER | STATIC
{procedure_specification | function_specification }]..] |
[PRAGMA RESTRICT REFERENCES (method_name, constraints)
  [PRAGMA RESTRICT REFERENCES (method_name, constraints)]..]
)
[[NOT] INSTANTIABLE]
[[NOT] FINAL];
```

where type_name is the name of the object type being created; schema is the owner of the object type; attribute_name is the name of an attribute; and datatype is an Oracle built-in data type, a user-defined data type, or a reference to an object type. The methods are specified following the attribute specification. The AUTHID clause specifies the execution privileges for the object type as DEFINER (i.e., owner) or CURRENT_USER.

The UNDER clause and the INSTANTIABLE and FINAL clauses of the object type, as well as the NOT INSTANTIABLE, FINAL, and OVERRIDING clauses of the member methods, refer to the inheritance feature of object types introduced in Oracle9*i* and are discussed in the section "Type Inheritance" later in this chapter. Here's an example:

```
CREATE OR REPLACE TYPE address AS OBJECT
                    (line1 VARCHAR2(20),
                     line2 VARCHAR2(20),
                     city  VARCHAR2(20),
                     state_code VARCHAR2(2),
                     zip   VARCHAR2(13));
/
```

Here's how you can verify the output of this code:

```
SQL> desc address
```

Here's the output:

Name	Null?	Type
LINE1		VARCHAR2(20)
LINE2		VARCHAR2(20)
CITY		VARCHAR2(20)
STATE_CODE		VARCHAR2(2)
ZIP		VARCHAR2(13)

The following points are worth noting:

- This statement creates an object type address that has five attributes defined: line1, line2, city, state_code, and zip.

- The object type has no member functions defined as yet.

- The forward slash (/) at the end of the statement is necessary.

TIP   *The CREATE OR REPLACE TYPE statement is a DDL statement. Hence, you can't use it in a PL/SQL block. However, you can use dynamic SQL using DBMS_SQL and native dynamic SQL to execute the CREATE OR REPLACE TYPE statement.*

Object types are stored in the data dictionary, so you can use the data dictionary objects USER_OBJECTS and ALL_OBJECTS to query metadata information about a created object type. For example, the following query:

```
SELECT * FROM USER_OBJECTS WHERE object_type = 'TYPE';
```

lists information about all object types created in a current schema.

TIP   *The system privilege CREATE TYPE is to be granted to the current user to create an object type. The CREATE TYPE privilege is part of the RESOURCE role provided by Oracle.*

The attributes of an object type can be of an Oracle built-in SQL data type except the following:

- LONG or LONG RAW

- ROWID or UROWID

- NCHAR, NVARCHAR2, and NCLOB

The data type can also be another user-defined object type or LOB type. Also, any PL/SQL-only data types or any PL/SQL constructs can't be used in an attribute data type specification. In particular, the following can't be used:

- BOOLEAN, BINARY_INTEGER, PLS_INTEGER, RECORD, and REF CURSOR

- %TYPE or % ROWTYPE

- A type defined in a PL/SQL package

The object type body is defined only if the object type has member methods. I discuss this further in the section "Methods" later in this chapter.

Object Instances and Initialization

An *instance* of an object type is a variable defined of that type. An instance represents an actual object with its own local memory and its own copy of the attributes of that object type.

Here's an example that shows an instance of the object type address:

```
DECLARE
   off_add address;
```

This code declares off_add as an instance of the object type address. Now off_add represents an address object and can have values assigned to its attributes. It can also have its methods called in a sample application.

Initialization

By default, when an object is defined, it represents a NULL object (i.e., the object as a whole is NULL). You can initialize this object using a special method called the constructor method. A constructor method has the same name as the object type and is a function that accepts as parameters the values for its type's attributes and returns an initialized object.

Here's an example that shows how the off_add object is initialized:

```
DECLARE
   off_add address := address('19 J', 'Reading Rd', 'Edison', 'NJ', '08817');
BEGIN
   . . .
END;
```

 TIP   *Once an object is initialized, read and write operations can be performed on its attributes. The attribute values can be accessed or assigned using the dot notation as object_variable.attribute_name.*

Here's a PL/SQL block that prints the attribute values of the off_add object created and initialized previously:

```
DECLARE
  off_add address := address('19 J', 'Reading Rd', 'Edison', 'NJ', '08817');
BEGIN
  DBMS_OUTPUT.PUT_LINE(off_add.line1||' '||off_add.line2);
  DBMS_OUTPUT.PUT_LINE(off_add.city||','||off_add.state_code||' '||off_add.zip);
END;
/
```

A constructor method is an implicitly defined function that returns an initialized object. However, Oracle9*i* Release 2 allows the definition of user-defined constructor functions.

NULL Objects and NULL Attributes

Uninitialized objects have an atomically NULL value. A NULL object can't have its attributes referred to by the dot notation. A NULL object is never equal to another object. Also, objects can be assigned a NULL value explicitly. Objects can be tested with the IS NULL condition for null. Here's an example:

```
DECLARE
  v_address address;
BEGIN
-- v_address has a value
  v_address := address('27 Mine Brook Rd', '#99-A', 'Edison', 'NJ','08820');
  v_address := NULL; -- v_address becomes atomically null.
  IF (v_address IS NULL) THEN  -- condition returns TRUE
    DBMS_OUTPUT.PUT_LINE('v_address is atomically null');
  END IF;
END;
/
```

In an expression, attributes of an uninitialized object have a NULL value. Setting the values to attributes of an uninitialized object raises the predefined exception ACCESS_INTO_NULL. An object initialized with all its attributes as NULL is *not* atomically NULL. Here's an example to illustrate these points:

```
DECLARE
  v_address address;
BEGIN
```

```
   IF (v_address IS NULL) THEN -- Returns TRUE
                DBMS_OUTPUT.PUT_LINE('v_address is atomically null');
   END IF;
   IF (v_address.line1 IS NULL) THEN -- Returns TRUE
                DBMS_OUTPUT.PUT_LINE('line1 is null');
   END IF;
-- v_address has a value
   v_address := address('27 Mine Brook Rd', '#99-A', 'Edison', 'NJ','08820');
   v_address := NULL; -- v_address becomes atomically null.
   IF (v_address IS NULL) THEN   -- condition returns TRUE
                DBMS_OUTPUT.PUT_LINE('v_address is atomically null');
   END IF;
   v_address.line1 := '1, Ethel Road'; -- raises ACCESS_INTO_NULL
EXCEPTION WHEN ACCESS_INTO_NULL THEN
   DBMS_OUTPUT.PUT_LINE('Access Into Null');
END;
/
```

Here's the output of this program:

```
v_address is atomically null
line1 is null
v_address is atomically null
Access Into Null

PL/SQL procedure successfully completed.
```

Methods

Methods of an object type are functions or procedures that are called by objects
(i.e., instances of the object type). These methods act upon the attributes of the
object type. In an object type specification, methods are defined after the attributes. Only the specification of the methods is given in the object type. The
methods are specified as a comma-separated list of subprogram declarations,
each preceded by the keyword MEMBER. You implement these methods in the
object type body. You create the type body with the CREATE TYPE BODY . . .
statement. Here's the syntax:

```
CREATE OR REPLACE TYPE BODY [schema.]type_name
{IS | AS}
   [{MAP | ORDER} MEMBER function_declaration;] |
```

```
      [[NOT INSTANTIABLE| FINAL| OVERRIDING] MEMBER | STATIC
{procedure_declaration | function_declaration };
      [[NOT INSTANTIABLE| FINAL| OVERRIDING] MEMBER | STATIC
{procedure_declaration | function_declaration }]. . . ]
END;
/
```

Note that each method declaration ends with a semicolon (;) instead of a comma (,).

Here's an example that illustrates the use of member specifications in the type and member declarations in the type body for the address object type created earlier:

```
CREATE OR REPLACE TYPE address AS OBJECT
                    (line1 VARCHAR2(20),
                     line2 VARCHAR2(20),
                     city  VARCHAR2(20),
                     state_code VARCHAR2(2),
                     zip   VARCHAR2(13),
      MEMBER FUNCTION get_address RETURN VARCHAR2,
      MEMBER PROCEDURE set_address
                                        (ip_line1 VARCHAR2,
                                         ip_line2 VARCHAR2,
                                         ip_city  VARCHAR2,
                                         ip_state_code VARCHAR2,
                                         ip_zip VARCHAR2)
                                        );
/
```

This code re-creates the address type with two new member functions added to it. Here's how you can verify the code:

```
SQL> desc address
```

Here's the output:

Name	Null?	Type
LINE1		VARCHAR2(20)
LINE2		VARCHAR2(20)
CITY		VARCHAR2(20)
STATE_CODE		VARCHAR2(2)
ZIP		VARCHAR2(13)

```
METHOD
------
 MEMBER FUNCTION GET_ADDRESS RETURNS VARCHAR2

METHOD
------
 MEMBER PROCEDURE SET_ADDRESS
 Argument Name                     Type                      In/Out Default?
 ----------------------------      ---------------------     ---------------
 IP_LINE1                          VARCHAR2                  IN
 IP_LINE2                          VARCHAR2                  IN
 IP_CITY                           VARCHAR2                  IN
 IP_STATE_CODE                     VARCHAR2                  IN
 IP_ZIP                            VARCHAR2                  IN
```

The corresponding type body is as follows:

```
CREATE OR REPLACE TYPE BODY address AS
      MEMBER FUNCTION get_address RETURN VARCHAR2
      IS
      BEGIN
        RETURN (SELF.line1||' '||SELF.line2||' '||SELF.city||','||
                         SELF.state_code||' '||SELF.zip);
      END get_address;
    MEMBER PROCEDURE set_address(ip_line1 VARCHAR2,
                                 ip_line2 VARCHAR2,
                                 ip_city  VARCHAR2,
                                 ip_state_code VARCHAR2,
                                 ip_zip VARCHAR2)
    IS
    BEGIN
      line1 := ip_line1;
      line2 := ip_line2;
      city  := ip_city;
      state_code := ip_state_code;
      zip := ip_zip;
    END set_address;
  END;
/
```

Invoking a Method

Similar to a packaged subprogram, a method is called using the dot notation as OBJECT_VARIABLE.METHOD(). An object variable is required because the method needs to reference a particular object instance. You can omit the parentheses if the method has no parameters, but giving them in the case of no parameters is also valid.

Here's an example that illustrates how to call the GET_ADDRESS() and SET_ADDRESS() methods on address object variables:

```
DECLARE
  off_add address;
  home_add address;
BEGIN
  off_add := address('10 Wood Avenue South', 'Suite 111', 'Edison', 'NJ',
'08830');
  home_add := address(null,null,null,null,null);
  DBMS_OUTPUT.PUT_LINE(off_add.get_address());
  home_add.set_address('161 Franklin Rd', '#180', 'Edison','NJ', '08820');
  DBMS_OUTPUT.PUT_LINE(home_add.get_address());
END;
/
```

TIP *Although referencing an uninitialized object's attributes is illegal, calls to methods of an uninitialized object are allowed. In this case, SELF evaluates to NULL.*

TIP *When passed as arguments to IN parameters, attributes of uninitialized objects evaluate to NULL. When passed as arguments to OUT or IN OUT parameters, they raise an exception.*

TIP *When called in SQL statements, calls to parameterless methods require an empty parameter list.*

You can chain method calls. First invoke function calls, and then invoke procedure calls. The methods are executed from left to right. In the previous example, the following is valid:

```
off_add.get_address().set_address(...)
```

However, while chaining, you can't chain additional method calls to the right of a procedure call. The following statement is invalid:

```
off_add.set_address(...).get_address()
```

If two function calls are chained, the first function must return an object that can be passed to the second function.

You can write methods in PL/SQL or Java, or in languages such as C and C++. Methods written in PL/SQL or Java are stored internally in the database, whereas methods written in other languages are stored externally. A method of an object type can be a MEMBER method, a STATIC method, or a comparison method.

As discussed previously, a MEMBER method is defined with the MEMBER keyword preceding the method name. A MEMBER method has an implicit SELF parameter and thus can act on the attributes of a specific object instance. For example, the method GET_ADDRESS() is a MEMBER method that uses the SELF parameter to access the object's attributes. Here, SELF refers to the instantiating object (i.e., off_add or home_add).

Inside a member method's implementation, the use of the SELF keyword is optional. When an object instance is passed as an argument to another procedure or method, use SELF. In the case of member functions, SELF is implicitly declared as an IN parameter. For member procedures, it's implicitly declared as an IN OUT parameter. In PL/SQL, a member method using SELF shouldn't be invoked on a NULL object. Otherwise, the exception SELF_IS_NULL is raised.

A STATIC method is a procedure or a function that doesn't have an implicit SELF parameter. STATIC methods are invoked as OBJECT_TYPE_NAME.METHOD(). STATIC methods are generally used for global data that isn't specific to a particular object instance. For example, consider a function that returns the constant value irrespective of the object. You can specify this function as STATIC. The best use of STATIC methods is to pass the corresponding object as a parameter or to create a new object inside it and make it reference the attributes of this new object. Here's an example to illustrate this:

```
CREATE OR REPLACE TYPE zip_code AS OBJECT
(five_digit_code NUMBER,
 four_digit_code NUMBER,
STATIC FUNCTION getZip(zip_in zip_code) RETURN zip_Code
);
```

```
/
CREATE OR REPLACE TYPE BODY zip_code AS
    STATIC FUNCTION getZip(zip_in zip_code) RETURN zip_code
    IS
      v_zip zip_code;
    BEGIN
        v_zip := zip_code(null,null);
        v_zip.five_digit_code := zip_in.five_digit_code;
        v_zip.four_digit_code := zip_in.four_digit_code;
        RETURN (v_zip);
    END;
END;
/
```

You perform a comparison of two objects of a given object type by defining MAP or ORDER methods. The values of a predefined scalar data type have a predefined order and thus can be compared. For example, you can compare two integers for less than, equal to, or greater than. However, objects of a given object type have no definite order. To put them in order, you should define MAP and ORDER methods.

MAP methods are defined by the MAP keyword and return a single value that maps to a predefined scalar data type. You can use this value for comparison. As an example, you can define a MAP method on the address object type by having an additional ID attribute of type NUMBER and having the MAP method return that attribute. Then you can compare two address objects using their respective IDs.

TIP *You should define MAP methods as functions that take no parameters and return NUMBER, VARCHAR2, DATE, CHAR, or REAL values.*

ORDER methods use an internal logic to compare two objects and return the following values:

- −1 if the first is smaller

- 0 if they're equal

- 1 if the first is larger

You can define either a MAP method or an ORDER method for an object type, but not both. MAP methods should be parameterless functions. ORDER methods should take one parameter of the type of object type. If no comparison methods are specified, there's no way to determine a greater-than or less-than relationship between two objects. However, Oracle determines an equal-to relationship as follows:

- If all the attributes are non-null and equal, the objects are equal.

- If at least one attribute has an unequal non-null value, the objects are unequal.

- In all other cases, the objects are unequal.

To summarize, the use of object types involves three steps:

1. Define an object type that specifies a template for an object.

2. Define an object type body that specifies the implementation of member methods.

3. Instantiate an object of the type and invoke member methods on it.

User-Defined Constructors

As explained earlier, a user-defined object is initialized using a constructor method. This method is an implicitly declared method accepting parameters, one for each attribute of the corresponding object type. Oracle9*i* Release 2 and onward allow the definition of user-defined constructors that can be defined in the type. The implementation of the user-defined constructor can be provided in the type body.

A *user-defined constructor* is a function with the same name as the object type name with any number of arbitrary parameters that returns an object of type SELF. The parameters need not necessarily map to type attributes. You define a user-defined constructor with the CONSTRUCTOR FUNCTION . . . RETURN SELF AS RESULT clause. Here's an example:

```
CREATE OR REPLACE TYPE address2 AS OBJECT
               (line1 VARCHAR2(20),
                line2 VARCHAR2(20),
                city  VARCHAR2(20),
```

```
                              state_code VARCHAR2(2),
                              zip    VARCHAR2(13),
                              country VARCHAR(3),
        CONSTRUCTOR FUNCTION address2(ip_line1 VARCHAR2,
                                      ip_line2 VARCHAR2,
                                      ip_city  VARCHAR2,
                                      ip_state_code VARCHAR2,
                                      ip_zip VARCHAR2)
        RETURN SELF AS RESULT);
    /
```

The preceding code creates an object type named address2 with six attributes and a customized constructor function with the same name accepting only
five parameters. Here's how you can verify this:

```
SQL> desc address2
```

Here's the output:

Name	Null?	Type
LINE1		VARCHAR2(20)
LINE2		VARCHAR2(20)
CITY		VARCHAR2(20)
STATE_CODE		VARCHAR2(2)
ZIP		VARCHAR2(13)
COUNTRY		VARCHAR2(3)

```
METHOD
------
FINAL CONSTRUCTOR FUNCTION ADDRESS2 RETURNS SELF AS RESULT
```

Argument Name	Type	In/Out Default?
IP_LINE1	VARCHAR2	IN
IP_LINE2	VARCHAR2	IN
IP_CITY	VARCHAR2	IN
IP_STATE_CODE	VARCHAR2	IN
IP_ZIP	VARCHAR2	IN

The implementation of the user-defined constructor is provided in the type
body. Here's the code:

```
CREATE OR REPLACE TYPE BODY address2 IS
    CONSTRUCTOR FUNCTION address2(ip_line1 VARCHAR2,
                                  ip_line2 VARCHAR2,
                                  ip_city  VARCHAR2,
                                  ip_state_code VARCHAR2,
                                  ip_zip VARCHAR2)
    RETURN SELF AS RESULT
    IS
    BEGIN
        SELF.line1 := ip_line1;
        SELF.line2 := ip_line2;
        SELF.city := ip_city;
        SELF.state_code := ip_state_code;
        SELF.zip := ip_zip;
        SELF.country := 'USA';
        RETURN;
    END;
END;
/
```

Notice that the value for the country attribute is not derived from an IN parameter, but instead is set in the body of the user-defined constructor. This way, there's no need to pass the value for country every time an object of type address2 is initialized.

Here's an example that shows how the user-defined constructor can be called:

```
declare
   v_address address2;
begin
   v_address := address2('Suite 288','San Street','San Jose','CA','11011');
   dbms_output.put_line(v_address.line1);
   dbms_output.put_line(v_address.line2);
   dbms_output.put_line(v_address.city||', '||v_address.state_code||
                                     ' '||v_address.zip);
   dbms_output.put_line(v_address.country);
end;
/
```

Here's the output of this code:

```
Suite 288
San Street
San Jose, CA 11011
USA

PL/SQL procedure successfully completed.
```

Notice that the value for the country attribute isn't passed while calling the constructor. It's derived from the implementation in the user-defined constructor.

> **TIP**   *A user-defined constructor has the SELF parameter implicitly passed to it in the IN OUT mode.*

> **TIP**   *When a new attribute is added to the object type, the user-defined constructor need not be modified, but the default constructor has to have an argument corresponding to the new attribute passed to it.*

User-defined constructors are useful for specifying default values for attributes and for validating attribute data for correctness.

Altering and Dropping Object Types

Object types once defined can be altered to recompile the type specification or the body, to add or remove attributes, and/or to add methods. You do this with the ALTER TYPE statement. Once you've defined an object type, you can also drop it using the DROP TYPE statement. Also, you can drop the type body only using the DROP TYPE BODY statement. I discuss this in more detail in the section "Type Evolution" later in this chapter.

Objects in the Database

So far, I've discussed the definition of object types in the database. However, objects based on these object types were local to a PL/SQL block. These are referred to as *transient objects*. Objects can also be *persistent,* meaning they can be stored in a database table and manipulated using SQL statements. Persistent objects have session scope and exist until they're explicitly deleted.

This section discusses the way in which you can store objects in the database and how you can perform DML operations on objects. You can store objects in the database in three ways:

- As row objects in object tables.

- As column objects in relational tables. I call these tables *object-relational tables.*

- As references to row objects defined in object tables. These are known as *object REFS.*

Once you create an object table or an object-relational table, you can perform DML operations on it, as in the case of a relational table. You can share row objects between more than one object-relational table using object REFS.

Object Tables

Object tables are composed of row objects that constitute an entire database row. The table is based entirely on the object type and has no other column. Here's how object tables are created:

```
CREATE TABLE table_name OF object_type_name;
```

where table_name is the name of the table being created and object_type_name is the name of an object type on which the object table is being based.

Here's an example that creates an object table address_master based on the address object type:

```
CREATE TABLE address_master OF address;
```

Each row of address_master contains an instance of address. Each attribute of the object type appears as a column in the object table. When you describe the object table using

```
DESC address_master
```

here's the output:

```
SQL> desc address_master
 Name                                       Null?    Type
 ------------------------------------------ -------- ------------
 LINE1                                               VARCHAR2(20)
 LINE2                                               VARCHAR2(20)
 CITY                                                VARCHAR2(20)
 STATE_CODE                                          VARCHAR2(2)
 ZIP                                                 VARCHAR2(13)
```

This means an object table provides a relational view of objects stored in it.

Now you can insert data into this object table in one of two ways. The first way is by inserting into the object table by calling the constructor for the object type:

```
INSERT INTO address_master
VALUES (address('19 J', 'Reading Rd','Edison','NJ', '08817'));
```

The second way is by inserting into the object table directly into the individual columns as in case of a relational table.

```
INSERT INTO address_master VALUES ('19 J', 'Reading Rd','Edison','NJ', '08817');
```

Here's how you can verify the output of the previous INSERT statement:

```
SQL> select * from address_master;
```

Here's the output:

LINE1	LINE2	CITY	ST ZIP
19 J	Reading Rd	Edison	NJ 08817

Object Identifiers

Just as rows in a relational table have ROWIDs, rows in object tables have object identifiers (OIDs) associated with them. An OID enables the corresponding row object to be referred to from other objects or object-relational tables. An OID is a 16-byte Oracle-generated column that's unique and can't be modified. Also, once an OID is generated, it isn't reused even if the corresponding row is deleted.

Object-Relational Tables

Object-relational tables have one or more object columns and one or more relational columns. You create these tables by specifying the object type as a data type for one or more columns of the table. Here's a statement that creates an object-relational table employee with an object column emp_address:

```
CREATE TABLE employee
(empid            number(10) PRIMARY KEY,
 lastname         varchar2(30) NOT NULL,
 firstname        varchar2(30) NOT NULL,
 middle_initial   varchar2(2) ,
 emp_address      address);
```

You insert into employee by directly specifying values for the relational columns and using the constructor for specifying the value for the object column. Here's an example:

```
INSERT INTO employee VALUES
(101, 'LAKSHMAN', 'BULUSU', null,
address('50 UNION SQUARE','SUITE 101','NEW YORK','NY', '10020'));
```

Object References

Oracle provides a built-in data type called REF that references an OID of an object table. In fact, a REF is a pointer to a row object in an object table. Here's how you define a REF:

```
variable_name REF object_type_name
```

You can specify a REF as a data type of a column object in an object-relational table. In this way, it represents a kind of foreign key reference for object columns that refer to an object row in a master object table. This ensures that data isn't replicated, and it also ensures that changes made to the master are propagated instantly to the shared objects.

In the example of the employee table described previously, there's no guarantee that the address specified for the emp_address column exists in the address_master table. The referential data integrity can be maintained by declaring the emp_address column as a REF column. Here's the definition of the employee table with a REF column included:

```
DROP TABLE employee;
CREATE TABLE employee
(empid            number(10) PRIMARY KEY,
 lastname         varchar2(30) NOT NULL,
 firstname        varchar2(30) NOT NULL,
 middle_initial   varchar2(2),
 emp_address      REF address);
```

A REF reference is required between two objects and/or object-relational tables for the following reasons:

- The scope of a nested object is limited to the context of the parent object. Hence, each row object (in the case of an object table) and column object (in the case of an object-relational table) can't be referenced outside of the object table.

- Each row of an object table will hold its own PRIVATE instance of the row or column object and thus will have no accessibility to a second object table.

DML on Objects

This section highlights the methods of performing DML (SELECT, INSERT, UPDATE, and DELETE) on row objects and column objects.

DML operations on row and columns objects have similar transaction scope and visibility to those being performed on relational tables. The same COMMIT, ROLLBACK, and SAVEPOINT issues apply to relational tables and row and column objects.

SELECT

Querying object tables and object-relational tables pertains to how column objects and row objects can be accessed in the database. I first discuss how column objects can be queried and then I describe the SELECT operation on row objects.

You can query column objects in one of two ways. The first way is by directly retrieving the column object into a PL/SQL variable whose data type is the corresponding object type. This is when the column object isn't a REF column. Here's an example to illustrate this (employee is assumed to contain an object column named emp_address and of type address):

```
DECLARE
  v_address address;
BEGIN
  SELECT emp_address
  INTO   v_address
  FROM employee
  WHERE  lastname = 'LAKSHMAN';
  DBMS_OUTPUT.PUT_LINE(' The address of the employee LAKSHMAN is');
  DBMS_OUTPUT.PUT_LINE(v_address.line1||' '||v_address.line2);
  DBMS_OUTPUT.PUT_LINE(v_address.city||','||v_address.state_code||' '||
                                              v_address.zip);
END;
/
```

The second method is to fully qualify the object in a SELECT statement WHERE. Here's an example to show this:

```
SELECT * FROM employee e WHERE e.emp_address.city = 'Edison';
```

To reference a column object in the WHERE clause, the statement has to be a SELECT statement, not a SELECT . . . INTO statement. However, you can reference a column object in a SELECT . . . INTO statement if you supply an alias for the object-relational table. For example:

```
SELECT empid, lastname, firstname
INTO   v_empid, v_lastname, v_firstname
FROM   employee e
WHERE  e.emp_address.city = 'Edison';
```

Here, v_empid, v_lastname, and v_firstname are assumed to be declared.

It's also possible to query column object methods. You do this using an alias for the object-relational table and then referring to column object method in SQL using this alias. Here's an example:

```
SELECT e.emp_address.get_address()
FROM   employee e;
```

Note the opening and closing parentheses in the SELECT clause. These are required for methods accepting no parameters when called from SQL. This isn't required when the same method is invoked from procedural statements.

You query row objects using three operators: VALUE, REF, and DEREF. The following sections provide a description of each operator.

VALUE

The function VALUE returns the value of an object. VALUE takes as its argument a correlation variable (i.e., a table alias associated with a row in an object table). Here's an example:

```
DECLARE
  v_address address;
BEGIN
  SELECT VALUE(a)
  INTO   v_address
  FROM   address_master a
  WHERE  a.city = 'EDISON';
END;
/
```

REF

REF returns the reference to the object rather than the object itself. It also takes a correlation variable as its argument. Here's an example:

```
DECLARE
  v_address_ref REF address;
BEGIN
  SELECT REF(a)
  INTO   v_address_ref
  FROM   address_master a
  WHERE  a.city = 'EDISON';
END;
/
```

Also, an individual attribute of an object can be selected along with REF. Here's an example:

```
DECLARE
  v_address_ref REF address;
  v_zip VARCHAR2(30);
BEGIN
  SELECT REF(a), a.zip
  INTO   v_address_ref, v_zip
  FROM   address_master a
  WHERE  a.city = 'EDISON';
```

```
END;
/
```

DEREF

DEREF returns the value of the object to which the corresponding REF points. DEREF takes as its argument a reference to an object, and then it returns the value of that object. Here's an example:

```
DECLARE
  v_address_ref REF address;
  v_address address;
BEGIN
  SELECT DEREF(v_address_ref)
  INTO    v_address
  FROM    DUAL;
END;
/
```

Here you assume that v_address_ref holds a valid reference to an object stored in the address_master table.

You can also dereference REF column objects using DEREF. Consider the employee table with the REF column emp_address created. Here's an example to illustrate how to get the address of a particular employee:

```
DECLARE
  v_address address;
BEGIN
    SELECT DEREF(e.emp_address)
    INTO    v_address
    FROM    employee e
    WHERE   e.lastname = 'LAKSHMAN';
  DBMS_OUTPUT.PUT_LINE(' The address of the employee LAKSHMAN is');
  DBMS_OUTPUT.PUT_LINE(v_address.line1||' '||v_address.line2);
  DBMS_OUTPUT.PUT_LINE(v_address.city||','||v_address.state_code||' '||
                                                 v_address.zip);
END;
/
```

> **TIP** *You can't use DEREF in procedural statements.*

If the object to which a REF points is deleted, the REF is said to be *dangling* (pointing to a nonexistent object). You can use the SQL predicate IS DANGLING to check for dangling REFS.

For example, if an address row is deleted from the address_master table, the corresponding object REF in the employee table is dangling. The following UPDATE statement sets all dangling REFS to NULL:

```
UPDATE employee SET emp_address = NULL WHERE emp_address IS DANGLING;
```

INSERT

You INSERT into row objects by directly specifying the values for the object type attribute or by using the constructor method for the object type. You INSERT into column objects by calling the constructor for the corresponding object type. This was illustrated in the sections "Object Tables" and "Object-Relational Tables." There's a special clause, the RETURNING clause, that you can use with INSERT, UPDATE, and DELETE statements on objects. This clause enables you to retrieve information from the inserted, updated, or deleted row without having to query again. Here's an example to illustrate this:

```
DECLARE
  v_address_ref REF address;
BEGIN
  INSERT INTO address_master a
VALUES (address('57-1 Fairlawn Street','#101C','Flushing','NY','10110'))
  RETURNING REF(a) INTO v_address_ref;
END;
/
```

Also, you can use a subquery to insert into an object table. For example, consider an employee_special table that has all employees belonging to New York City:

```
INSERT INTO employee_special
  SELECT VALUE(e)
```

```
FROM    employee e
WHERE   e.emp_address.city = 'NEW YORK';
```

 TIP *No OIDs are copied from the employee table. New OIDs are generated for the rows in the employee_special table.*

UPDATE

You can perform an UPDATE in one of two ways. The first is by directly modifying the attributes of an object in the object table. Here's an example:

```
UPDATE address_master a SET a.zip = '08820-3307' WHERE a.zip = '08820';
```

The second method is by modifying the entire object. Here's an example:

```
DECLARE
  v_address address;
  v_address_ref REF address;
BEGIN
  INSERT INTO address_master a
VALUES (address('10 Metroplex Complex','Suite 202','Boston','MA', '01701'))
  RETURNING REF(a) INTO v_address_ref;
UPDATE employee
SET emp_address = v_address_ref
WHERE empid = 101;
END;
/
```

DELETE

You can use the DELETE statement to delete objects from an object table. You can also use an optional WHERE clause. Here's an example:

```
BEGIN
  DELETE FROM address_master a
  WHERE (a.line1 IS NULL) AND (a.line2 IS NULL);
END;
/
```

Using %TYPE and %ROWTYPE on Row Objects

The use of %TYPE and %ROWTYPE is allowed on object tables as on relational tables. Declarations using %TYPE on an object table are valid and work well. Here's an example:

```
DECLARE
    v_line1 address_master.line1%TYPE;
BEGIN
  SELECT line1
  INTO    v_line1
  FROM   address_master
  WHERE  city = 'EDISON';
  DBMS_OUTPUT.PUT_LINE(v_line1);
END;
/
```

However, when %ROWTYPE is used on a row object, it returns the corresponding object type on which the object table is based and not a PL/SQL record as in the case of relational tables. Hence, fetching into %ROWTYPE variables on an object table results in a type mismatch error. Here's an example to illustrate this:

```
declare
    cursor c1 is select * from address_master;
    v_add address_master%ROWTYPE;
begin
  open c1;
  loop
    fetch c1 into v_add;
    exit when c1%notfound;
    dbms_output.put_line(v_add.line1);
  end loop;
  close c1;
end;
/
fetch c1 into v_add;
                   *
ERROR at line 7:
ORA-06550: line 7, column 19:
PLS-00386: type mismatch found at 'V_ADD' between FETCH cursor and INTO
variables
ORA-06550: line 7, column 5:
PL/SQL: SQL Statement ignored
```

To rectify this error, either select the object type from the table rather than * (the individual columns) or use a cursor for loop with an implicitly declared index that points to the correct type. Here's the previous example modified to select the object type:

```
declare
    cursor c1 is select VALUE(a) from address_master a;
    v_add address_master%ROWTYPE;
begin
  open c1;
  loop
    fetch c1 into v_add;
    exit when c1%notfound;
    dbms_output.put_line(v_add.line1);
  end loop;
  close c1;
end;
/
```

Here's an example that uses a cursor FOR LOOP with an implicitly declared index that points to the correct type:

```
declare
    cursor c1 is select * from address_master;
    v_add address_master%ROWTYPE;
begin
  for i in c1 loop
    dbms_output.put_line(i.line1);
  end loop;
end;
/
```

Objects and Native Dynamic SQL

You can use native dynamic SQL with object types and object tables. The native dynamic SQL statements for performing dynamic object DDL and DML are the same as those you use when working with relational tables. The difference is that instead of relational tables, object tables and/or tables with objects as columns are used. This section discusses the use of native dynamic SQL with objects.

Dynamic DDL Involving Objects

Consider an application in which there are different regions and the different addresses in each region are to be stored separately. The region data is stored in the region_tab table and the address data for each region is to be stored in separate tables created for each region. This involves dynamically creating the address table for each region. Assume that this address table is based on the address object type created earlier. To summarize the requirement, an object table for each region is to be created dynamically based on the rows in the region_tab table. This involves dynamic DDL with objects and is done with the EXECUTE IMMEDIATE statement. Here's the syntax:

```
EXECUTE IMMEDIATE dyn_ddl_string;
```

where dyn_ddl_string is a string variable whose value is a DDL statement determined at runtime.

The dynamic object tables are created in two steps:

1. The procedure create_dyn_obj_table creates the individual address_master_for_<region> table using native dynamic SQL.

2. The procedure create_dyn_obj_for_all calls this procedure for each region in region_tab.

Here's the code for these procedures:

```
Create or replace Procedure create_dyn_obj_table
                            (i_region_name VARCHAR2,
                             retcd OUT NUMBER,
                             errmsg OUT VARCHAR2)
authid current_user
Is
  Dyn_string VARCHAR2(1000);
  Dyn_Table_name VARCHAR2(30);
Begin
  Dyn_table_name := 'ADDRESS_MASTER_FOR_'||replace(trim(i_region_name),' ','_');
  Dyn_string := ' CREATE TABLE ' ||dyn_table_name||' OF address ';

  EXECUTE IMMEDIATE dyn_string ;

  retcd := 0;

EXCEPTION WHEN OTHERS THEN
```

```
    retcd := SQLCODE;
    errmsg := 'ERR: Creating table '||dyn_table_name ||' - '||SQLERRM;
End;
/
```

This procedure does the following:

- Creates a dynamic table name concatenating the input region name with the constant ADDRESS_MASTER_FOR_ and places it in a PL/SQL variable named dyn_table_name. This is for the address_master table for each region.

- Creates a dynamically generated CREATE TABLE statement using the dyn_table_name variable and places it in a PL/SQL variable named dyn_string. The table structure is that of an object table based on the address object type.

- Executes this dynamic string using the EXECUTE IMMEDIATE statement.

- Outputs a return code of 0 on success in the form of an OUT parameter named retcd. On error it outputs the corresponding SQLCODE and SQLERRM in the form of two OUT parameters, retcd and errmsg.

Next, here's the code for the create _dyn_obj_for_all procedure:

```
Create or replace Procedure create_dyn_obj_for_all
                                  (retcd OUT NUMBER, errmsg OUT VARCHAR2)
Authid current_user
Is
   CURSOR csr_region IS
     SELECT region_name
     FROM   region_tab;
BEGIN
   FOR idx IN csr_region LOOP
     create_dyn_obj_table(idx.region_name, retcd, errmsg);
     IF retcd <> 0 THEN
        EXIT;
     END IF;
   END LOOP;
EXCEPTION WHEN OTHERS THEN
   Retcd := SQLCODE;
   Errmsg := SQLERRM;
END;
/
```

This procedure does the following:

- Declares a cursor for all the region names in the region_tab table.

- For each row in the cursor, it invokes the create_dyn_obj_table procedure, passing the region name as an IN parameter to both. This creates the ADDRESS_MASTER_FOR_<region> object table, where <region> stands for each region name in the region_tab table.

- Outputs a return code of 0 on success in the form of an OUT parameter named retcd. On error it outputs the corresponding SQLCODE and SQLERRM in the form of two OUT parameters, retcd and errmsg.

Here's the code for executing this procedure:

```
DECLARE
  Retcd NUMBER;
  Errmsg VARCHAR2(32767);
BEGIN
  Create_dyn_obj_for_all(retcd, errmsg);
  IF (retcd <> 0) THEN
    RAISE_APPLICATION_ERROR(-20190, errmsg);
  END IF;
EXCEPTION WHEN OTHERS THEN
  RAISE_APPLICATION_ERROR(-20191, SQLERRM);
END;
/
```

Here's the code to verify the output of this program:

```
column object_name format a30;
select object_name, object_type from user_objects
where  object_name like 'ADDRESS%FOR%';
```

Here's the output of this query:

```
OBJECT_NAME                     OBJECT_TYPE
------------------------------  -----------
ADDRESS_MASTER_FOR_REGION1      TABLE
ADDRESS_MASTER_FOR_REGION2      TABLE
ADDRESS_MASTER_FOR_REGION3      TABLE
ADDRESS_MASTER_FOR_REGION4      TABLE
ADDRESS_MASTER_FOR_REGION5      TABLE
ADDRESS_MASTER_FOR_REGION6      TABLE

6 rows selected.
```

Dynamic INSERT Involving Objects

In addition to DDL statements, INSERT, UPDATE, and DELETE statements involving objects can be constructed dynamically and executed at runtime. This section demonstrates the use of dynamic INSERTs involving objects using native dynamic SQL.

The statements

```
EXECUTE IMMEDIATE <dyn_string>;
EXECUTE IMMEDIATE <dyn_string> INTO <plsql_variables_list_comma_separated>
USING <bind_variables_list_comma_seperated>;
```

are used to execute dynamic INSERT, UPDATE, and DELETE statements. The dynamic SQL string can also have a RETURNING clause if needed. As an example, consider a procedure to insert into each of the address_master_for_<region> object tables created earlier. Here's the code:

```
Create or replace Procedure insert_dyn_obj_table
                        (i_region_name VARCHAR2, i_line1 VARCHAR2,
                         i_line2 VARCHAR2, i_city VARCHAR2,
                         i_state_code VARCHAR2, i_zip VARCHAR2,
                         retcd OUT NUMBER, errmsg OUT VARCHAR2)
authid current_user
Is
  Dyn_ins_string VARCHAR2(1000);
  Dyn_Table_name VARCHAR2(30);
Begin
  Dyn_table_name := 'ADDRESS_MASTER_FOR_'||replace(trim(i_region_name),' ','_');
```

```
      Dyn_ins_string :=
         ' INSERT INTO '||dyn_table_name||' VALUES (address(:1,:2,:3,:4,:5)) ';
      EXECUTE IMMEDIATE dyn_ins_string
         USING i_line1, i_line2, i_city, i_state_code, i_zip;
      retcd := 0;
EXCEPTION WHEN OTHERS THEN
   retcd := SQLCODE;
   errmsg := 'ERR: '||SQLERRM;
End;
/
```

This procedure does the following:

- Creates a dynamic table name concatenating the input region name with the constant ADDRESS_MASTER_FOR_ and places it in a PL/SQL variable named dyn_table_name. This is for the address master table for each region.

- Creates a dynamically generated INSERT statement using the dyn_table_name variable and places it in a PL/SQL variable named dyn_ins_string. This is for inserting into the ADDRESS_MASTER_FOR_<region> table for each region name. It uses five bind variables for setting the values of each column in this table, with the passed input parameters as arguments for each of them.

- Executes this dynamic string using the EXECUTE IMMEDIATE . . . USING statement. This inserts a row into the ADDRESS_MASTER_FOR_<region> table for the input region.

- Outputs a return code of 0 on success in the form of an OUT parameter named retcd. On error it outputs the corresponding SQLCODE and SQLERRM in the form of two OUT parameters, retcd and errmsg.

Here's the code to call this procedure:

```
DECLARE
   Retcd NUMBER;
   Errmsg VARCHAR2(32767);
BEGIN
   insert_dyn_obj_table('REGION1','20 James St.', null, 'Edison', 'NJ', '08825',
                                       retcd, errmsg);
   IF (retcd <> 0) THEN
     RAISE_APPLICATION_ERROR(-20193, errmsg);
```

```
  END IF;
insert_dyn_obj_table('REGION1','11 Woodstock Ave.', '#2D', 'Blue Bells', 'VA',
                                '17864', retcd, errmsg);
  IF (retcd <> 0) THEN
    RAISE_APPLICATION_ERROR(-20194, errmsg);
  END IF;
insert_dyn_obj_table('REGION2','15 Highs Blvd', 'Suite 201', 'Sunnyvale', 'CA',
                                '12456', retcd, errmsg);
  IF (retcd <> 0) THEN
    RAISE_APPLICATION_ERROR(-20195, errmsg);
  END IF;
insert_dyn_obj_table('REGION4','1 Woodfield Ct.', null, 'Dallas', 'TX',
                                '94567', retcd, errmsg);
  IF (retcd <> 0) THEN
    RAISE_APPLICATION_ERROR(-20196, errmsg);
  END IF;
  COMMIT;
EXCEPTION WHEN OTHERS THEN
  RAISE_APPLICATION_ERROR(-20197, SQLERRM);
END;
/
```

Dynamic Multirow Querying Involving Objects

Like native dynamic SQL for relational tables, dynamic multirow querying involving objects is done by using a weak cursor variable that is opened for a dynamic query string. Here are the basic steps:

1. Declare a weak REF CURSOR type.

2. Declare a cursor variable of this type.

3. Construct the dynamic query string involving object tables.

4. Open the cursor variable for this dynamic query string.

5. FETCH in a loop the rows one by one and process them. Fetching into variables of type as the object type is allowed.

6. Close the cursor variable.

The statements

```
OPEN <cursor_var> FOR <dyn_query_string>;
OPEN <cursor_var> FOR <dyn_query_string>
USING <plsql_variables_list_comma_seperated>;
FETCH <cursor_var> INTO <plsql_variables_of_type_object_type>;
CLOSE <cursor_var>;
```

are used to execute dynamic multirow SELECTs.

As an example, consider a procedure for displaying the addresses for each region that was created earlier. This procedure accepts a particular region_name as input. Here's the code:

```
Create or replace Procedure display_dyn_obj_for_region
                                    (i_region_name VARCHAR2,
                                     retcd OUT NUMBER,
                                     errmsg OUT VARCHAR2)
Is
    Dyn_table_name  VARCHAR2(100);
    Dyn_query_string VARCHAR2(1000);
    Type csr_dyn IS REF CURSOR;
    csr_dyn1 csr_dyn;
    v_address address;
BEGIN
    Dyn_table_name := 'ADDRESS_MASTER_FOR_'||replace(trim(i_region_name), ' ',
'_');
    Dyn_query_string := 'SELECT VALUE(a) FROM '||dyn_table_name||' a ';
    DBMS_OUTPUT.PUT_LINE('The addresses for region: '||i_region_name||' are :-');
    DBMS_OUTPUT.NEW_LINE;
    OPEN csr_dyn1 FOR dyn_query_string;
    LOOP
      FETCH csr_dyn1 INTO v_address;
      EXIT WHEN csr_dyn1%NOTFOUND;
        DBMS_OUTPUT.PUT_LINE(v_address.line1||' '||v_address.line2||' '||
          v_address.city||', '||v_address.state_code||' '||v_address.zip);
    END LOOP;
    CLOSE csr_dyn1;
EXCEPTION WHEN OTHERS THEN
  Retcd := SQLCODE;
  Errmsg := SQLERRM;
END;
/
```

This procedure does the following:

- Declares a type definition of type REF CURSOR named csr_dyn and a cursor variable named csr_dyn1 as an instance of the csr_dyn type. This is for processing multiple rows of a dynamic query.

- Creates a dynamic table name concatenating the input region name with the constant ADDRESS_MASTER_FOR_ and places it in a PL/SQL variable named dyn_table_name. This is for the address master table for each region.

- Creates a dynamically generated SELECT statement using the dyn_table_name variable and places it in a PL/SQL variable named dyn_query_string. This is for selecting each object row from the ADDRESS_MASTER_FOR_<region> table. This SELECT returns multiple rows from each ADDRESS_MASTER_FOR_<region> table.

- Executes this dynamic string using the OPEN FOR and FETCH . . . INTO statements. First, the REF CURSOR variable is opened for the dynamic SELECT. Next, the cursor variable is fetched into a local object variable named v_address. Each row returned by the query is displayed using DBMS_OUTPUT.PUT_LINE.

- Outputs a return code of 0 on success in the form of an OUT parameter named retcd. On error it outputs the corresponding SQLCODE and SQLERRM in the form of two OUT parameters, retcd and errmsg.

You can further extend this procedure to encompass all addresses in all regions. I call this procedure display_dyn_obj_global. The logic for this procedure doesn't require dynamic SQL. For all regions in the region_tab table, it loops through to execute display_dyn_obj_for_region with region_name pointing to the current cursor row as the first input parameter. Here's the code:

```
Create or replace Procedure display_dyn_obj_global
                                    (retcd OUT NUMBER,
                                     errmsg OUT VARCHAR2)
Is
  CURSOR csr_region IS
     SELECT region_name FROM region_tab;
BEGIN
    FOR idx IN csr_region LOOP
    display_dyn_obj_for_region(idx.region_name, retcd, errmsg);
    IF retcd <> 0 THEN
```

```
        EXIT;
      END IF;
    END LOOP;
EXCEPTION WHEN OTHERS THEN
   Retcd := SQLCODE;
   Errmsg := SQLERRM;
END;
/
```

This procedure does the following:

- Declares a cursor for all the region names in the region_tab table.

- For each row in the cursor, it invokes the display_dyn_obj_for_region procedure, passing the region name as an IN parameter.

- Outputs a return code of 0 on success in the form of an OUT parameter named retcd. On error it outputs the corresponding SQLCODE and SQLERRM in the form of two OUT parameters, retcd and errmsg.

Here's the code for executing this procedure:

```
DECLARE
   Retcd NUMBER;
   Errmsg VARCHAR2(32767);
BEGIN
   display_dyn_obj_global(retcd, errmsg);
   IF (retcd <> 0) THEN
      RAISE_APPLICATION_ERROR(-20190, errmsg);
   END IF;
EXCEPTION WHEN OTHERS THEN
   RAISE_APPLICATION_ERROR(-20191, SQLERRM);
END;
/
```

Here's the output of this program:

```
The addresses for region: REGION1 are :-
20 James St.  Edison, NJ 08825
11 Woodstock Ave. #2D Blue Bells, VA 17864
The addresses for region: REGION2 are :-
15 Highs Blvd Suite 201 Sunnyvale, CA 12456
The addresses for region: REGION4 are :-
1 Woodfield Ct.  Dallas, TX 94567
The addresses for region: REGION5 are :-
The addresses for region: region6 are :-
The addresses for region: REGION3 are :-

PL/SQL procedure successfully completed.
```

> **TIP** *Variables or parameters of object types can be used as arguments to bind variables used in native dynamic SQL statements.*

> **TIP** *Exceptions raised when using objects with native dynamic SQL statements are handled with an exception handler in an enclosing block.*

Type Inheritance

Inheritance relates to two or more objects where one object behaves as a child of a parent object and derives the properties of the base (parent) object. The child object is said to "inherit" the properties of the parent object. For example, a *literature book* object can inherit the common properties pertaining to a *book* object.

In object-oriented languages such as Java and C++, inheritance is implemented by means of superclasses and subclasses constructed to form a class hierarchy. In PL/SQL, an object type takes the role of a Java or C++ class and PL/SQL 9*i* supports object type inheritance by means of supertypes and subtypes. Objects are organized as instances of types, and types can be related in a tree fashion by means of type hierarchies. The hierarchy so formed constitutes a supertype/subtype hierarchy with subtypes inheriting attributes (data) and methods (behavior) from their supertypes. In fact, a subtype inherits all of the attributes and methods from all its supertypes in the resulting object type hierarchy and not just the immediate subtype.

Inheritance leads to substitutability and dynamic polymorphism. PL/SQL 9*i* supports *substitutability*—that is, the ability to use the value of a subtype where a supertype is expected. PL/SQL 9*i* also supports dynamic polymorphism by means of *dynamic method dispatch,* which is the ability to determine at runtime and execute the most specific method in the object hierarchy that corresponds to the instance of the object type that invokes the method.

This section discusses the inheritance features of object types and the construction of a type hierarchy in PL/SQL. Dynamic polymorphism is discussed in a subsequent section.

Typical inheritance hierarchies are shown in Figures 10-2 and 10-3.

A Typical Book Hierarchy

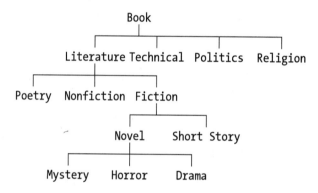

Figure 10-2. A typical Book hierarchy

A Typical Vehicle Hierarchy

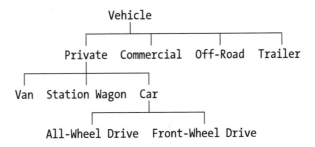

Figure 10-3. A typical Vehicle hierarchy

A careful analysis of the hierarchy shown in Figure 10-2 reveals the following:

- The root type of the hierarchy is Book.

- Four subtypes evolve from Book: Literature, Technical, Politics, and Religion.

- A Literature book in turn can be a Fiction book, a Nonfiction book, or a Poetry book.

- A Fiction book can be a Novel or a Short Story.

- Finally, a Novel can be on a Mystery topic, a Horror topic, or a Drama topic.

- The Book hierarchy has five levels, including the root level, and all types defined at a level other than the root level are subtypes of their preceding level types and supertypes of their succeeding level types.

- All the categories of books defined share certain common properties, such as title, author, ISBN#, publisher, and so on. The type of the book, whether Literature, Fiction, Novel, or Mystery, is immature while describing these common properties. Also, each type can have properties specific only to that type. For example, a Novel type can have a property called can_be_filmed that's not common to the Poetry type.

- The common properties and behavior of a supertype that a subtype inherits are defined only once in the supertype and are available to all its subtypes in the hierarchy.

PL/SQL 9*i* supports *single inheritance*, where a subtype can inherit attributes and methods from only one direct supertype. However, a subtype can inherit from another subtype that in turn inherits from a supertype and so on, indirectly making it inherit from multiple supertypes. The following features are significant to the implementation of supertypes and subtypes in SQL and PL/SQL in Oracle9*i*:

- A "root" type that acts as the primary supertype and forms the basis for all subtypes

- The UNDER clause of the CREATE OR REPLACE TYPE statement for all subtypes

- The INSTANTIABLE, NOT INSTANTIABLE, and FINAL, NOT FINAL clauses of the CREATE OR REPLACE statement for the object type

- The INSTANTIABLE, NOT INSTANTIABLE; FINAL, NOT FINAL; and OVER-RIDING clauses in the member method specification of the CREATE OR REPLACE TYPE statement

Here's an example of defining a supertype and one of its subtypes using the Book hierarchy outlined previously:

```
CREATE OR REPLACE TYPE book_type AS OBJECT
( title VARHCHAR2(50),
  author VARCHAR2(30),
  ISBN  NUMBER,
  publisher VARCHAR2(50),
  prize_awarded VARCHAR2(1)
)
```

```
INSTANTIABLE
NOT FINAL;
/
CREATE OR REPLACE TYPE literature_type UNDER book_type
( category VARCHAR2(20),
  award_name VARCHAR2(20)
)
INSTANTIABLE
NOT FINAL;
/
```

The following points are worth noting:

- The book_type object type serves as the root in the object type hierarchy and has five attributes: title, author, ISBN, publisher, and prize_awarded.

- The book_type is defined as INSTANTIABLE and NOT FINAL. INSTANTIABLE specifies that object instances of this type can be defined. In other words, variables of this object type can be declared in PL/SQL. NOT FINAL specifies that subtypes can be defined with this type as the parent. If, on the other hand, FINAL is specified, this type can't be a supertype.

- The literature_type is a subtype of book_type. The UNDER clause is used to specify this. It has two attributes, category and award_name, and is INSTANTIABLE and NOT FINAL.

CAUTION   *Never specify the combination NOT INSTANTIABLE and FINAL when you define an object type. Doing so would mean it's not a base for a subtype and object instances can't be defined based on it, which means it can't be used in any way.*

Constructing a Type Hierarchy in PL/SQL

As mentioned previously, object types enable you to build a type hierarchy by means of supertypes and subtypes. You can implement the hierarchy depicted in Figure 10-2 in PL/SQL using inheritance concepts. This section focuses on the method to do this. Here are the steps involved:

1. Create a root type with the NOT FINAL clause.

2. Create subtypes starting from the root type and proceeding to the successive level, providing specification of each subtype at each node in the hierarchy. For each such subtype, decide whether it should be INSTANTIABLE or NOT, and whether it should be FINAL or NOT. Specifying FINAL leaves the object type as a leaf node in the hierarchy.

3. Within each object type, define member methods. For each method, decide whether it should be INSTANTIABLE or NOT, meaning it can be overridden in a subtype or is an abstract method in a supertype, which means it specifies only the method signature and the actual implementation is done in each subtype inherited from it. A method is defined with the OVERRIDING clause in two cases: to provide an implementation of a NOT INSTANTIABLE method in the supertype or to override a generic method defined in a supertype. Also, decide whether any method is FINAL or NOT, meaning it can't be overridden in a subtype.

4. Implement the type body for each type in the hierarchy that isn't declared as FINAL.

5. Decide whether to overload, override, or inherit or create new methods at each node of the hierarchy.

6. Finally, write code that performs specific functions using the types and their methods.

Keeping in mind these steps, here's the code that constructs the Book hierarchy depicted in Figure 10-2. First, I create type specifications:

```
CREATE OR REPLACE TYPE book_type AS OBJECT
( title VARCHAR2(50),
  author VARCHAR2(30),
  ISBN  NUMBER,
  publisher VARCHAR2(50),
  prize_awarded VARCHAR2(1),
  NOT INSTANTIABLE MEMBER PROCEDURE display_info
)
NOT INSTANTIABLE
NOT FINAL;
/
CREATE OR REPLACE TYPE literature_type UNDER book_type
( category VARCHAR2(20),
  award_name VARCHAR2(20),
  OVERRIDING MEMBER PROCEDURE display_info
)
INSTANTIABLE
NOT FINAL;
/
CREATE OR REPLACE TYPE fiction_type UNDER literature_type
( based_upon VARCHAR2(20),
  OVERRIDING MEMBER PROCEDURE display_info
)
INSTANTIABLE
NOT FINAL;
/
CREATE OR REPLACE TYPE novel_type UNDER fiction_type
( can_be_filmed VARCHAR2(1),
  OVERRIDING MEMBER PROCEDURE display_info
)
INSTANTIABLE
NOT FINAL;
/

CREATE OR REPLACE TYPE mystery_type UNDER novel_type
( type_of_mystery VARCHAR2(20),
  OVERRIDING MEMBER PROCEDURE display_info
)
INSTANTIABLE
FINAL;
/
```

The following points are worth noting:

- A five-level hierarchy of types is defined by this code. The root type is book_type and is NOT INSTANTIABLE. It's also NOT FINAL, meaning subtypes can be defined based on the book_type.

- The remaining four types, literature_type, fiction_type, novel_type, and mystery_type, are subtypes of the type in the level preceding them and supertypes for the types in the level succeeding each of them.

- The root type defines a NON INSTANTIABLE method named display_info. This declaration acts as a template for the method and its implementation is to be provided in each of its subtypes. Each subtype must define its own version of this procedure.

Next, I define the type bodies with corresponding member methods. Here's the code:

```
CREATE OR REPLACE TYPE BODY literature_type
IS
  OVERRIDING MEMBER PROCEDURE display_info
  IS
  BEGIN
    DBMS_OUTPUT.PUT_LINE(rpad('Category',20)||' '||rpad('Books',60));
    DBMS_OUTPUT.PUT_LINE(rpad('-',20,'-')||' '||rpad('-',60,'-'));
    DBMS_OUTPUT.PUT_LINE(rpad(SELF.category,20)||' '||SELF.title||' by '||
                                                   SELF.author);
  END;
END;
/
CREATE OR REPLACE TYPE BODY fiction_type
IS
  OVERRIDING MEMBER PROCEDURE display_info
  IS
  BEGIN
    DBMS_OUTPUT.PUT_LINE(rpad('Category',20)||' '||rpad('Books',60));
    DBMS_OUTPUT.PUT_LINE(rpad('-',20,'-')||' '||rpad('-',60,'-'));
    DBMS_OUTPUT.PUT_LINE(rpad(SELF.category,20)||' '||SELF.title||' by '||
                                                   SELF.author);
    DBMS_OUTPUT.PUT_LINE('This title is based upon '||SELF.based_upon);
  END;
END;
/
```

```
CREATE OR REPLACE TYPE BODY novel_type
IS
  OVERRIDING MEMBER PROCEDURE display_info
  IS
     v_can_be_filmed VARCHAR2(20);
BEGIN
    SELECT decode(SELF.can_be_filmed, 'Y', 'can be filmed',
                                'N', 'cannot be filmed')
    INTO       v_can_be_filmed
    FROM    dual;
    DBMS_OUTPUT.PUT_LINE(rpad('Category',20)||' '||rpad('Books',60));
    DBMS_OUTPUT.PUT_LINE(rpad('-',20,'-')||' '||rpad('-',60,'-'));
    DBMS_OUTPUT.PUT_LINE(rpad(SELF.category,20)||' '||SELF.title||' by '||
                                                SELF.author);
    DBMS_OUTPUT.PUT_LINE('This title is a novel based upon '||SELF.based_upon||
                                        'and'||v_can_be_filmed);
  END;
END;
/
CREATE OR REPLACE TYPE BODY mystery_type
IS
  OVERRIDING MEMBER PROCEDURE display_info
  IS
     v_can_be_filmed VARCHAR2(20);
  BEGIN
    SELECT decode(SELF.can_be_filmed, 'Y', 'can be filmed',
                                'N', ' cannot be filmed')
    INTO       v_can_be_filmed
    FROM    dual;
    DBMS_OUTPUT.PUT_LINE(rpad('Category',20)||' '||rpad('Books',60));
    DBMS_OUTPUT.PUT_LINE(rpad('-',20,'-')||' '||rpad('-',60,'-'));
    DBMS_OUTPUT.PUT_LINE(rpad(SELF.category,20)||' '||SELF.title||' by '||
                                                SELF.author);
    DBMS_OUTPUT.PUT_LINE('This title is a novel based upon '||SELF.based_upon||
                                        ', '||v_can_be_filmed||
                   'and is a mystery of'||SELF.type_of_mystery||' type');
  END;
END;
/
```

The following points are worth noting:

- The type body of each subtype overrides the noninstantiable member method display_info in the root type.

- The display_info procedure displays the information specific to it and the information derived from all of its supertypes. This is evident from the fact that all the attributes of all supertypes of each subtype can be accessed from that subtype. This is one of the main advantages of inheritance.

- The display_info procedure in each subtype OVERRIDES the nonimplemented method with the same name in the root supertype.

Now that the methods are in place, I can write code to use the type hierarchy. Basically, this consists of instantiating objects starting from any type declared as INSTANTIABLE, initializing these objects, and invoking the methods on them. In the example type hierarchy, I can start from any subtype (excluding the root book_type). Here are two examples to illustrate this.

First, I start with literature_type. Here's the code:

```
SQL> declare
  2    lit_classic literature_type;
  3  begin
  4    lit_classic := literature_type('DREAMS UNLIMITED','Bulusu Lakshman',
  5                                    0112224444,'Books International', 'Y',
  6                                    'Fiction','Booker Prize');
  7    lit_classic.display_info;
  8  end;
  9  /
Category             Books
-------------------- ------------------------------------
Fiction              DREAMS UNLIMITED by Bulusu Lakshman

PL/SQL procedure successfully completed.
```

Second, I start with the lowest level subtype, mystery_type. Here's the code:

```
SQL> declare
  2    classic_book mystery_type;
  3  begin
  4    classic_book := mystery_type('DREAMS UNLIMITED','Bulusu Lakshman',
  5                                  0112224444,'Books International', 'Y',
  6                                  'Fiction','Booker Prize','Scientific',
```

```
  7                                           'Y','Medical Related');
  8     classic_book.display_info;
  9   end;
 10   /
Category                 Books
-------------------      ------------------------------------
Fiction                  DREAMS UNLIMITED by Bulusu Lakshman
This title is a novel based upon Scientific, can be filmed and is a mystery of
Medical Related type

PL/SQL procedure successfully completed.
```

Dynamic Method Dispatch

Inheritance with type hierarchies leads to dynamic method dispatch. Dynamic method dispatch is the method by which Oracle implements dynamic polymorphism. Polymorphism is ability to use multiple methods with the same name with different data. There are two types of polymorphism: static and dynamic. Static polymorphism refers to choosing the appropriate method based on the data at compile time and ideally is implemented using method overloading. Dynamic polymorphism refers to selecting the appropriate method to be executed depending on the data at runtime. In PL/SQL 9*i* this is implemented using dynamic method dispatch. In other words, dynamic method dispatch is the ability to determine at runtime and execute the most specific method in the object hierarchy that corresponds to the instance of the object type that invokes the method.

As evident from the previous section, you can override a method of an object type in the subtypes in a type hierarchy. In the Book hierarchy described earlier, the display_info method is first specified in the supertype book_type and overridden in each of the subtypes literature_type, fiction_type, novel_type, and mystery_type. This resulted in multiple implementations of display_info depending on the subtype. Now, when you use the type hierarchy, objects are defined based on the supertypes and subtypes. Then member methods are invoked based on the type of object defined. The method call is dispatched to the corresponding type's implementation and then executed.

How does PL/SQL determine which method implementation to use on the particular object instance? As an example, in the case of the lit_classic and classic_book objects defined earlier, how does PL/SQL know what method implementation of the display_info method is to be used? It does this by using dynamic method dispatch. PL/SQL uses that method implementation in the type hierarchy that is "nearest" to the type of object on which the method is invoked.

It does this by checking, starting with the current type and navigating through the hierarchy to its supertypes, if any. This is done at runtime depending on the object instance on which the particular method is invoked. Here's an example:

```
declare
      lit_classic literature_type;
     classic_book mystery_type;
begin
      lit_classic := literature_type('DREAMS UNLIMITED','Bulusu Lakshman',
                            0112224444,'Books International', 'Y',
                            'Fiction','Booker Prize');
      lit_classic.display_info;
     classic_book := mystery_type('DREAMS UNLIMITED','Bulusu Lakshman',
                            0112224444,'Books International', 'Y','Fiction',
                  'Booker Prize','Scientific','Y','Medical Related');
      classic_book.display_info;
    end;
/
```

Here's the output of this program:

```
Category            Books
------------------- ----------------------------------
Fiction             DREAMS UNLIMITED by Bulusu Lakshman

Fiction             DREAMS UNLIMITED by Bulusu Lakshman
This title is a novel based upon Scientific, can be filmed and is a mystery
of Medical Related type

PL/SQL procedure successfully completed.
```

The following points are worth noting:

- Two different book objects are defined using the subtypes literature_type and mystery_type. Each of these objects is instantiated and its attributes populated using the appropriate constructor for the corresponding object type.

- The display_info method is invoked on each object instance. The method name is the same for both the lit_classic and classic_book objects. For the lit_classic object, this displays the attribute information for its type as well as its supertype (i.e., book_type). For the classic_book object, this works out from the root of the type hierarchy and displays all information from all of its supertypes as well as its own specific attributes.

- Compiling the types in the type hierarchy resolves the display_info method in each of the types and the code compiles successfully. But during execution of the previous PL/SQL block, dynamic method dispatch comes into play. The PL/SQL runtime engine does the following:

  - For the method call lit_classic.display_info, it knows the type of the object instance as literature_type. It checks whether this method is defined in literature_type. It is, and so it executes that implementation of this method.

  - For the method call classic_book.display_info, it recognizes the object instance as of type mystery_type and thus executes the implementation of display_info that's specific to the mystery_type object type.

TIP   *If a method is defined in one of the supertypes and not defined in a subtype, but the subtype calls this method, PL/SQL still executes the implementation of this method that's "nearest" to the supertype implementation. For example, consider a method called display_basic_lit_info in literature_type that isn't defined in any of its subtypes. If the classic_book object calls the display_basic_lit_info method and then the display_info method, the implementation of the display_basic_lit_info method is the one found in literature_type, but the implementation of the display_info method is the one given in mystery_type. This holds true for supertype methods calling methods that are overridden in the subtypes.*

Type Evolution

Oracle9*i* has introduced the feature of type evolution for object types. *Type evolution* refers to the ability to change the attributes and methods of an existing object type without having to re-create the type and its data, and all of its dependent types. Attributes and methods can be added to and dropped from existing object types. In addition, the changes so made can be explicitly propagated to the dependent types and tables. Type evolution also refers to making changes to supertypes in a type hierarchy—for example, dropping a method in a supertype.

Specifically, type evolution lets you perform the following functions:

- Changes to object type member attributes such as adding, dropping, and changing the length of an attribute

- Changes to object type member methods such as adding and dropping methods

- Modifications to the INSTANTIABLE and FINAL properties of an object type in a type hierarchy

- Propagation of the changes made to a type to dependent types and tables

I discuss each of these functions in the sections that follow.

You perform type evolution using the ALTER TYPE statement in SQL. Here's the syntax:

```
ALTER TYPE type_name COMPILE {SPECIFICATION | BODY}
        REPLACE [AUTHID {CURRENT_USER|DEFINER}] AS OBJECT (type_spec)
                            {ADD |DROP} function_spec|proc_spec
                            {ADD|MODIFY} ATTRIBUTE attribute_spec
                            DROP ATTRIBUTE attribute_name
                            [NOT] {INSTANTIABLE|FINAL}
                        {INVALIDATE|CASCADE [[NOT] INCLUDING TABLE DATA]};
```

where type_name refers to the object type being changed and type_spec refers to the complete object type specification with new member methods. function_spec and proc_spec are the signatures of the member function or procedure being added in the case of the add operation and the name of the function or procedure in the case of the drop operation. attribute_spec refers to the complete specification of the attribute being added or modified that includes its name, data type, and length; and attribute_name is the name of the attribute being dropped.

In addition to type evolution, the ALTER TYPE statement allows separate recompilation of the type specification or the type body. Also, you can compile both the specification and body together by specifying the compile option without the keyword SPECIFICATION or BODY.

Changes to Object Type Attributes

You can add, drop, or change the length of an attribute of an object type using the ALTER TYPE statement with the ADD, MODIFY, or DROP ATTRIBUTE clause. When you add or change an attribute, you specify the complete specification of the attribute, including its name, data type, and length. Here's the syntax:

```
ALTER TYPE type_name ADD ATTRIBUTE (attr_name data_type(length))
[INVALIDATE| CASCADE [NOT] INCLUDING TABLE DATA];
```

When you drop an attribute, you specify only the attribute name. Here's the syntax:

```
ALTER TYPE type_name DROP ATTRIBUTE attr_name
[INVALIDATE| CASCADE [NOT] INCLUDING TABLE DATA];
```

Here's an example:

```
ALTER TYPE address ADD ATTRIBUTE
(country_code VARCHAR2(4)) CASCADE INCLUDING TABLE DATA;
```

This statement adds a new attribute country_code to the address object type created previously and propagates the change to the dependent tables address_master and employee. Here's how you can verify the output of this statement.

Here's the code to describe the address object type:

```
SQL> desc address
```

Here's the output:

Name	Null?	Type
LINE1		VARCHAR2(20)
LINE2		VARCHAR2(20)
CITY		VARCHAR2(20)
STATE_CODE		VARCHAR2(2)
ZIP		VARCHAR2(13)
COUNTRY_CODE		VARCHAR2(4)

```
METHOD
------
 MEMBER FUNCTION GET_ADDRESS RETURNS VARCHAR2
```

```
METHOD
-------
MEMBER PROCEDURE SET_ADDRESS
Argument Name                        Type                    In/Out Default?
----------------------------         ------------------      ---------------
IP_LINE1                             VARCHAR2                IN
IP_LINE2                             VARCHAR2                IN
IP_CITY                              VARCHAR2                IN
IP_STATE_CODE                        VARCHAR2                IN
IP_ZIP                               VARCHAR2                IN
IP_COUNTRY_CODE                      VARCHAR2                IN
```

Here's the code to describe the address_master table:

```
SQL> desc address_master
```

Here's the output:

```
Name                                              Null?    Type
------------------------------------------------- -------- -----------
LINE1                                                      VARCHAR2(20)
LINE2                                                      VARCHAR2(20)
CITY                                                      VARCHAR2(20)
STATE_CODE                                                VARCHAR2(2)
ZIP                                                       VARCHAR2(13)
COUNTRY_CODE                                              VARCHAR2(4)
```

Here's the code to describe the employee table:

```
SQL> desc employee
```

Here's the output:

```
Name                                              Null?    Type
------------------------------------------------- -------- -----------
EMPID                                             NOT NULL NUMBER(10)
LASTNAME                                          NOT NULL VARCHAR2(30)
FIRSTNAME                                         NOT NULL VARCHAR2(30)
MIDDLE_INITIAL                                             VARCHAR2(2)
EMP_ADDRESS                                               REF OF ADDRESS
```

> **TIP** *You can make changes to multiple attributes by speci-fying add, modify, or drop operations separated by a comma.*

Changes to Object Type Methods

You can add or drop member methods of an object type with the ALTER TYPE statement. You have two ways of doing so:

- Use the ALTER TYPE . . . REPLACE AS OBJECT statement to provide a complete specification of the type, including newly added member methods. The corresponding type body has to be re-created with the implementation of the new methods using the CREATE OR REPLACE TYPE BODY statement.

- Use the ALTER TYPE . . . ADD MEMBER statement. The corresponding type body has to be re-created with the implementation of the new methods using the CREATE OR REPLACE TYPE BODY statement.

Modify the INSTANTIABLE and FINAL Properties of an Object Type in a Type Hierarchy

You can alter an object type's INSTANTIABLE or FINAL properties using the ALTER TYPE statement. Here's the syntax:

```
ALTER TYPE type_name {[NOT] INSTANTIABLE | [NOT] FINAL};
```

In a type hierarchy, the following rules apply:

- You can't replace or drop a type if subtypes are defined based on it.

- Changing a type's property from INSTANTIABLE to NOT INSTANTIABLE is possible only if the type has no dependent types or isn't referenced in columns, views, and tables, either directly or indirectly through another type or subtype.

- Changing a type's property from NOT FINAL to FINAL is possible only if the type has no subtypes defined based on it.

Propagate the Changes Made to a Type to Dependent Types and Tables

One of the primary features of type evolution is that changes made to object types can be propagated to dependent object types, object tables, and object columns referencing the type. You do this by specifying the CASCADE option with an optional [NOT] INCLUDING TABLE DATA clause. Here's the syntax:

```
ALTER TYPE ... CASCADE [NOT] INCLUDING TABLE DATA;
```

Here's the previous example rewritten to include the CASCADE option:

```
ALTER TYPE address ADD ATTRIBUTE
(country_code VARCHAR2(4)) CASCADE INCLUDING TABLE DATA;
```

This propagates the changes to the dependent object table address_master and the object-relational table employee. It also converts the data in these tables to a format that's consistent with the modified version of the address type. You can verify this by selecting the value of the objects stored in the address_master table. Here's the code to do so:

```
SQL> SELECT VALUE(a)
  2  FROM   address_master a;

VALUE(A)(LINE1, LINE2, CITY, STATE_CODE, ZIP, COUNTRY_CODE)
-----------------------------------------------------------
ADDRESS('19 J', 'Reading Rd', 'Edison', 'NJ', '08817', NULL)
```

The CASCADE option added the extra column to the address_master table and the INCLUDING TABLE DATA clause converted the data in the rows of the address_master table by adding a NULL value to the extra country_code attribute.

 TIP *If you don't specify CASCADE, you must specify the INVALIDATE option. This option invalidates the dependent types and tables, and they have to be re-created.*

Java Object Storage: SQL Types of Language Java or SQLJ Object Types

The integration of Java in the Oracle database allowed one main function: accessing SQL object types from Java applications using JDBC or SQLJ. This was possible by mapping Java classes to the object types. Oracle9*i* introduced Java object persistence with SQLJ object types that enable the reverse mapping (i.e., SQL object types mapped to Java classes).

SQLJ object types are SQL object types of the Java language. You can use these types wherever you can use a SQL object type—for example, as the type of an object table, an attribute of a type, or a column of an object-relational table. You can query and manipulate schema objects of SQLJ object types using SQL.

You create SQLJ object types using the extended CREATE TYPE statement with the USING clause and the EXTERNAL clause.

To implement SQLJ object types, you need the following:

- A mapping between the SQLJ object type attributes and member methods to the corresponding Java equivalents, and a mapping between the SQLJ object type as a whole to the Java class as a whole. You do this with the EXTERNAL clause.

- An interface to use the SQLJ object type functionality. You do this with the USING clause. The USING clause can specify one of the interfaces java.sql.SQLData or oracle.sql.ORAData, along with oracle.sql.ORADataFactory, and the corresponding Java class must implement one of these interfaces.

Here are the steps involved in creating and using SQLJ object types:

1. Create the custom Java class that the SQLJ object type maps to.

2. Load the class into the Oracle9*i* database.

3. Create a SQLJ object type specifying the mappings from the object type to the Java class.

4. Use the SQLJ object type in PL/SQL and/or SQL just like any object type.

The following sections describe how to perform each of these steps.

Create the Custom Java Class That the SQLJ Object Type Maps To

This class should implement the java.sql.SQLData or oracle.sql.ORAData interface. I use the definition similar to that of the address object type described earlier. Here's the code for the custom Java class:

```
import java.sql.*;
import oracle.sql.*;
public class Address implements SQLData {
  public String line1;
  public String line2;
  public String city;
  public String state_code;
  public String zip;
  String sql_type = "ADDRESS_SQLJ";

  public Address() {
  }

  public Address (String iline1, String iline2, String icity,
                             String istate, String izip) {
    this.line1 = iline1;
    this.line2 = iline2;
    this.city = icity;
    this.state_code = istate;
    this.zip = izip;
  }

  public String getSQLTypeName() throws SQLException
  {
    return sql_type;
  }

  public void readSQL(SQLInput stream, String typeName)
    throws SQLException
  {
    sql_type = typeName;

    line1 = stream.readString();
    line2 = stream.readString();
    city = stream.readString();
    state_code = stream.readString();
```

```
    zip = stream.readString();
  }

  public void writeSQL(SQLOutput stream)
    throws SQLException
  {
    stream.writeString(line1);
    stream.writeString(line2);
    stream.writeString(city);
    stream.writeString(state_code);
    stream.writeString(zip);
  }

 public static Address setAddress (String iline1, String iline2,
                                    String icity, String istate, String zip) {
    return new Address(iline1, iline2, icity, istate, izip);
  }

  public String getAddress() {
    return this.line1 + " " + this.line2 + " " + this.city + ", " +
             this.state_code + " " + this.zip;
  }
}
```

Once you've defined the Java source, you have to compile into a .class file using the command

```
javac Address.java
```

Load the Class into the Oracle9i Database

You do this using the loadjava utility provided by Oracle. Refer to the "Oracle9*i* Java Stored Procedures Developers Guide" and the "Oracle9*i* Java Developers Guide" in the Oracle documentation for a description of the loadjava utility.

Here's how the Address.class Java class file is loaded into the plsql9i/plsql9I schema:

```
loadjava -u -plsql9i/plsql9i -r -oci8 Address.class
```

The –r option resolves external references inside in the schema.

To verify that the Address.class file is loaded into the database, use the following query:

```
SQL> column object_name format a30;
SQL> select object_name, object_type
  2  from    user_objects
  3  where   object_type like '%JAVA%';


OBJECT_NAME                          OBJECT_TYPE
------------------------------       -----------
Address                              JAVA CLASS
```

Create a SQLJ Object Type Specifying the Mappings from the Object Type to the Java Class

Once you've defined the custom Java class and compiled and loaded it into the database, the next step is to define the object type based on the Java class. You do this with the CREATE TYPE statement using the EXTERNAL and USING clauses. Here's an example that defines an object type based on the Address class:

```
CREATE TYPE address_sqlj AS OBJECT
  EXTERNAL NAME 'Address' LANGUAGE JAVA
  USING SQLData(
    line1_sqlj varchar2(20) EXTERNAL NAME 'line1',
    line2_sqlj varchar2(20) EXTERNAL NAME 'line2',
    city_sqlj varchar2(20) EXTERNAL NAME 'city',
    state_code_sqlj varchar2(2) EXTERNAL NAME 'state_code',
    zip_sqlj varchar2(13) EXTERNAL NAME 'zip',
    STATIC FUNCTION set_address (p_line1 VARCHAR2, p_line2 VARCHAR2,
        p_city VARCHAR2, p_state_code VARCHAR2, p_zip VARCHAR2)
      RETURN address_sqlj
      EXTERNAL NAME 'setAddress (java.lang.String, java.lang.String,
        java.lang.String, java.lang.String, java.lang.String) return Address',
    MEMBER FUNCTION get_address RETURN VARCHAR2
      EXTERNAL NAME 'Address.getAddress() return java.lang.String'
  )
NOT FINAL;
/
```

Here's how you can verify the output of this statement:

```
SQL> desc address_sqlj
```

Here's the output:

```
address_sqlj is NOT FINAL
Name                                    Null?    Type
--------------------------------------- -------- ------------
LINE1_SQLJ                                       VARCHAR2(20)
LINE2_SQLJ                                       VARCHAR2(20)
CITY_SQLJ                                        VARCHAR2(20)
STATE_CODE_SQLJ                                  VARCHAR2(2)
ZIP_SQLJ                                         VARCHAR2(13)

METHOD
------
 STATIC FUNCTION SET_ADDRESS RETURNS ADDRESS_SQLJ
 Argument Name                   Type                     In/Out Default?
 ------------------------------- ------------------------ ---------------
 P_LINE1                         VARCHAR2                 IN
 P_LINE2                         VARCHAR2                 IN
 P_CITY                          VARCHAR2                 IN
 P_STATE_CODE                    VARCHAR2                 IN
 P_ZIP                           VARCHAR2                 IN

METHOD
------
 MEMBER FUNCTION GET_ADDRESS RETURNS VARCHAR2
```

The USING clause specifies the interface that the SQLJ object type implements. It's one of the interfaces of java.sql.SQLData or oracle.sql.ORAData, along with oracle.sql.ORADataFactory, and the corresponding Java class must implement one of these interfaces.

The EXTERNAL clause specifies the mapping between each SQLJ object type attribute and member methods to the corresponding Java equivalents, and a mapping between the SQLJ object type as a whole to the Java class as a whole.

Use the SQLJ Object Type in PL/SQL and/or SQL Just Like Any Object Type

Once you've created the SQLJ object type, you can use it just like any other object type. For example, you can use it to build an object table or you can use it as the data type of a column in an object-relational table. Here's an example to illustrate this.

First, I create an object table based on the SQLJ object type address_sqlj. Here's the code:

```
CREATE TABLE address_master_sqlj OF address_sqlj;
```

Then I use an INSERT statement with the set_address member method invoked on the object type to insert a row into this table. Here's the code:

```
insert into address_master_sqlj
values(address_sqlj.set_address('1 Oracle parkway',null,'Redwood Shores',
                                             'CA ', '41246 '));
```

Next, I query the object table to select columns that are mapped to the attributes of the SQLJ object type. Here's the code:

```
SELECT a.line1_sqlj, a.line2_sqlj FROM address_master_sqlj a;
```

Here's the output of this query:

```
SQL> SELECT a.line1_sqlj, a.line2_sqlj FROM address_master_sqlj a;
LINE1_SQLJ           LINE2_SQLJ
-------------------- ----------
1 Oracle parkway
```

Also, I can invoke member methods of the SQLJ object type as follows:

```
SELECT a.get_address() FROM address_master_sqlj;
```

Here's the output of this query:

```
SQL> select a.get_address() from address_master_sqlj a;

A.GET_ADDRESS()
-----------------------------------------------
1 Oracle parkway null Redwood Shores, CA 41246
```

>
> **TIP**   *You can declare member methods of a SQLJ object type as STATIC. STATIC member functions can map to static Java methods of the corresponding mapping Java class, and they're used in INSERT statements to invoke either a user-defined constructor of the Java class or a static Java method that returns the class type.*

User-Defined Operators

One of the features with regard to objects in the database is the introduction of user-defined operators. This section discusses the methods of defining and invoking user-defined operators in the database. The similarity and differences between user-defined operators and functions and when to use user-defined operators are highlighted.

Defining User-Defined Operators

A user-defined operator is an operator identified by a name that takes a set of operands as input and returns a result. It's a top-level schema object that's created with the CREATE OPERATOR statement and has an operator binding associated with it. An *operator binding* identifies the operator with a unique signature via argument data types and allows associating a function that provides an implementation for the operator. This function is executed when the operator is invoked. You can evaluate the binding associated with an operator using a user-defined function that could be one of the following:

- Stand-alone functions

- Packaged functions

- OBJECT member methods

You create a user-defined operator by specifying the operator name and its bindings. To do so, first you create a function to implement the binding. Here's an example:

```
CREATE OR REPLACE FUNCTION f_eq (p1 VARCHAR2, p2 VARCHAR2) RETURN NUMBER
IS
```

```
BEGIN
   IF p1 = p2 THEN
      RETURN 1;
   ELSE
        RETURN 0;
   END IF;
END f_eq;
/
```

This function gives the functional implementation of EQ.

Next, you define the operator with binding. Here's an example:

```
CREATE OR REPLACE OPERATOR eq
BINDING (VARCHAR2, VARCHAR2) RETURN NUMBER
USING f_eq;
```

The argument's data type list enclosed within parentheses is called the signature of the binding and uniquely determines the binding associated with a particular operator. The return data type is not part of the signature.

The RETURN data type of the BINDING clause should be a valid SQL data type and not a PL/SQL data type. For example, if I define a second function f_eq1 in the lines of the f_eq function but returning BOOLEAN values, and then I proceed to define the operator with the associated binding based on f_eq1, I get an error, as shown here:

```
CREATE OR REPLACE FUNCTION f_eq1 (p1 VARCHAR2, p2 VARCHAR2)
RETURN BOOLEAN
IS
BEGIN
   IF p1 = p2 THEN
      RETURN TRUE;
   ELSE
        RETURN FALSE;
   END IF;
END f_eq1;
/
```

Creating an operator based on this function yields an error. This is shown here:

```
CREATE OR REPLACE OPERATOR eq1
BINDING (VARCHAR2, VARCHAR2) RETURN BOOLEAN
USING f_eq1;
```

Here's the error:

```
CREATE OR REPLACE OPERATOR eq1
*
ERROR at line 1:
ORA-06552: PL/SQL: Declaration ignored
ORA-06553: PLS-201: identifier 'SYSTEM.BOOLEAN' must be declared
```

TIP *The argument's data type list and the RETURN data type of the BINDING clause should match exactly with those in the actual function implementation of the binding.*

TIP *You can define multiple bindings on an operator as along as each binding has a different signature.*

You can define multiple operators using the same binding function. Here's the code to illustrate this:

```
CREATE OR REPLACE OPERATOR eq1
BINDING (VARCHAR2, VARCHAR2) RETURN NUMBER
USING f_eq;
```

User-Defined Operators and Functions

User-defined operators are domain-specific operators that you can use as native SQL built-in operators and integrate into the Oracle9*i* server. They are another way of defining function-like functionality, especially when the functional logic is complex. When to use user-defined operators is more of a project-specific need than a technical issue. For example, to simulate a complex mathematical function in a way similar to a built-in operator, you can define a user-defined operator.

However, there a few subtle differences between function bindings in operators and user-defined functions:

- The signatures of the bindings of a user-defined operator can't have OUT or INOUT parameters. A function can have OUT or INOUT parameters in addition to a return value.

- The binding functions of a user-defined operator can't perform INSERT, UPDATE, or DELETE operations, whereas these operations are allowed in regular functions.

- The return value of a user-defined operator or the parameters of the corresponding function can't be a REF type, whereas regular functions can return REF types and pass REF types as parameters.

When Should Operators Be Used?

User-defined operators are a second way of defining function-like functionality, especially when the functional logic is complex. *The question regarding when to use a user-defined operator is more of a project-specific need and design issue than a technical issue.* For example, to simulate a complex mathematical function in a way similar to a built-in operator, you can use a user-defined operator. However, for implementing simple functional logic, using an operator would involve an administrative overhead.

An operator is simply a way of calling a function. There's no place where you can use an operator where you couldn't use a function just as well. Why would you want to use operators? Traditionally, when you create a function to use within SQL, it's placed in a package with a RESTRICT REFERENCES PRAGMA. The invocation of that function is "package.<function name>."

It's not necessary to place functions in packages, but failure to do so is considered bad programming practice. If you want to create a reusable component whose status as either an Oracle built-in or a custom package is seamless to the developer (for example, as part of a template library), you can build your function, place it in a package, and place an operator wrapper around it. When operators are used in this way, their limitations (only IN parameters) actually strengthen the case for their use.

Invoking a User-Defined Operator

You can invoke a user-defined operator anywhere you can use a built-in operator in SQL DML. Specifically, you can invoke user-defined operators in

- The select list of a SELECT statement

- The condition of a WHERE clause

- The GROUP BY and ORDER BY clauses

- The VALUES clause of an INSERT statement

- The SET clause of an UPDATE statement

- The WHERE clause of a DELETE statement

Here's an example that provides a simple use of EQ in the WHERE clause of a SELECT statement:

```
SELECT * FROM employee_test
WHERE EQ(lastname, 'SMITH') = 1;
```

Here's the output of this SELECT statement:

EMPID LASTNAME	FIRSTNAME	MI
101 SMITH	JOHN	

Here's an example that illustrates the use of EQ in the VALUES clause of an INSERT statement. First, I create a table named test:

```
SQL> create table test (test number);

Table created.
```

Next, I insert into this table using EQ:

```
SQL> insert into test values (eq('ROBERT','SMITH'));

1 row created.
```

Querying the test table now yields the following:

```
SQL> select * from test;

      TEST
----------
         0
```

Also, EQ can be used in an INSERT statement with a SELECT query. Here's an example:

```
SQL> insert into test select eq('ROBERT','SMITH') from dual;

1 row created.
```

To use a user-defined operator in an expression, the operator must have been created in the user schema or must have the EXECUTE privilege on it granted to the user schema.

Using User-Defined Operators in PL/SQL

You can use user-defined operators in PL/SQL blocks in the same way you use them in SQL. However, you must use them in SQL statements inside the PL/SQL block. Here's an example that demonstrates the use of the EQ operator described earlier in PL/SQL:

```
declare
    v_empid number;
    v_lastname varchar2(30);
    v_firstname varchar2(30);
 begin
    select empid, lastname, firstname
    into   v_empid, v_lastname, v_firstname
    from   employee_test
    where  EQ(lastname, 'SMITH') = 1;
    dbms_output.put_line(to_char(v_empid)||' '||v_lastname||' '||v_firstname);
end;
/
```

Here's the output of this program:

```
101 SMITH JOHN

PL/SQL procedure successfully completed.
```

Also, you can use user-defined operators in stand-alone procedures, functions, and packaged procedures and functions in a manner similar to the PL/SQL block outlined earlier.

You can't use user-defined operators in PL/SQL constructs such as the IF clause. The following code causes a compilation error:

```
declare
  string1 varchar2(10) := 'ROBERT';
  string2 varchar2(10) := 'SMITH';
begin
  if eq(string1, string2) = 1 then
    dbms_output.put_line('String1 equals String2');
  else
    dbms_output.put_line('String1 does not equal String2');
  end if;
end;
/
```

Here's the output of this program:

```
if eq(string1, string2) = 1 then
        *
ERROR at line 5:
ORA-06550: line 5, column 6:
PLS-00548: invalid use of operator.
ORA-06550: line 5, column 3:
PL/SQL: Statement ignored
```

TIP *You can use user-defined operators in SQL DML statements such as SELECT, INSERT, UPDATE, and DELETE. You can't use user-defined operators in PL/SQL constructs such as the IF clause, WHILE and FOR loops, PL/SQL assignment statements, and so on.*

Dropping a User-Defined Operator

You can drop user-defined operators using the DROP OPERATOR statement. Here's an example that illustrates this:

```
SQL> drop operator eq;

Operator dropped
```

You can drop an operator that's being referenced by other schema objects such as index types, procedures, functions, packages, and so on using the FORCE option. Here's the syntax:

```
DROP OPERATOR operator_name FORCE;
```

Here's an example:

```
SQL> drop operator eq FORCE;
```

This invalidates the referencing objects of the operator.

TIP   *When a user-defined operator is dropped, the underlying binding function isn't dropped.*

TIP   *For large projects, you should consider using operators as part of template construction. They can effectively be used to provide developer access to functions that can be safely used within SQL. Although they don't provide any additional functionality in comparison with functions, operators can assist with the organization of a code library.*

Summary

In this chapter, I discussed the object-relational extensions in Oracle9*i*. Specifically, I highlighted the use of object types, object tables, and object-relational tables. I then discussed the new object features of Oracle9*i* such as type evolution, inheritance, and dynamic method dispatch. I highlighted the use of SQLJ object types. Finally, I covered the implementation of user-defined operators in Oracle9*i*.

The next chapter covers collections in PL/SQL.

CHAPTER 11

Collections (VARRAYS and Nested Tables)

Oracle9i supports three types of collection data types: index-by tables, VARRAYS (variable size arrays), and nested tables. Index-by tables are unbounded single-dimensional arrays. They were introduced in PL/SQL 2 (with Oracle7) and enhanced in PL/SQL 2.3 (with Oracle7.3) with the addition of table attributes. Chapter 3 covered index-by tables. This chapter highlights the features of the other two types of collections, VARRAYS and nested tables.

Creating and Using Collections in PL/SQL

This section presents the use of collections as independent objects in PL/SQL. Basically, it defines VARRAYS and nested tables in PL/SQL and explains how to initialize and manipulate them. First, I discuss VARRAYS, and then I move on to cover nested tables.

VARRAYS

VARRAYS are bounded single-dimensional arrays that are limited by a maximum number of elements. You can change the upper bound for VARRAYS. You use VARRAYS to store a fixed number of elements in a definite order. This helps to materialize fixed-size collections. All the elements of the variable array are of the same data type. Each element has an index associated with it that corresponds to the position of the element in the array. Elements are inserted into a VARRAY starting with index 1 and extending to the maximum limit. The maximum size of a VARRAY is 2GB.

A VARRAY is generally a one-dimensional array unless otherwise defined to a multilevel collection, in which case it simulates an array of more than one dimension.

As with index-by tables, you define a VARRAY by first defining a VARRAY type and then declaring a variable of that type. The following sections detail the steps involved.

Defining the VARRAY Type

A VARRAY type is defined using the TYPE . . . IS VARRAY statement. Here's the syntax:

```
TYPE type_name IS {VARRAY| VARRAYING ARRAY} (max_size) OF data_type [NOT NULL];
```

where type_name is the name of the VARRAY type; max_size is the maximum number of elements in the VARRAY specified as an integer; and data_type is one of a PL/SQL scalar, record, or object type. Here's an example of a VARRAY type:

```
TYPE num_varray IS VARRAY(5) OF NUMBER;
```

This declares a numeric VARRAY with a maximum of five elements.
The following rules apply when you specify the data_type:

- You can use %TYPE and %ROWTYPE.

- The data_type can be another VARRAY or TABLE type as of Oracle9*i*.

- The data_type can't be a BOOLEAN, NCHAR, NVARCHAR2, NCLOB, or REF CURSOR type.

Declaring a Variable of the VARRAY Type

Once you've defined a VARRAY type, you need to declare variables of that type that represent the actual VARRAYS. Here's the syntax:

```
<var_name> <VARRAY_type_name>;
```

where VARRAY_type_name is the VARRAY type defined using the TYPE . . . IS VARRAY specification and var_name is an arbitrary variable name having a data type of this VARRAY type. Here's an example:

```
v_numvarray num_varray;
```

Here's a complete example combining the previous two steps:

```
DECLARE
    TYPE num_varray IS VARRAY(5) OF NUMBER;
    v_numvarray num_varray;
```

```
BEGIN
     /* Do some processing */
     null;
END;
/
```

TIP   *A TYPE . . . IS VARRAY definition is only abstract, and as such it can't be used by itself.*

TIP   *Creating a VARRAY doesn't allocate space. It only defines a data type that can be used as the data type of a column of an object-relational table, an object-type attribute, or the type of a PL/SQL variable, parameter, or function return value.*

TIP   *A VARRAY declared as NOT NULL must have a value specified for each of its elements.*

Initializing a VARRAY

By default, when a variable of type VARRAY is defined, it represents a NULL object (i.e., the VARRAY as a whole is NULL). You have to initialize this VARRAY variable using a special method: the constructor method. Similar to object types, a constructor method for a VARRAY has the same name as the VARRAY type and is a function that accepts as parameters values whose data type is of the VARRAY element type and returns an initialized VARRAY. The number of elements in the VARRAY evaluates to the number of arguments passed to the constructor. This again is limited by the maximum size specified while defining the VARRAY.

Here's an example that shows how the v_numvarray object is initialized:

```
DECLARE
     TYPE num_varray IS VARRAY(5) OF NUMBER;
     v_numvarray num_varray := num_varray(10,  20, 30, 40);
```

```
BEGIN
    dbms_output.put_line('The first element of v_numvarray is '||
                                        TO_CHAR(v_numvarray(1)));
END;
/
```

In the preceding code, the statement

```
v_numvarray num_varray := num_varray(10,  20, 30, 40)
```

creates a VARRAY of four elements.

TIP   *Once a VARRAY is initialized, elements are created. The number of elements created is equal to the number of arguments passed to the constructor while initializing. Also, read and write operations can be performed on the VARRAY elements. You can reference the individual elements using the notation varray_variable(subscript_index). This index should start with 1 and must be positive.*

The previous PL/SQL block accessed the first element of the v_numvarray VARRAY and printed its value.

A VARRAY constructor method is an implicitly defined function that returns an initialized VARRAY.

NULL VARRAYS and NULL Elements

VARRAYS declared and uninitialized objects have an atomically NULL value. You can assign VARRAYS a NULL value explicitly and you can also test them with the IS NULL condition for null. Here's an example:

```
declare
  Type num_varray is VARRAY(5) OF NUMBER;
  v_numvarray num_varray;
begin
-- checking for NULL after declaring and before initializing
if v_numvarray IS NULL then
```

```
        dbms_output.put_line('v_numvarray is atomically null');
end if;
    v_numvarray := NULL;
-- checking for NULL after explicitly assigning to NULL
    if v_numvarray IS NULL then
        dbms_output.put_line('v_numvarray is atomically null after assignment');
    end if;
end;
/
```

Here's the output of this program:

```
v_numvarray is atomically null
v_numvarray is atomically null after assignment

PL/SQL procedure successfully completed.
```

Also, you can initialize a VARRAY to contain a NULL element. Here's the code to do so:

```
    v_numvarray := num_varray(NULL);
```

This creates one element in the v_numvarray whose value is null. This is different from an entirely NULL VARRAY, which is uninitialized. Here's the first of two examples:

```
declare
    Type num_varray is VARRAY(5) OF NUMBER;
    v_numvarray1 num_varray;
begin
if v_numvarray1 IS NULL then
        dbms_output.put_line('v_numvarray1 is atomically null');
end if;
if v_numvarray1(1) IS NULL then
        dbms_output.put_line('The first element of v_numvarray1 is null');
end if;
end;
/
```

Here's the output of the preceding program:

```
v_numvarray1 is atomically null
declare
*
ERROR at line 1:
ORA-06531: Reference to uninitialized collection
ORA-06512: at line 10
```

In this example, a VARRAY named v_numvarray1 is defined and checked for NULL without initializing it. Referencing an element of this VARRAY results in an error, as you can see from the previous output.

Here's the second example:

```
declare
  Type num_varray is VARRAY(5) OF NUMBER;
  v_numvarray2 num_varray;
begin
  v_numvarray2 := num_varray(NULL);
-- checking for NULL after initialization
  if v_numvarray2 IS NULL then
    dbms_output.put_line('v_numvarray2 is atomically null');
  else
    dbms_output.put_line('v_numvarray2 is not atomically null');
end if;
if v_numvarray2(1) IS NULL then
    dbms_output.put_line('The first element of v_numvarray2 is null');
end if;
end;
/
```

Here's the output of this program:

```
v_numvarray2 is not atomically null
The first element of v_numvarray2 is null

PL/SQL procedure successfully completed.
```

In this example, a VARRAY named v_numvarray2 is defined and initialized using the VARRAY constructor. Doing so creates one element whose value is NULL. Referencing this element succeeds, as you can see from the previous output.

Referencing the elements of an uninitialized VARRAY raises the error

```
ORA-06531: Reference to uninitialized collection
```

TIP *A VARRAY initialized with all its elements as NULL is not atomically NULL.*

Accessing VARRAY Elements

You can access the individual elements of a VARRAY using valid subscription notation. Here's the syntax:

```
varray_variable(subscript_index)
```

This is for both read and write operations on the VARRAY. Here's an example:

```
v_numvarray(1)
```

Here, the first element of the v_numvarray VARRAY defined earlier can be accessed as v_numvarray(1).

Here's a complete example:

```
declare
  Type num_varray is VARRAY(5) OF NUMBER;
  v_numvarray num_varray;
begin
  v_numvarray := num_varray(10, 20, 30, 40);
-- Referencing individual elements
  dbms_output.put_line('The elements in the v_numvarray are: ');
  dbms_output.put_line(to_char(v_numvarray(1))||', '||to_char(v_numvarray(2))||
                                ', '||to_char(v_numvarray(3))||', '||
                                to_char(v_numvarray(4)));
-- assignment
  v_numvarray(4) := 60;
dbms_output.put_line('The elements in the v_numvarray are: ');
  dbms_output.put_line(to_char(v_numvarray(1))||', '||to_char(v_numvarray(2))||
                                ', '||to_char(v_numvarray(3))||', '||
                                to_char(v_numvarray(4)));
end;
/
```

Here's the output of this program:

```
The elements in the v_numvarray are:
10, 20, 30, 40
The elements in the v_numvarray are:
10, 20, 30, 60

PL/SQL procedure successfully completed.
```

However, the subscript can't be a value beyond the initial size of the VARRAY. This is determined during the time of initialization of the VARRAY. If this rule is violated, Oracle raises the error "ORA-6533: Subscript beyond count." Also, assigning values outside of the VARRAY maximum limit or extending the VARRAY past the maximum size isn't allowed. If this rule is violated, PL/SQL raises the predefined exception SUBSCRIPT_OUTSIDE_LIMIT.

Nested Tables

A *nested table* is an unbounded and unordered single-dimensional array of data elements, all of the same data type. It's similar to an index-by table except that the INDEX BY BINARY_INTEGER clause is missing in its definition. A nested table array has no maximum limit and can be sparse, meaning that elements at any given random index can be deleted. However, you must create a nested table with all its elements in a sequential order. The maximum number of elements in a nested table is 2GB. The elements in a nested table are also ordered.

A nested table is generally a one-dimensional array unless otherwise defined to a multilevel collection, in which case it simulates an array of more than one dimension.

As with a VARRAY, you define a nested table by first defining a TABLE type and then declaring a variable of that type. The following sections detail the steps involved.

Defining the TABLE Type

A nested table type is defined using the TYPE . . . IS TABLE statement. Here's the syntax:

```
TYPE table_name IS TABLE OF data_type [NOT NULL];
```

where table_name is the name of the nested table type and data_type is one of a PL/SQL scalar, record, or object type.

Here's an example of a nested TABLE type:

```
TYPE num_table IS TABLE OF NUMBER;
```

This declares a numeric nested table of unbounded size.

The following rules apply when you specify the data_type:

- You can use %TYPE and %ROWTYPE.

- The data_type can be another VARRAY or TABLE type as of Oracle9*i*.

- The data_type can't be a BOOLEAN, NCHAR, NVARCHAR2, NCLOB, or REF CURSOR type.

Declaring a Variable of the TABLE Type

Once you've defined a nested TABLE type, you need to declare variables of that type that represent the actual nested tables. Here's the syntax:

```
<var_name> <TABLE_type_name>;
```

where TABLE_type_name is the nested TABLE type defined using the TYPE . . . IS TABLE specification and var_name is an arbitrary variable name having a data type of this nested TABLE type. Here's an example:

```
v_numarray num_table;
```

Here's a complete example combining the previous two steps:

```
DECLARE
    TYPE num_table IS TABLE OF NUMBER;
    v_numarray num_table;
BEGIN
    /* Do some processing */
    null;
END;
/
```

TIP *A TYPE . . . IS TABLE definition is only abstract, and as such it can't be used by itself. This means variables of the said type need to be declared and used in PL/SQL manipulations.*

TIP *Creating a nested table doesn't allocate space. It only defines a data type that can be used as the data type of a column of an object-relational table, an object-type attribute, or the type of a PL/SQL variable, parameter, or function return value.*

TIP *A nested table declared as NOT NULL must have a value specified for each of its elements.*

Initializing a Nested Table

When a variable of type TABLE is defined, it represents a NULL nested table. You have to initialize this variable using the constructor method. Similar to a VARRAY, a constructor method for a nested table has the same name as the nested table type and is a function that accepts as parameters values whose data type is of the nested table element type and returns an initialized nested table. The number of elements in the nested table evaluates to the number of arguments passed to the constructor.

Here's an example that shows how the v_numarray object is initialized:

```
DECLARE
    TYPE num_table IS TABLE OF NUMBER;
    v_numarray num_table := num_table(10,  20, 30, 40);
BEGIN
    dbms_output.put_line('The first element of v_numarray is '||
                                    TO_CHAR(v_numarray(1)));
END;
/
```

In the preceding code, the statement

```
v_numarray num_table := num_table(10,  20, 30, 40)
```

creates a nested table of four elements.

> **TIP**   *Once a nested table is initialized, elements are created. The number of elements created is equal to the number of arguments passed to the constructor while initializing. Also, read and write operations can be performed on the nested table elements. You can reference the individual elements using the notation nested_table_variable(subscript_index). This index should start with 1 and must be positive.*

The previous PL/SQL block accessed the first element of the v_numarray nested table and printed its value.

A nested table constructor method is an implicitly defined function that returns an initialized nested table.

NULL and Empty Nested Tables and NULL Elements

Nested tables declared and uninitialized have an atomically NULL value. You can assign nested tables a NULL value explicitly and you can also test them with the IS NULL condition for null. Here's an example:

```
declare
  Type num_table is TABLE OF NUMBER;
  v_numarray num_table;
begin
-- checking for NULL after declaring and before initializing
if v_numarray IS NULL then
    dbms_output.put_line('v_numarray is atomically null');
end if;
  v_numarray := NULL;
-- checking for NULL after explicitly assigning to NULL
  if v_numarray IS NULL then
    dbms_output.put_line('v_numarray is atomically null after assignment');
  end if;
end;
/
```

Here's the output of this program:

```
v_numarray is atomically null
v_numarray is atomically null after assignment

PL/SQL procedure successfully completed.
```

You can initialize a nested table to an empty table of the same type. You specify an empty table by a constructor with no arguments. In this case, the opening and closing parentheses should be specified following the constructor name. Here's an example of an empty table:

```
v_emptyarray num_table := num_table();
```

A nested table initialized to an empty table is *not* atomically null. It's an initialized nested table with no elements. Hence, the individual elements of an empty nested table don't exist. Here's an example to illustrate this:

```
declare
  Type num_table is TABLE OF NUMBER;
  v_emptyarray num_table := num_table();
begin
if v_emptyarray IS NULL then
    dbms_output.put_line('v_emptyarray is atomically null');
else
    dbms_output.put_line('v_emptyarray is NOT atomically null');
end if;
end;
/
```

Here's the output of this program:

```
v_emptyarray is NOT atomically null

PL/SQL procedure successfully completed.
```

Also, a nested table can be initialized to contain a NULL element. Here's the code:

```
v_numarray := num_table(NULL);
```

This creates one element in the v_numarray nested table whose value is null. This is different from an entirely NULL nested table, which is uninitialized. Here's the first of two examples:

```
declare
  Type num_table is TABLE OF NUMBER;
  v_numarray1 num_table;
begin
if v_numarray1 IS NULL then
    dbms_output.put_line('v_numarray1 is atomically null');
end if;
if v_numarray1(1) IS NULL then
    dbms_output.put_line('The first element of v_numarray1 is null');
end if;
end;
/
```

Here's the output of the preceding program:

```
v_numarray1 is atomically null
declare
*
ERROR at line 1:
ORA-06531: Reference to uninitialized collection
ORA-06512: at line 10
```

Here's the second example:

```
declare
  Type num_table is TABLE OF NUMBER;
  v_numarray2 num_table;
begin
  v_numarray2 := num_table(NULL);
-- checking for NULL after initialization
  if v_numarray2 IS NULL then
    dbms_output.put_line('v_numarray2 is atomically null');
  else
    dbms_output.put_line('v_numarray2 is not atomically null');
  end if;
  if v_numarray2(1) IS NULL then
    dbms_output.put_line('The first element of v_numarray2 is null');
  end if;
end;
/
```

Here's the output of the second program:

```
v_numarray2 is not atomically null
The first element of v_numarray2 is null

PL/SQL procedure successfully completed.
```

TIP *Referencing the elements of an uninitialized nested table raises the error "ORA-06531: Reference to uninitialized collection." This corresponds to the predefined PL/SQL exception COLLECTION_IS_NULL.*

TIP *A nested table initialized with all its elements as NULL or initialized with an empty table is not atomically NULL.*

Accessing Nested Table Elements

You can access the individual elements of a nested table using valid subscription notation. Here's the syntax:

```
nested_table_variable(subscript_index)
```

This is for both read and write operations on the nested table. Here's an example:

```
v_numarray(1)
```

Here, the first element of the v_numarray nested table defined earlier can be accessed as v_numarray(1).

Here's a complete example:

```
declare
  Type num_table is TABLE OF NUMBER;
  v_numarray num_table;
begin
  v_numarray := num_table(10, 20, 30, 40);
-- Referencing individual elements
```

```
  dbms_output.put_line('The elements in the v_numarray are: ');
  dbms_output.put_line(to_char(v_numarray(1))||', '||to_char(v_numarray(2))||
                                      ', '||to_char(v_numarray(3))||', '||
                                      to_char(v_numarray(4)));
-- assignment
  v_numarray(4) := 50;
  dbms_output.put_line('The elements in the v_numarray are: ');
  dbms_output.put_line(to_char(v_numarray(1))||', '||to_char(v_numarray(2))||
                                      ', '||to_char(v_numarray(3))||', '||
                                      to_char(v_numarray(4)));
end;
/
```

Here's the output of this program:

```
The elements in the v_numarray are:
10, 20, 30, 40
The elements in the v_numarray are:
10, 20, 30, 50

PL/SQL procedure successfully completed.
```

However, the subscript can't be a value beyond the initial size of the nested table. This is determined during the time of initialization of the nested table. Elements with subscripts beyond the count of elements of the nested table aren't yet created and therefore don't exist. If this rule is violated, Oracle raises the error "ORA-6533: Subscript beyond count." Here's an example to show this:

```
declare
  Type num_table is TABLE OF NUMBER;
  v_numarray num_table;
begin
  v_numarray := num_table(10, 20, 30, 40);
-- Referencing individual elements
  dbms_output.put_line('The elements in the v_numarray are: ');
  dbms_output.put_line(to_char(v_numarray(1))||', '||to_char(v_numarray(2))||
                                      ', '||to_char(v_numarray(3))||', '||
                                      to_char(v_numarray(4)));
  dbms_output.put_line(to_char(v_numarray(5)));
end;
/
```

Here's the output of this program:

```
declare
*
ERROR at line 1:
ORA-06533: Subscript beyond count
ORA-06512: at line 10
```

Referencing the fifth element of a VARRAY of four elements caused this error.

However, you can add any number of elements beyond the count by using special methods. I discuss how to do this in the next section.

Collection Methods

PL/SQL has certain predefined methods that you can invoke on both VARRAY and nested table instances. These methods enable an already implemented way of performing functions on collections, such as checking for the existence of a collection element, getting the count of elements in a collection, or deleting elements from a collection. Here's the syntax to use these methods:

```
collection_variable.method_name
```

where collection_variable is the name of the collection variable and method_name is the name of the particular method. Table 11-1 lists these methods.

Table 11-1. Collection Methods and Their Use

METHOD	USE	SYNTAX
EXISTS	A function that checks for the existence of a particular element. It returns TRUE if the element exists and FALSE otherwise.	collection_variable.EXISTS(index)
COUNT	A function that returns the number of elements contained in the collection.	collection_variable.COUNT
DELETE	A procedure that deletes one, more than one, or all elements from a nested table.	table_name.DELETE to remove all the elements; table_name.DELETE(index) to remove a particular element with the specified index; table_name.DELETE(start_index, end_index) to remove all elements defined between and including the start and end indices

(continued)

Table 11-1. Collection Methods and Their Use (continued)

METHOD	USE	SYNTAX
FIRST	A function that returns the index of the first element in a collection. It returns NULL if the collection is empty.	collection_variable.FIRST
LAST	A function that returns the index of the last element in a collection. It returns NULL if the collection is empty.	collection_variable.LAST
NEXT	A function that returns the index of the element in a collection that is next to the element indicated by the specified index. It returns NULL if such an element doesn't exist.	collection_variable.NEXT(index)
PRIOR	A function that returns the index of the element in the collection that immediately precedes the element indicated by the specified index. It returns NULL if such an element doesn't exist.	collection_variable.PRIOR(index)
LIMIT	A function that returns the maximum number of elements that can be created in a VARRAY. It returns NULL for a nested table.	varray_variable.LIMIT
EXTENDS	A procedure that adds elements to the end of a collection.	collection_variable.EXTEND to add one NULL element; collection_variable.EXTEND(n) to add *n* NULL elements; collection_variable.EXTEND(n, index) to add *n* copies of an element at index specified by index
TRIM	A procedure that deletes elements from the end of a collection.	collection_variable.TRIM to delete the last element; collection_variable.TRIM(n) to delete *n* elements from the end

The following sections present a description of each of these methods.

EXISTS

You use EXISTS to determine whether or not the referenced element exists. Here's the syntax:

```
collection_variable.EXISTS(n)
```

where collection_variable refers to the collection instance and *n* is an integer or integer expression denoting the index. It returns TRUE if the element at index *n* exists, even if it's NULL. If *n* is out of range, EXISTS returns FALSE. Here's an example:

```
DECLARE
    TYPE num_varray IS VARRAY(5) OF NUMBER;
    v_numarray num_varray := num_varray(10, 20, 30, 40, 50);
  BEGIN
    IF v_numarray.EXISTS(4) THEN
        DBMS_OUTPUT.PUT_LINE('The element 4 exists in the variable array.');
    END IF;
END;
/
```

Here's the output of this program:

```
The element 4 exists in the variable array.

PL/SQL procedure successfully completed.
```

COUNT

COUNT is a function that returns the number of elements currently in the collection. In the case of a VARRAY, this may be different from the maximum number elements allowed in the VARRAY. Here's the syntax:

```
collection_variable.COUNT
```

where collection_variable refers to the collection instance. Here's an example:

```
DECLARE
     TYPE num_varray IS VARRAY(10) OF NUMBER;
     v_numarray num_varray := num_varray(10, 20, 30, 40, 50);
     TYPE num_table IS TABLE OF NUMBER;
     v_numlist num_table := num_table(101, 201, 301, 401);
BEGIN
     DBMS_OUTPUT.PUT_LINE('Varray Count = '||TO_CHAR(v_numarray.COUNT));
     DBMS_OUTPUT.PUT_LINE('Nested Table Count = '||TO_CHAR(v_numlist.COUNT));
END;
/
```

Here's the output of this program:

```
Varray Count = 5
Nested Table Count = 4

PL/SQL procedure successfully completed.
```

LIMIT

When applied to a VARRAY, LIMIT returns the maximum number of elements allowed in the VARRAY. When applied to nested tables, it always returns NULL because nested tables have no maximum size. It's important to note the difference between LIMIT and COUNT. LIMIT returns the maximum number of elements allowed in the VARRAY, whereas COUNT returns the number of elements currently existing in the VARRAY. Here's the syntax:

```
collection_variable.LIMIT
```

where collection_variable refers to the collection (VARRAY) instance. Here's an example:

```
DECLARE
     TYPE num_varray IS VARRAY(10) OF NUMBER;
     v_numarray num_varray := num_varray(10, 20, 30);
BEGIN
     DBMS_OUTPUT.PUT_LINE('Varray Count = '||TO_CHAR(v_numarray.COUNT));
     DBMS_OUTPUT.PUT_LINE('Varray Limit = '||TO_CHAR(v_numarray.LIMIT));
END;
/
```

Here's the output of this program:

```
Varray Count = 3
Varray Limit = 10

PL/SQL procedure successfully completed.
```

FIRST and LAST

FIRST is a function that returns the index of the first element of a collection, and LAST returns the index of the last element of a collection. For a VARRAY, FIRST always returns 1 and LAST always returns the value of COUNT, since a VARRAY is dense and elements can't be deleted. Here's the syntax:

```
collection_variable.FIRST
collection_variable.LAST
```

NEXT and PRIOR

NEXT and PRIOR are functions that return the index of the element immediately following the element at position *n* and the index of the element immediately preceding the element at position *n*. You use NEXT and PRIOR to increment and decrement the index for a collection. Here's the syntax:

```
collection_variable.NEXT(n)
collection_variable.PRIOR(n)
```

where collection_variable refers to the collection instance and *n* is an integer or an integer expression denoting the index.

EXTEND

You use the EXTEND procedure to add elements to the end of a nested table or VARRAY. Here's the syntax:

```
collection_variable.EXTEND
collection_variable.EXTEND(n);
collection_variable.EXTEND(n, i)
```

where collection_variable refers to the collection instance, *n* is an integer or an integer expression denoting the index, and *i* is an integer denoting the index of an already existing element of the collection.

EXTEND with no arguments adds a NULL element to the end of the collection with index LAST + 1. EXTEND(n) adds *n* NULL elements starting with index LAST+1. EXTEND(n, i) adds *n* copies of element *i* to the end of the collection. Here's an example:

```
DECLARE
    TYPE num_varray IS VARRAY(10) OF NUMBER;
    v_numarray num_varray := num_varray(NULL, NULL);
    TYPE num_table IS TABLE OF NUMBER;
    v_numlist     num_table   := num_table(NULL);
BEGIN
    v_numarray(1) := 1001;
    v_numarray(2) := 1002;
    v_numarray.EXTEND;
    v_numarray(3) := 1003;

    v_numlist(1) := 101;
    v_numlist.EXTEND(5);
    v_numlist(5) := 105;
END;
/
```

EXTEND operates on the internal size of a collection, which includes any deleted elements for a nested table.

TRIM

You use TRIM to remove elements from the end of a VARRAY or nested table. Here's the syntax:

```
collection_variable.TRIM
collection_variable.TRIM(n)
```

where collection_variable refers to the collection instance and *n* is an integer or an integer expression denoting the number of elements to be trimmed.

When specified with no arguments, TRIM removes one element from the end of the collection. Otherwise, *n* elements are removed. If *n* is greater than COUNT, the SUBSCRIPT_BEYOND_COUNT exception is raised. Like EXTEND, TRIM operates on the internal size of a collection.

DELETE

DELETE removes one, more than one, or all elements from a nested table. DELETE has no affect on a VARRAY. It's illegal to call DELETE on a VARRAY. Here's the syntax:

```
collection_variable.DELETE
collection_variable.DELETE(index)
collection_variable.DELETE(start_index,end_index)
```

where collection_variable refers to the collection instance and index, start_index, and end_index denote the indices of elements in the collection.

When invoked with no arguments, DELETE removes the entire table. DELETE(index) removes the element at the specified index, and DELETE(start_index, end_index) removes all the elements between indices start_index and end_index, both inclusive. If an element of a table to be deleted doesn't exist, DELETE simply skips that element.

Collections in the Database

Unlike index-by tables, both VARRAYS and nested tables can be stored in the database as columns of object-relational tables. They are used as data types of columns of an object-relational table. In order to figure as a data type of database columns, the collection type must be visible to both PL/SQL and SQL. This requires it to be defined using a CREATE OR REPLACE TYPE statement rather than being local to a PL/SQL block. Here's the syntax using a VARRAY:

```
CREATE OR REPLACE TYPE type_name IS VARRAY(size) OF data_type;
```

where type_name is the VARRAY type name, size specifies the maximum size of the VARRAY, and data_type is the data type of the elements of the VARRAY.

Here's the syntax using a nested table:

```
CREATE OR REPLACE TYPE table_name IS TABLE OF data_type;
```

where table_name is the nested table type name and data_type is the data type of the elements of the nested table. Here's an example:

```
CREATE OR REPLACE TYPE num_varray IS VARRAY(10) OF NUMBER;
/
```

This creates a VARRAY type of NUMBER of five elements.
    The following example:

```
CREATE OR REPLACE TYPE num_table IS TABLE OF NUMBER;
/
```

creates a nested table type of NUMBER. The DDL information is recorded in the data dictionary objects in both cases.

Stored VARRAYS

You can use a VARRAY as the data type of a database column. In this case, the whole VARRAY is stored in one database row along with other relational columns. Memory allocation is contiguous for the column value in each row. Here are the definitions that highlight this:

```
CREATE OR REPLACE TYPE add_list AS VARRAY(10) OF NUMBER(10);
/
CREATE TABLE direct_address_list (list_id VARCHAR2(6) PRIMARY KEY,
                                  direct_addresses add_list );
```

    The direct_address_list table contains a list of direct addresses identified by a list_id. The list is stored as a VARRAY column. This VARRAY column is stored in the data dictionary. In Oracle9*i*, VARRAYS less than or equal to 4KB are stored inline, and those larger than 4KB are stored in a LOB in the containing table.

DML on Whole VARRAYS

You can manipulate a stored VARRAY in its entirety using SQL DML statements. The following sections explain how to do so.

INSERT

You use the INSERT statement to insert a VARRAY into a database row. You must first create and initialize the VARRAY. Here are the steps:

1. Directly use a VARRAY constructor with the elements list specified.

2. Use a PL/SQL variable of the VARRAY type preinitialized with elements.

Here's an example of how to INSERT a VARRAY using a constructor:

```
INSERT INTO direct_address_list VALUES
('OFF101', add_list(1001, 1002, 1003, 1004));
```

Also, a PL/SQL variable of type VARRAY can be used. Here's the code that illustrates this:

```
DECLARE
    v_add_varray add_list := add_list(2001, 2002);
BEGIN
    INSERT INTO direct_address_list VALUES ('OFF102', v_add_varray);
END;
/
```

UPDATE

You can use an UPDATE statement to modify a stored VARRAY. Here are the steps to do this:

1. Use a VARRAY instance variable that is preinitialized with elements.

2. Directly use a new VARRAY constructor.

Here's the code to illustrate this using a VARRAY instance variable:

```
DECLARE
    v_add_varray add_list := add_list(1011, 1012, 1013);
BEGIN
    UPDATE direct_address_list
    SET direct_addresses = v_add_varray
    WHERE list_id = 'OFF102';
END;
/
```

Also, instead of using a VARRAY instance variable, you can use a new VARRAY constructor as shown here:

```
UPDATE direct_address_list
SET direct_addresses = add_list(1011, 1012, 1013)
WHERE list_id = 'OFF102';
```

DELETE

You can use a DELETE statement to delete a row containing a VARRAY. Here's the code:

```
DELETE FROM direct_address_list
 WHERE  list_id = 'OFF102';
```

SELECT

You have two methods of querying VARRAYS:

- You can directly query the VARRAY into a PL/SQL variable of the same type.

- You can use the SQL TABLE operator to retrieve the individual elements.

The first method provides a way to manipulate the individual elements. VARRAYS are retrieved from the database into PL/SQL variables using the SELECT statement. The whole VARRAY is fetched into the PL/SQL variable. Once the VARRAY is available as a PL/SQL variable, you can manipulate it using procedural statements. Here's the code to illustrate this:

```
DECLARE
     v_add_varray direct_address_list.direct_addresses%TYPE;
BEGIN
    SELECT direct_addresses
    INTO       v_add_varray
    FROM     direct_address_list
    WHERE   list_id = 'OFF101';

DBMS_OUTPUT.PUT_LINE (
    'The address list for OFF101 contains the following address IDs :');
FOR idx IN 1..v_add_varray.COUNT LOOP
     DBMS_OUTPUT.PUT_LINE(TO_CHAR(v_add_varray(idx)));
END LOOP;
EXCEPTION WHEN OTHERS THEN
     DBMS_OUTPUT.PUT_LINE(SQLERRM);
END;
/
```

Here's the output of this program:

```
The address list for OFF101 contains the following address IDs :
1001
1002
1003
1004
PL/SQL procedure successfully completed.
```

> **TIP**   *You can't manipulate elements of stored VARRAYS directly with SQL. You can manipulate them using PL/SQL only.*

> **TIP**   *Use the SQL TABLE operator to retrieve the individual elements.*

SQL provides a TABLE operator to retrieve the individual elements of a VARRAY. Here's the syntax:

```
SELECT column_value FROM TABLE(varray_column);
```

where column_value is a predefined column name to be used every time the TABLE operator is used and varray_column is the database table column of VARRAY type. Here's an example:

```
SELECT list_id, column_value
FROM    direct_address_list, TABLE(direct_addresses);
```

Here's the output of this query:

```
LIST_I COLUMN_VALUE
------------- ------
OFF101       1001
OFF101       1002
OFF101       1003
OFF101       1004
```

Stored Nested Tables

You can use a nested table as the data type of a database column in a relational table or as an attribute of the underlying object type of an object table. In these cases, Oracle stores all of the nested table data in a separate single table, which it associates with the enclosing relational or object table. Here are the definitions that highlight this:

```
CREATE OR REPLACE TYPE home_add_list AS TABLE OF NUMBER(10);
/
CREATE TABLE home_address_list (list_id VARCHAR2(6) PRIMARY KEY,
                                home_addresses home_add_list )
NESTED TABLE home_addresses STORE AS home_addresses_tab;
```

The home_address_list table contains a list of home addresses identified by a list_id. The list is stored as a nested table column. For each nested table in a given database table, the NESTED TABLE clause is required. This clause specifies the name of the store table. A *store table* is an Oracle-generated table that stores the actual data in the nested table. The data for the nested table isn't stored inline with the rest of the relational columns. It's stored separately in the store table. The home_addresses column actually stores a REF into the home_addresses_tab table, where the list of home address IDs are stored.

DML on Whole Nested Tables

You can manipulate a stored nested table in its entirety using SQL DML statements.

INSERT

You use the INSERT statement to insert a nested table into a database row. You must first create and initialize the nested table. Here are the ways to do this:

- Directly use a constructor.

- Use a PL/SQL variable of nested table type, declared and preinitialized with nested table elements.

Here are examples:

```
INSERT INTO home_address_list VALUES
('H101', home_add_list(1001, 1002, 1003, 1004));
```

Also, you can use a PL/SQL variable of type nested table. The following code illustrates this:

```
DECLARE
    v_add_list home_add_list := home_add_list(2001, 2002);
BEGIN
    INSERT INTO home_address_list VALUES ('H102', v_add_list);
END;
/
```

UPDATE

You can use an UPDATE statement to modify a stored nested table. Here are the ways to do this:

- Use a PL/SQL variable of nested table type, declared and preinitialized with nested table elements.

- Directly use a constructor.

Here's the code:

```
DECLARE
    v_add_list home_add_list := home_add_list(1011, 1012, 1013);
BEGIN
    UPDATE home_address_list
    SET home_addresses = v_add_list
    WHERE list_id = 'H102';
END;
/
```

Also, instead of an instance variable, you can use a new nested table constructor as shown here:

```
UPDATE home_address_list
SET home_addresses= home_add_list(1011, 1012, 1013)
WHERE list_id = 'H102';
```

DELETE

You can use a DELETE statement to delete a row containing a nested table. The following code illustrates this:

```
DELETE FROM home_address_list
WHERE  list_id = 'H102';
```

SELECT

Nested tables are retrieved from the database into PL/SQL variables using the SELECT statement. There are two ways to do this:

- Directly retrieve the nested column into a PL/SQL variable of the same type.

- Use the SQL TABLE operator.

In the case of the first method, the entire nested table is fetched into the PL/SQL variable. The nested table so retrieved is assigned keys starting at 1 and ranging to the number of elements in the nested table. Once the nested table is available as a PL/SQL variable, you can manipulate it using procedural statements.

I first insert a record into home_address_list for H102:

```
DECLARE
    v_add_list home_add_list := home_add_list(2001, 2002);
BEGIN
    INSERT INTO home_address_list VALUES ('H102', v_add_list);
END;
/
DECLARE
    v_add_list home_address_list.home_addresses%TYPE;
BEGIN
    SELECT home_addresses
    INTO       v_add_list
    FROM     home_address_list
    WHERE    list_id = 'H102';

DBMS_OUTPUT.PUT_LINE (
    'The home address list for H102 contains the following address IDs :');
FOR idx IN 1..v_add_list.COUNT LOOP
```

```
        DBMS_OUTPUT.PUT_LINE(TO_CHAR(v_add_list(idx)));
END LOOP;
EXCEPTION WHEN OTHERS THEN
    DBMS_OUTPUT.PUT_LINE(SQLERRM);
END;
/
```

Here's the output of this program:

```
The home address list for H102 contains the following address IDs :
2001
2002


PL/SQL procedure successfully completed.
```

TIP *As a result of the sequential allocation of the index of a nested table column retrieved from the database, the original order of the indices of the nested table gets changed even if elements were inserted nonsequentially while INSERTING into the corresponding database column.*

TIP *Once a nested table column value is retrieved into a PL/SQL variable of the same type, you can invoke any of the collection methods that apply to a nested table on it and you can manipulate it using PL/SQL.*

Using the SQL TABLE operator allows you to retrieve the individual elements of a stored nested table and use them in PL/SQL. This is in contrast to the first method, where the nested table column is first selected into a PL/SQL variable, its individual elements are then accessed and modified if necessary, and then those elements are updated back in the database. Here's the syntax:

```
TABLE(sub_query)
```

where sub_query is the query that returns a nested table column. Also, you can use the TABLE operator in DML statements.

Here's an example of using the TABLE operator to query the homes_addresses table previously created:

```
SELECT *
FROM TABLE(SELECT home_addresses FROM home_address_list WHERE list_id = 'H101');
```

Here's the output of this query:

```
COLUMN_VALUE
------------
        1001
        1002
        1003
        1004
```

Starting with Oracle8*i* PL/SQL 8.1, Oracle provides support for SQL queries on local variables of nested table or VARRAY types. In other words, you can specify a PL/SQL local variable or parameter of a nested table or VARRAY type in the FROM clause of a SQL query. You can also accomplish this using the TABLE operator. Here's an example:

```
create table num_tab (col1 number(10));

declare
    v_add_list home_add_list := home_add_list(NULL, NULL, NULL);
begin
  v_add_list(1) := 1001;
  v_add_list(2) := 1002;
  v_add_list(3) := 1003;
  insert into num_tab
    select column_value
    from   TABLE(CAST(v_add_list AS home_add_list));
end;
/
```

Querying the num_tab table yields the following result:

```
SQL> select * from num_tab;

     COL1
---------
     1001
     1002
     1003
```

Table Functions

A *table function* is a PL/SQL function that returns a resultset and can be called in
the FROM clause of a SQL SELECT clause. Typically, the resultset is returned as
a collection. Here are the steps involved:

1. Create a collection type using the CREATE TYPE statement.

2. Create a function that returns this collection type.

3. Invoke this function using a SELECT statement, specifying it in the
   FROM clause using the TABLE and CAST operators.

Here's an example:

```
create or replace type num_table is table of number;
/
create or replace function f_table return num_table
is
  v_numarray num_table := num_table();
begin
  FOR i in 1..10 loop
     v_numarray.EXTEND;
     v_numarray(i) := i+100;
  END LOOP;
  RETURN (v_numarray);
end;
/
SELECT * FROM TABLE(f_table);
```

Here's the output of this query:

```
SQL> SELECT * FROM TABLE (f_table);

COLUMN_VALUE
------------
         101
         102
         103
         104
         105
         106
         107
         108
         109
         110
```

> **TIP**   *In Oracle8i, you use the CAST operator in conjunction with the TABLE operator to make the previous query work. Here's what the query looks like:*
> ```
> select * from table ( cast(f_table() as num_table));
> ```

Table Functions Involving Object Types

The num_table nested table type created earlier wasn't based on an object type. However, you can also use a nested table of an object type as the return type of a table function.

I use the address object type created in Chapter 10 to demonstrate this. Here's the code:

```
CREATE TYPE temp_adds IS TABLE OF address;
/
CREATE OR REPLACE FUNCTION f_table_obj RETURN temp_adds
IS
    v_temp_adds temp_adds := temp_adds();
BEGIN
    v_temp_adds.EXTEND(5);
    v_temp_adds(1) :=
        address('20 Spring St.', null, 'New York','NY','10020','USA');
    v_temp_adds(2) :=
        address('Suite 206', 'Prospect Blvd', 'Bloomington','IL','60610','USA');
    v_temp_adds(3) :=
        address('1 Woodlake Dr.', null, 'Piscataway','NJ','08540','USA');
    v_temp_adds(4) :=
        address('#9', 'Hayes Avenue', 'Dallas','TX','11134','USA');
    v_temp_adds(5) :=
        address('1 Franklin Ct.', null, 'Franklin','MA','17012','USA');
    RETURN (v_temp_adds);
END;
/
SELECT * FROM TABLE(f_table_obj);
```

Here's the output of this query:

```
SQL> SELECT * FROM TABLE(f_table_obj);

LINE1                 LINE2                 CITY                  ST ZIP
COUN
-------------------   --------------------  --------------------  -------------
20 Spring St.                               New York              NY 10020      USA
Suite 206             Prospect Blvd         Bloomington           IL 60610      USA
1 Woodlake Dr.                              Piscataway            NJ 08540      USA
#9                    Hayes Avenue          Dallas                TX 11134      USA
1 Franklin Ct.                              Franklin              MA 17012      USA
```

New Features of Table Functions in Oracle9i

As you learned in the previous section, PL/SQL versions prior to Oracle9*i* supported table functions, but they did so in an elementary form in that they could return only collections of schema-level types and not PL/SQL types. Also, the CAST operator had to be used in the syntax of calling a table function. In addition, the entire collection had to be materialized before it could be used. As of PL/SQL 9*i*, a table function can

- Be pipelined so that rows of data can be returned incrementally rather than waiting for the function to execute completely and the entire set of rows to be stored in memory. The entire collection need not be instantiated in memory. This results in a better response time and lower memory consumption.

- Be passed from one table function to the next in a pipelined fashion without the need to store data in intermediate tables.

- Be parallelized for execution, which improves speed and scalability.

- Be pipelined and return a PL/SQL type (i.e., a packaged PL/SQL type based on a table of records).

I explain these points in more detail in the sections that follow.

Pipelined Table Functions

A typical table function works in this manner:

- The function executes completely.

- The entire set of rows returned by the collection gets stored in memory.

This has a performance bottleneck while returning a large set of rows. Oracle9*i* introduces *pipelined* table functions, where rows of data can be returned incrementally rather than waiting for the function to execute completely, and the entire collection need not be instantiated in memory. As stated earlier, this results in a better response time and lower memory consumption.

The rows are returned as they're determined, and each row is piped and returned. Here are the steps involved:

1. The table function is defined as pipelined using the PIPELINED construct.

2. The PIPE ROW statement is used to return a single element of a collection.

3. An empty RETURN statement is used to specify the completion of the pipelined table function.

Here's how you can modify the f_table_obj table function to make it pipelined:

```
CREATE OR REPLACE FUNCTION f_table_obj_pipelined
RETURN temp_adds PIPELINED
IS
    v_address address;
BEGIN
    FOR i IN 1..5 LOOP
        IF (i=1) THEN
            v_address :=
                address('20 Spring St.', null, 'New York','NY','10020','USA');
        ELSIF (i=2) THEN
            v_address :=
        address('Suite 206', 'Prospect Blvd', 'Bloomington','IL','60610','USA');
        ELSIF (i=3) THEN
            v_address :=
                address('1 Woodlake Dr.', null, 'Piscataway','NJ','08540','USA');
```

```
        ELSIF (i=4) THEN
            v_address :=
                address('#9', 'Hayes Avenue', 'Dallas','TX','11134','USA');
        ELSIF (i=5) THEN
            v_address :=
                address('1 Franklin Ct.', null, 'Franklin','MA','17012','USA');
        END IF;
        PIPE ROW(v_address);
    END LOOP;
    RETURN;
END;
/
```

You can use this pipelined table function in a SELECT statement. Here's the query:

```
SELECT * FROM TABLE(f_table_obj_pipelined);
```

Here's the output of this query:

```
SQL> SELECT * FROM TABLE(f_table_obj_pipelined);

LINE1                LINE2                CITY                  ST ZIP          COUN
-------------------- -------------------- --------------------- ------------- ---
20 Spring St.                             New York              NY 10020        USA
Suite 206            Prospect Blvd        Bloomington           IL 60610        USA
1 Woodlake Dr.                            Piscataway            NJ 08540        USA
#9                   Hayes Avenue         Dallas                TX 11134        USA
1 Franklin Ct.                            Franklin              MA 17012        USA
```

The following points are worth noting:

- Inside the pipelined table function, a reference is made to each element of the collection rather than populating the entire collection.

- The PIPE ROW statement is used in a loop.

TIP   *A pipelined table function must return a collection.*

A Pipelined Table Function That Returns a PL/SQL Type

The f_table_obj function is a table function that returns a table of objects. However, Oracle9*i* enables the definition of table functions based on PL/SQL types instead of schema-level types. Two conditions must be met:

- The PL/SQL type must be a packaged type.

- The table function must be pipelined.

You can modify the previous example of using the address object type and a table of this type to include a PL/SQL type in a package. Instead of an object type, you can use a PL/SQL record type and the corresponding table function can return a nested table of this record. Here's the code:

```
CREATE OR REPLACE PACKAGE pkg_table_func
IS
    TYPE address_rec IS RECORD
(LINE1                                    VARCHAR2(20),
LINE2                                     VARCHAR2(20),
CITY                                      VARCHAR2(20),
STATE_CODE                                VARCHAR2(2),
ZIP                                        VARCHAR2(13),
COUNTRY_CODE                               VARCHAR2(4)  );
    TYPE temp_adds IS TABLE OF address_rec;
END;
/
```

Next, define the table function that returns temp_adds. Here's the code:

```
CREATE OR REPLACE FUNCTION f_table_plsql_pipelined
RETURN pkg_table_func.temp_adds
PIPELINED
IS
   v_address pkg_table_func.address_rec;
BEGIN
    FOR i IN 1..3 LOOP
        IF (i=1) THEN
            v_address.line1 := '20 Spring St.';
            v_address.line2 := null;
            v_address.city := 'New York';
            v_address.state_code := 'NY';
            v_address.zip := '10020';
```

```
                        v_address.country_code := 'USA';
                ELSIF (i=2) THEN
                    v_address.line1 := 'Suite 206';
                    v_address.line2 := 'Prospect Blvd';
                    v_address.city := 'Bloomington';
                    v_address.state_code := 'IL';
                    v_address.zip := '60610';
                    v_address.country_code := 'USA';
                ELSIF (i=3) THEN
                    v_address.line1 := '1 Woodlake Dr.';
                    v_address.line2 := null;
                    v_address.city := 'Piscataway';
                    v_address.state_code := 'NJ';
                    v_address.zip := '08540';
                    v_address.country_code := 'USA';
                  END IF;
                    PIPE ROW(v_address);
                  END LOOP;
                  RETURN;
END;
/
```

Then, use a SELECT statement to query the table function:

```
SELECT * FROM TABLE(f_table_plsql_pipelined);
```

Here's the output of this query:

```
SQL> SELECT * FROM TABLE(f_table_plsql_pipelined);

LINE1                 LINE2                  CITY                   ST ZIP          COUN
--------------------  ---------------------  ---------------------  --------------  ---
20 Spring St.                                New York               NY 10020        USA
Suite 206             Prospect Blvd          Bloomington            IL 60610        USA
1 Woodlake Dr.                               Piscataway             NJ 08540        USA
```

 TIP *You can't use the CAST operator while querying the table function using a SELECT statement, if that table function returns a collection of a PL/SQL type.*

Passing Data from One Table Function to Another in a Pipelined Fashion

You can pass data from one pipelined table function to another. This eliminates the need to store the data in intermediate tables. Here are the steps to do this:

1. Define a pipelined table function in the normal way.

2. Define a second pipelined function that takes as input the output of querying the first pipelined table function. To do this, you must define the input parameter as of type REF CURSOR.

3. Invoke the second pipelined table function with a CURSOR expression that returns the collection returned by the first pipelined table function.

Here's an example to illustrate this. The table function f_table_plsql_pipelined serves as the first pipelined table function. Next, you define a second pipelined table function with an IN parameter of type SYS_REFCURSOR. Here's the code:

```
CREATE OR REPLACE FUNCTION f_table_plsql2_pipelined(p_ref_cursor SYS_REFCURSOR)
RETURN pkg_table_func.temp_adds PIPELINED
IS
    v_address1 pkg_table_func.address_rec;
    v_address2 pkg_table_func.address_rec;
BEGIN
    LOOP
            FETCH p_ref_cursor INTO v_address1;
            EXIT WHEN p_ref_cursor%NOTFOUND;
        IF (v_address1.city='New York') THEN
            v_address2.line1 := 'P.O. Box 2215';
            v_address2.line2 := null;
          v_address2.city := 'New York';
          v_address2.state_code := 'NY';
          v_address2.zip := '10020-2215';
          v_address2.country_code := 'USA';
        ELSIF (v_address1.city='Bloomington') THEN
            v_address2.line1 := 'P.O. Box 6615';
            v_address2.line2 := null;
          v_address2.city := 'Bloomington';
          v_address2.state_code := 'IL';
          v_address2.zip := '60610-6615';
          v_address2.country_code := 'USA';
```

```
    ELSIF (v_address1.city='Piscataway') THEN
            v_address2.line1 := 'P.O. Box 0001';
            v_address2.line2 := null;
            v_address2.city := 'Piscataway';
            v_address2.state_code := 'NJ';
            v_address2.zip := '08540';
            v_address2.country_code := 'USA';
    END IF;
                    PIPE ROW(v_address2);
    END LOOP;
    close p_ref_cursor;
    RETURN;
END;
/
```

Finally, call this table function with an argument that is a cursor expression that returns the collection returned by f_table_plsql_pipelined. Here's the query:

```
SELECT * FROM TABLE(f_table_plsql2_pipelined(CURSOR(SELECT * FROM
TABLE(f_table_plsql_pipelined()))));
```

Here's the output of this query:

```
SQL> SELECT * FROM TABLE(f_table_plsql2_pipelined(CURSOR(SELECT * FROM
TABLE(f_table_plsql_pipelined()
)))));
```

LINE1	LINE2	CITY	ST	ZIP	COUN
P.O. Box 2215		New York	NY	10020-2215	USA
P.O. Box 6615		Bloomington	IL	60610-6615	USA
P.O. Box 0001		Piscataway	NJ	08540	USA

TIP *You can't use PIPE ROW with nonpipelined table functions. Doing so results in the compilation error "PLS-00629: PIPE statement cannot be used in non-pipelined functions."*

> **TIP**   *Table functions can specify the AUTONOMOUS_TRANSACTION PRAGMA, and INSERT, UPDATE, or DELETE operations can be done inside the body of such a table function.*

Multilevel Collections

So far the collections that I've described, such as VARRAYS and nested tables have been collections containing scalar types. Also, a collection can contain elements that are instances of an object type. These are termed *collections of one dimension*. Oracle9*i* supports *collections of two or more dimensions*. These are collections each of whose elements is in turn a collection and are termed *multi-level collections*. This type of nesting of collections can typically be of five types:

- A VARRAY containing VARRAY elements

- A VARRAY containing nested table elements

- A nested table containing VARRAY elements

- A nested table containing nested table elements

- A VARRAY or nested table of an object type one of whose attributes is a VARRAY or nested table type

> **TIP**   *Oracle9i supports collection nesting of arbitrary dimensions.*

> **TIP**   *Collection nesting is allowed for both schema-level types and PL/SQL types.*

Here's an example of multilevel collections of schema-level types:

```
CREATE OR REPLACE TYPE varray_one IS VARRAY(10) OF NUMBER;
/
CREATE OR REPLACE TYPE varray_one_nested IS VARRAY(10) OF varray_one;
/
CREATE OR REPLACE TYPE varray_two_nested IS VARRAY(10) OF varray_one_nested;
/
```

This example declares a VARRAY type named varray_one of one dimension and two multilevel VARRAY types named varray_one_nested and varray_two_nested of dimensions two and three, respectively. Once created, instances of these collections can be declared in PL/SQL and manipulated as desired. Here's the code that illustrates this:

```
DECLARE
    v1 varray_one;
    v2 varray_one_nested;
    v3 varray_two_nested;
BEGIN
    v1 := varray_one(1, 2, 3);
    v2 := varray_one_nested(varray_one(11,12, 13), varray_one(21,22,23));
    v3   := varray_two_nested(
varray_one_nested(varray_one(111,112,113), varray_one(121,122,123)),
varray_one_nested(varray_one(211,212,213), varray_one(221,222,223)));
dbms_output.put_line('The elements of one-dimensional VARRAY v1 are:');
for i in 1..v1.count loop
    dbms_output.put_line(v1(i));
end loop;
dbms_output.put_line('The elements of two-dimensional VARRAY v2 are:');
for i in 1..v2.count loop
    for j in 1..v2(i).count loop
      dbms_output.put_line(v2(i)(j));
    end loop;
end loop;
dbms_output.put_line('The elements of three-dimensional VARRAY v3 are:');
for i in 1..v3.count loop
    for j in 1..v3(i).count loop
      for k in 1..v3(i)(j).count loop
        dbms_output.put_line(v3(i)(j)(k));
      end loop;
```

```
    end loop;
end loop;
END;
/
```

Here's the output of this program:

```
The elements of one-dimensional VARRAY v1 are:
1
2
3
The elements of two-dimensional VARRAY v2 are:
11
12
13
21
22
23
The elements of three-dimensional VARRAY v3 are:
111
112
113
121
122
123
211
212
213
221
222
223

PL/SQL procedure successfully completed.
```

The following points are worth noting:

- The constructors for each nested VARRAY call the constructor of its element VARRAY. This is evident from the initializations of v2 and v3.

- Individual elements of multilevel collections are referenced by multiple parentheses to refer to the element of the nested collection. Thus, v2(i)(j) refers to the jth element of type varray of the ith element of type varray_one. v3; being a three-dimensional collection, it has one set of parentheses to the right, as in v3(i)(j)(k).

- The FOR LOOPs for displaying all the elements of multilevel collections have nested loops, one loop for each dimension involved.

Similar to schema-level types of nested collections, you can have PL/SQL types of nested collections. Here's an example of this:

```
DECLARE
    TYPE varray_one IS VARRAY(10) OF NUMBER;
    TYPE varray_one_nested IS VARRAY(10) OF varray_one;
    TYPE varray_two_nested IS VARRAY(10) OF varray_one_nested;
    v1 varray_one;
    v2 varray_one_nested;
    v3 varray_two_nested;
BEGIN
    /* Continue further logic */
    null;
END;
/
```

Once you declare multilevel collections in PL/SQL, you can manipulate them in a similar fashion to the way you manipulate them when they're declared as schema-level types. You can modify the previous example of populating and displaying one-, two-, and three-dimensional VARRAYS to deal with multilevel collections of PL/SQL types. Here's the code:

```
DECLARE
    TYPE varray_one IS VARRAY(10) OF NUMBER;
    TYPE varray_one_nested IS VARRAY(10) OF varray_one;
    TYPE varray_two_nested IS VARRAY(10) OF varray_one_nested;
    v1 varray_one;
    v2 varray_one_nested;
    v3 varray_two_nested;
BEGIN
  v1 := varray_one(1, 2, 3);
    v2 := varray_one_nested(varray_one(11,12, 13), varray_one(21,22,23));
    v3  := varray_two_nested(
varray_one_nested(varray_one(111,112,113), varray_one(121,122,123)),
varray_one_nested(varray_one(211,212,213), varray_one(221,222,223)));
dbms_output.put_line('The elements of one-dimensional VARRAY v1 are:');
for i in 1..v1.count loop
   dbms_output.put_line(v1(i));
end loop;
dbms_output.put_line('The elements of two-dimensional VARRAY v2 are:');
for i in 1..v2.count loop
   for j in 1..v2(i).count loop
     dbms_output.put_line(v2(i)(j));
```

```
      end loop;
   end loop;
dbms_output.put_line('The elements of three-dimensional VARRAY v3 are:');
for i in 1..v3.count loop
   for j in 1..v3(i).count loop
      for k in 1..v3(i)(j).count loop
         dbms_output.put_line(v3(i)(j)(k));
      end loop;
   end loop;
end loop;
END;
/
```

Here's the output of this program:

```
The elements of one-dimensional VARRAY v1 are:
1
2
3
The elements of two-dimensional VARRAY v2 are:
11
12
13
21
22
23
The elements of three-dimensional VARRAY v3 are:
111
112
113
121
122
123
211
212
213
221
222
223

PL/SQL procedure successfully completed.
```

TIP   *It's recommended that you include multilevel collection type definitions of PL/SQL type in a package so that they're available persistently across sessions.*

Summary

This chapter discussed the use of collections in Oracle9*i*. Specifically, I high-lighted the use of VARRAYS and nested tables in PL/SQL and inside the database. I then outlined two new features of Oracle9*i* with regard to collections: table functions and multilevel collections.

The next chapter explores the capabilities of using large objects in PL/SQL.

CHAPTER 12

Large Objects

ORACLE9*I* IS AN INTERNET-enabled database that supports storage, retrieval, and manipulation of data of all forms. Data in character or number form is easy to store and retrieve. Oracle provides VARHCAR2 and NUMBER types that can store these types of data. Data such as text documents, video, sound, or images is usually large and in an unstructured format such as binary format. This type of data is relatively huge compared to character data. Oracle7 first provided the ability to store unstructured data in columns of LONG and LONG RAW data types. However, this was limited to a maximum size of 2GB. Also, only one LONG or LONG RAW column was allowed per table. To overcome these limitations, Oracle8 introduced large objects (LOBs) in three major forms: binary large objects (BLOBs), character large objects (CLOBs), and binary files (BFILEs) stored external to the database, in the operating system (OS). The features of these large objects were enhanced in Oracle8*i* and Oracle9*i*. LOBs provide the following advantages over LONG and LONG RAW:

- LOBs can store up to 4GB of unstructured data.

- More than one LOB column can be defined in a single table.

- LOBs can be used as part of conditions in the WHERE clause.

- The data in a LOB can be accessed randomly rather than sequentially as in LONG or LONG RAW columns.

In this chapter, I discuss the methods of storing and retrieving LOBs in the database. I explain how to manipulate LOB data using the PL/SQL interface by means of the DBMS_LOB package. Finally, I outline the conversion of LONG to LOB data.

LOBs Overview

LOBs are divided into two major types: internal and external. *Internal* LOBs are stored inline in a database row or in a separate segment or tablespace. Inline storage is for LOBs less than or equal to 4000 bytes in size. LOBs of a size greater than this are stored in a separate segment or tablespace. BLOBs and CLOBs fall into this category.

Internal LOBs can take part in transactions and can be manipulated using SQL DML statements. All the features of transactions, such as read consistency, the ability to preview changes before making them permanent, and the ability to group related SQL statements into a single logical unit, are available for internal LOBs.

External LOBs are stored outside the database in OS files. BFILEs are external LOBs.

Immaterial of whether a LOB is internal or external, a LOB locator is always stored in a database row. The LOB locator is pointer to where the actual LOB is stored. If there are multiple LOB columns in a table, each column has a unique LOB locator stored in it for each row. The actual LOB data is also distinct for each column in each row. In the case of BFILEs, two different BFILE locators can point to the same OS file.

The manner in which LOBs are stored is an advantage because such storage encompasses a large amount of data and its access is also optimized for such huge data. Also, LOB data can be accessed from within the database or from outside it, such as from the Internet.

BLOBs

A BLOB is a binary large object that can store up to 4GB of unstructured or binary data. You can define attributes of an object type or columns of a database table as of type BLOB. You can have multiple columns of type BLOB in a single table. Here's an example:

```
CREATE TABLE blob_tab
(id NUMBER PRIMARY KEY,
 blob_data BLOB);
```

Once you've defined such a table, you can perform DML operations (specifically, INSERT, UPDATE, and DELETE) on the BLOB column.

You can assign a BLOB column in three ways:

- Set to NULL

- Set to an empty BLOB

- Set to a particular value

Assigning a BLOB to NULL consists of inserting into the table using the constant NULL. In this case, there is no BLOB locator created and no BLOB value exists for the BLOB column. Here's an example using the blob_tab table:

```
INSERT INTO blob_tab VALUES (1, null);
```

Assigning a BLOB column to NULL in this manner doesn't assign a BLOB locator in the corresponding row. Thus, the row with ID 1 doesn't have a valid BLOB locator.

Assigning a BLOB to an empty BLOB consists of setting the BLOB column using the EMPTY_BLOB() function. Doing so sets a locator for the corresponding row with a BLOB of 0 length. Here's an example:

```
UPDATE blob_tab
SET    blob_data = EMPTY_BLOB()
WHERE id = 1;
```

TIP   *You can't manipulate NULL BLOBs in any way. However, you can retrieve the corresponding locator of empty BLOBs and then populate them with data using PL/SQL or any other programmatic interface such as Pro*C/C++, JDBC, and so on.*

Assigning a BLOB to a particular value consists of setting to a fixed value of binary data. You can use the function HEXTORAW to do this. This function converts data in hexadecimal format to RAW or binary format. Here's an example:

```
INSERT INTO blob_tab VALUES (2, HEXTORAW('ABCDEFABCDEFABCDEF'));
```

TIP   *You can initialize object type attributes of type BLOB only to NULL or empty.*

You can obtain the BLOB locator in two ways, one of which is by selecting the BLOB column into a PL/SQL variable of type BLOB. Here's an example:

```
DECLARE
    v_blob BLOB;
BEGIN
    INSERT INTO blob_tab VALUES (3, HEXTORAW('ABCDEFABCDEFABCDEF')) ;
    SELECT blob_data
    INTO    v_blob
    FROM    blob_tab
    WHERE id = 3;
/* ... Use this blob locator to populate the BLOB with large binary data. */
END;
/
```

You can also use the RETURNING clause to return the current value of the LOB locator when setting the BLOB value to empty or a fixed value. Here's an example:

```
DECLARE
    v_blob BLOB;
BEGIN
    INSERT INTO blob_tab VALUES (4, HEXTORAW('ABCDEFABCDEFABCDEF'))
    RETURNING blob_data INTO v_blob;
/* ... Use this blob locator to populate the BLOB with large binary data. */
END;
/
```

CLOBs

A CLOB is a character large object that can store up to 4GB of character data. CLOBs are of two types, CLOB and NCLOB. CLOB refers to character data in the database character set. NCLOB refers to character data in the national character data set. The data in the CLOB or NCLOB column can be of fixed width or variable width, and single byte or multiple byte. You can define attributes of an object type or columns of a database table as of type CLOB. You can have multiple columns of type CLOB in a single table. For example:

```
CREATE TABLE clob_tab
(id NUMBER PRIMARY KEY,
 clob_data CLOB);
```

Once you've defined such a table, you can perform DML operations (specifically, INSERT, UPDATE, and DELETE) on the CLOB column. You can't declare an attribute of an object type as of type NCLOB.

You can assign a CLOB column in three ways:

- Set to NULL

- Set to an empty CLOB

- Set to a particular value

Assigning a CLOB to NULL consists of inserting into the table using the constant NULL. In this case, there's no CLOB locator created and no CLOB value exists for the CLOB column. Here's an example using the clob_tab table:

```
INSERT INTO clob_tab VALUES (101, null);
```

Assigning a CLOB column to NULL doesn't assign a CLOB locator in the corresponding row. Thus, the row with ID 101 doesn't have a valid CLOB locator.

Assigning a CLOB to an empty CLOB consists of setting the CLOB column using the EMPTY_CLOB() function. Doing so sets a locator for the corresponding row with a CLOB of 0 length. Here's an example:

```
UPDATE clob_tab
SET   clob_data = EMPTY_CLOB()
WHERE id = 101;
```

 TIP *You can't manipulate NULL CLOBs in any way. However, you can retrieve the corresponding locator of empty CLOBs and then populate them with data using PL/SQL or any other programmatic interface such as Pro*C/C++, JDBC, and so on.*

Assigning a CLOB to a particular value consists of setting to a fixed value of character data. Here's an example:

```
INSERT INTO clob_tab VALUES (102, RPAD('ABCDEFABCDEFABCDEF',40000,'A'));
```

TIP *You can initialize object type attributes of type CLOB only to NULL or empty.*

You can obtain the CLOB locator in two ways. One way is by selecting the CLOB column into a PL/SQL variable of type CLOB. Here's an example:

```
DECLARE
    v_clob CLOB;
BEGIN
    INSERT INTO clob_tab VALUES (103, EMPTY_CLOB()) ;
    SELECT clob_data
    INTO    v_clob
    FROM    clob_tab
    WHERE id = 103;
/* ... Use this clob locator to populate the CLOB with large character data. */
END;
/
```

The other way is to use the RETURNING clause to return the current value of the LOB locator when setting the CLOB value to empty or a fixed value. Here's an example:

```
DECLARE
    v_clob CLOB;
BEGIN
    INSERT INTO clob_tab VALUES (104, EMPTY_CLOB())
    RETURNING clob_data INTO v_clob;
/* ... Use this clob locator to populate the CLOB with large character data. */
END;
/
```

As of Oracle9*i*, seamless integration of CLOB with VARCHAR2 is possible. Assignment of VARCHAR2 to CLOB and using string functions on CLOB and NCLOB is now possible in PL/SQL 9*i*. Also, 9*i* provides implicit data conversion between VARCHAR2 and NVARCHAR2. You can now use the PL/SQL string functions such as INSTR, LIKE, REPLACE, CONCAT, LENGTH, SUBSTR, TRIM, LOWER, UPPER, RPAD, LPAD, and so forth on CLOB columns and variables holding CLOB values. Also, the functions TO_CHAR and TO_CLOB are available to perform conversion from CLOB to CHAR and vice versa. However, assignment of CLOB to VARCHAR2 variables results in an error if the VARCHAR2 variable is not long enough to hold the CLOB data.

BFILEs

A BFILE is a large binary file that can store up to 4GB of binary data and is located in the OS file system. Only a pointer to this external file is stored in the database. You can define attributes of an object type or columns of a database table as of type BFILE. You can have multiple columns of type BFILE in a single table. Here's an example:

```
CREATE TABLE bfile_tab
(id NUMBER PRIMARY KEY,
 bfile_data BFILE);
```

Once you've defined such a table, you can perform DML operations (specifically, INSERT, UPDATE, and DELETE) on the BFILE column.

You can assign a BFILE column in two ways:

- Set to NULL

- Set to a particular value using the BFILENAME() function

Assigning a BFILE to NULL consists of inserting into the table using the constant NULL. In this case, there is no BFILE locator created. Here's an example using the bfile_tab table:

```
INSERT INTO bfile_tab VALUES (201, null);
```

Assigning a BFILE column to NULL doesn't assign a BFILE locator in the corresponding row. Thus, the row with ID 201 doesn't have a valid BFILE locator.

 TIP *You can't manipulate NULL BFILEs in any way.*

Assigning a BFILE to a particular value consists of pointing it to an external file using the BFILENAME() function. Here's an example:

```
INSERT INTO bfile_tab VALUES (202, BFILENAME('BFILE_DIR', 'test.bmp'));
```

where bfile_dir is a directory object created using the CREATE DIRECTORY statement and test.bmp is the actual OS file name of a binary file residing in the directory pointed to by bfile_dir.

Here's the syntax of the CREATE DIRECTORY statement:

```
CREATE DIRECTORY dir_alias AS '<physical_dir_name>';
```

where dir_alias is the alias for a physical directory named physical_dir_name. Here's an example:

```
CREATE DIRECTORY bfile_dir AS 'c:\proj';
```

Once a directory object is created, the READ privilege must be granted on it to the schema using the directory object. Here's the code for this:

```
GRANT READ ON DIRECTORY BFILE_DIR TO PLSQL9I;
```

where PL/SQL9I is assumed to be a valid username.

You can obtain the BFILE locator in two ways. The first is by selecting the BFILE column into a PL/SQL variable of type BFILE. Here's an example:

```
DECLARE
    v_bfile BFILE;
BEGIN
    INSERT INTO bfile_tab VALUES (203, BFILENAME('BFILE_DIR', 'test.bmp'));
    SELECT bfile_data
    INTO     v_bfile
    FROM   bfile_tab
    WHERE id = 203;
/* ... Use this bfile locator to read the BFILE */
END;
/
```

The second method is using the RETURNING clause to return the current value of the BFILE locator when setting the BFILE value to a fixed value. Here's an example:

```
DECLARE
    v_bfile BFILE;
BEGIN
    INSERT INTO bfile_tab VALUES (204, BFILENAME('BFILE_DIR', 'test.bmp'))
    RETURNING bfile_data INTO v_bfile;
/* ... Use this bfile locator to read the BFILE */
END;
/
```

TIP *BFILEs provide only read-only access to external files.*

DBMS_LOB Package

Once you've obtained a LOB locator, you can manipulate the actual data in the LOB by using several programmatic interfaces. As mentioned earlier, you can use SQL DML on internal LOBs of up to 4KB in size. Beyond this size, you should use one of the programmatic interfaces. Also, you can't read BFILE data using SQL; you have to read it using the API only. Several programmatic interfaces are available to read and manipulate LOBs. These are the PL/SQL interface using the DBMS_LOB package, Oracle Call Interface (OCI) for C, Oracle C++ Call Interface (OCCI), Pro*C/C++, Pro*COBOL, Visual Basic using Oracle Objects for OLE (OO4O), and Java using the JDBC API. This section discusses the manipulation of LOBs using the PL/SQL interface with the DBMS_LOB package.

Basically, there are two steps involved in accessing and manipulating LOB data using the PL/SQL interface:

1. Read the LOB locator. This is done using SQL.

2. Once the LOB locator is obtained, read and/or write the actual LOB data. This is done using PL/SQL with the DBMS_LOB package.

The DBMS_LOB package contains procedures and functions that you can use to perform various read and write operations on internal and external LOBs. Table 12-1 lists the functions you can perform using this interface.

Table 12-1. List of Functions Using the DBMS_LOB Interface

TYPE OF LOB	FUNCTION
BLOB/CLOB	Populating an internal LOB (BLOB or CLOB) with data from an external file (BFILE)
	Testing if an internal LOB is open, and checking in and checking out an internal LOB
	Displaying internal LOB data
	Reading data from an internal LOB
	Reading a part of an internal LOB
	Comparing two internal LOBs in whole or in part
	Searching for patterns in an internal LOB
	Displaying the length of an internal LOB
	Copying one internal LOB to another in whole or in part
	Appending one internal LOB to another
	Writing to the end of an internal LOB
	Working with internal LOB locators (for example, testing if one exists, checking for equality, or copying a LOB locator)
	Writing data to an internal LOB
	Trimming internal LOB data
	Erasing part of the data from an internal LOB
BFILE	Testing if the file pointed to by a BFILE exists
	Opening a BFILE, checking if it is open or not
	Reading and displaying BFILE data
	Reading a portion of a BFILE
	Displaying the length of a BFILE
	Comparing two BFILEs in whole or in part
	Getting the directory alias and the file name pointed to by the BFILE.
	Closing a BFILE and closing all open BFILEs

What follows is a list of procedures and functions included in the DBMS_LOB package. You can perform the functions in Table 12-1 using the procedures and functions listed in Tables 12-2 and 12-3. Table 12-2 lists the procedures and functions pertaining to BLOBs and CLOBs. The procedures DBMS_LOB.LOADBLOBFROMFILE and DBMS_LOB.LOADCLOBFROMFILE are available as of Oracle9*i* Release 2.

Table 12-2. List of Procedures and Functions in the DBMS_LOB Package Pertaining to BLOBs and CLOBs

NAME	SYNTAX	PARAMETERS	DESCRIPTION
OPEN()	DBMS_LOB.OPEN (lob_loc IN OUT NOCOPY lob_type, open_mode IN BINARY_INTEGER)	lob_loc is the locator of the lob_type, which is a BLOB or CLOB, and open_mode is one of 0 (readonly) or 1 (readwrite).	Opens a BLOB or CLOB in specified mode.
ISOPEN()	DBMS_LOB.ISOPEN (lob_loc IN lob_type) RETURN INTEGER	lob_loc is the locator of the lob_type, which is either a BLOB or CLOB.	Tests if a BLOB or CLOB is open and returns 1 if so.
CLOSE()	DBMS_LOB.CLOSE (lob_loc IN OUT NOCOPY lob_type)	lob_loc is the locator of the lob_type, which is either a BLOB or CLOB.	Closes an already opened BLOB or CLOB.
APPEND()	DBMS_LOB.APPEND (dest_lob_loc IN OUT NOCOPY lob_type, src_lob_loc IN lob_type)	src_lob_loc and dest_lob_loc are locators for the source and destination LOB of lob_type, which is a BLOB or CLOB.	Appends a whole source LOB to a destination lob of the same type. COMMIT is to be done explicitly.
COPY()	DBMS_LOB.COPY (dest_lob_loc IN OUT NOCOPY lob_type, src_lob_loc IN lob_type, amount IN INTEGER, dest_offset IN INTEGER := 1, src_offset IN INTEGER := 1)	src_lob_loc and dest_lob_loc are locators for the source and destination LOB of lob_type, which is a BLOB or CLOB; amount is the number of bytes or characters to copy; and dest_offset and src_offset are the start positions in the destination and source lobs where the copy begins.	Copies all or a part of the data in source to the destination LOB.
ERASE()	DBMS_LOB.ERASE (lob_loc IN OUT NOCOPY lob_type, amount IN OUT NOCOPY INTEGER, offset IN INTEGER := 1)	lob_loc is the lob locator for the LOB of lob_type, which is a BLOB or CLOB; amount is the number of bytes or characters to erase; and offset is the start position in the lob where the erase begins.	Deletes all or part of the data in a BLOB or CLOB.

(continued)

Table 12-2. List of Procedures and Functions in the DBMS_LOB Package Pertaining to BLOBs and CLOBs (continued)

NAME	SYNTAX	PARAMETERS	DESCRIPTION
TRIM()	DBMS_LOB.TRIM (lob_loc IN OUT NOCOPY lob_type, newlen IN INTEGER)	lob_loc is the locator of the LOB of lob_type, which is a BLOB or CLOB, and newlen is the resulting length of the LOB after trimming.	Trims the specified LOB to a specified length.
WRITE()	DBMS_LOB.WRITE (lob_loc IN OUT NOCOPY lob_type, amount IN BINARY_INTEGER, offset IN INTEGER, buffer IN RAW|VARCHAR2)	lob_loc is the locator of the LOB of lob_type, which is a BLOB or CLOB; amount is the number of bytes or characters to be written to the BLOB or CLOB, starting from a position given by offset; and buffer is RAW (for BLOB) or VARCHAR2 (for CLOB), holding the data to be written.	Writes data to a BLOB or CLOB.
WRITEAPPEND()	DBMS_LOB.WRITEAPPEND (lob_loc IN OUT NOCOPY lob_type, amount IN BINARY_INTEGER, buffer IN RAW|VARCHAR2)	lob_loc is the locator of the LOB of lob_type, which is a BLOB or CLOB; amount is the number of bytes or characters to be appended to the BLOB or CLOB; and buffer is RAW (for BLOB) or VARCHAR2 (for CLOB), holding the data to be appended.	Appends data to the end of a BLOB or CLOB.
LOADFROMFILE()	DBMS_LOB.LOADFROMFILE (dest_lob_loc IN OUT NOCOPY lob_type, src_file_loc IN BFILE, amount IN INTEGER, dest_offset IN INTEGER := 1, src_offset IN INTEGER := 1)	dest_lob_loc is the locator for the destination internal LOB of lob_type, which is a BLOB or CLOB; src_file_loc is the BFILE locator for the input external file; amount is the number of bytes or characters to copy from the input file: dest_offset is the start position in the destination LOB where the copy begins; and src_offset is the start position in the input file where the copy begins.	Loads all or part of an input external BFILE to a BLOB or CLOB.

(continued)

Table 12-2. List of Procedures and Functions in the DBMS_LOB Package Pertaining to BLOBs and CLOBs (continued)

NAME	SYNTAX	PARAMETERS	DESCRIPTION
LOADBLOBFROMFILE()	DBMS_LOB.LOADBLOBFROMFILE (dest_lob_loc IN OUT NOCOPY BLOB, src_file_loc IN BFILE, amount IN INTEGER, dest_offset IN OUT INTEGER := 1, src_offset IN OUT INTEGER := 1)	dest_lob_loc is the locator for the destination internal BLOB; src_file_loc is the BFILE locator for the input external file; amount is the number of bytes or characters to copy from the input file; dest_offset is the start position in the destination BLOB where the copy begins; and src_offset is the start position in the input file where the copy begins.	Loads all or part of an input external BFILE to a BLOB.

(continued)

Table 12-2. List of Procedures and Functions in the DBMS_LOB Package Pertaining to BLOBs and CLOBs (continued)

NAME	SYNTAX	PARAMETERS	DESCRIPTION
LOADCLOBFROMFILE()	DBMS_LOB.LOADCLOBFROMFILE (dest_lob_loc IN OUT NOCOPY CLOB, src_file_loc IN BFILE, amount IN INTEGER, dest_offset IN OUT INTEGER := 1, src_offset IN OUT INTEGER := 1, src_csid IN NUMBER, lang_context IN OUT INTEGER, warning OUT INTEGER)	dest_lob_loc is the locator for the destination internal CLOB; src_file_loc is the BFILE locator for the input external file; amount is the number of bytes or characters to copy from the input file; dest_offset is the start position in the destination CLOB where the copy begins; src_offset is the start position in the input file where the copy begins; src_csid is the character set of the input BFILE; lang_context is the shift status; and warning is a message in case of abnormal loading.	Loads all or part of an input external BFILE to a CLOB.

(continued)

Table 12-2. List of Procedures and Functions in the DBMS_LOB Package Pertaining to BLOBs and CLOBs (continued)

NAME	SYNTAX	PARAMETERS	DESCRIPTION
COMPARE()	DBMS_LOB.COMPARE (lob_1 IN lob_type, lob_2 IN lob_type, amount IN INTEGER := 4294967295, offset_1 IN INTEGER := 1, offset_2 IN INTEGER := 1) RETURN INTEGER	lob_1 and lob_2 are locators of the first and second LOBs to be compared of lob_type, which is a BLOB or CLOB; amount is the number of bytes or characters to compare; and offset_1 and offset_2 are the starting positions for comparison in the first and second LOBs.	Compares two LOBs of the same type and returns 0 if equal, nonzero if unequal, and null otherwise.
GETCHUNKSIZE()	DBMS_LOB.GETCHUNKSIZE (lob_loc IN lob_type) RETURN INTEGER	lob_loc is the locator of the LOB of lob_type, which is a BLOB or CLOB.	Returns the number of bytes or characters used in the LOB chunk to store the LOB value.
GETLENGTH()	DBMS_LOB.GETLENGTH (lob_loc IN lob_type) RETURN INTEGER	lob_loc is the locator of the LOB of lob_type, which is a BLOB or CLOB.	Returns the length of an input LOB.
INSTR()	DBMS_LOB.INSTR (lob_loc IN lob_type, pattern IN RAW, offset IN INTEGER := 1, nth IN INTEGER := 1) RETURN INTEGER	lob_loc is the locator of the LOB of lob_type, which is a BLOB or CLOB; pattern is the pattern to be searched in the LOB; offset is the start position for the search; and nth specifies the *n*th occurrence of the searched pattern in the LOB.	Returns the position of the *n*th occurrence of a pattern in a BLOB or CLOB.

(continued)

Table 12-2. List of Procedures and Functions in the DBMS_LOB Package Pertaining to BLOBs and CLOBs (continued)

NAME	SYNTAX	PARAMETERS	DESCRIPTION
READ()	DBMS_LOB.READ (lob_loc IN lob_type, amount IN OUT NOCOPY BINARY_INTEGER, offset IN INTEGER, buffer OUT RAW|VARCHAR2)	lob_loc is the locator of the LOB of lob_type, which is a BLOB or CLOB; amount is the number of bytes or characters to read; offset is the start position at which the read begins; and buffer is a RAW (for BLOB) or VARCHAR2 (for CLOB) variable holding the data to read.	Reads from a BLOB or CLOB in a random manner.
SUBSTR()	DBMS_LOB.SUBSTR (lob_loc IN lob_type, amount IN INTEGER := 32767, offset IN INTEGER := 1) RETURN RAW|VARCHAR2	lob_loc is the locator of the LOB of lob_type, which is a BLOB or CLOB; amount is the number of bytes or characters to read; and offset is the starting position for the read operation.	Reads a portion of a LOB in RAW or VARCHAR2 form.

Table 12-3 lists the procedures and functions pertaining to BFILEs.

Table 12-3. List of Procedures and Functions in the DBMS_LOB Package Pertaining to BFILEs

NAME	SYNTAX	PARAMETERS	DESCRIPTION
OPEN()	DBMS_LOB.OPEN (bfile_loc IN OUT NOCOPY BFILE, open_mode IN BINARY_INTEGER := file_readonly)	bfile_loc is the locator of the BFILE and open_mode is 0 for file_readonly.	Opens a BFILE in read-only mode.
ISOPEN()	DBMS_LOB.ISOPEN (bfile_loc IN BFILE) RETURN INTEGER	bfile_loc is the locator of the BFILE.	Tests if a BFILE is open. It returns 1 if so and 0 otherwise.

(continued)

Table 12-3. List of Procedures and Functions in the DBMS_LOB Package Pertaining to BFILEs (continued)

NAME	SYNTAX	PARAMETERS	DESCRIPTION
FILEOPEN()	DBMS_LOB.FILEOPEN (bfile_loc IN OUT NOCOPY BFILE, open_mode IN BINARY_INTEGER := file_readonly)	bfile_loc is the locator of the BFILE and open_mode is 0 for file_readonly.	Opens a BFILE in read-only mode.
FILEISOPEN()	DBMS_LOB.FILEISOPEN (bfile_loc IN BFILE) RETURN INTEGER	bfile_loc is the locator of the BFILE.	Tests if a BFILE is open. It returns 1 if so and 0 otherwise.
CLOSE()	DBMS_LOB.CLOSE (bfile_loc IN OUT NOCOPY BFILE)	bfile_loc is the locator of the BFILE.	Closes an already opened BFILE.
FILECLOSE()	DBMS_LOB.FILECLOSE (bfile_loc IN OUT NOCOPY BFILE)	bfile_loc is the locator of the BFILE.	Closes an opened BFILE.
FILECLOSEALL()	DBMS_LOB.FILECLOSEALL		Closes all BFILEs opened within a session.
FILEEXISTS()	DBMS_LOB.FILEEXISTS (bfile_loc IN BFILE) RETURN INTEGER	bfile_loc is the locator of the BFILE.	Tests if the input BFILE locator points to an existing file. It returns 1 if so and 0 otherwise.
FILEGETNAME()	DBMS_LOB.FILEGETNAME (bfile_loc IN BFILE, dir_alias OUT VARCHAR2, filename OUT VARCHAR2)	bfile_loc is the locator of the BFILE, and dir_alias and filename are the directory alias and file name pointed to by bfile_loc.	Retrieves the directory alias and actual OS file name pointed to by a BFILE.
COMPARE()	DBMS_LOB.COMPARE (lob_1 IN BFILE, lob_2 IN BFILE, amount IN INTEGER, offset_1 IN INTEGER := 1, offset_2 IN INTEGER := 1) RETURN INTEGER	lob_1 and lob_2 are locators of the first and second BFILEs to be compared, amount is the number of bytes to compare, and offset_1 and offset_2 are the starting positions for comparison in the first and second BFILEs.	Compares two BFILEs and returns 0 if equal, nonzero if unequal, and null otherwise.

(continued)

Table 12-3. List of Procedures and Functions in the DBMS_LOB Package Pertaining to BFILEs (continued)

NAME	SYNTAX	PARAMETERS	DESCRIPTION
GETLENGTH()	DBMS_LOB.GETLENGTH (bfile_loc IN BFILE) RETURN INTEGER	bfile_loc is the locator of the BFILE.	Returns the length of an input BFILE.
INSTR()	DBMS_LOB.INSTR (bfile_loc IN BFILE, pattern IN RAW, offset IN INTEGER := 1, nth IN INTEGER := 1) RETURN INTEGER	bfile_loc is the locator of the BFILE, pattern is the pattern to be searched in the BFILE, offset is the start position for the search, and nth specifies the *n*th occurrence of the searched pattern in the BFILE.	Returns the position of the *n*th occurrence of a pattern in a BFILE.
READ()	DBMS_LOB.READ (bfile_loc IN BFILE, amount IN OUT NOCOPY BINARY_INTEGER, offset IN INTEGER, buffer OUT RAW)	bfile_loc is the locator of the BFILE, amount is the number of bytes to read, offset is the start position at which the read begins, and buffer is a RAW variable holding the data to be read.	Reads from a BFILE in a random manner.
SUBSTR()	DBMS_LOB.SUBSTR (bfile_loc IN BFILE, amount IN INTEGER := 32767, offset IN INTEGER := 1) RETURN RAW	bfile_loc is the locator of the BFILE, amount is the number of bytes to read, and offset is the starting position for the read operation.	Reads a portion of a BFILE in RAW form.

In the sections that follow, I discuss the following examples with regard to using the DBMS_LOB package:

- Populating a BLOB column from an external BFILE

- Reading and writing to a CLOB

- Getting the length of a BFILE

Populating a BLOB Column from an External BFILE

Consider the blob_tab table. This example populates binary data from a .bmp file into the BLOB column blob_data of this table. Here are the steps involved:

1. Insert a row with an empty BLOB.

2. Select the BLOB locator for this row into a PL/SQL BLOB variable.

3. Obtain the BFILE locator for the input binary file.

4. Open the input BFILE.

5. Open the BLOB.

6. Populate the BLOB with data from the whole BFILE.

7. Obtain the length of the populated BLOB.

8. Close the BLOB.

9. Close the BFILE.

10. Perform a COMMIT.

11. Display the length of the populated BLOB obtained in step 7.

Here's the code:

```
DECLARE
    bfile_loc    BFILE;
    blob_loc     BLOB;
    bfile_offset  NUMBER := 1;
    blob_offset   NUMBER := 1;
    tot_len INTEGER;
BEGIN
    -- First INSERT a row with an empty blob
    INSERT INTO blob_tab VALUES (5, EMPTY_BLOB());
    COMMIT;
    -- SELECT the blob locator FOR UPDATE
    SELECT blob_data INTO blob_loc FROM blob_tab
        WHERE id = 5 FOR UPDATE;
    - Obtain the BFILE locator
```

```
      bfile_loc := bfilename('BFILE_DIR','test.bmp');
   --  Open the input BFILE */
      dbms_lob.fileopen(bfile_loc, dbms_lob.file_readonly);
    -- Open the BLOB
      dbms_lob.OPEN(blob_loc, dbms_lob.lob_readwrite);
-- Populate the blob with the whole bfile data
dbms_lob.LOADBLOBFROMFILE(blob_loc,bfile_loc,dbms_lob.lobmaxsize,bfile_offset,
      blob_offset) ;
   --   Obtain length of the populated BLOB
      tot_len := DBMS_LOB.GETLENGTH(blob_loc);
    -- Close the BLOB
      dbms_lob.close(blob_loc);
    -- Close the BFILE
      dbms_lob.fileclose(bfile_loc);
      COMMIT;
- Display the length of the BLOB
DBMS_OUTPUT.PUT_LINE('The length of the BLOB after population is: '||
                                            TO_CHAR(tot_len));
    END ;
/
```

Here's the output of this program:

```
The length of the BLOB after population is: 861382

PL/SQL procedure successfully completed.
```

You can see that the length of the populated BLOB is equal to the size of the .bmp file.

Reading and Writing to a CLOB

Consider the clob_tab table. This example consists of two parts. The first part populates character data into the CLOB column clob_data of this table. The second part reads the data from the populated CLOB into an output file.

Here are the steps involved in the first part:

1. Insert a row with an empty CLOB.

2. Select the CLOB locator for this row into a PL/SQL CLOB variable.

3. Populate a VARCHAR2 buffer variable with data of length 1000.

4. Open the CLOB.

5. Populate the CLOB with data from the buffer. This is done in a loop to create a large amount of data.

6. Close the CLOB.

Here's the code for this part:

```
DECLARE
    clob_loc            CLOB;
    v_buf               VARCHAR2(1000);
    Amount              BINARY_INTEGER := 1000;
    Position            INTEGER := 1;
BEGIN
    v_buf := rpad('A',1000,'A');
    insert into clob_tab values (5, EMPTY_CLOB());
    commit;
        SELECT clob_data INTO clob_loc
        FROM clob_tab
        WHERE id = 5 FOR UPDATE;

    DBMS_LOB.OPEN (clob_loc, DBMS_LOB.LOB_READWRITE);

    FOR i IN 1..500 LOOP
        DBMS_LOB.WRITE (clob_loc, Amount, Position, v_buf);
        Position := Position + Amount;
    END LOOP;
    DBMS_LOB.CLOSE (clob_loc);
END;
/
```

Here are the steps involved in the second part:

1. Select the CLOB locator for the row containing the CLOB data into a PL/SQL CLOB variable.

2. Open the CLOB.

3. Open the output file for writing.

4. Read from the CLOB in amounts of 1000 into a VARCHAR2 buffer variable and write a line of this buffer into the output file. This is done in a loop to read until the end of data is reached in the CLOB.

5. Close the output file.

6. Close the CLOB.

Here's the code:

```
DECLARE
    clob_loc  CLOB;
    v_Buf   VARCHAR2(1000);
    Amount   BINARY_INTEGER := 1000;
    Position INTEGER := 1;
    fp UTL_FILE.FILE_TYPE;
BEGIN
    -- Select the CLOB locator for row with id 5 in clob_tab table
    SELECT clob_data INTO clob_loc
        FROM clob_tab WHERE id = 5;
    -- Open the CLOB
    if (DBMS_LOB.ISOPEN(clob_loc)!=1) then
    DBMS_LOB.OPEN (clob_loc, DBMS_LOB.LOB_READONLY);
     end if;
    -- Open the output file for writing
    fp := UTL_FILE.FOPEN('BFILE_DIR', 'output.dat','w');
- Read from the CLOB in chunks of 1000 characters and write to the output file
LOOP
    BEGIN
        DBMS_LOB.READ (clob_loc, Amount, Position, v_Buf);
        UTL_FILE.PUT_LINE(fp, v_Buf, TRUE);
        Position := Position + Amount;
    EXCEPTION
        WHEN NO_DATA_FOUND THEN -- This indicates end of data in CLOB
                EXIT;
     END;
    END LOOP;
    -- Close the output file
    UTL_FILE.FCLOSE(fp);
-- Close the CLOB
    DBMS_LOB.CLOSE (clob_loc);
 END;
 /
```

The output file output.dat can be verified to contain all of the data in the entire CLOB.

Getting the Length of a BFILE

Consider the bfile_tab table. This example populates a BFILE locator pointing to a .bmp file into the BFILE column bfile_data of this table and gets the length of this binary file. Here are the steps involved:

1. Insert a row using the BFILENAME function to populate the bfile_data column with a BFILE locator.

2. Check for the existence of the file pointed to by the BFILE locator.

3. Open the input BFILE.

4. Get the length of the .bmp binary file pointed to by the BFILE locator.

5. Close the BFILE.

Here's the code:

```
declare
    bfile_loc BFILE;
    tot_len INTEGER;
begin
    INSERT INTO bfile_tab VALUES (5, BFILENAME('BFILE_DIR','test.bmp'));
    COMMIT;
    SELECT bfile_data
    INTO    bfile_loc
    FROM    bfile_tab
    WHERE   id = 5;
    IF (DBMS_LOB.FILEEXISTS(bfile_loc)!=0) THEN
       IF (DBMS_LOB.FILEISOPEN(bfile_loc)!=1) THEN
          DBMS_LOB.FILEOPEN(bfile_loc, DBMS_LOB.FILE_READONLY);
          tot_len := DBMS_LOB.GETLENGTH(bfile_loc);
       END IF;
    END IF;
    DBMS_LOB.FILECLOSE(bfile_loc);
    DBMS_OUTPUT.PUT_LINE('The size of the external BMP file is '||
TO_CHAR(tot_len));END;
/
```

Here's the output of this program:

```
The size of the external BMP file is 861382

PL/SQL procedure successfully completed.
```

The operation of reading from a BFILE is similar to that of reading from a BLOB, except that a BFILE locator is used instead of a BLOB locator.

TO_LOB Function

The TO_LOB function converts data in a LONG or LONG RAW column to a LOB column of the appropriate type. In fact, it copies the contents of the LONG or LONG RAW column to a CLOB or BLOB column, regardless of the size. The TO_LOB function is available as of Oracle8*i*, and it provides a handy method of converting LONG and LONG RAW columns to a CLOB or BLOB, respectively. Here are the steps involved:

1. Create a table with the LOB column.

2. Use an INSERT ... SELECT statement with the TO_LOB function applied to the LONG or LONG RAW column and insert into the LOB table.

3. Drop the LONG table.

Here's an example to illustrate this:

```
CREATE TABLE long_test (id NUMBER, long_data LONG);
INSERT INTO long_test VALUES (100, RPAD('A',200000,'A'));
CREATE TABLE lob_test (id NUMBER, clob_data CLOB);
INSERT INTO lob_test
    SELECT id, TO_LOB(long_data)
    FROM    long_test;
/* DROP TABLE long_test; */
```

Alternatively, you can combine steps 1 and 2 into a single step using the CREATE TABLE ... AS SELECT ... statement. Here's the code:

```
CREATE TABLE lob_test AS SELECT id, TO_LOB(long_data) clob_data FROM long_test;
```

There are some restrictions on using the TO_LOB function. First, you can only use it in INSERT . . . SELECT and CREATE TABLE . . . AS SELECT . . . statements in SQL. Using it on PL/SQL variables of type LONG or CLOB causes an error. Here's an example to illustrate this:

```
declare
  x long := rpad('A',100000,'B');
  y clob;
begin
  y := to_lob(x);
  insert into lob_test values (200, y);
end;
/
```

This gives the following error:

```
y := to_lob(x);
        *
ERROR at line 5:
ORA-06550: line 5, column 8:
PLS-00201: identifier 'TO_LOB' must be declared
ORA-06550: line 5, column 3:
PL/SQL: Statement ignored
```

Also, using the TO_LOB function in an UPDATE statement raises an error. Here's the code to illustrate this:

```
update lob_test set clob_data = (select to_lob(long_data) from
long_test where id = 100)
where id = 200;
```

This raises the following error:

```
update lob_test set clob_data = (select to_lob(long_data) from
                                         *
ERROR at line 1:
ORA-00932: inconsistent datatypes: expected - got LONG
```

Oracle9*i* provides two ways of converting a LONG or LONG RAW to a CLOB or BLOB:

- Use the ALTER TABLE . . . MODIFY statement in SQL.

- Use the TO_CLOB and TO_BLOB functions in PL/SQL.

Copying LONG to LOB with the ALTER TABLE . . . MODIFY Statement

You can use the ALTER TABLE . . . MODIFY statement to convert a LONG to a CLOB or a LONG RAW to a BLOB. Here's an example to illustrate this:

```
CREATE TABLE long_test1 (id NUMBER, long_data LONG);
INSERT INTO long_test1 VALUES (100, RPAD('A',200000,'A'));
ALTER TABLE long_test1 MODIFY (long_data CLOB);
```

Here's how you can verify the output of this code:

```
SQL> desc long_test1
```

Here's the output:

Name	Null?	Type
ID		NUMBER
LONG_DATA		CLOB

With this method, the data in the LONG column is converted to CLOB and any constraints on the LONG column are valid on the CLOB column as well. However, any indexes on the LONG column have to be rebuilt.

Copying LONG to LOB with the TO_CLOB and TO_BLOB Functions

You can covert a LONG or LONG RAW column to a CLOB or BLOB using the TO_CLOB and TO_BLOB functions, respectively. Here's an example to illustrate this:

```
declare
    x long;
    y clob;
```

```
begin
  select long_data
  into    x
  from    long_test
  where id = 100;
  y := to_clob(x);
  insert into lob_test values (200, y);
end;
/
```

You can also use the TO_CLOB function on VARCHAR2 data. Here's an example to illustrate this:

```
declare
  x varchar2(32767) := rpad('A',32767, 'B');
  y clob;
begin
  y := to_clob(x);
  insert into lob_test values (200, y);
end;
/
```

These two functions work only in PL/SQL. Using them in SQL causes the following error:

```
ORA-00932: inconsistent datatypes
```

Summary

In this chapter, I discussed the implementation of large objects in Oracle9*i*. I outlined the use of LOBs in SQL and PL/SQL. I explained the use of the PL/SQL API for manipulating LOBs in detail, and I provided specific examples for populating a BLOB column from an external BFILE, reading and writing to a CLOB, and getting the length of a BFILE. Finally, I described the TO_LOB function in detail. I presented code segments to highlight the concepts.

The next chapter presents the creation and use of Java stored procedures in Oracle9*i*.

Part Four

PL/SQL with Java and the Web

Floating in Java

THE INTRODUCTION OF Java in the database opened a more viable alternative to PL/SQL for implementing business logic. Java in the Oracle database server was first introduced in Oracle8*i* by means of an Oracle Java Virtual Machine (JVM) tightly integrated into the database server. This enabled database access using Java as a database language. Oracle provided three ways to access the database using Java: Java stored procedures, Java Database Connectivity (JDBC), and SQLJ. Of these, Java stored procedures enabled Java code to be executed within the Oracle database. Specifically, a Java stored procedure is a Java class compiled and resolved that's stored in the database and executed from there. The Java class could implement data-intensive application logic in Java. The second and third ways of accessing the database using Java, JDBC and SQLJ, allowed Java applications outside of the database to access the database by means of an open API. Oracle9*i* went a step further and enhanced the capability of Java stored procedures.

This chapter highlights the details of using Java stored procedures in Oracle9*i*, including new techniques introduced in Oracle9*i*. It starts with a discussion of why you need Java in the database.

Using Java in the Database

Oracle9*i* provides a seamless environment in which Java and PL/SQL can interoperate as two major database languages. The advantages of using both languages are many.

PL/SQL can be used for the following:

- Intensive database access that's faster than Java. PL/SQL is optimized for running SQL statements within PL/SQL blocks and more so with the native compilation introduced in Oracle9*i*.

- Oracle-specific functionality that has no equivalent in Java, such as using DBMS_LOCK and DBMS_ALERT.

- Seamless access to the database. PL/SQL has the same data types and language constructs as SQL.

- Platform independence.

Java in the database has many advantages, such as:

- Optimization for compute-intensive tasks that don't need database access.

- Extension of database functionality by allowing extremely complex application logic to be implemented in the database.

- A safer type system, automatic garbage collection, polymorphism, inheritance, and multithreading.

- Access to system resources outside of the database such as operating system (OS) commands, files, and so forth.

- Functionality not available in PL/SQL such as OS commands, fine-grained security policies, and easy sending of e-mails with attachments using JavaMail.

- Database independence in addition to the platform independence provided by Java stored procedures.

- Broader ability to share business logic across applications provided by Java stored procedures. Java stored procedures can be developed using any Java IDE and then deployed on any tier of the network architecture. This means Java code can be moved from the database to the client side or the application server (middle tier) and vice versa. Moreover, Java stored procedures can be invoked by applications using any of the standard interfaces such as JDBC, EJB, SQLJ, JSP, Servlets, and so on.

To illustrate the advantages of Java over PL/SQL, the next section explores an area where Java outperforms PL/SQL: file I/O.

Performing File I/O

With PL/SQL file I/O, there are no user-level file permissions, but with Java, granting user-level file permissions is possible. Java provides a more fine-grained permission policy while reading and writing files to the OS. In addition,

- You can specify recursive directories in the case of Java

- You can't perform directory management functions such as creating a directory or listing the contents of a directory in PL/SQL

New Features of Java Stored Procedures in Oracle9i

Oracle9*i* enhances the functionality of Java stored procedures by enabling the following:

- Oracle9*i* JVM compliance with JDK 1.3.*x* and J2SE 1.3

- Return of resultsets to Oracle from Java

- As of Oracle9*i* Release 2, autogeneration of PL/SQL call specifications while loading Java classes into the database

- As of Oracle9*i* Release 2, integration of the database with a J2EE environment by means of callouts to JSP, Servlets, Web components, and Enterprise JavaBeans deployed in the application server tier

PL/SQL Calling Java: Java Stored Procedures

A *Java stored procedure* is a method in a Java class loaded into the database and published in PL/SQL. It's stored as a database object inside the database. Java methods written and compiled as part of a Java class are published in PL/SQL by using *call specifications* or *call specs*. A PL/SQL call spec provides the PL/SQL equivalent of a Java method with corresponding mapping of Java method names, parameter types, and return types to its PL/SQL counterparts. When the PL/SQL call spec is invoked at runtime, it in turn executes the corresponding Java method. At runtime the JVM, along with the database engine, dispatches the call with minimum overhead. It's interesting to note that both SQL and Java run in the same runtime session.

Once it's published, a Java stored procedure can be accessed by PL/SQL or Java applications using a syntax similar to calling any PL/SQL procedure or function. It can be called with arguments, and it can reference Java classes and return values. As of Oracle9*i*, the value returned can also be a resultset. The type of the application that can invoke a Java stored procedure is determined by the runtime context. Any Java method that doesn't include GUI methods can be stored and run in the RDBMS as a stored procedure or function.

Calling Java Stored Procedures from Server-Side PL/SQL

Server-side PL/SQL applications can use the following runtime contexts to call Java stored procedures:

- Stand-alone functions and procedures

- Packaged procedures and functions

- Database triggers

- Object type methods

void Java methods can use a call spec as a procedure, and methods returning values can be published as functions. Also, packaged procedures and functions can be used as call specs.

In addition to these execution contexts, you can reference Java methods published as procedures and functions in anonymous PL/SQL blocks and SQL CALL statements. You can call published functions from SQL DML, such as the INSERT, UPDATE, DELETE, SELECT, EXPLAIN PLAN, and MERGE statements. You can also use the CALL statement to invoke a Java method in a database trigger. Alternatively, the Java stored procedure can be called in the trigger body. You can define object types with attributes and methods that operate on these attributes that reference Java class methods.

Calling Java Stored Procedures from Non-Server-Side PL/SQL

Java stored procedures can also be called from non-server-side PL/SQL applications or non-PL/SQL applications such as

- A Java application via JDBC or SQLJ

- A Pro*, OCI, or ODBC client

- JSP, Servlets, and Enterprise JavaBeans in a J2EE environment

- An Oracle Developer Forms client

- A Web services client

Comparing Java Stored Procedures and PL/SQL Stored Procedures

Although Java stored procedures provide the same advantages as PL/SQL stored procedures in terms of reduced network traffic, better performance, and scalability, there are at least two major differences between them:

- Unlike PL/SQL stored procedures, Java stored procedures are executed by default with invoker rights.

- By default, the Java code, though it resides in the database, is converted into intermediate bytecode that is executed by a Java 2 bytecode interpreter and associated Java runtime system embedded in the Oracle JServer. PL/SQL code is stored as p-code by default and executed by the PL/SQL engine. However, both PL/SQL and Java have the capability of native compilation. In native compilation, the PL/SQL p-code or Java bytecode is converted into machine-independent C code that is then translated into machine code using the C compiler. In PL/SQL, this is done by native compilation and in the case of Java, the Oracle JVM uses an accelerator or native compiler to do the job. This is called *ahead-of-time compilation* because it occurs before execution.

Creating Java Stored Procedures

To create Java stored procedures, you need the Oracle9*i* Database Server, which installs the Oracle9*i* JVM and configures it for Java use. You also need an IDE, such as the Java Development Kit (JDK) or Oracle9*i* JDeveloper, for coding, compiling, and executing Java classes. You can download the JDK from Sun's Java Web site (`http://java.sun.com`), and you can download Oracle9*i* JDeveloper from the Oracle Web site (`http://technet.oracle.com`), where you can also find the installation, configuration, and setup instructions.

I use the JDK as the IDE for developing, compiling, and executing Java classes.

Basic Steps in Creating Java Stored Procedures

Starting from coding a Java class to calling the Java stored procedure, here are the steps involved:

1. Code a custom Java class containing the Java method and compile it.

2. Load the Java method into the database and resolve external references.

3. Publish the Java method in PL/SQL by means of a PL/SQL call spec.

4. If needed, grant the appropriate privileges to invoke the Java stored procedure.

5. Call the Java stored procedure from SQL, PL/SQL, and/or Java.

I explain each step in the following sections.

Coding a Custom Java Class

Consider a Java method that lists the contents of an OS directory passed to it as an argument. I'll name the class "Directory" with a method named "list" in it. This method returns an array of file names listed in the directory passed to it as an argument. Here's the code:

```
import java.io.*;
public class Directory
{
                public static String[] list(String dirName)
            {
            String[] files = null;

                        File file = new File(dirName);
                        if (file.exists())
                        {
                                        if (file.isDirectory())
                                        {
                                            if (file.canRead())
                                            {
                                                files = file.list();
                                            }

                                        }

                }
                        return files;
            }
}
```

Once you've written a custom class, it's saved as a .java source file. You can then compile it before you load it into the database. To compile this class, use the javac command from the command line with the source file name as the argument. Note that the current directory should be the directory in which the source file resides. Here's the code for this:

```
javac Directory.java
```

This results in a Directory.class file.

To test it, I write another class named DirMain with a main() method that calls the Directory.list() method and prints the file names returned by it. Here's the code for this:

```
import java.io.*;
public class DirMain
{
        public static void main(String args[])
        {
                String[] fileNames;
                // listing of directory
                fileNames = Directory.list("C:\\lax\\plsql9i\\latest");
                if (fileNames != null)
                {
                        for (int i=0;i<fileNames.length;i++)
                                System.out.println(fileNames[i]);
                }
        }
}
```

Now that I've tested the Directory.list() method, I can incorporate it into the database. To do this, I have to modify it in the following manner.

Initially, the return type of the list method is an array of strings in Java. In Oracle, this has to be an array of VARCHAR2, which in turn means it can be a collection type such as a VARRAY or a nested table. Since the number of files in a directory is a random number, I choose to use a nested table. The corresponding Java equivalent for a nested table of VARCHAR2 is defined in the class oracle.sql.ARRAY. This class is specified in one of the JDBC APIs. To use it, I have to write some amount of JDBC code.

To use JDBC, you'll need to perform a minimal setup of the environment for Java and JDBC to work, as follows:

- Set the CLASSPATH to include the current working directory and [OracleHome]\jdbc\lib\classes12.zip.

- Set the PATH to include the [JavaHome]\bin and [OracleHome]\bin directories.

With all this in place, here's the code for the modified Directory class:

```
import java.io.*;
import java.sql.*;
import oracle.sql.*;
import oracle.jdbc.driver.*;
public class Directory
{
                public static oracle.sql.ARRAY list(String dirName)
                                throws SQLException
                { Connection conn = null; int ret_code ;
                      String[] files = null ; File file = new File(dirName);
                      if (file.exists())
                      {
                                    if (file.isDirectory())
                                    {
                                                if (file.canRead())
                                                {
                                                  files = file.list(); }
                                    }
                      }
      try {

//       DriverManager.registerDriver(new oracle.jdbc.driver.OracleDriver());

   //   conn = DriverManager.getConnection(
// "jdbc:oracle:thin:@ASSOCIAT-SZECHG:1521:Oracle9", "plsql9i", "plsql9i");
          conn = new OracleDriver().defaultConnection();

    ArrayDescriptor x_ad
              = ArrayDescriptor.createDescriptor("X_NESTED_TABLE", conn);
   ARRAY x_array = new ARRAY(x_ad, conn, files);
   conn.close();
   return x_array;
          } catch (SQLException e) {ret_code = e.getErrorCode();
     System.err.println(ret_code + e.getMessage()); conn.close(); return null;}
      }
}
```

Loading the Java Method into the RDBMS and Resolving External References

Now that the custom Java method is in place, coded, and compiled, it has to be loaded into the database. You use the utility loadjava for this. loadjava is a command-line utility provided by Oracle to load Java code files (.java source files, .class files, .jar files, and Java resource files) into the database. Here's the code for using loadjava:

```
loadjava -user PLSQL9i/PLSQL9i -oci8 -resolve Directory.class
```

Once it's loaded, the Java class is stored in the database and recorded in the data dictionary views just like any other regular database object. The object type for it is JAVA CLASS.

To verify that the class has been loaded, query the data dictionary view USER_OBJECTS. Here's the code to do so:

```
column object_name format a30;
select object_name, object_type, status, timestamp
from   user_objects
where  object_type like 'JAVA%'
order by object_type, object_name;
```

Here's the output of this code:

OBJECT_NAME	OBJECT_TYPE	STATUS	TIMESTAMP
Directory	JAVA CLASS	VALID	2002-08-03:17:34:25

Publishing the Java Method into the Database

After you've loaded the Java method into the database, you need to publish it in PL/SQL by writing a PL/SQL call specification (call spec). The call spec maps the Java method names, parameter types, and return types to their SQL counterparts. You write the call spec using the CREATE PROCEDURE or CREATE FUNCTION statements, or the CREATE PACKAGE or CREATE TYPE statements.

Methods with return values are published as functions and void Java methods are published as procedures. Inside the function or procedure body, you specify the LANGUAGE JAVA clause. This clause maintains information about the name, parameter types, and return type of the Java method. Here's the code for publishing the Directory.list Java method:

```
create or replace type x_nested_table is table of varchar2(100);
/

create or replace function list_dir(p_dir_name VARCHAR2)
return x_nested_table
is language java
  name 'Directory.list(java.lang.String) return oracle.sql.ARRAY';
/
```

The following points are worth noting:

- The full name of the Java method is specified using the class_name.method_name syntax.

- Any parameters to the Java method aren't specified by the parameter names. Instead, the fully qualified data type name is specified. For the Directory.list() method, java.lang.String is the String class with the full name of the package containing this class. There's a one-to-one mapping between the fully qualified Java type names specified in the call spec parameter list and the Java method formal parameters. The main() method is an exception to this rule.

- The fully qualified data type of the return type is specified for the RETURN clause of the Java method.

- Here the call spec is a stored function that returns a nested table of VAR-CHAR2. Executing this function in turn executes the Java method Directory.list() with the appropriate mapping of the parameters and return types and returns the list of files contained in the directory passed as an argument.

Granting the Appropriate Privileges to Invoke the Java Stored Procedure

By default, Java stored procedures execute with invoker rights and all references, including those of class execution, are resolved in the schema of the invoker. You can override this default behavior by specifying the loadjava option -definer. Also, you can give execute privileges on a particular class to other schemas using the -grant option of loadjava while loading the class into the database.

In addition to this authorization, if the Java method accesses any resources outside of the database, permissions must be explicitly granted to the schema for accessing these resources.

Oracle9*i* provides Java 2 security by means of two roles named JAVAUSER-PRIV and JAVASYSPRIV. These roles provide permissions to access resources outside of the database. However, they provide the very basic level privileges needed to access outside resources. To provide extended fine-grained access control, you can use the procedure dbms_java.grant_permission. For the Directory.list routine to be callable from PL/SQL, fine-grained permissions should be granted. Here's the code for this:

```
connect system/manager
begin
   dbms_java.grant_permission( 'PLSQL9I', 'SYS:java.io.FilePermission',
 '<<ALL FILES>>', 'read,write,execute,delete' );
end;
/



begin
   dbms_java.grant_permission( 'PLSQL9I', 'SYS:java.net.SocketPermission',
   'ASSOCIAT-SZECHG', 'resolve' );
end;
/

begin
   dbms_java.grant_permission( 'PLSQL9I',
 'SYS:java.net.SocketPermission', '127.0.0.1:1521', 'connect,resolve' );
end;
/
```

Alternatively, you could execute one grant command to implement this security. Here's the code:

```
connect system/manger
GRANT JAVASYSPRIV TO PLSQL9i;
```

Calling the Java Stored Procedure from SQL and/or PL/SQL

Once it's published, the Java method is called from SQL and/or PL/SQL using the standard procedure for calling PL/SQL procedures or functions. Here's the code for calling the Directory.list Java method:

```
declare
  v_tab x_nested_table;
begin
  v_tab := list_dir('c:\lax\plsql9I\latest');
  for i in 1..v_tab.COUNT loop
    dbms_output.put_line(v_tab(i));
  end loop;
end;
/
```

The output of this PL/SQL program is a list of files contained in the specified directory.

This section outlined the basic steps for creating Java stored procedures. The subsequent sections in this chapter elaborate on the issues involved in each of these steps.

Loading the Java Method

Once a Java class is coded and compiled, it can be loaded into the database in three ways:

- Using the CREATE JAVA . . . DDL statement in SQL. This can also be used to load Java source files.

- Using a BLOB column in the database.

- Using the loadjava utility.

Once they're loaded into the database, Java source, class, and resource files are stored as Java schema objects of type JAVA SOURCE, JAVA CLASS, and JAVA RESOURCE, respectively. Typically, these are stored as library units inside the database schema. In a Java execution environment, the CLASSPATH determines the path where referencing Java classes can be found. The CLASSPATH is a list of OS-specific directories. Analogous to CLASSPATH, Oracle9*i* uses a RESOLVER specification to determine the schemas where referencing Java classes can be found in the database. This makes sense because all Java classes are stored in a database schema as schema objects. In fact, all JVM classes, such as java.io.* and java.lang.*, are loaded in the PUBLIC database schema.

A RESOLVER specification is a combination of Java class names and schema names. Here's the syntax:

```
RESOLVER ((<class name> <schema name>) ... )
```

where <class name> is either a Java name or a wildcard name that can appear in a Java language import statement or the single wildcard * that matches any name. The <schema name> specifies a schema to be searched for a corresponding "library unit." Here's an example:

```
RESOLVER (("oracle.sql.*" PLSQL9I) (* PUBLIC))
```

Using the CREATE JAVA . . . DDL Statement in SQL

You can use the CREATE JAVA . . . statement to load Java source files directly or Java class files as binaries pointed to by a BFILE. Here's an example to load the Directory class created earlier using this method:

```
CREATE OR REPLACE AND COMPILE JAVA SOURCE NAMED "Directory" AS
import java.io.*;
import java.sql.*;
import oracle.sql.*;
import oracle.jdbc.driver.*;
public class Directory
{
        public static oracle.sql.ARRAY list(String dirName)
                    throws SQLException
        { Connection conn = null; int ret_code ;
              String[] files = null ; File file = new File(dirName);
              if (file.exists())
              {
                    if (file.isDirectory())
                    {
                            if (file.canRead())
                            {
                                    files = file.list(); }
                    }
              }
```

```
        try {
            conn = new OracleDriver().defaultConnection();
          ArrayDescriptor x_ad
              = ArrayDescriptor.createDescriptor("X_NESTED_TABLE", conn);
     ARRAY x_array = new ARRAY(x_ad, conn, files);
      conn.close();
      return x_array;
              }catch (SQLException e) {ret_code = e.getErrorCode();
        System.err.println(ret_code + e.getMessage()); conn.close(); return null;}
      }
  }
  /
```

This example creates a JAVA SOURCE object named Directory and a JAVA CLASS object also named Directory. This is because the AND COMPILE clause has been specified.

Alternatively, you can load Java class files as binaries pointed to by a BFILE. Here are the steps involved:

1. Create a BFILE directory to point to a specific OS directory and grant the relevant permissions.

2. Load the Java class using the CREATE OR REPLACE JAVA CLASS USING BFILE statement.

Here's an example:

```
CREATE DIRECTORY bfile_dir AS 'c:\proj';
GRANT READ ON DIRECTORY bfile_dir TO PLSQL9I;
CREATE OR REPLACE JAVA CLASS USING BFILE(bfile_dir, 'Directory.class');
```

This code creates a JAVA CLASS object named Directory in the database schema specified.

TIP   *One good reason to load a Java source file into the database is to preserve the Java source code.*

Using a BLOB Column

You can also load a Java class into the database using a BLOB column in a table. Here are the steps:

1. Load the Java .class file into a BLOB column in the database. You can do this using the DBMS_LOB PL/SQL API.

2. Use the CREATE OR REPLACE JAVA RESOLVER USING BLOB statement to load the Java class from the BLOB column.

Here's an example. First, load the Java class into a BLOB column:

```
DECLARE
      bfile_loc    BFILE;
      blob_loc     BLOB;
      bfile_offset  NUMBER := 1;
      blob_offset  NUMBER := 1;
    tot_len INTEGER;
   BEGIN
     -- First INSERT a row with an empty blob
     INSERT INTO blob_tab VALUES (6, EMPTY_BLOB());
     COMMIT;
    -- SELECT the blob locator FOR UPDATE
    SELECT blob_data INTO blob_loc FROM blob_tab
        WHERE id = 6 FOR UPDATE;
  -- Obtain the BFILE locator
    bfile_loc := bfilename('BFILE_DIR','Directory.class');
   --   Open the input BFILE
     dbms_lob.fileopen(bfile_loc, dbms_lob.file_readonly);
    -- Open the BLOB
    dbms_lob.OPEN(blob_loc, dbms_lob.lob_readwrite);
-- Populate the blob with the whole bfile data
dbms_lob.LOADBLOBFROMFILE(blob_loc,bfile_loc,dbms_lob.lobmaxsize,bfile_offset,
      blob_offset) ;
-- Close the BLOB
      dbms_lob.close(blob_loc);
    -- Close the BFILE
     dbms_lob.fileclose(bfile_loc);
     COMMIT;
END ;
/
```

Next, load the Java class using data from the BLOB column:

```
create or replace and resolve Java class using blob
(select blob_data from blob_tab where id = 6);
/
```

Using the loadjava Utility

loadjava is a utility provided by Oracle9*i* that loads Java classes into the database
and creates the corresponding schema objects of type JAVA SOURCE, JAVA
CLASS, or JAVA RESOURCE. With loadjava, you can load different types of Java
files into the database. More specifically, you can load the following type of files:

- Java source files (files with the .java extension).

- Java binary files compiled outside the database (files with the .class
  extension or archive files with the .jar and .zip extensions). Archive files
  should be uncompressed and non-nested. .jar and .zip files can't be stored
  as schema objects, and loadjava loads these files individually. Only the
  most recently modified files are uploaded.

- Java resource files such as files with the .properties extension, SQLJ profile
  files with the .ser extension, or data files.

Here's the syntax of loadjava:

```
loadjava {-user | -u} username/password[@database]
[ -option_name -option_name ... ] filename filename ...
```

where option_name stands for the following:

```
[action]
[andresolve]
[casesensitivepub]
[cleargrants]
[debug]
[definer | d]
[dirprefix <dir_prefix>]
[encoding encoding_schema_name]
```

```
[fileout file_name
[force | f]
[grant | g username [, username] ... ]
[genmissing]
[genmissingjar jar_file_name]
[help]
[jarasresource]
[noaction]
[nocasesensitivepub]
[nocleargrants]
[nodefiner]
[nogrant]
[norecursivejars]
[noschema]
[noserverside]
[nosynonym]
[nousage]
[noverify]
[oci8 | oci | o]
[optionfile file_name]
[optiontable table_name]
[publish package_name]
[pubmain number]
[recursivejars]
[resolve | r]
[resolver | R "resolver_spec"]
[resolveonly]
[schema | S schema_name]
[stdout]
[stoponerror]
[synonym | s]
[tableschema schema_name]
[thin | t]
[time]
[unresolvedok]
[verbose | v]
```

The loadjava utility is located in the bin directory under the [ORACLE_HOME] directory. You can specify multiple options and file names by separating them with spaces.

Table 13-1 describes the loadjava command-line options.

Table 13-1. loadjava Options

OPTION	DESCRIPTION
action	To perform all the functions.
andresolve	Compiles uploaded source files and resolves external references in each class file as it is loaded.
casesensitivepub	Autogenerates call specs with case-sensitive names.
cleargrants	Revokes any existing execute privileges before granting to users and roles as given with the –grant option.
debug	Generates and displays debugging information.
definer	Overrides default execution with invoker rights and executes the uploaded class methods with definer rights.
dirprefix dir_prefix	For resource files, deletes the specified prefix from the name and then creates the schema object with the new name obtained.
encoding	Sets (or resets) the option -encoding in the database table JAVA$OPTIONS to the specified value.
fileout file_name	Outputs all messages to the specified file.
force	Loads Java class files irrespective of whether they've been loaded before. By default, previously loaded files are discarded.
grant	Grants the EXECUTE privilege on uploaded classes to the listed users.
genmissing	Autogenerates dummy definitions for any missing classes that the main class being loaded references. This isn't done for Java source files.
genmissingjar	Autogenerates dummy definitions for missing classes and places their definitions in a specified .jar file.
help	Displays the loadjava help screen.
jarasresource	Overrides the default behavior of loading .jar files by loading the .jar file as a resource.
noaction	Skips doing the default actions.
nocasesensitivepub	Autogenerates call specs with names in uppercase.
nocleargrants	Doesn't revoke any existing privileges before granting execute privileges to users specified in the -grant option.

(continued)

Table 13-1. loadjava Options (continued)

OPTION	DESCRIPTION
nodefiner	Executes the loaded classes with invoker rights.
nogrant	Doesn't grant any execute privileges to the loaded classes.
norecursivejars	Loads nested JARs as resource schema objects.
noschema	Loads classes into the schema specified in the -user option.
nosynonym	Doesn't create a public synonym for the loaded classes.
noserverside	Determines whether server-side loadjava should use a JDBC driver.
nousage	Suppresses the usage message when no options are given or the –help option is given.
noverify	Disables the bytecode verifier so that uploaded classes aren't verified.
oci8 locilo	Uses the JDBC OCI driver to communicate with the database.
optionfile file_name	Specifies a sequence of patterns and options in a file.
optiontable table_name	Specifies a sequence of patters and options in a database table.
publish package_name	Autogenerates call specs in a package specified by the package_name.
pubmain number	Autogenerates multiple variants of call specs for the main() method or methods with exactly one argument of type java.lang.String.
recursivejars	Loads nested JAR members by exploding them into individual classes, sources, or resources.
resolve	Compiles if required and resolves all external references in those classes.
resolver	Binds newly created class schema objects to a user-defined RESOLVER spec. The default RESOLVER is as follows: "((* definer's_schema) (* public))".
resolveonly	Omits the initial creation step.
schema	Uploads newly created Java schema objects into the specified schema. If this option isn't specified, then the logon schema specified in the –user option is used.

(continued)

Table 13-1. loadjava Options (continued)

OPTION	DESCRIPTION
stdout	Redirects the output to stdout rather than stderr.
stoponerror	Overrides the default behavior of continuing on error and halts uploading at that point.
synonym	Creates a PUBLIC synonym for each of the loaded classes.
tableschema schema_name	Causes the loadjava internal tables to be created in this specified schema.
thin	Uses the JDBC thin driver to communicate with the database.
time	Creates a timestamp for every message.
unresolvedok	Causes unresolved errors to be ignored when used with the -resolve option.
user	Specifies the username, password, and database connect string for loading the Java classes.
verbose	Directs loadjava to display progress messages.

loadjava Options New to Oracle9i

The loadjava options added in Oracle9*i* Release 2 are as follows:

-action

-casesensitivepub

-cleargrants

-dirprefix

-genmissing

-genmissingjar

-noaction

-nocasesensitivepub

-nocleargrants

-nodefiner

-nogrant

-norecursivejars

-noschema

-nosynonym

-nousage

-optionfile

-optiontable

-publish

-pubmain

-resursivejars

-resolveonly

-stoponerror

How loadjava Works

The loadjava utility does the following:

- Creates a system-generated database table named create$java$lob$table, into which Java sources, classes, and/or resources can be loaded.

- Loads the Java binaries into a BLOB column of the system-generated database table.

- Implicitly executes the CREATE JAVA . . . command to load Java from the BLOB column into database library units.

- Compiles Java source files into class files if the -resolve option is specified. Otherwise, it compiles source files at runtime when the class method is invoked. You can specify compilation options, such as the JDK encoding scheme and whether it's online or not, during compilation. This can be either in the command line while using the –resolve option with the –encoding option or by means of an API into a database table JAVA$OPTIONS called the *options table*. Command-line options override options set in the options table. The API used for this is a set of procedures and a function of the DBMS_JAVA package. Here are their definitions:

```
PROCEDURE set_compiler_option
          (name VARCHAR2, option VARCHAR2, value VARCHAR2);
FUNCTION get_compiler_option
          (name VARCHAR2, option VARCHAR2);
PROCEDURE reset_compiler_option
          (name VARCHAR2, option VARCHAR2);
```

where name stands for the name of a Java package, the full name of a class, or an empty string. While compiling, the compiler selects the row that most closely matches the full name of the schema object. In the case of an empty string, it should match the name of any schema object. The options table is created when the procedure DBMS_JAVA.SET_COMPILER_OPTION is called.

- After all the Java classes are loaded, loadjava resolves external references for referencing classes using the default RESOLVER spec of the current schema and PUBLIC, or a resolver spec specified in the -resolver option.

- loadjava doesn't load previously uploaded class files. You can override this default behavior by specifying the -force option. However, both the source and class file for the same class can't be loaded. The source schema object has to be dropped first. To determine whether a class file has been loaded or not in a given schema, loadjava queries a hash table named JAVA$CLASS$MD5$TABLE. This table is called the *digest table*. Every time a Java schema object is loaded, the digest table is updated and only the most recent files are loaded. So, all files not changed since the last load are skipped. Also, before you reload, you must use the dropjava command to remove the corresponding entry from the digest table. However, if you specify the -force option, the digest table lookup is bypassed.

TIP *It's recommended that a Java class once loaded with the loadjava command be dropped with the dropjava command. Otherwise, the digest table doesn't update properly.*

Publishing the Java Method into the Database

Once Java methods are loaded into the database, they must be published in PL/SQL. You do this using call specs. A call spec is one of the following:

- A stand-alone stored subprogram

- A packaged subprogram

- An object type member method

A call spec provides the PL/SQL equivalent of the Java method signature, and as such, the return type and parameter modes must be mapped appropriately from PL/SQL and SQL to their Java equivalents. This raises two concerns:

- Mapping of data types between SQL and Java

- Mapping of parameter modes from SQL and Java

Mapping of Data Types Between SQL and Java

When a Java method published in PL/SQL is executed, there's a transfer of data from SQL to Java and vice versa. As SQL and Java differ in their data type definitions, the need to map data types from Java to SQL and vice versa arises. This mapping ensures that the return types and actual parameters have compatible data types. To enable this, Oracle has provided mappings between SQL data types and Java classes. Table 13-2 lists these mappings.

Table 13-2. Mappings Between SQL and Java Types

SQL TYPE	JAVA CLASS
CHAR, LONG, VARCHAR2	oracle.sql.CHAR
	java.lang.String
	java.sql.Date
	java.sql.Time
	java.sql.Timestamp
	java.lang.Byte
	java.lang.Short
	java.lang.Integer
	java.lang.Long
	java.lang.Float
	java.lang.Double
	java.math.BigDecimal
	byte, short, int, long, float, double
DATE	oracle.sql.DATE
	java.sql.Date
	java.sql.Time
	java.sql.Timestamp
	java.lang.String
NUMBER	oracle.sql.NUMBER
	java.lang.Byte
	java.lang.Short
	java.lang.Integer
	java.lang.Long
	java.lang.Float
	java.lang.Double
	java.math.BigDecimal
	byte, short, int, long, float, double
OPAQUE	oracle.sql.OPAQUE

(continued)

Table 13-2. Mappings Between SQL and Java Types (continued)

SQL TYPE	JAVA CLASS
RAW, LONG RAW	oracle.sql.RAW
	byte[]
ROWID	oracle.sql.CHAR
	oracle.sql.ROWID
	java.lang.String
BFILE	oracle.sql.BFILE
BLOB	oracle.sql.BLOB
	oracle.jdbc2.Blob
CLOB, NCLOB	oracle.sql.CLOB
	oracle.jdbc2.Clob
Object types and SQLJ types	oracle.sql.STRUCT
	java.sql.Struct
	java.sql.SqlData
	oracle.sql.ORAData
REF	oracle.sql.REF
	java.sql.Ref
	oracle.jdbc2.Ref
	oracle.sql.ORAData
Nested table types and VARRAY types	oracle.sql.ARRAY
	java.sql.Array
	oracle.jdbc2.Array
	oracle.sql.ORAData
Any of the preceding SQL types	oracle.sql.CustomDatum
	oracle.sql.Datum

When you map SQL native types to Java native types, there's a chance of information being lost. For example, a SQL NUMBER type mapped to a Java int type could result in loss of information when the data is large. Also, SQL allows the handling of NULLS, and Java native types can't handle NULL values. To overcome this problem, use Java classes corresponding to the Java native types. For example, you can use a data type of java.lang.Integer to allow for NULL values while mapping NUMBER to int. However, since data conversion occurs between Java native format and SQL format, there still there may be a loss of information.

Oracle9*i* provides the oracle.sql package, which contains Java wrapper classes for native SQL types (e.g., oracle.sql.NUMBER, oracle.sql.DATE, and so on). Using these classes when mapping from SQL to Java prevents any loss of information and also handles NULL values.

Mapping of Parameter Modes from SQL and Java

PL/SQL provides three parameter modes: IN, OUT, and IN OUT. IN parameters are similar to call by value in Java and are mapped directly to their Java counterparts. IN OUT and OUT parameters refer to call by reference in Java, and the corresponding Java parameter must be declared as a one-element array. For example, an OUT parameter of type NUMBER can be mapped to a Java parameter of type

```
int[]   p
```

Then a new value can be assigned to p[0].

TIP   *You can map the String[] parameter of main()to multiple VARCHAR2 parameters of the corresponding call spec.*

TIP   *You can't give boolean parameters in call specs. You can define NUMBER parameters instead.*

TIP   *If the Java method has no parameters, you have to specify an empty parameter list for it, but not for the PL/SQL procedure or function.*

Stand-alone Procedures and Functions As Call Specs

You can define top-level call specs using a stand-alone procedure or function. You use procedures for void Java methods, and you use functions for Java methods returning values. Here's the syntax of defining such a call spec:

```
CREATE [OR REPLACE]
{  PROCEDURE procedure_name [(param[, param] ... )]
 | FUNCTION function_name [(param[, param] ... )] RETURN sql_type}
[AUTHID {DEFINER | CURRENT_USER}]
[PARALLEL_ENABLE]
[DETERMINISTIC]
{IS | AS} LANGUAGE JAVA
NAME 'method_name (java_type_name[, java_type_name] ... )
  [return java_type_name]';
```

The NAME clause must specify the full name of the Java method using the class_name.method_name syntax.

Also, the java_type_name must be the fully qualified Java class name corresponding to the Java data type. The number of parameters in the PL/SQL call spec should have a one-to-one correspondence with the java_type_names in the Java method.

The list_dir function created earlier illustrates how to create top-level call specs.

Packaged Procedures and Functions As Call Specs

In addition to stand-alone procedures and/or functions, procedures and/or functions defined as part of a package can be defined as call specs to publish Java methods. In this case, the individual procedures and/or functions inside the package body use the AS LANGUAGE NAME clause to refer to the Java method.

I use the Directory class defined earlier to illustrate the concept of publishing Java methods using PL/SQL packages. The Directory class contains a list() method to list the contents of the directory passed to it as an argument. This is extended to perform directory management functions such as deleting a directory recursively and creating a directory. To do this, I add two more methods to the Directory class:

- A delete() method that takes as an argument a valid directory name, including the path, and returns 1 on successful deletion of all the files contained in it (including those of any subdirectories) and 0 otherwise.

- A create() method that takes as an argument a valid path and a valid directory name and returns 1 on successful creation of the specified directory in the specified path and 0 otherwise.

Here's the Directory class modified in this way:

```
import java.io.*;
import java.sql.*;
import oracle.sql.*;
import oracle.jdbc.driver.*;
public class Directory
{
        public static oracle.sql.ARRAY list(String dirName)
                        throws SQLException
        { Connection conn = null; int ret_code ;
            String[] files = null ; File file = new File(dirName);
            if (file.exists())
            {
                if (file.isDirectory())
                {
                        if (file.canRead())
                        {
                            files = file.list(); }
                }
            }
    try {

    conn = new OracleDriver().defaultConnection();
    ArrayDescriptor x_ad
            = ArrayDescriptor.createDescriptor("X_NESTED_TABLE", conn);
 ARRAY x_array = new ARRAY(x_ad, conn, files);
    conn.close();
    return x_array;
        }catch (SQLException e) {ret_code = e.getErrorCode();
     System.err.println(ret_code + e.getMessage()); conn.close(); return null;}
    }
       public static int delete(String dirName) throws Exception
       {boolean status=false;
        String[] files = null; File dirFile; File file = new File(dirName);
        if (file.exists())
        {
            if (file.isDirectory())
            {
```

```
        if (file.exists())
        {
            if (file.isDirectory())
            {
                if (file.canRead())
                {
                    files = file.list(); }
            }
        }

        if (files != null)
        {
            if (files.length>0)
            {
                for (int i=0;i<files.length;i++)
                {
                 dirFile =
                 new File(file.getPath()+File.separator+files[i]);
                 if  (dirFile.isFile())
                 {
                    dirFile.delete(); }
                  else
                 {
                 delete(file.getPath()+File.separator+files[i]);}
                 }
                }
             }
            status = file.delete(); }
        }
        if (status)
        {
          return 1; }
        else
        {
          return 0; }

    }

public static int create(String path,String dirName)
{
boolean status = false;
File file = new File(path+File.separator+dirName);
status = file.mkdir();
```

```
        if (status)
        {
          return 1; }
        else
        {
          return 0; }
    }
}
```

Now that the Directory class is in place, I define a package to publish these methods. I create a package named PKG_DIR with three functions named LIST_DIR, DEL_DIR, and CREATE_DIR that correspond to the Java methods Directory.list(), Directory.delete(), and Directory.create(), respectively. Thus, these three methods are published using the packaged functions PKG_DIR.LIST_DIR, PKG_DIR.DEL_DIR, and PKG_DIR.CREATE_DIR, respectively. Here's the code for the package specification:

```
create or replace package pkg_dir
is
   function list_dir(p_dir_name VARCHAR2)
   return x_nested_table;
   function del_dir(p_dir_name VARCHAR2)
   return number;
   function create_dir(p_path VARCHAR2, p_dir_name VARCHAR2)
   return number;
end pkg_dir;
/
```

Here's the code for the corresponding package body:

```
create or replace package body pkg_dir
is
   function list_dir(p_dir_name VARCHAR2)
   return x_nested_table
   is language java
   name 'Directory.list(java.lang.String) return oracle.sql.ARRAY';
   function del_dir(p_dir_name VARCHAR2)
   return number
   is language java
   name 'Directory.delete(java.lang.String) return int';
  function create_dir(p_path VARCHAR2, p_dir_name VARCHAR2)
   return number
   is language java
```

```
    name 'Directory.create(java.lang.String, java.lang.String) return int';
end pkg_dir;
/
```

Once published, the Java stored procedure can be called using an anonymous PL/SQL block. Here's the code:

```
declare
  ret_code NUMBER;
begin
  ret_code := pkg_dir.create_dir('C:\proj','dir1');
  if (ret_code = 1) then
    dbms_output.put_line('Directory dir1 successfully created.');
  else
    dbms_output.put_line('Directory dir1 creation failed.');
  end if;
end;
/
```

Here's the output of this program:

```
Directory dir1 successfully created.

PL/SQL procedure successfully completed.
```

Member Methods of a SQL Object Type As Call Specs

Another way to publish Java methods is to use member methods of a SQL object type as call specs. This allows you to use object features and publish Java methods as part of processing objects. Unlike SQL object types, where a type body is created to provide implementation of each member method defined in the object type specification, for member methods used as call specs, there is no type body defined. The type specification itself uses the IS LANGUAGE JAVA clause to refer to the Java methods being published.

I use an AddressJsp Java class with two methods, set_address and get_address, that populate and retrieve the attributes of an object instantiated from the AddressJsp Java class. These two methods are published in PL/SQL as member functions of an object type named address_jsp to describe an address_jsp object type. Here's the code for the AddressJsp Java class:

```java
import java.sql.*;
import oracle.sql.*;
public class AddressJsp implements SQLData {
  public String line1;
  public String line2;
  public String city;
  public String state_code;
   public String zip;
  String sql_type = "ADDRESS_JSP";

  public AddressJsp() {
  }

  public AddressJsp (String iline1, String iline2, String icity, String istate,
                               String izip) {
    this.line1 = iline1;
    this.line2 = iline2;
    this.city = icity;
    this.state_code = istate;
    this.zip = izip;
  }

  public String getSQLTypeName() throws SQLException
  {
    return sql_type;
  }

  public void readSQL(SQLInput stream, String typeName)
    throws SQLException
  {
    sql_type = typeName;

    line1 = stream.readString();
    line2 = stream.readString();
    city = stream.readString();
    state_code = stream.readString();
    zip = stream.readString();
  }

  public void writeSQL(SQLOutput stream)
    throws SQLException
  {
    stream.writeString(line1);
```

```
      stream.writeString(line2);
      stream.writeString(city);
      stream.writeString(state_code);
      stream.writeString(zip);
   }

 public AddressJsp setAddress (String iline1, String iline2, String icity,
                               String istate, String izip) {
      return new AddressJsp(iline1, iline2, icity, istate, izip);
   }

   public String getAddress() {
      return this.line1 + " " + this.line2 + " " + this.city + ", "
               + this.state_code + " " + this.zip;
   }
}
```

Next, I create a call spec using an object type address_jsp with member methods set_address and get_address that publish the Java methods AddressJsp.setAddress() and AddressJsp.getAddress(), respectively. Here's the code for this:

```
CREATE TYPE address_jsp AS OBJECT
(
    line1 varchar2(50),
    line2 varchar2(50),
    city varchar2(50),
    state_code varchar2(2),
    zip varchar2(20),
    MEMBER FUNCTION set_address (p_line1 VARCHAR2, p_line2 VARCHAR2,
                                 p_city VARCHAR2, p_state_code VARCHAR2,
                                     p_zip VARCHAR2) RETURN address_jsp
    IS LANGUAGE JAVA
    NAME 'AddressJsp.setAddress (java.lang.String, java.lang.String,
      java.lang.String, java.lang.String, java.lang.String) return AddressJsp',
    MEMBER FUNCTION get_address RETURN VARCHAR2
    IS LANGUAGE JAVA
    NAME 'AddressJsp.getAddress() return java.lang.String'
  )
NOT FINAL;
/
```

These object type methods can then be called on instances of this object type. This is illustrated in the next section.

TIP *Java methods declared as static are published as STATIC member methods, and nonstatic Java methods are published as MEMBER procedures or functions in the call spec.*

TIP *To be published as member methods of an object type, the Java class containing the Java methods must implement the java.sql.SQLData interface or the oracle.sql.ORAData interface. The SQLData interface is a Java interface for accessing the object attributes of an object type. This calls for the implementation of two methods named readSQL() and writeSQL(), which are defined in the SQLData interface. These methods have to be defined in the Java class and are executed by the JDBC driver to read values from and write values to the database and the instance of the Java class.*

Autogenerating Call Specs Using loadjava

By default, loaded methods aren't published automatically. However, as of Oracle9*i* Release 2, the loadjava utility has a –publish option that autogenerates call specs as part of a package. You can specify the package name to be generated when you give the –publish option.

As an example, I copy the Directory class to a new class named Directory1. This contains the same methods as the original class. This copying is done so as to not mess up the Directory class that's being used for other purposes.

I compile and load the Directory1.java file into the database using the load-java command with the –publish option. Here's the code:

```
loadjava -user plsql9i/plslq9i -r -publish Directory1 Directory1.class
```

where the name Directory1 immediately following the option –publish specifies that a call spec of type package should be autogenerated with the package name as DIRECTORY1. This command loads the Directory1.class file into the database, creating a schema object named Directory1 of type JAVA CLASS and a call spec named DIRECTORY1 of type PACKAGE. No package body is created. I can verify the contents of the DIRECTORY1 package specification by querying the USER_SOURCE data dictionary view. Here's the code:

```
select text from user_source where name = 'DIRECTORY1' and
type = 'PACKAGE'
order by line;
```

Here's the output of this query:

```
TEXT
----------------------------------------------------------------------------
PACKAGE DIRECTORY1 AUTHID CURRENT_USER AS
    FUNCTION DELETE(arg0 VARCHAR) RETURN NUMBER AS LANGUAGE JAVA NAME
'Directory1.delete(java.lang.String ) return int ';
FUNCTION CREATE(arg0 VARCHAR,arg1 VARCHAR) RETURN NUMBER AS LANGUAGE JAVA NAME
'Directory1.create(java.lang.String ,java.lang.String ) return int ';
```

Once the packaged call specs have been generated, they can be called in a similar manner as explicitly coded call specs. No call spec was generated for the list_dir() method, because the –publish option doesn't generate call specs for methods returning collections. In fact, object types, collections, and OUT and IN OUT parameters are exceptions to the rules for autogenerating call specs.

Call specs are generated for only those methods that meet the following criteria:

- The method is defined in a public class.

- The method is defined as public and static.

- The method arguments or return types are byte, int, long, float, double, char, or java.lang.String.

- Arguments or return types of byte, int, long, float, and double types are mapped to NUMBER. Arguments or return types of char and java.lang.String types are mapped to VARCHAR.

- Void methods are created as procedures, and methods with return values are created as functions.

Executing Java Stored Procedures

The final step in developing Java stored procedures is executing them after the Java classes have been loaded and the Java methods have been published in PL/SQL.

The following are several execution contexts for calling Java stored procedures:

- Executing from the top level

- Executing from database triggers

- Executing from SQL DML

- Executing from PL/SQL

I discuss these contexts in the sections that follow.

Executing from the Top Level

Executing from the top level means not executing from an anonymous PL/SQL block or from another procedure or function. Java methods published as procedures and functions can be called using SQL CALL statements at the top level.

Here's the syntax of the CALL statement:

```
CALL [schema_name.] [{package_name. | object_type_name.}] [@dblink_name]
{procedure_name( {param[, param] ... ) |
 function_name ( {param[, param] ... ) INTO :host_variable};
```

where host _variable is a host variable defined in SQL*Plus and is prefixed with a colon (:) to distinguish it from other variables such as local PL/SQL variables, parameters, and packaged variables.

Here's an example that calls the PKG_DIR.CREATE_DIR function using the CALL statement. First, I define a host variable of type NUMBER:

```
SQL> VAR ret_code NUMBER;
```

Second, I execute the Java stored procedure using the CALL statement:

```
SQL> CALL pkg_dir.create_dir('C:\proj','dir2') INTO :ret_code;
Call completed.
```

This CALL statement executes the specified function and assigns its return value to the host variable ret_code.

Third, I print the value of the ret_code host variable:

```
SQL> PRINT ret_code;
RET_CODE
-------------------
        1
```

A value of 1 confirms the successful creation of the dir2 directory.

Executing from Database Triggers

The CALL statement is used to execute a Java method in a database trigger. Alternatively, the Java stored procedure can be called in the trigger body.

Executing from SQL DML

Published functions can be called from SQL DML, such as INSERT, UPDATE, DELETE, SELECT, EXPLAIN PLAN, and MERGE statements.

As an example, consider the pkg_dir.list_dir function. It can be used to insert into a table with a nested table column. I define such a table as follows:

```
CREATE TABLE dir_list (list_id VARCHAR2(6) PRIMARY KEY,
                       files x_nested_table )
NESTED TABLE files STORE AS files_tab;
```

Next, I insert into a row into this table by calling the Java stored function pkg_dir.list_dir in an INSERT statement:

```
insert into dir_list values (100, pkg_dir.list_dir('c:\lax\plsql9I\latest'));
```

Finally, I query the nested table to verify the outcome of this INSERT statement:

```
SELECT *
FROM TABLE(SELECT files FROM dir_list WHERE list_id = 100);
```

Here's the output of this query:

```
COLUMN_VALUE
-----------------
ch12_01.sql
0115ch11.doc
0115ch10.doc
Address_orig.java
0115ch13.doc
test.bmp
0115ch12.doc
Person.java
ch12_02.sql
ch12_03.sql
ch12_04.sql
0115ch14.doc
ch12_05.sql
ch12_06.sql
ch12_07.sql
```

The following restrictions apply for calling Java stored functions from SQL DML:

- The function can't declare any OUT or IN OUT parameters.

- The method can't modify any database tables if it's called from a SELECT statement.

- The method can't query or modify any database tables specified in the INSERT, UPDATE, or DELETE statement if it's called in this statement.

- The method can't execute any Data Definition Language (DDL) statements, transaction control statements such as COMMIT, session control statements such as SET ROLE, or system control statements such as ALTER SYSTEM if it's called from a SELECT, INSERT, UPDATE, or DELETE statement.

Executing from PL/SQL

Java stored procedures can be executed from PL/SQL using anonymous PL/SQL blocks. The published Java method is called using the corresponding call spec in the same way any PL/SQL procedure or function is called.

As an example, I illustrate calling the PKG_DIR.LIST_DIR Java stored function from PL/SQL and calling the object type ADDRESS_JSP member methods used as call specs in the following sections.

Calling the PKG_DIR.LIST_DIR Java Stored Function from PL/SQL

Here's the code for executing this Java stored function:

```
declare
  v_tab x_nested_table;
begin
  v_tab := pkg_dir.list_dir('c:\lax\plsql9I\latest');
  for i in 1..v_tab.COUNT loop
    dbms_output.put_line(v_tab(i));
  end loop;
end;
/
```

This code declares a variable of x_nested_table type and assigns the return value of the Java stored function pkg_dir.list_dir to it. This executes the Java method Directory.list_dir(). You can then display the contents of the nested table v_tab by traversing through each of its elements.

Calling the Object Type ADDRESS_JSP Member Methods Used As Call Specs

To execute the Java methods published as object member methods of the object type ADDRESS_JSP, I define an object table called address_master_jsp. Here's the code for this:

```
create table address_master_jsp of address_jsp;
```

Here's the code to view the structure of this table:

```
SQL> desc address_master_jsp;
```

Here's the output of this code:

Name	Null?	Type
LINE1		VARCHAR2(50)
LINE2		VARCHAR2(50)
CITY		VARCHAR2(50)
STATE_CODE		VARCHAR2(2)
ZIP		VARCHAR2(20)

Next, I define a PL/SQL block to call the member methods of the published object type. Here's the code:

```
declare
  a1 address_jsp := address_jsp(null,null, null,null, null);
begin
  insert into address_master_jsp values
  (a1.set_address('20 Sycamore Dr.',null, 'Fremont','CA','94126'));
end;
/
```

This program declares an instance variable of the object type address_jsp and instantiates it by using the default constructor. It then inserts a record into the address_master_jsp table by calling the set_address function that returns an object of type address_jsp. This in turn executes the AddressJsp.setAddress() Java method.

I can verify the output of this code in two ways. First, I can directly select from the address_master_jsp table. Here's the code:

```
SQL> select * from address_master_jsp;
```

Here's the output:

```
LINE1
------------------------
LINE2
------------------------
CITY                                               ST ZIP
-------------------------------------------------- -- -------
20 Sycamore Dr.

Fremont                                            CA 94126
```

Second, I can use the member method get_address. Here's the code:

```
SQL> select a.get_address() from address_master_jsp a;
```

Here's the output:

```
A.GET_ADDRESS()
---------------------------------------
20 Sycamore Dr. null Fremont, CA 94126
```

This in turn executes the Java method AddressJsp.getAddress().

TIP   *You can use only top-level and packaged procedures and functions as call specs.*

In addition to the previously specified execution contexts, Java stored procedures can be called from non-server-side PL/SQL applications or non-PL/SQL applications such as

- A Java application via JDBC or SQLJ

- A Pro*, OCI, or ODBC client

- JSP, Servlets, and Enterprise JavaBeans in a J2EE environment

- An Oracle Developer Forms client

- A Web services client

Java Stored Procedures Returning Resultsets

The functionality of Java stored procedures in Oracle8*i* was limited by the fact that it wasn't possible to return a resultset directly from them. This means that Java stored procedures couldn't return the results of multirow query to the calling environment. In PL/SQL, this is possible by means of REF CURSOR. PL/SQL functions or procedures can return sets of rows as a weak REF CURSOR defined in a package. Java applications could use the JDBC resultset feature to do the same thing. However, there was no mapping available in Java of the type ResultSet->REF CURSOR. Oracle9*i* has incorporated this mapping, thus allowing you to return a resultset from a function or as an OUT parameter to a procedure. This conversion also uses the JDBC API and is made possible by using a special procedure introduced in it.

In the following sections, I use the Organizational Hierarchy System described in Appendix A as an example to write a function that returns details of all organizations for a particular hierarchy.

Writing the Java Method That Returns a Resultset and Compiling It to Obtain a .class File

I define a Java class RefCursor containing a Java function RefCursor_func(). This function uses the JDBC API to access the database and return a set of rows from a multirow query. Here are the steps:

1. Import the JDBC-specific packages such as java.sql.*, oracle.jdbc.driver.*, and oracle.sql.*:

```
import java.sql.*;
import oracle.jdbc.driver.*;
import oracle.sql.*;
```

2. Get the default server-side Oracle connection:

```
Connection conn = new OracleDriver().defaultConnection();
```

3. Create the Statement or PreparedStatement as a REF CURSOR by calling the method setCreateStatementAsRefCursor(true) on the Connection object cast to an OracleConnection object:

```
((OracleConnection)conn).setCreateStatementAsRefCursor(true);
```

4. Define the Statement object:

```
Statement sql_stmt = conn.createStatement();
```

5. Define a ResultSet object to execute the appropriate query. This query returns the resultset so desired. Here's the code:

```
ResultSet rset = sql_stmt.executeQuery("SELECT hrc_descr, org_long_name " +
    "FROM org_tab o, hrc_tab h where o.hrc_code = h.hrc_code");
```

6. Return the ResultSet object (as a REF CURSOR):

```
return rset;
```

Here's the complete program (saved as RefCursor.java):

```
//Import JDBC packages
import java.sql.*;
import oracle.jdbc.driver.*;
import oracle.sql.*;

public class RefCursor {
  public static ResultSet RefCursor_func() throws SQLException {
    try {
    Connection conn = new OracleDriver().defaultConnection();
    ((OracleConnection)conn).setCreateStatementAsRefCursor(true);

  //Create a Statement object
  Statement sql_stmt = conn.createStatement();
  //Create a ResultSet object, execute the query and return a
  // resultset
  ResultSet rset = sql_stmt.executeQuery("SELECT hrc_descr, org_long_name " +
  "FROM org_tab o, hrc_tab h where o.hrc_code = h.hrc_code");
  return rset;
    } catch (SQLException e) {System.out.println(e.getMessage()); return null;}
  }
}
```

TIP   *The Java method, if it's a function, should return a resultset of type java.sql.ResultSet. If it's a procedure, the Java method should be declared as a parameter of type java.sql.ResultSet[] (i.e., an array of type java.sql.ResultSet).*

TIP   *Only OUT parameters in the call spec are allowed. You can't use IN or IN OUT parameters because there's no mapping from REF CURSOR to ResultSet.*

TIP   *You should invoke the method setCreateStatementAsRefCursor(true) prior to creating the Statement or PreparedStatement object. Otherwise, the error message "ORA-00932: inconsistent datatypes" is generated when the Java stored procedure is executed.*

Once this Java program is defined, you can compile it into a .class file as follows:

```
javac RefCursor.java
```

Loading the .class File into the Oracle9i Database

I do this using the loadjava utility as follows:

```
loadjava -user plsql9i/plsql9i -r -oci8 RefCursor.class
```

Publishing the Java Method in Oracle9i Using a PL/SQL Call Spec

I define a packaged function to correspond to the Java function. Here's the code:

```
create or replace package pkg_rc as
  TYPE rc IS REF CURSOR;
  function f_rc return rc;
end pkg_rc;
/
create or replace package body pkg_rc as
  function f_rc return rc
  is language java
    name 'RefCursor.RefCursor_func() return java.sql.Resultset';
end pkg_rc;
/
```

TIP   *The return type of the PL/SQL packaged function is of type REF CURSOR.*

TIP   *The Java method should specify the fully qualified type name for its return type. So, java.sql.ResultSet should be specified, not just ResultSet.*

Calling the Java Stored Procedure Using the PL/SQL Call Spec

This is a simple PL/SQL program to call the packaged function pkg_rc.f_rc. Here's the code:

```
declare
  TYPE rc IS REF CURSOR;
  r1 rc;
  v_hrc_descr varchar2(20);
  v_org_long_name varchar2(60);
begin
  r1:= pkg_rc.f_rc;
  dbms_output.put_line('Hierarchy  Org Long Name');
  dbms_output.put_line('-----  ---------');
  fetch r1 into v_hrc_descr, v_org_long_name;
  while r1%FOUND loop
    dbms_output.put_line(rpad(v_hrc_descr, 9)||'  '||v_org_long_name);
    fetch r1 into v_hrc_descr, v_org_long_name;
  end loop;
  close r1;
end;
/
```

The Java stored procedure gets executed based on the data in the org_tab table. Here's the output:

```
Hierarchy  Org Long Name
---------  ----------------------
CEO/COO    Office of CEO ABC Inc.
CEO/COO    Office of CEO XYZ Inc.
CEO/COO    Office of CEO DataPro Inc.
VP         Office of VP Sales ABC Inc.
VP         Office of VP Mktg ABC Inc.
VP         Office of VP Tech ABC Inc.
Director   Office of Director Tech ABC Inc.
Director   Office of Dir. SSL
```

Summary

In this chapter, I highlighted the technique of defining Java stored procedures in Oracle9*i*. I explained the new features of Oracle9*i* related to Java stored procedures: autogenerating PL/SQL call specifications and returning resultsets from Java stored procedures.

The next chapter presents a discussion of Web enabling PL/SQL applications.

CHAPTER 14

PL/SQL and the Web

No application, either developed from scratch or converted from an older version, seems complete without its being Web enabled. This is especially the case with an Oracle database. PL/SQL is the primary procedural language for Oracle, and PL/SQL applications can be made globally accessible through deployment on the Web. Web enabling a PL/SQL application involves the use of HTML and/or XML and requires deployment using a Web server. The combination of PL/SQL and HTML/XML brings an altogether new technology to the world of PL/SQL. For related links, refer to the Oracle Technology Network Web site at `http://technet.oracle.com/`.

This chapter highlights the methods of running PL/SQL applications on the Web. It details building a Web application using PL/SQL. It also discusses the method of sending e-mail from within the database using the PL/SQL API. Typically, you can run a PL/SQL application on the Web in two ways:

- Using HTML in PL/SQL

- Using PL/SQL in HTML

To run PL/SQL on the Web, you use the Oracle HTTP Server component of Oracle9*i* Application Server (Oracle9*i*AS). Specifically, you use the mod_plsql module of the Oracle9*i* HTTP Server component. The software you need is as follows:

- Oracle9*i* database, installed and configured

- Oracle9*i*AS, installed and configured

You can download both from the Oracle Web site (`http://www.oracle.com`) or the Oracle Technology Network Web site (`http://technet.oracle.com`).

I begin this chapter with an explanation of how to use HTML in PL/SQL.

Using HTML in PL/SQL

This section details the method of using HTML in PL/SQL for running PL/SQL on the Web. You use HTML in PL/SQL by means of a set of packages in the PL/SQL Web toolkit. Of the packages in the PL/SQL Web toolkit, you'll primarily use the HTP package. The HTP package consists of a set of procedures and functions to embed HTML inside PL/SQL code.

Consider a simple HTML script that displays two rows of data in tabular form. Here's the code:

```
<HTML>
<HEAD>
<TITLE>Organization Records</TITLE>
</HEAD>
<BODY>
<H1>Organization Records</H1>
<TABLE BORDER="1 ">
<TR><TH>Hierarchy</TH><TH>Org Long Name</TH></TR>
<TR>
<TD>Director</TD>
<TD>Office of Director Tech ABC Inc.</TD>
</TR>
<TR>
<TD>Director</TD>
<TD>Office of Dir. SSL</TD>
</TR>
</TABLE>
</BODY>
</HTML>
```

The output of this code when invoked from a browser is shown in Figure 14-1.

Figure 14-1. Organization records output

More specifically, the procedures HTP.PRINT or HTP.P in the HTP package enable you to embed HTML in PL/SQL. HTP.P is a short form of HTP.PRINT. The calls to any of these procedures invoke the mod_plsql module of the Oracle9*i* HTTP Server.

Here are the steps involved:

1. Create a Database Access Descriptor (DAD). You specify the DAD as a string name and associate it with a database schema. The function of the DAD is to convert the URL specified in the Web browser to a call to a stored procedure in the specified database schema.

2. Create a stored procedure in the specified schema by calling the HTP.P procedure multiple times. In fact, wrap each line in HTML script with a call to the HTP.P procedure by prefixing `htp.p('` and suffixing `');` to each line. The HTP.P procedure redirects output back to the Web browser.

3. Invoke the stored procedure as a URL from the Web browser using the DAD.

The following sections describe these steps in more detail.

Creating a Database Access Descriptor

A *Database Access Descriptor,* or DAD for short, is a name that maps a Web address (otherwise known as a URL) specified in a Web browser to a call to a stored procedure. The schema where this stored procedure is created is specified during the DAD's creation. Here are the steps involved:

1. Access the Oracle HTTP Server's main page, which is shown in Figure 14-2. You do this by specifying the UTL `http://hostname/`, where hostname is the name of the host machine on which the Oracle HTTP Server is installed. The hostname is generally suffixed with a colon (:) followed by port number; the port number for the Oracle HTTP Server is 80.

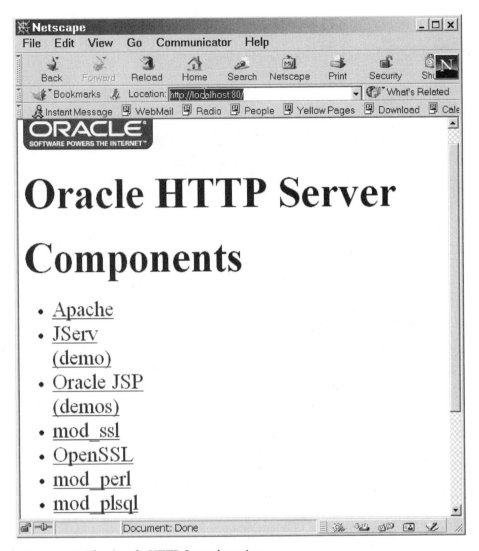

Figure 14-2. The Oracle HTTP Server's main page

2. Select the mod_plsql option by clicking the mod_plsql link. This takes you to the Gateway Configuration Menu page shown in Figure 14-3.

Chapter 14

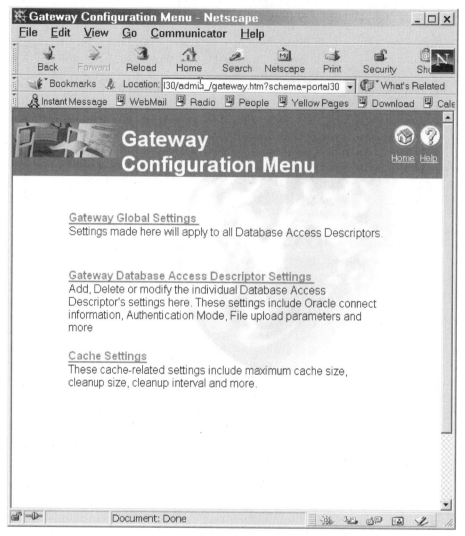

Figure 14-3. The Gateway Configuration Menu page

3. Click the Gateway Database Access Descriptor Settings link. This takes
    you to the Administer DAD Entries page shown in Figure 14-4.

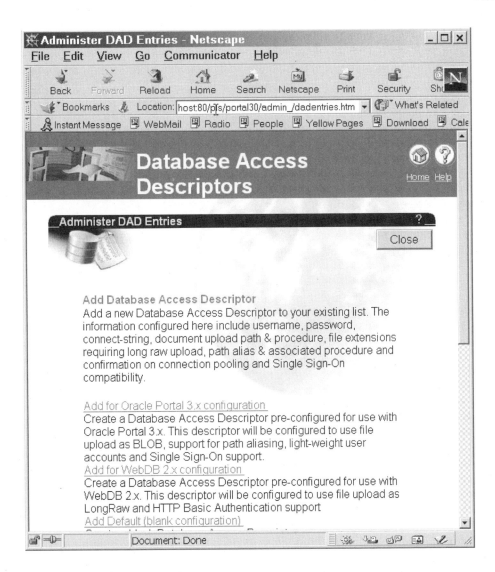

Figure 14-4. The Administer DAD Entries page

4. Click the Add Default (blank configuration) link. This takes you to the
   Database Access Descriptor page shown in Figure 14-5. Enter the name
   of the DAD to be created. I chose to enter the name **webdad**.

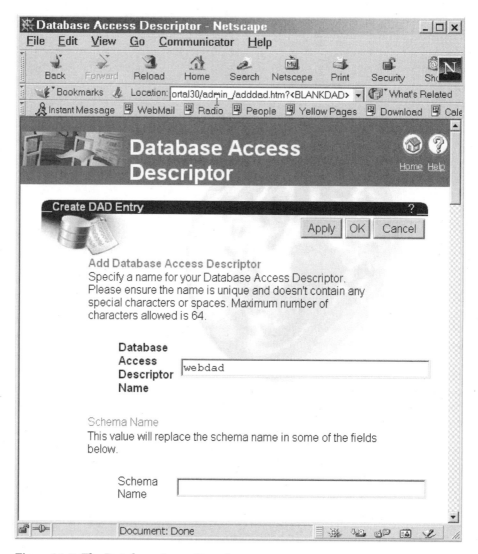

Figure 14-5. The Database Access Descriptor page

5. Scroll down the Database Access Descriptor page to the Database
   Connectivity Information section (see Figure 14-6). Enter the username,
   password, and connect string of the database schema to be associated
   with this DAD.

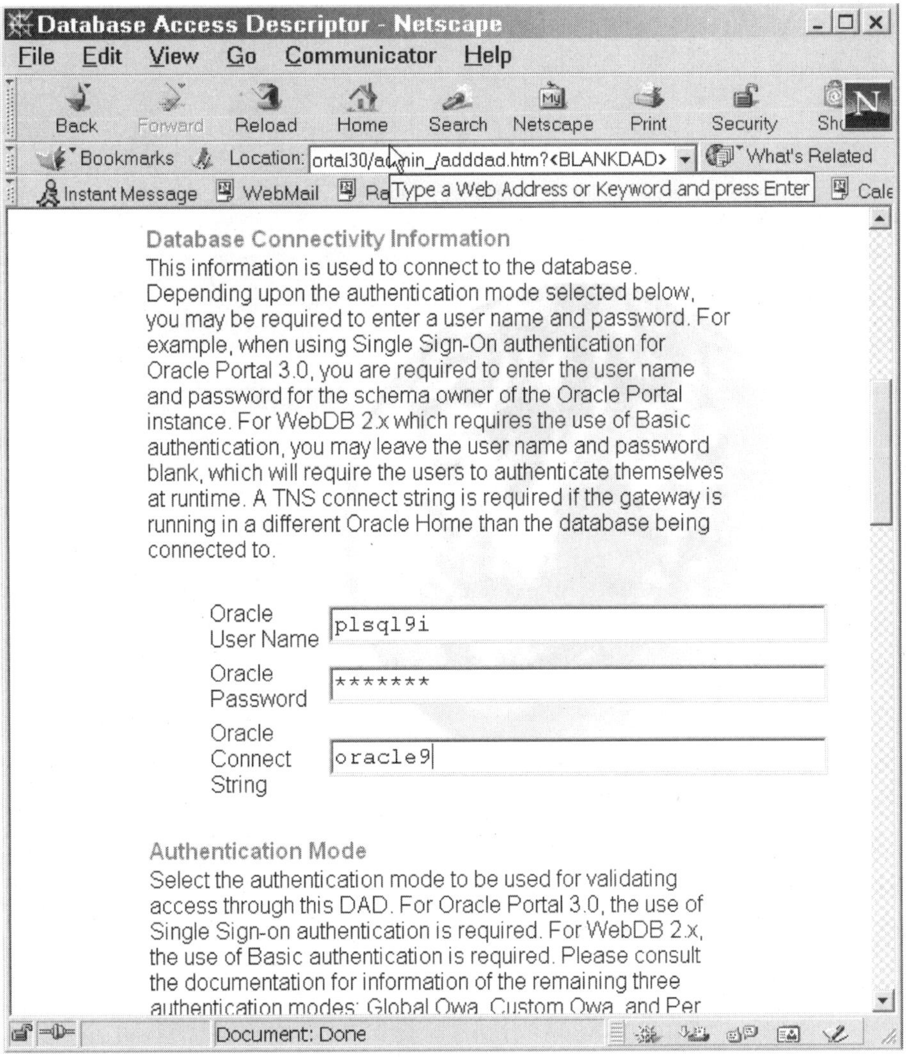

Figure 14-6. The Database Connectivity Information section of the Database Access Descriptor page

6. Click OK at the top of this page. You are notified that the DAD was successfully created with the message shown in Figure 14-7.

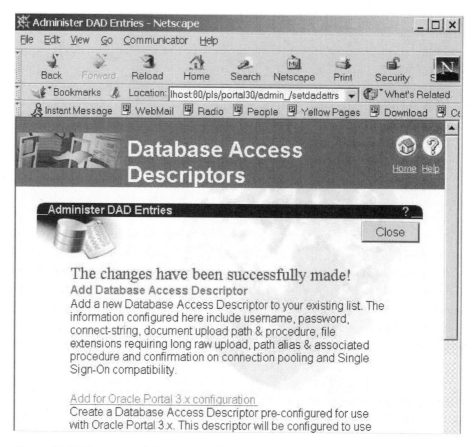

Figure 14-7. The successful creation of a DAD

7. Close the browser.

Creating the Stored Procedure

Now that you've created the DAD, you'll need to create the stored procedure to embed HTML in PL/SQL. You do this by creating a stored procedure with calls to the HTP.P procedure for each line of HTML. Here's the code for the test.html script written earlier:

```
CREATE OR REPLACE PROCEDURE p_test
IS
BEGIN
    htp.p('<HTML>');
    htp.p('<HEAD>');
    htp.p('<TITLE>Organization Records</TITLE>');
    htp.p('</HEAD>');
    htp.p('<BODY>');
    htp.p('<H1>Organization Records</H1>');
    htp.p('<TABLE BORDER="1 ">');
    htp.p('<TR><TH>Hierarchy</TH><TH>Org Long Name</TH></TR>');
    htp.p('<TR>');
    htp.p('<TD>Director</TD>');
    htp.p('<TD>Office of Director Tech ABC Inc.</TD>');
    htp.p('</TR>');
    htp.p('<TR>');
    htp.p('<TD>Director</TD>');
    htp.p('<TD>Office of Dir. SSL</TD>');
    htp.p('</TR>');
    htp.p('</TABLE>');
    htp.p('</BODY>');
    htp.p('</HTML>');
end;
/
```

Invoking the Stored Procedure As a URL

Now that you've put the procedure to embed HTML in PL/SQL in place, you have to invoke it as a URL from the browser. This URL takes the following syntax:

```
http://hostname/mod_plsql_directory/dad_name/proc_name
```

where hostname is the name of the host machine on which the Oracle HTTP Server is installed. The hostname is usually suffixed with a colon (:) followed by a port number; the port number for the Oracle HTTP Server is 80. mod_plsql_directory is the directory alias of the mod_plsql module of the HTTP Server (usually, this is pls), dad_name is the name of the DAD created in step 1 of the "Using HTML in PL/SQL" section, and proc_name is the name of the PL/SQL procedure created in step 2 of the "Using HTML in PL/SQL" section.

With all this in place, you can invoke the p_test procedure as follows:

```
http://localhost:80/pls/webdad/p_test
```

The output of this Web address is shown in Figure 14-8.

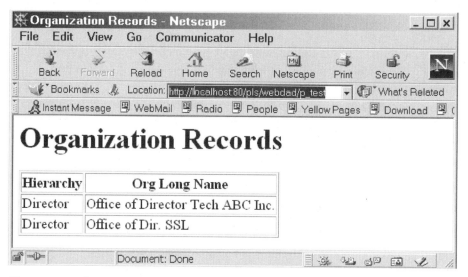

Figure 14-8. The output of calling p_test from a Web browser

The p_test procedure illustrates a way of embedding HTML in PL/SQL. A more constructive method of doing this is to use PL/SQL statements in conjunction with HTP.P calls containing embedded HTML. Here's an example procedure that illustrates this method:

```
CREATE OR REPLACE PROCEDURE p_displayOrgs
IS
BEGIN
    htp.p('<HTML>');
    htp.p('<HEAD>');
    htp.p('<TITLE>Organization Records</TITLE>');
    htp.p('</HEAD>');
    htp.p('<BODY>');
    htp.p('<H1>Organization Records</H1>');
    htp.p('<TABLE BORDER="1 ">');
    htp.p('<TR><TH>Hierarchy</TH><TH>Org Long Name</TH></TR>');
    for idx in (select h.hrc_descr, o.org_long_name
```

```
                    from    org_tab o, hrc_tab h
                    where o.hrc_code = h.hrc_code
                    order by h.hrc_code ) loop
        htp.p('<TR>');
        htp.p('<TD>'||idx.hrc_descr||'</TD>');
        htp.p('<TD>'||idx.org_long_name||'</TD>');
        htp.p('</TR>');
    end loop;
    htp.p('</TABLE>');
    htp.p('</BODY>');
    htp.p('</HTML>');
end;
/
```

Once you've created this procedure, you can call it from a browser using the following URL:

```
http://localhost:80/pls/webdad/p_displayOrgs
```

The output of this procedure is shown in Figure 14-9.

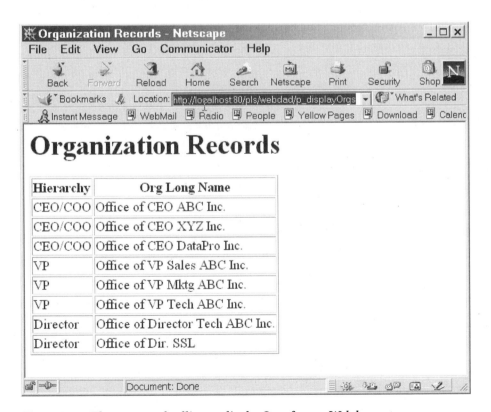

Figure 14-9. The output of calling p_displayOrgs from a Web browser

Passing Parameters When Using HTML in PL/SQL

Passing parameters to a procedure results in more generic code with the capability to retrieve information based on user-input criteria. You can pass parameters from HTML to PL/SQL in two ways:

- Specifying the parameter value in the URL

- Using an HTML form to accept user input

I discuss these two methods in the sections that follow.

Specifying the Parameter Value in the URL

In this case, you define the parameter as an input parameter to the corresponding PL/SQL procedure. When the procedure is invoked from a browser, the (name, value) pair for the parameter is used as follows:

```
name=value
```

You specify the parameters by adding them as a suffix to the procedure name with multiple parameters being separated by an ampersand (&).

TIP   *There is no need to read the parameter when you use PL/SQL. This is done automatically when the parameter is defined as an input parameter to the corresponding procedure.*

As an example, consider the p_displayOrgs procedure defined earlier. This procedure outputs data for all organizations of all hierarchies. You can modify this procedure to accept hrc_code as an input parameter. Here's the code for this:

```
CREATE OR REPLACE PROCEDURE p_displayOrgs_with_param(ip_hrc_code NUMBER)
IS
BEGIN
    htp.p('<HTML>');
    htp.p('<HEAD>');
    htp.p('<TITLE>Organization Records</TITLE>');
    htp.p('</HEAD>');
    htp.p('<BODY>');
    htp.p('<H1>Organization Records</H1>');
    htp.p('<TABLE BORDER="1 ">');
    htp.p('<TR><TH>Hierarchy</TH><TH>Org Long Name</TH></TR>');
    for idx in (select h.hrc_descr, o.org_long_name
                    from   org_tab o, hrc_tab h
                    where o.hrc_code = h.hrc_code
                        and h.hrc_code = ip_hrc_code
                    order by h.hrc_code ) loop
        htp.p('<TR>');
        htp.p('<TD>'||idx.hrc_descr||'</TD>');
        htp.p('<TD>'||idx.org_long_name||'</TD>');
        htp.p('</TR>');
    end loop;
    htp.p('</TABLE>');
    htp.p('</BODY>');
    htp.p('</HTML>');
end;
/
```

You call this procedure as follows:

```
http://localhost:80/pls/webdad/p_displayOrgs_with_param?ip_hrc_code=1
```

The output of this URL is shown in Figure 14-10.

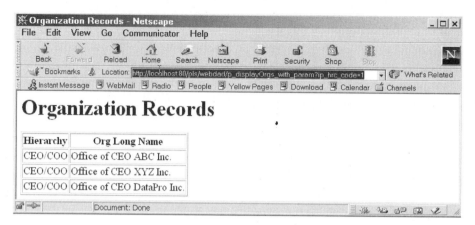

Figure 14-10. The output of calling p_displayOrgs_with_param from a Web browser

The following points are worth noting:

- A question mark (?) is used immediately after the procedure name.

- The parameter is specified by using the actual name of the parameter as defined in the procedure.

- Multiple parameters are separated by an ampersand (&).

Using an HTML Form to Accept User Input

In this case, you construct an HTML form with input text fields and a Run button. The values entered in the text fields are passed to the PL/SQL procedure that is invoked when the Run button is clicked. Here's what the HTML for this looks like:

```
<HTML>
<HEAD>
<TITLE>Organization Records</TITLE>
</HEAD>
<BODY>
<H1>Organization Records</H1>
<P>Enter Hrc Code and Press the <b> Run </b> button. </P>
<FORM method="post" action="p_displayOrgs_with_param">
    <P>Hrc Code
                <INPUT type="text" name="ip_hrc_code" maxlength="4" size="4">
    </P>
    <P>
                <INPUT type="submit" value="Run">
    </P>
</FORM>
</BODY>
</HTML>
```

The next step is to convert this HTML into a PL/SQL procedure to be invoked from a URL. Here's the code:

```
CREATE OR REPLACE PROCEDURE p_displayOrgs_with_param_form
IS
BEGIN
    htp.p('<HTML>');
    htp.p('<HEAD>');
    htp.p('<TITLE>Organization Records</TITLE>');
    htp.p('</HEAD>');
    htp.p('<BODY>');
    htp.p('<H1>Organization Records</H1>');
    htp.p('<P>Enter Hrc Code and Press the <b> Run </b> button. </P>');
    htp.p('<FORM method="get" action="p_displayOrgs_with_param">');
    htp.p('<P>Hrc Code
                <INPUT type="text" name="ip_hrc_code" maxlength="4" size="4">
    </P>');
    htp.p('<P>
                <INPUT type="submit" value="Run">
    </P>');
    htp.p('</FORM>');
    htp.p('</BODY>');
    htp.p('</HTML>');
end;
/
```

Once you've put the procedure in place, you can invoke it by means of URL. Here's the URL:

```
http://localhost:80/pls/webdad/p_displayOrgs_with_param_form
```

The output of this procedure is shown in Figure 14-11.

 NOTE *You can perform the validation for the input form data on the browser side before it gets to the server. This way, only valid data can be passed on to the server.*

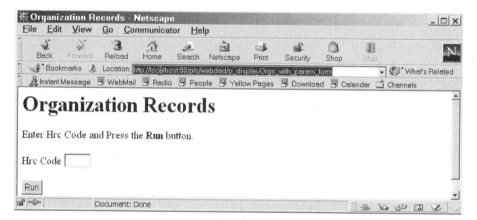

Figure 14-11. The output of calling p_displayOrgs_with_param_form from a Web browser

Entering **1** in the Hrc Code box and clicking the Run button displays the same output as in Figure 14-10. Entering **2** in the Hrc Code box and clicking the Run button displays a different output, as shown in Figure 14-12.

Note that clicking Run generates the URL

```
http://localhost:80/pls/webdad/p_displayOrgs_with_param?ip_hrc_code=1
```

automatically. This means the value entered in the Hrc Code box is passed to the p_displayOrgs_with_param procedure when the Run button is clicked. This procedure in turn is executed with the appropriate parameter to display the output records.

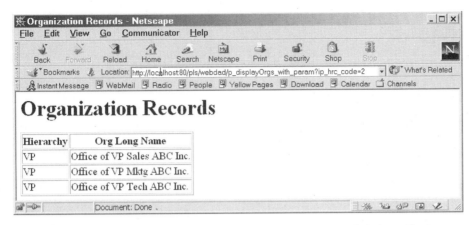

Figure 14-12. The output of entering 2 in the Hrc Code box and clicking the Run button in a Web browser

PL/SQL in HTML: PL/SQL Server Pages

Using PL/SQL in HTML is a second way of Web enabling PL/SQL applications. You do this by embedding PL/SQL within HTML using special PL/SQL tags. This kind of Web page is called a *PL/SQL Server Page* (PSP). PL/SQL is placed within special script tags known as *PSP tags*. These PSP tags are similar to scriptlets in a Java Server Page (JSP), with the only difference being that they're written in PL/SQL. You can write a PSP in HTML or XML.

The primary advantage of a PSP is that it enables inclusion of dynamic content within static HTML. The dynamic content is nothing but PL/SQL logic that's executed on the server side (i.e., on the database server) when the PSP page is submitted by a Web browser. This minimizes network round-trips, thus increasing efficiency.

To run a PSP, you need an Oracle database server in conjunction with a PL/SQL Web gateway. Oracle 8.1.6 and higher support PSPs. Also, for the PL/SQL Web gateway, you can use Oracle9*i*AS (i.e., Oracle HTTP Server) with the mod_plsql module.

PSP Basics

A PSP is a file stored with the .psp extension that contains a combination of HTML and PL/SQL. It has various elements that are defined by means of PSP tags. This section highlights the various syntax elements that make up a PSP page. More specifically, it describes PSP directives, declarations, scriptlets, and comments. The syntax elements are specified by means of special characters called *tags*.

Directives

You specify directives using the <%@ . . . %> tag. Here's the syntax:

```
<%@ directive attribute="value" %>
```

where attribute is case sensitive and refers to one of the following:

- *page:* This directive signifies any page-dependent attributes such as the scripting language, Multipurpose Internet Mail Extensions (MIME) content type, character set, and so forth. Here are examples:

```
<%@ page language="PL/SQL" %>
<%@ page contentType="text/html" %>
```

- *plsql:* This directive refers to a PL/SQL-specific directive such as specifying a procedure name or a parameter. Here's an example:

```
<%@ plsql procedure="p_displayOrgs_psp" %>
<%@ plsql parameter="ip_hrc_code" type="number" default="null" %>
```

  The type is optional and must be a PL/SQL data type when specified. If the type isn't specified, the default is VARCHAR2.

- *include:* This directive is used to specify a file that contains HTML or PL/SQL scriptlets to be included in the PSP when it's translated. Here's an example:

```
<%@ include file="test1.html" %>
```

  This specifies that the PSP should include the contents of the file test1.html at the time of translation.

Declarations

You specify declarations using the <%! . . . %> tags. Here's an example:

```
<%! v_code NUMBER;
    v_descr VARCHAR2(20);
%>
```

The DECLARE keyword isn't necessary.

Expressions

You specify expressions using the <%= . . . %> tag. Here's an example:

```
<P> The error is <%= SQLERRM %>.</P>
```

In this case, expression can refer to any PL/SQL expression such as a NUMBER, DATE, or VARCHAR2 variable; a function; or an arithmetic expression.

Scriptlets

Scriptlets are any executable PL/SQL statements that you specify using the <% . . . %> tag. You can specify here any number of PL/SQL statements; DECLARE . . . BEGIN . . . END; PL/SQL blocks; and control, loop, or other PL/SQL executable statements. Here's an example:

```
<% IF (ip_hrc_code = 1) THEN %>
```

Comments

You specify comments using the <%-- . . . --%> tag. Here's an example:

```
<%-- This is a test PSP --%>
```

However, you specify comments within PL/SQL scriptlets using standard PL/SQL comment syntax.

PSP Architecture

A PSP should first be loaded into the database. It is then translated into a procedure within the associated schema and executed on the server side when requested by means of a URL in a Web browser.

No database connection need be made. The connection is implicitly established when the DAD is specified in the URL.

When the PSP is loaded into the database, the HTML part is translated into calls to the HTP.P procedure and the PL/SQL scriptlets and tags are left unchanged.

Developing a PL/SQL Server Page

A typical PSP development process consists of the following steps:

1. Write the PSP by using PSP tags and placing PL/SQL scriptlets within HTML.

2. Load the PSP into the database.

3. Invoke the PSP from a Web browser by means of a URL.

A discussion of each of these steps follows.

Writing PSP

In this section, I rewrite as a PSP the p_displayOrgs procedure created earlier. To do so, I use the various PSP tags. Here's the code:

```
<%@ page language="PL/SQL"%>
<%@ plsql procedure="p_displayOrgs_psp"%>
<HTML>
<HEAD>
<TITLE>Organization Records</TITLE>
</HEAD>
<BODY>
<H1>Organization Records</H1>
<TABLE BORDER="1 ">
<TR><TH>Hierarchy</TH><TH>Org Long Name</TH></TR>
<%
 for idx in (select h.hrc_descr, o.org_long_name
             from   org_tab o, hrc_tab h
```

```
             where o.hrc_code = h.hrc_code
             order by h.hrc_code ) loop
%>
<TR>
<TD> <%= idx.hrc_descr %> </TD>
<TD> <%= idx.org_long_name %> </TD>
</TR>
<%  end loop; %>
</TABLE>
</BODY>
</HTML>
```

This is saved in an OS file named displayOrgs.psp.

Loading the PSP into the Database

Once a PSP is written and saved in .psp file, the next step is to load the PSP into
the database. You do this using the loadpsp utility. This utility performs two functions. First, it reads the PSP file and generates a PL/SQL procedure in the schema
into which the PSP is loaded. The name of the procedure generated is specified
by the

```
<%@ plsql procedure="p_displayOrgs_psp"%>
```

tag in the PSP file. The PSP is loaded into the database as a stored procedure.
    Second, the loadpsp utility converts all HTML in the PSP file to calls to the
HTP.P procedure, leaving all PL/SQL scriptlet code as is.
    Here's the syntax of using loadpsp:

```
loadpsp -user username/password@connect_string -replace errorfile psp_file
```

In this command,

- user specifies a database schema into which the PSP is loaded. It should be
  specified as username/password@connect_string. This is the schema
  where the corresponding converted procedure is created, and it's the same
  schema as the one associated with the DAD that was created earlier.

- replace specifies that the converted procedure should be replaced with a new one if it already exists. If this option isn't specified and the procedure already exists, loadpsp exits with an error.

- errorfile specifies a error file name corresponding to a

```
<%@ page errorPage="errorfile.psp" %>
```

directive specified in the PSP file. This is optional. errorfile should appear before the list of actual .psp files.

- psp_file is the file name of the PSP being loaded into the database. You can load multiple files by specifying them one after another and separating them with spaces.

You can load displayOrgs.psp into the database using the following command:

```
loadpsp -user plsql9i/plsql9i@oracle9 -replace displayOrgs.psp
```

The output of this command is shown in Figure 14-13.

Figure 14-13. Output of loadpsp Invoking the PSP from a Web browser

Invoking the PSP from a Web browser

Once you've loaded the PSP, you can call it from a Web browser by means of a URL. The URL contains the procedure name the PSP is translated into. Here's the URL for calling the displayOrgs.psp PSP via the procedure p_displayOrgs_psp: .

```
http://localhost:80/pls/webdad/p_displayOrgs_psp
```

The output of this URL is shown in Figure 14-14.

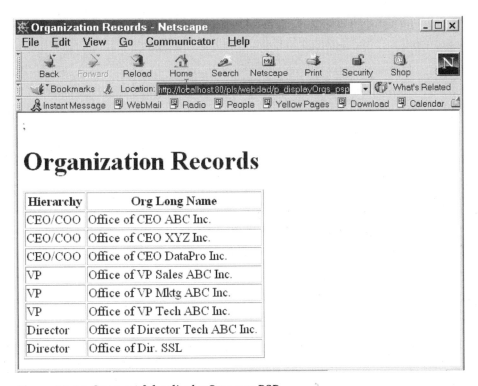

Figure 14-14. Output of the displayOrgs.psp PSP

Building an Application for the Web Using PL/SQL

Building a PL/SQL application for the Web involves writing a PSP that contains
the HTML part for the page display and interaction with the user for input, as
well as coding the background business logic in PL/SQL. In this section,
I describe a Web-based application that depicts an organization system in which
the user interacts with the Web page to add, modify, and delete organizations.
I break this application into two parts: user interface and business logic.

The User Interface

The user interface consists of three input text fields and three buttons. When the
user enters values for these input fields and clicks on one of the buttons, behind
the scenes the PSP performs the DML operations of INSERT, UPDATE, and
DELETE by calling appropriate PL/SQL procedures. These procedures contain
the business logic for the DML operations and are coded as part of a PL/SQL
package.

Here's the PSP code for the user interface:

```
<%@ page language="PL/SQL"%>
<%@ plsql procedure="p_webapporg_psp"%>
<HTML>
<HEAD>
<TITLE> Organization Web Page </TITLE>
</HEAD>
<BODY>
<H1>Add, Modify or Delete Organizations</H1>
<P> Enter Hrc Code, Org Id, Short Name, Long Name and click on
        <b> ADD, MODIFY </b> or <b>DELETE</b> buttons</P>
<form method=post action="WebAppOrg.run">
<BR> <BR>
<B> Hrc Code: </B>   <input name="ip_hrc_code" value=""> <BR>
<B> Org Id: </B>   <input name="ip_org_id" value=""> <BR>
<B> Short Name: </B>   <input name="ip_org_short_name" value=""> <BR>
<B> Long Name: </B>   <input name="ip_org_long_name" value=""> <BR>
<BR><BR>
<input type="submit" name="ip_op" value="Add">
<input type="submit" name="ip_op" value="Delete">
<input type="submit" name="ip_op" value="Modify">
</FORM>
</BODY>
</HTML>
```

This is saved in the OS file WebAppOrg.psp.

Now that the PSP is in place, it has to be loaded into the database. Here's the command to do so:

```
loadpsp -user plsql9i/plsql9i@oracle9 -replace WebAppOrg.psp
```

The procedure p_webapporg_psp gets created in the specified schema.

Business Logic

The business logic for the Organization Web application consists of a package named WebAppOrg with four procedures:

- *insertOrg:* To insert a new organization.

- *updateOrg:* To modify an existing organization.

- *deleteOrg:* To delete an existing organization.

- *run:* To call one of these three procedures depending on DML operation (i.e., Add, Modify, or Delete). It first checks for the correct input. If the input is incorrect, an error message is displayed.

Here's the code for the package specification:

```
CREATE OR REPLACE PACKAGE WebAppOrg
IS
    PROCEDURE insertOrg (ip_hrc_code NUMBER,
                         ip_org_id NUMBER,
                         ip_org_short_name VARCHAR2,
                         ip_org_long_name VARCHAR2);
    PROCEDURE updateOrg(ip_org_id NUMBER,
                        ip_org_short_name VARCHAR2,
                        ip_org_long_name VARCHAR2);
    PROCEDURE deleteOrg(ip_org_id NUMBER);
    PROCEDURE run (ip_op VARCHAR2,
                   ip_hrc_code NUMBER,
                   ip_org_id NUMBER,
                   ip_org_short_name VARCHAR2,
                   ip_org_long_name VARCHAR2);
END WebAppOrg;
/
```

Here's the code for the package body:

```
CREATE OR REPLACE PACKAGE BODY WebAppOrg
IS
-- Procedure to delete records from the org_site_tab table
-- before deleting from org_table. This procedure is called
-- from the deleteOrg procedure
PROCEDURE deleteOrgSites(ip_org_id NUMBER,
                         op_retcd OUT NUMBER,
                         op_err_msg OUT VARCHAR2)
   IS
   BEGIN
       DELETE org_site_tab WHERE org_id = ip_org_id;
       op_retcd := 0;
   EXCEPTION WHEN OTHERS THEN
           op_retcd := SQLCODE;
           op_err_msg := SQLERRM;
   END deleteOrgSites;
-- Procedure to insert a new record  in the org_tab table
```

```
      PROCEDURE insertOrg (ip_hrc_code NUMBER,
                           ip_org_id NUMBER,
                           ip_org_short_name VARCHAR2,
                           ip_org_long_name VARCHAR2)
   IS
   BEGIN
        INSERT INTO org_tab VALUES
        (ip_hrc_code, ip_org_id, ip_org_short_name, ip_org_long_name);
        htp.p('Organization with Id '||TO_CHAR(ip_org_id)||
                ' successfully inserted.');
   EXCEPTION WHEN DUP_VAL_ON_INDEX THEN
        htp.p('Organization with Id '||TO_CHAR(ip_org_id)||' already exists.');
        WHEN OTHERS THEN
           htp.p(SQLERRM);
   END insertOrg;
-- Procedure to modify the long and short names for a
-- given org_id in the org_tab table
   PROCEDURE updateOrg(ip_org_id NUMBER,
                       ip_org_short_name VARCHAR2,
                       ip_org_long_name VARCHAR2)
   IS
   BEGIN
        UPDATE org_tab
        SET org_short_name = ip_org_short_name,
               org_long_name = ip_org_long_name
        WHERE org_id = ip_org_id;
        IF (SQL%NOTFOUND) THEN
           htp.p('Organization with Id '||TO_CHAR(ip_org_id)||
                                  ' does not exist.');
           RETURN;
        END IF;
        htp.p('Organization with Id '||TO_CHAR(ip_org_id)||
                ' successfully modified.');
   EXCEPTION WHEN OTHERS THEN
        htp.p(SQLERRM);
   END updateOrg;
-- Procedure to delete a record from the org_tab table
   PROCEDURE deleteOrg(ip_org_id NUMBER)
   IS
     op_retcd NUMBER;
     op_err_msg VARCHAR2(1000);
   BEGIN
        deleteOrgSites(ip_org_id, op_retcd, op_err_msg);
```

```
        IF (op_retcd <> 0) then
            htp.p('Delete of Org Sites failed with error '||op_err_msg);
            RETURN;
        END IF;
         DELETE org_tab WHERE org_id = ip_org_id;
        IF (SQL%NOTFOUND) THEN
            htp.p('Organization with Id '||TO_CHAR(ip_org_id)||
                                      ' does not exist.');

            RETURN;
        END IF;
        htp.p('Organization with Id '||TO_CHAR(ip_org_id)||' successfully deleted.');
      EXCEPTION WHEN OTHERS THEN
            htp.p(SQLERRM);
END deleteOrg;
PROCEDURE run (ip_op VARCHAR2,
                  ip_hrc_code NUMBER,
                  ip_org_id NUMBER,
                  ip_org_short_name VARCHAR2,
                  ip_org_long_name VARCHAR2)
IS
BEGIN
  IF (ip_op = 'Add') THEN
     IF ((ip_hrc_code IS NULL) or (ip_org_id IS NULL) or
          (ip_org_short_name IS NULL) or (ip_org_long_name IS NULL)) THEN
          htp.p('All input fields must be entered for the Add operation.');
          RETURN;
     END IF;
     insertOrg (ip_hrc_code,
                 ip_org_id,
                 ip_org_short_name,
                 ip_org_long_name);
  ELSIF (ip_op = 'Modify') THEN
      IF ((ip_hrc_code IS NULL) or (ip_org_id IS NULL) or
          (ip_org_short_name IS NULL) or (ip_org_long_name IS NULL)) THEN
          htp.p('All input fields must be entered for the Modify operation.');
          RETURN;
      END IF;
          updateOrg(ip_org_id,
                     ip_org_short_name,
                     ip_org_long_name);
  ELSIF (ip_op = 'Delete') THEN
     IF (ip_org_id IS NULL) THEN
          htp.p('Org Id must be entered for the Delete operation.');
```

```
            RETURN;
        END IF;
        deleteOrg(ip_org_id);
     END IF;
  END run;
END WebAppOrg;
/
```

Invoking the Organization Web Application

Now that the user interface and the business logic are in place, you can invoke the WebAppOrg.psp PSP by means of a URL via the p_webapporg_psp procedure. Here's the syntax for this:

```
http://localhost:80/pls/webdad/p_webapporg_psp
```

The output of this URL is shown in Figure 14-15.

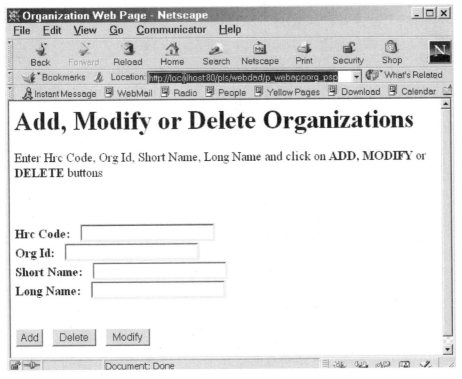

Figure 14-15. The output of calling p_webapporg_psp from a Web browser

Now let's test the Add, Modify, and Delete operations one after the other. The Add operation is illustrated in Figure 14-16.

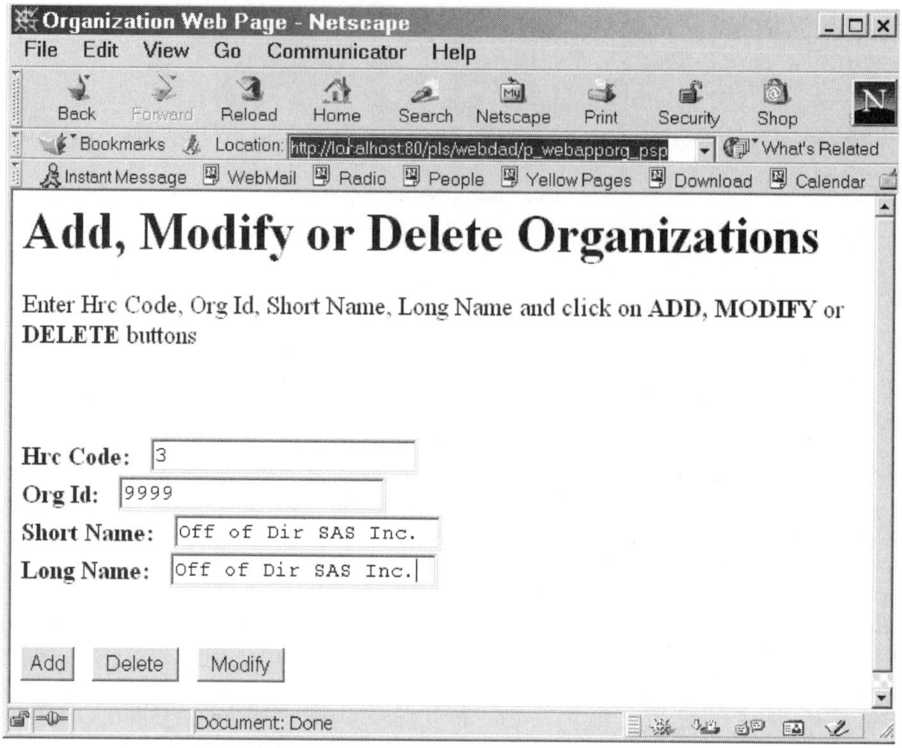

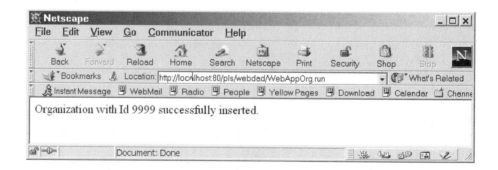

Figure 14-16. The Add operation

The output of the Add operation is shown in Figure 14-17.

Figure 14-17. The output of the Add operation

The PL/SQL packaged procedure WebAppOrg.run returned the given message by executing the WebAppOrg.insertOrg procedure behind the scenes. You can verify the output in the database as follows:

```
SQL> select * from org_tab where org_id = 9999;
```

Here's the output:

```
  HRC_CODE     ORG_ID ORG_SHORT_NAME
-------------- --------- -------------------
ORG_LONG_NAME
--------------------------------------------------
        3       9999 Off of Dir SAS Inc.
Off of Dir SAS Inc.
```

If the user doesn't enter all the input fields, an error message is thrown, as shown in Figure 14-18.

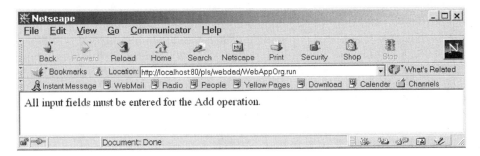

Figure 14-18. Error message for the Add operation

Figure 14-19 shows the Modify operation.

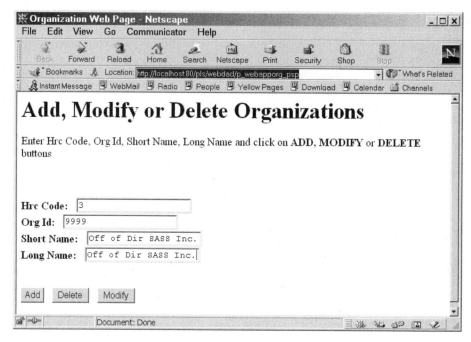

Figure 14-19. The Modify operation

You can verify the output in the database as follows:

```
SQL> select * from org_tab where org_id = 9999;
```

Here's the output:

```
   HRC_CODE     ORG_ID ORG_SHORT_NAME
-------------- --------- -------------------
ORG_LONG_NAME
--------------------------------------------------
        3      9999 Off of Dir SASS Inc.
Off of Dir SASS Inc.
```

Finally, you can verify the Delete operation as follows:

```
SQL> select * from org_tab where org_id = 9999;
```

Here's the output:

```
no rows selected
```

Unhandled exceptions result in the error "HTP-404 Not Found," as shown in Figure 14-20.

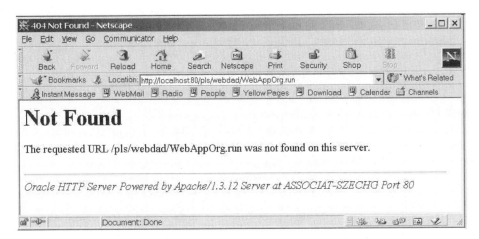

Figure 14-20. The error shown in the case of an unhandled exception

 TIP *COMMIT is implicit by PL/SQL gateway. There's no need to COMMIT in a PL/SQL procedure, but you can specify it.*

Sending E-mail Using PL/SQL

You can use PL/SQL to access resources outside of the database. In Chapter 13 you used Java stored procedures to access file system resources outside of the database. In this section I demonstrate how to access an e-mail server and send e-mail from PL/SQL. Oracle9*i* allows you to send e-mail from within the database using the Simple Mail Transfer Protocol (SMTP). SMTP is an Internet protocol for sending e-mail across mail servers over the Internet. There are a few parameters necessary for sending e-mail:

- Address of the mail server

- E-mail address of the sender

- E-mail address of the recipient

- Subject of the message being sent

- Actual body of the message

- Any attachments being included with the message

Oracle9*i* PL/SQL provides a built-in package called UTL_SMTP that provides an API to send e-mail from within the database. Functions and procedures of this package are called from a PL/SQL procedure executed within the database to send e-mail. Here are the steps involved in using UTL_SMTP to send e-mail:

1. Identify the mail host address, from e-mail address, and to e-mail address. Store these in PL/SQL variables.

2. Store the message subject and message body in VARCHAR2 variables.

3. Declare a connection object of type UTL_SMTP.Connection.

4. Open a connection with the mail server by using the UTL_SMTP.OPEN_CONNECTION function. This returns a Connection object.

5. Identify the domain for the mail host using the standard the SMTP protocol. You do this by calling the UTL_SMTP.HELO procedure, passing the connection and mail host address as input parameters to it.

6. Notify the mail server of the from e-mail address. You do this by calling the UTL_SMTP.MAIL procedure, passing the connection and from e-mail address as input parameters to it.

7. Notify the mail server of the to e-mail address. You do this by calling the UTL_SMTP.RCPT procedure, passing the connection and to e-mail address as input parameters to it.

8. Notify the mail server that what follows will be the subject and body of the e-mail message. You do this by calling the UTL_SMTP.OPEN_DATA procedure, passing the connection as an input parameter to it.

9. Send the e-mail subject and body of the message on to the mail server. You do this by calling the UTL_SMTP.WRITE_DATA procedure, passing the connection and the message text as input parameters to it. You can make multiple calls to this procedure to specify large messages.

10. Notify the mail server that the sending of the message is completed. You do this by calling the UTL_SMTP.CLOSE_DATA procedure, passing the connection as an input parameter to it.

11. Close the mail server connection. You do this by calling the UTL_SMTP.QUIT procedure, passing the connection as an input parameter to it.

I implement a procedure called p_send_email to illustrate these steps. Here's the code for this procedure:

```
CREATE OR REPLACE PROCEDURE p_send_email
                    (p_mailhost VARCHAR2,
                     p_from_address VARCHAR2,
                     p_to_address VARCHAR2,
                     p_message_text VARCHAR2,
                     p_retcd OUT NUMBER,
                     p_err_msg OUT VARCHAR2)
  IS
     mail_conn   utl_smtp.connection;
  BEGIN
     mail_conn := utl_smtp.open_connection(p_mailhost, 25);
     utl_smtp.helo(mail_conn, p_mailhost);
     utl_smtp.mail(mail_conn, p_from_address);
     utl_smtp.rcpt(mail_conn, p_to_address);
     utl_smtp.open_data(mail_conn);
     utl_smtp.write_data(mail_conn, p_message_text);
     utl_smtp.close_data(mail_conn);
     utl_smtp.quit(mail_conn);
       p_retcd := 0;
     EXCEPTION
         WHEN OTHERS THEN
             p_retcd   := SQLCODE;
             p_err_msg := SQLERRM;
  END;
  /
```

Here's the code to execute this procedure:

```
declare
  retcd number;
  err_msg varchar2(1000);
begin
  p_send_email('mail.compunnel.com',
               'blakshman@compunnel.com',
               'blakshman@compunnel.com',
               'From: '||'Bulusu'||CHR(13)||CHR(10)||
               'Subject: '||'Message from Bulusu '||CHR(13)||CHR(10)||
               CHR(13)||CHR(10)||
               'This is a test message.',
               retcd,
               err_msg);
  IF (retcd <> 0) THEN
    dbms_output.put_line('ERR: '||err_msg);
  END IF;
end;
/
```

TIP   *If the message to be sent is available in a single string variable, you can replace calls to UTL_SMTP.OPEN_DATA, UTL_SMTP.WRITE_DATA, and UTL_SMTP.CLOSE_DATA with a single call to UTL_SMTP.DATA that accepts the connection and message as input parameters.*

TIP   *The connection to the SMTP server via the Internet or otherwise should be on for UTL_SMTP to work.*

NOTE *There are other ways of sending e-mail from the database. You can use a Java stored procedure called via a PL/SQL call spec from PL/SQL. The custom Java class can code the e-mail sending routine using the JavaMail API or any other Java e-mailing mechanism that can then be called using a call spec from PL/SQL. Also, you can use C++ or C and code the e-mail sending procedure as a function that can be invoked from PL/SQL as an external procedure. Whatever method you use, the functionality remains the same.*

Summary

In this chapter, I highlighted the methods of running PL/SQL applications on the Web. I discussed how to build a Web application using PL/SQL by means of a case study application. I also outlined the method of sending e-mail from within the database using the PL/SQL API.

The next chapter covers performance considerations in PL/SQL.

Part Five

PL/SQL Performance and Standards

CHAPTER 15

Performance Considerations

PERFORMANCE OF ANY software application is always one of the top considerations in designing and developing the application. The abilities to execute quickly and in an efficient manner are critical factors in determining the suitability of the application in terms of output, throughput, and customer satisfaction. This is even more critical when it comes to database applications. The size of the database and the number of users using the application are primary factors in tuning the application for maximum performance. PL/SQL applications also need to be tailored to perform optimally in terms of throughput and scalability of a large number of users.

This chapter highlights some of the ways to achieve optimal performance when using PL/SQL in an Oracle9*i* database. I've presented a detailed discussion of each of these topics in previous chapters. In this chapter, I'll provide a brief summary of each topic, along with some general PL/SQL tuning tips. In particular, this chapter covers the following:

- Some PL/SQL tuning procedures

- Native compilation of PL/SQL code

- Parameter passing by reference

- Using native dynamic SQL

- Using bulk binds

- Using the RETURNING clause

- Using object types and collections

- Using pipelined table functions

Some PL/SQL Tuning Procedures

The following is a list of some PL/SQL tuning procedures that often speed up execution:

- PL/SQL permits sets of SQL statements to be combined and submitted in one call to the SQL server engine. This reduces network traffic in two-tier or three-tier application structures and thus improves performance.

- Stored procedures, functions, and packages result in better performance with fewer database calls. Since they're stored in compiled form, there's no need to reparse SQL statements within PL/SQL. In addition, packages improve performance by reducing disk I/O. This is because when a packaged subprogram is referenced for the first time, the entire package is loaded into memory, so subsequent calls don't consume disk I/O. Also, packages can be pinned in the shared pool to prevent on-demand paging of the package to and from the shared pool. This is very useful for huge packages.

- SQL and PL/SQL parsers are integrated, which results in the availability of SQL features in PL/SQL in Oracle9*i* and onward.

- Using PL/SQL in place of SQL in certain cases can result in reduced overhead. For example, when a DML statement affects a huge set of rows, it's better to use PL/SQL because you can do incremental COMMITs. This reduces the rollback segment problems.

- Calling PL/SQL functions from SQL statements—keeping in mind the side effects for tasks that can't be achieved by using SQL—can result in in-memory saving and reduced network traffic.

- When coding IF statements, place the condition that's most likely to be TRUE as the very first condition. You should do this because subsequent conditions will not need to be evaluated if the first one evaluates to TRUE.

- Using fewer iterations in a PL/SQL loop will result in better response time.

- Using explicit cursors will eliminate the need to query a second time to check for the TOO_MANY_ROWS exception, as is the case with SELECT . . . INTO statements.

- Specifying the WHEN clause where appropriate will eliminate trigger execution on unnecessary rows.

- Using serially reusable packages can free up the user global area (UGA) by making the runtime state of a package persist only for the duration of the call rather than the entire session.

Native Compilation of PL/SQL Code

As of Oracle9*i*, PL/SQL provides native compilation. By default, PL/SQL uses an interpreter to convert code into p-code that's then invoked at runtime. In native compilation, the PL/SQL code is converted into machine-independent C code that is then translated into machine code using the C compiler. In PL/SQL, this is done by native compilation. This is called *ahead-of-time compilation* because it occurs before execution.

How Native Compilation Works

There's an initialization parameter called PLSQL_COMPILER_FLAGS involved in enabling native compilation. You must change the value of this parameter to NATIVE from the default INTERPRETED. You can do this in three ways:

- In the init.ora file, which affects any stored parameter file settings (spfile settings)

- Using the ALTER SYSTEM command

- Using the ALTER SESSION command

Here's an example of the ALTER SESSION command method:

```
ALTER SESSION SET PLSQL_COMPILER_FLAGS = 'NATIVE';
```

Using this command causes all subsequent recompilations of PL/SQL stored subprograms to be natively compiled. Whether interpreted or natively compiled, this information is recorded within the subprogram metadata in the data dictionary view USER_STORED_SETTINGS. If the subprogram is automatically recompiled as a result of dependency checking, the setting in this view is used. Here's an example to show this:

```
select uo.object_name, uo.object_type, uss.param_value
from user_stored_settings uss, user_objects uo
where uss.object_id = uo.object_id
and uss.param_name = 'plsql_compiler_flags'
and uo.object_type in ('PROCEDURE', 'FUNCTION' );
```

Here's the output of this SELECT statement:

```
SQL> column object_name format a30;
SQL> column object_type format a15;
SQL> column param_value format a30;
SQL> set pages 100
SQL> select uo.object_name, uo.object_type, uss.param_value
  2    from user_stored_settings uss, user_objects uo
  3    where uss.object_id = uo.object_id
  4    and uss.param_name = 'plsql_compiler_flags'
  5    and uo.object_type in ('PROCEDURE', 'FUNCTION' );
OBJECT_NAME                     OBJECT_TYPE     PARAM_VALUE
------------------------------- --------------- --------------------
LIST_DIR                        FUNCTION        INTERPRETED,NON_DEBUG
```

The param_value is INTERPRETED, meaning the procedure or function is stored as p_code. If natively compiled, it will be NATIVE.

Here are the steps involved in native compilation:

1. Translate into C code from PL/SQL code.

2. Write this code to the file system in the form of a shared library.

3. Invoke and run the C compiler.

4. Link the resulting object code into Oracle.

5. Invoke the natively compiled code on execution.

 NOTE   *PL/SQL stored subprograms, such as stand-alone procedures, functions, and packages, can be natively compiled. Anonymous PL/SQL blocks can't use native compilation.*

Translation into C code is done first, followed by compilation using a C compiler. Finally, the resulting code is linked into Oracle processes. Executing the subprogram invokes the natively compiled program. When the particular stored subprogram is invoked, the natively compiled program is mapped to the PGA.

PL/SQL 9*i* allows native compilation of PL/SQL packages, procedures, and functions and subsequent conversion to native C code and then storage in machine code. The PL/SQL is translated into C code rather than p-code, which is in interpreted mode, and compiled using the C compiler on the given platform and then linked directly into Oracle processes. When the particular stored subprogram is invoked, the natively compiled program is mapped to the PGA. This native compilation results in better performance.

Performance Benefit

The performance of native compilation is a function of the code written. It's most optimal when you're writing compute-intensive PL/SQL subprograms that perform database-independent tasks. In this case, native compilation results in faster execution of PL/SQL. However, when the PL/SQL code consists of many SQL statements embedded in it, native compilation isn't very useful. This is because there are the additional steps of parsing and analyzing SQL code prior to execution. However, it's recommended that you don't natively compile a large number of subprograms, because too many shared units in the same directory can result in decreased efficiency.

Additional Parameters

You must have a C compiler installed on the system to compile and link the converted C code into a shared library.

As mentioned earlier, you must set the initialization parameter PLSQL_COMPILER_FLAGS to NATIVE for native compilation to take place. You have to consider a number of other related parameters when activating native compilation, which I've summarized here:

- *PLSQL_NATIVE_C_COMPILER:* Full path name of the C compiler. This setting is optional.

- *PLSQL_NATIVE_LIBRARY_DIR:* Directory where the shared objects are stored, as a result of native compilation.

- *PL/SQL_NATIVE_LIBRARY_SUBDIR_COUNT:* The number of subdirectories created under the previously specified directory. This parameter is recommended if the number of subprograms to be natively compiled exceeds 10,000.

- *PLSQL_NATIVE_LINKER:* The full path name of a linker used to link the object file into a shared object or DLL. This is optional.

- *PLSQL_NATIVE_MAKE_FILE_NAME:* The full name of the make file used by the make utility to generate shared objects.

- *PLSQL_NATIVE_MAKE_UTILITY:* The full path name of the make utility used to generate the shared object from the C source.

Parameter Passing by Reference

Parameter passing by reference refers to the ability to pass a pointer to the actual parameter instead of making a copy of it into the formal parameter. This is available as of Oracle8*i*.

How Parameter Passing Works

Recall that subprogram parameters are governed by two major factors: type of parameter and parameter mode. The type of parameter refers to actual and formal parameters. Actual parameters are the arguments used when calling the stored subprogram. Formal parameters refer to the definition of parameters that's specified in the signature of the subprogram. Both actual and formal parameters must have a one-to-one correspondence. The parameter mode refers to formal parameters and specifies whether the parameter is used for input, output, or both. There are three parameter modes: IN, OUT, and IN OUT, respectively.

When actual parameters are passed, there are two inherent ways in which they are passed: call by value and call by reference. In call by value, the value of the actual parameter is copied into the formal parameter. That is, a copy of the actual parameter is made. In call by reference, a pointer to the actual parameter is passed to the corresponding formal parameter. Thus, no copy is made and both actual and formal parameters refer to the same memory location.

PL/SQL uses call by reference for IN mode and call by value for OUT and IN OUT mode. Because a copy is made, call by value can take more execution time and consume more memory when large data structures are passed as OUT or IN

OUT parameters. This is especially true when passing resultsets, collections, index-by tables of records, or objects. To overcome this, call by reference for parameters in OUT and IN OUT mode was introduced in PL/SQL 8*i* using a compiler hint called NOCOPY. Here are the steps involved:

1. Specify the NOCOPY keyword following the IN OUT or OUT keyword.

2. The actual parameter is passed by reference and no copy of it is made.

3. In case of exceptions, the value of actual parameters isn't reliable.

However, NOCOPY is a compiler hint and not a directive, so PL/SQL may not always apply it. That is, even if it's specified, the parameter may still be passed by value. Here's an example:

```
CREATE OR REPLACE FUNCTION f_nocopy
                (ip_1 IN NUMBER,
                 op_2 OUT NOCOPY VARCHAR2)
IS
BEGIN
     NULL;
END;
/
```

Table 15-1 depicts the behavior of specifying IN, IN OUT, OUT, and NOCOPY.

Table 15-1. Behavior of Various Parameter Modes

IN	IN OUT	OUT	IN OUT NOCOPY, OUT NOCOPY
The actual parameter is passed by reference.	The actual parameter is passed by value.	The actual parameter is passed by value.	The actual parameter is passed by reference.
A pointer (address) to the value is passed.	A copy of the value is passed out.	A copy of the value is passed in and out.	The address of the value is passed.
N/A	The out value is rolled back in the case of an unhandled exception.	The out value is rolled back in the case of an unhandled exception.	Can't predict the correctness of the OUT value always, as no rollback occurs in the case of an unhandled exception.

Performance Benefit

Using call by reference is faster than using call by value because it avoids copying the actual parameter into the formal parameter. This is significant when you're passing huge collections of data. Chapter 5 contains an example that illustrates the performance benefit of NOCOPY in the section "Parameter Passing by Reference." As you can see from the output of the example in Chapter 5, using NOCOPY is faster than passing by simply using OUT or IN OUT.

Though the time difference between using NOCOPY and not using it is a function of the hardware and software configuration, the difference is still significant.

Using Native Dynamic SQL

Native dynamic SQL refers to the execution of SQL statements dynamically constructed at runtime using declarative statements.

How Native Dynamic SQL Works

Here are the steps involved in native dynamic SQL:

1. Native dynamic SQL is built-in support for dynamic SQL inside the PL/SQL interpreter. It's also integrated with SQL.

2. There's no API involved, and SQL statements and PL/SQL blocks are executed by means of two declarative statements, EXECUTE IMMEDIATE and OPEN FOR.

3. You can specify bind variables to link program values to variables at runtime. Specify the bind variables in the dynamic SQL statement string by prefixing a colon (:) to the bind variable names. Then provide the actual values for the bind variables using the USING clause of the EXECUTE IMMEDIATE statement or OPEN FOR statement.

EXECUTE IMMEDIATE is used for dynamically executing DDL, DML, and single-row queries. OPEN FOR is used for multirow queries.

Performance Benefit

The performance response of using native dynamic SQL is a function of the number of times the dynamic SQL statement is used in a single session. If the dynamic SQL statement is executed a few times in a session, native dynamic SQL is faster than static SQL. This is because native dynamic SQL parses the SQL statement each time it's executed.

In addition, native dynamic SQL can improve performance in the following ways:

- Being declarative in syntax, native dynamic SQL has no API involved, so it minimizes procedure call overhead.

- Binding variables in native dynamic SQL execute the code faster. This is because the same SQL statement is executed with different values of the bind variables so that a single cursor is shareable by multiple SQL statements. Also, binding takes care of data type conversion implicitly since native data types are involved; otherwise, conversion functions such as TO_DATE, TO_CHAR, and so on should be used.

Using Bulk Binds

Bulk binding refers to the ability to INSERT rows into, UPDATE rows in, and DELETE rows from a table using a collection input, or SELECT or FETCH rows from a table into a collection in a single shot without multiple context switches between SQL and PL/SQL. Bulk binding was first introduced in Oracle8*i*. Oracle9*i* enhanced bulk binding by allowing the use of bulk dynamic SQL.

How Bulk Binding Works

SQL in PL/SQL is executed by forwarding the SQL statement to the SQL engine. The output of the SQL statement is then forwarded back to the PL/SQL engine for further processing. This results in a context switch from PL/SQL to SQL and from SQL back to PL/SQL. Considering this fact, if a SQL statement is executed iteratively, the number of context switches from PL/SQL to SQL and vice versa is very large. This hinders performance.

Bulk binding minimizes this context switching. Here are the steps involved:

1. Use the FORALL statement for bulk binding INSERT, UPDATE, and DELETE statements. Specify the SAVE EXCEPTIONS clause to filter rows rejected in the FORALL operation.

2. Use the BULK COLLECT statement for retrieving multiple rows from a multirow query or fetching multiple rows from a cursor.

3. The set of rows are inserted, updated, deleted, or queried in a single call with a context switch occurring from PL/SQL to SQL once and then once again from SQL to PL/SQL.

4. Use dynamic bulk binding with EXECUTE IMMEDIATE with BULK COLLECT for SELECT queries and FETCH . . . BULK COLLECT INTO for bulk fetch from cursors dynamically defined in native dynamic SQL.

5. Use EXECUTE IMMEDIATE with a FORALL statement for bulk DML and EXECUTE IMMEDIATE with a FORALL . . . RETURNING INTO . . . statement for bulk DML in native dynamic SQL.

6. Perform multirow updates and deletes with a RETURNING clause using dynamic SQL. Prior to 9*i*, native dynamic SQL supported a RETURNING clause only in the case of single-row output.

Performance Benefit

As I mentioned earlier, bulk binding reduces the number of context switches between PL/SQL and SQL, resulting in faster execution of sets of DML statements. Chapter 9 contains an example in the section "Bulk DML" that verifies the performance improvement of bulk binds by performing a massive INSERT with a normal FOR LOOP and a bulk-binding FORALL statement. The example shows the time for the FORALL operation to be significantly less than that for the FOR LOOP operation.

Bulk dynamic SQL drastically improves performance by combining the performance advantage of using bulk binds to reduce context switching with the ability to execute quickly using native dynamic SQL statements.

Using the RETURNING Clause

The RETURNING clause refers to the ability to return column values from the inserted rows of an INSERT statement or updated rows from an UPDATE OR DELETE statement without performing a query to obtain this information.

How the RETURNING Clause Works

Normally, when an INSERT, UPDATE, or DELETE statement is executed in PL/SQL, the information about the new row being inserted or the existing row being changed isn't available until a query is done following the currently executing DML statement. To avoid this query, you can specify the RETURNING clause for an INSERT, UPDATE, or DELETE statement.

To do this, first specify the RETURNING clause following the INSERT, UPDATE, or DELETE statement. Here's the syntax:

```
INSERT INTO table_name VALUES ( ... , ... , ... )
RETURNING col1, col2, ... INTO plsql_variable1, plsql_variable2, ... ;
```

where table_name is the table being inserted into, and col1, col2, and so on are column names of this table. plsql_variable1, plsql_variable2, and so on are PL/SQL variables with a one-to-one correspondence in data type and length with the column names.

For bulk binding operations, specify the RETURNING BULK COLLECT INTO clause after the FORALL statement syntax. Here's the syntax:

```
FORALL index IN start..end
    sql_statement
     RETURNING column_name BULK COLLECT INTO collection_name;
```

where index is the index variable of the FORALL statement; start and end are the starting and ending values for executing the FORALL statement; sql_statement is an INSERT, UPDATE, or DELETE statement; and collection_name is a collection corresponding to the column_name column being modified.

Next, specify the RETURNING INTO clause when you use native dynamic SQL and/or bulk dynamic SQL. This method of multiple ROW updates and deletes with a RETURNING clause using dynamic SQL is possible only in Oracle9*i*. Here's the syntax:

```
FORALL index IN start..end
    EXECUTE_IMMEDIATE 'sql_statement_using_bind_variables_and_returning_clause'
    USING collection_name
    RETURNING BULK COLLECT INTO output_collection_name;
```

Performance Benefit

Using the RETURNING clause eliminates the extra step of querying the database after doing the INSERT, UPDATE, or DELETE to retrieve the modified rows. This in turn reduces the additional round-trip in a network and also the context switching from PL/SQL to SQL and vice versa. This increases performance by saving time and resources.

Using Object Types and Collections

Object types model real-world entities. Object types and methods that operate on these types combine data and methods into a single construct. This eliminates the need for multiple tables.

Object REFS and the introduction of REF columns in the database are better alternatives to foreign key relationships; hence, you can avoid complicated joins. This improves performance by eliminating the overhead for join processing.

Also, object methods can replace code otherwise stored as PL/SQL program units. You can store and manipulate objects as a whole in both SQL and PL/SQL. This increases efficiency and productivity.

Using Pipelined Table Functions

Pipelined table functions refer to functions returning collections in a pipelined manner using the PIPELINED clause in the function signature and the PIPE ROW statement inside the function body.

How Pipelined Table Functions Work

Pipelined table functions are available in Oracle9*i*. Here are the steps involved in creating pipelined table functions:

1. Create an object type or PL/SQL record.

2. Create a collection of this object type or PL/SQL record.

3. Create a function that returns this collection.

4. Define this function as pipelined using the PIPELINED construct.

5. Use the PIPE ROW statement to return a single element of a collection.

6. Code an empty RETURN statement that is used to specify the completion of the pipelined table function.

7. The rows are returned as they're determined and each row is piped and returned. This means rows are returned incrementally rather than waiting for the function to execute completely.

 CROSS-REFERENCE   *Chapter 11 discusses pipelined table functions in detail with examples.*

Performance Benefit

Pipelined table functions improve performance when returning a large set of rows. The function need not execute completely and the entire collection need not be instantiated in memory. This results in better response time and less memory consumption. Pipelined table functions can be passed from one table function to the next in a pipelined fashion. This increases performance by eliminating the need to store data in intermediate tables. Finally, pipelined table functions can execute in parallel, which results in improved speed and scalability.

Summary

This chapter highlighted some techniques of achieving improved PL/SQL performance. Specifically, I presented some general tips for tuning PL/SQL and other in-depth details related to native compilation of PL/SQL code, parameter passing by reference, using native dynamic SQL and bulk binds, using the RETURNING clause, using object types and collections, and using pipelined table functions. The next chapter discusses certain PL/SQL coding standards.

CHAPTER 16

PL/SQL Coding Standards

CODING STANDARDS are part of any software application, and PL/SQL is no exception. These standards are generally devised before beginning the development phase of the software development life cycle. They serve as rules of thumb while coding, and when they are followed they allow standardized and efficient code to be developed. These standards are "tricks of the trade" that assert often ignored facts and provide solutions to certain technical problems, saving time and effort on the part of developers in addition to providing well-written, well-maintained, and efficient PL/SQL code.

This chapter highlights some coding standards for when you're using PL/SQL in Oracle9*i*, including using new features introduced in Oracle9*i*. Some of the standards are general guidelines, whereas others are must-follow rules. And still others show the optimal way to query and perform DML on the database. I've outlined these standards in the following major categories:

- Introduction to PL/SQL

- Cursors

- PL/SQL records and index-by tables

- Error message handling

- Subprograms

- Database triggers

- Native dynamic SQL

- Autonomous transactions

- Native bulk binds

- Objects in the database

- Collections

- Large objects

- Java in the database

 NOTE *Many of these topics are covered in some detail in the relevant areas of the book.*

Coding Standards

When you write an application, proper planning is required. Just as when you design a database, when you work with PL/SQL you need to create and maintain proper documentation. I'm fed up with going into an organization and not finding one word written anywhere about procedures and functions. In many cases, code contains no comments. Sometimes it takes longer to work out what something is doing than it does to actually rewrite it.

The following list provides several guidelines for your PL/SQL coding practices. The specific standards in each of the previously mentioned categories are outlined. You can refer to the relevant chapter in this book for examples and to see why the particular standard is to be followed.

Introduction to PL/SQL

The following are guidelines to start with PL/SQL coding:

Design a guidelines document with proper design criteria for coding before you start coding a PL/SQL application.

Identify inputs and outputs to the application being coded along with information to be logged or audited.

Partition the whole application into modules with each partition tailored to a specific task. Again, separate any independent modules to be run once before you run the main application.

Format the code with proper indentation for easy readability.

Follow a standard convention for variables, constants, and globals. Separate naming convention of variables from that of schema objects in PL/SQL such as subprograms and database triggers.

Anchor declarations with %TYPE and %ROWTYPE.

Use ELSIF instead of defining nested IFS wherever possible. Also, avoid defining multiple IF statements when you can use ELSIF.

Use CASE statements and expressions instead of IFS to simplify code writing.

Never declare the index of a FOR LOOP.

Use a FOR LOOP to process all iterations from the start to the end loop index. Don't use a FOR LOOP for conditional execution.

Avoid abnormal termination of loops. This is especially useful for WHILE and FOR LOOPS, where you should avoid specifying an explicit EXIT condition.

Commit or rollback incrementally to release any held-up locks and physical storage errors such as rollback segment errors.

Cursors

The following are guidelines/practices for dealing with cursors:

Always use cursors for dealing with multirow SELECTS. In this way, you can process the results of multirow SELECTS, row by row, in a PL/SQL block.

Always check for the explicit cursor attribute %ISOPEN before opening a cursor. You can do this with a negation specified. Follow a similar guideline for closing a cursor.

Always check for implicit cursor attributes with SQL% after performing a DML inside a PL/SQL block. Also, use the RETURNING clause to output information inserted or updated by the DML statement. Using

SQL%FOUND, SQL%NOTFOUND, or SQL%ROWCOUNT replaces a SELECT COUNT(*). Even if a SELECT COUNT(*) isn't used, at least a SELECT . . . INTO should be used instead. Using implicit cursor attributes saves this overhead.

Follow the standard way of OPEN, FETCH (in a loop if necessary), and CLOSE in this order to process explicit cursors not using a CURSOR FOR loop.

Always fetch into a cursor-oriented record of the form cursor_name%ROWTYPE or, if not, at least fetch into a record type compatible with the cursor SELECT rather than into individual variables. For cursors defined with SELECT *, use a table-oriented record. This is less error-prone and also improves program readability.

Use a cursor FOR LOOP when processing *all* the rows in a cursor unconditionally. Use OPEN, FETCH, and CLOSE to process some of the rows or to skip some rows on a certain condition.

Always avoid declaring cursors in the declaration and specify them in the cursor FOR LOOP itself when you're dealing with cursors to process all rows unconditionally.

Use an explicit cursor instead of a SELECT . . . INTO in client-side PL/SQL. This eliminates the extra call to the database to check for the TOO_MANY_ROWS exception in addition to the call for checking the NO_DATA_FOUND exception.

Parameterize cursors. Parameterized cursors are very useful in processing nested cursor loops in which an inner cursor is opened with data values passed to it from an outer opened cursor.

Use the SELECT FOR UPDATE cursor only when you want to update the table that you're selecting from. In this case, specify the column names being updated. Doing so not only locks the rows after the cursor is opened and the resultset rows are identified for UPDATE, but it also eliminates a second fetch of the rows for doing the update and preserves the current row by the WHERE CURRENT OF clause.

Don't COMMIT or ROLLBACK inside the cursor loop while processing a SELECT FOR UPDATE cursor. Do so after the loop.

Always check for the attribute %NOTFOUND *immediately after* the FETCH statement to terminate a cursor FETCH loop normally. When you use multiple FETCH statements to fetch a row set at a time, specify the EXIT WHEN cursor_name%NOTFOUND condition *immediately after every* FETCH statement.

Close all opened cursors irrespective of whether the PL/SQL program terminates normally or with an error. In the latter case, close all opened cursors in the exception handling section. This frees the resources otherwise occupied.

Make use of dynamic cursors by using cursor variables. However, the same rules apply to cursor variables and static cursors: OPEN, FETCH (in a loop if necessary), and CLOSE, in this order.

Make use of dynamism in cursor variables by reusing the same cursor variable for opening multiple queries or assigning different queries to the same cursor variable depending on runtime conditions.

Cursor variables and cursors aren't interoperable. You can't use one in place of the other.

Make use of cursor variables to return resultsets from subprograms. In this case, always define their REF CURSOR type in a package. However, when you pass cursor variables as formal parameters to subprograms, don't open them inside the body of the subprogram.

Make use of cursor expressions to eliminate the use of complex joins in cursors.

PL/SQL Records and Index-by Tables

When you use PL/SQL records and index-by tables, the following standards can serve as rules of thumb:

Encapsulate record and table type definitions in a package for global access.

While accessing the individual elements of a record, use the record variable name and not the record type name.

Use aggregate assignment wherever possible instead of individual field assignment. This saves code and time.

Use a table-oriented record when there is a need to include all the columns in the underlying database table as fields in the record. This ensures that the changes are automatically reflected in the table-oriented record when the structure of the table is altered.

Use cursor-oriented records when a greater degree of flexibility is desired—for example, when you're choosing columns from multiple tables.

Use entire PL/SQL records in INSERT and UPDATE statements wherever possible. This ensures that you avoid the declaration of too many variables. (This is available as of Oracle9*i* Release 2.)

Use index-by tables to transform database table data into PL/SQL structures.

Use a LOOP to populate an index-by table when it's necessary to create the rows sequentially.

Check for the existence of an index-by table element before referencing it for the first time in PL/SQL control structures for reading its value.

Use aggregate assignment of index-by tables wherever possible instead of individual field assignment.

Simulate multidimensional arrays using multiple index-by tables.

Use the FIRST, LAST, and NEXT methods to access the elements in an index-by table.

Use associative arrays when dealing with index-by tables of VARCHAR2 data. This improves performance by enabling fast lookup of individual array elements, eliminates the need to know the position of the individual element, and avoids looping through all array elements.

Error-Message Handling

Error-message handling can be more elegant when you follow these practices:

Categorize errors in an application by segregating them into predefined exceptions, non-predefined Oracle errors, user-defined exceptions, and user-defined PL/SQL error messages. For all of these types of errors, write generic error-handling routines that separate error processing from business logic processing.

Log the error in an error table with information such as the error code and the error message text.

Define user-defined exceptions for trapping and handling application-specific errors. You can further define user-defined error messages into information, warning, and error messages, and handle each in a proper way. Also, you can categorize the messages based on their severity level.

Use EXCEPTION_INIT to associate a non-predefined Oracle error with a user-defined exception. Although you can also use EXCEPTION_INIT to associate user-defined error messages with user-defined exceptions, don't use it for this purpose. Instead, code an error-raising procedure that makes a call to RAISE_APPLICATION ERROR within it for providing user-defined error messages in PL/SQL.

For messages of type error, you can use RAISE_APPLICATION_ERROR. Determine when to continue program execution after an exception occurs. This can be normally done for informative and warning messages. In the case of error messages, the normal behavior should be to halt program execution at that point. However, a careful analysis can reveal when to continue after errors in some exceptional cases.

Don't forget the benefit of using RAISE_APPLICATION_ERROR. It not only raises the customized error and stops further execution, but it also returns the customized error number and error message as the SQLCODE and SQLERRM to the calling environment.

Define user-defined exceptions in a package for global access. Don't define duplicate user-defined exceptions while dealing with nested blocks. Handle all user-defined exceptions explicitly by coding an exception handler for each of them. Don't try to associate more than one user-defined exception with the same error number.

Be careful about exceptions raised in declaration and exception-handling sections of a PL/SQL block.

Don't let exceptions fall through. Code an exception handler exclusively for each PL/SQL block or subprogram defined in the application.

Define a WHEN OTHERS handler in each exception handling section. This traps any errors not handled explicitly or otherwise. In this case, trap the Oracle error raised using SQLCODE and SQLERRM.

Don't declare user-defined exceptions with names that are the same as predefined ones. Always follow a naming pattern when you define user-defined exceptions.

In the case of nested blocks, always include a WHEN OTHERS handler in the topmost level of every PL/SQL program.

Subprograms

The following are standards for when you deal with PL/SQL subprograms:

Modularize code into subprograms based on specific functions and place logically related functional units in packages. Even in the case of a single program unit, if it performs huge tasks and is compute-intensive, or if it processes multiple SQL statements, it's good practice to place it in a package.

 NOTE   *Packages insulate code from other programs, provide a greater degree of modularity, and increase performance. Also, packages have the advantage that referencing programs need not be recompiled when the package body changes.*

Pin frequently used packages in memory to optimize performance of the shared pool.

When declaring only global variables and cursors, only code the package specification.

Code an initialization section for performing one-time package tasks.

Use the CREATE or REPLACE clause to avoid errors due to the prior existence of the objects.

Overload similarly functioning subprograms that differ only in their parameter types or number of parameters.

Don't code multiple RETURN statements in a function. Use local variables to handle return values on multiple conditions and code the return value by using one RETURN statement.

Don't use OUT parameters with functions. If multiple values are to be returned to the calling environment, use procedures with multiple OUT parameters.

Code multirow SELECTS as a cursor in a package specification. However, you can code multirow SELECTS using REF CURSORS if the resultset rows are returned by means of a subprogram. Always use weak cursor variables defined in a package to return resultsets from subprograms. This ensures that the definition of the cursor variable isn't constrained.

Take care with object dependencies when dropping subprograms.

Use parameter passing by reference using NOCOPY when passing huge sets of data as parameters. This improves performance.

Use invoker rights to take care of centralization of code and decentralization of data. Use definer rights otherwise. Using invoker rights provides the added advantage of localizing data specific to a particular user.

Always implement customized access control tailored toward the specific application by using invoker rights in addition to the default authentication and authorization schemes provided by Oracle.

Use serially reusable packages for the runtime package state to persist across database calls.

Use package variables to define PL/SQL globals and always define get and set methods to retrieve and populate these globals. Use a package initialization section to initialize any package variables needed for a session's duration.

Explicitly assign values to OUT formal parameters.

Use native compilation of PL/SQL code when writing compute-intensive PL/SQL subprograms that perform database-independent tasks. In this case, native compilation results in faster execution of PL/SQL.

Database Triggers

The following are certain guidelines for when you use database triggers:

Use row-level auditing by introducing audit columns in each table and populate these columns via database triggers. In addition, perform DDL auditing by using user-event triggers.

Assign unique names to database triggers that are different from the names of database tables.

Make sure your trigger body size does not exceed the executable size limit.

Don't duplicate triggers for performing multiple DML operations. Specify multiple DML operations in the same trigger and use conditional predicates inside the trigger body to identify them.

Use a customized error-reporting mechanism when defining errors from triggers.

Use system-event and user-event trigger attributes to reference system events, object owner, or object name when a system-level trigger fires. These are available through the SYS.% attributes or by means of public synonyms named ORA_%.

Code triggers in such a way as to avoid mutating and constraining table errors. The perfect scenario in which to use autonomous transactions to avoid mutating table errors is when the logic of the trigger isn't affected by the fact that changes made to the triggering table (i.e., the main transaction) aren't visible to the autonomous transaction until the main transaction is committed.

Code DML operations on a view by means of INSTEAD-OF triggers.

It's a good practice to analyze schema after logon using a user-event trigger to estimate statistics on the tables in the schema.

Avoid defining the same type of trigger at multiple levels. Also, avoid defining triggers of the same type multiple times.

Native Dynamic SQL

The following points can help you code better using native dynamic SQL:

Use native dynamic SQL over DBMS_SQL to perform dynamic SQL operations on the server side. This improves performance because execution is faster.

Use only weak REF CURSORS for processing multirow queries using native dynamic SQL.

Use bind variables when defining dynamic SQL statements. Using bind variables for data values in native dynamic SQL makes the code execute faster and also makes the code easier to maintain. It's faster because the same SQL statement is executed with different values of the bind variables so that a single cursor is shareable by multiple SQL statements. Also, binding takes care of data type conversion implicitly since native data types are involved.

Always use invoker rights when using dynamic SQL and dynamic PL/SQL.

Don't explicitly declare a bind variable.

Only use bind variables for data values and not for values that hold metadata values such as table names, column names, and SQL statement clauses. Use PL/SQL variables to hold the latter type of values. Using bind variables for specifying schema object names can result in errors that can cause confusion.

When using native dynamic SQL, always define an exception-handling section by specifying it an enclosing PL/SQL block.

Use DBMS_SQL over native dynamic SQL when the same SQL statement is executed multiple times in the same session.

Autonomous Transactions

The following are guidelines to follow when you use autonomous transactions:

Use autonomous transactions in cases where there's a need to partition transactions so that the commit or rollback of the main transaction should be independent of the commit or rollback of the subtransaction. A good example is error logging.

Make sure to avoid deadlocks when defining autonomous transactions. Deadlocks with the main transaction for resources and locks can occur.

Code an explicit COMMIT or ROLLBACK in an autonomous transaction program to end it normally.

Don't attempt to jump to ROLLBACK to a save point issued in the main transaction from inside the autonomous transaction.

Define the PRAGMA AUTONOMOUS_TRANSACTION for each subprogram defined in a package.

Use autonomous transactions to avoid side effects of functions callable from SQL.

Native Bulk Binds

The following are some practices to follow when you deal with native bulk binds:

Use bulk binding binds to improve performance with respect to overall PL/SQL execution when processing sets of DML statements in PL/SQL such as multirow inserts, updates, and deletes, so that traffic to and from PL/SQL and SQL is reduced.

Combine the features of native dynamic SQL and bulk binding. Using bulk binding with dynamic SQL combines the performance advantage of using bulk binds to reduce context switching with the ability to execute quickly using native dynamic SQL statements.

Use the RETURNING clause with bulk binds to output information from INSERT and UPDATE statements into collections.

Don't mistake a FORALL statement with a cursor FOR LOOP. They are quite different concepts.

Use record types for bulk DML instead of multiple individual collections. Also use BULK COLLECT into records. This is available as of Oracle9*i* Release 2.

Use the SAVE EXCEPTIONS clause introduced in Oracle9*i* to continue processing in the case of bulk bind operations using the FORALL statement, when an error occurs in the process.

Objects in the Database

The following are points to keep in mind when you use objects in the database and in PL/SQL:

Use objects to model real-world entities in PL/SQL. The inherent advantages of object orientation help leverage objects in PL/SQL, such as richer encapsulation and binding of methods to data.

Use get and set methods to retrieve and populate attributes of an object type.

Use type hierarchies to model hierarchical relationships involving objects. Features such as superclass and subclass definition, substitutability, and dynamic method dispatch enable you to model efficiently and with ease.

Leverage the benefit of using large objects with object types.

Always initialize object type instances by using a constructor. Make use of user-defined constructors to customize the initialization. This enables you to provide proper validation rules for attribute data.

Although it's allowed, don't invoke object type methods on uninitialized object instances.

Always use invoker rights on object member methods. This provides a greater degree of flexibility to be used by a large number of users.

Don't define both MAP and ORDER methods for an object type.

Use object REFS for defining referential integrity in the case of object tables and object-relational tables (tables with object columns). You can use variables or parameters of object types as arguments to bind variables used in native dynamic SQL statements.

Use object views to present an object-relational view of relational table data using INSTEAD-OF triggers on these views.

Use native dynamic SQL with objects. This gives the same performance benefits as when you use relational tables with the ability to execute code involving objects in the database efficiently.

Always define an enclosing block with an explicit exception handler for tracking errors raised when using objects with native dynamic SQL statements.

Never specify the combination NOT INSTANTIABLE and FINAL when defining an object type. Doing so would mean the object type so defined is not a base for a subtype and object instances can't be defined based on it, which means it can't be used in any way.

Make use of type evolution to alter object types.

Understand that when user-defined operators are used, it is more of a project-specific need and a design issue than a technical issue. For example, to simulate a complex mathematical function in a way similar to a built-in operator, you can use a user-defined operator. However, for implementing simple functional logic, using an operator would involve an administrative overhead.

Use user-defined operators in large PL/SQL applications as part of template construction. You can effectively use them to provide developer access to functions that can be safely used within SQL. Although they don't provide any additional functionality in comparison with functions, operators can assist with the organization of a code library.

Collections

Follow these guidelines to improve coding using collections:

Encapsulate collection type definitions in a package when defining them in PL/SQL.

Use collections to return resultsets from subprograms, especially when the resultset returned is not conformable to data returned by a SELECT query. Using table functions is one way of returning resultsets from subprograms. When you use table functions, pipeline them to incrementally return data for maximum efficiency.

Always initialize a PL/SQL collection before using it.

Leverage the advantage of collections. Collections can be stored in the database to efficiently store list data in the form of arrays, including multi-dimensional arrays using multilevel collections.

Don't try to manipulate VARRAY elements in PL/SQL. Doing so can result in illegal program termination.

Use the SQL TABLE operator to retrieve the individual elements of a nested table.

It's recommended that you include multilevel collection type definitions of PL/SQL type in a package so that they're available persistently across sessions.

Large Objects

The following are standards to follow when you use large objects in PL/SQL:

Use large objects (LOBs) for handling unstructured data of large size and for random access. You can access LOB data from within the database or from outside the database (e.g., from the Internet).

Use binary large objects (BLOBs) and character large objects (CLOBs) only after initializing them, preferably to an empty LOB.

Use binary files (BFILEs) only after obtaining a valid locator.

Always lock the row containing the LOB column when updating the LOB.

Be careful when performing string operations or assignment of CLOB columns to VARCHAR2 columns and vice versa so as not to lose data.

When using the PL/SQL API to manipulate LOBs, always obtain a LOB locator first, then open a LOB before using it, and finally close the LOB.

Java in the Database

You can use Java in the database more effectively when you follow these standards:

Use Java in the database for optimizing compute-intensive tasks that don't need database access and for extending database functionality not available in PL/SQL. Java also implements a safer type system, automatic garbage collection, polymorphism, inheritance, and multithreading.

When you use Java stored procedures, load a Java source file into the database to preserve the Java source code.

Always use the AND COMPILE clause when loading a Java source into the database using the CREATE JAVA command.

Always specify the -resolve option when loading a Java class into the database using loadjava. This eliminates compilation of the Java source at runtime.

Use the autogeneration of the call spec feature provided by loadjava to generate call specs for Java methods that don't have any complex return types or don't involve objects.

Always drop a Java class loaded with loadjava using the dropjava command to ensure proper update of the digest table.

Always specify the Java class as public and its methods as public static when defining a Java stored procedure.

Always use integer return values to map to Java boolean types.

Always specify the fully qualified name of the Java data type and Java class when defining a PL/SQL call specification to a Java stored procedure.

Always specify the Java class to implement the java.sql.SQLData interface or the oracle.sql.ORAData interface when publishing it as a member method of an object type.

Use Java stored procedures to return resultsets when there's a requirement to return multiple row query output to the server side from Java.

Use fine-grained access control when accessing resources outside of the database such as operating system files from Java stored procedures.

Summary

This chapter highlighted some coding standards for you to follow when programming using PL/SQL. Specifically, these standards related to general coding standards as well as to must-follow rules covering various aspects of PL/SQL, from cursors, error-message handling, and subprograms to objects, collections, and Java in the database.

Part Six

Appendix A

APPENDIX A

Case Studies and Schema Objects

THE FOLLOWING CASE studies and schema objects are used in various chapters of this book. SQL and PL/SQL code can be executed in a number of ways, such as from a Java/JDBC application, as embedded SQL/PL/SQL calls from Java, from an IDE such as SQL*Plus, or invoked as SQL/PL/SQL calls from a front application such as Oracle Forms or Visual Basic. For the purposes of this book, the environment used for compiling and executing SQL and PL/SQL code is SQL*Plus. Remember that all PL/SQL commands should be terminated by a semicolon (;) and a forward slash (/). I use the schema plsql9i, with the SQL*Plus connection clause plsql9i/plsql9i@ORCL (where ORCL is the tnsnames alias in tnsnames.ora).

In the connection string plsql9i/plsql9i@ORCL, plsql9i denotes the username as well as the password. ORCL denotes the tnsnames alias of the database as specified in the file tnsnames.ora. This file is located in the [Oracle_Home]\NETWORK\ADMIN directory. You can create this schema by running the following code:

```
connect system/manager@ORCL;
create user plsql9i identified by plsql9i;
grant connect, resource, dba to plsql9i;
```

Once you create the plsql9i schema, you can connect as the plsql9i user by typing the following command:

```
connect plsql9i/plsql9i@ORCL;
```

Not all schema objects used are listed. There are some of them to be created as the chapters progress. The basic ones listed are here:

```
CREATE TABLE items_tab (item_code varchar2(6) PRIMARY KEY,
                        item_descr varchar2(20) NOT NULL);
CREATE TABLE employee_test
(empid           number(10) PRIMARY KEY,
```

631

```
    lastname          varchar2(30) NOT NULL,
    firstname         varchar2(30) NOT NULL,
    middle_initial  varchar2(2));
```

The data for this table is populated using the following INSERT statements:

```
begin
    insert into employee_test values (101,'SMITH','JOHN',null);
    insert into employee_test values (102,'JOHNSON','ROBERT','L');
    insert into employee_test values (103,'LAKSHMAN','BULUSU',null);
    insert into employee_test values (104,'KNOP','VICTORIA','A');
    commit;
end;
/
```

Organizational Hierarchy System

This is first described in Chapter 2. Figure 2-1 shows the data model. The following are the schema table and sequence definitions for this case study. Note that you first create the tables and then use the ALTER TABLE statement to create primary and foreign keys.

```
create table site_tab
( site_no       number(4)     not null,
   site_descr varchar2(20) not null);

alter table site_tab add primary key (site_no);

create table hrc_tab
(hrc_code    number(4)       not null,
   hrc_descr   varchar2(20) not null);

alter table hrc_tab add primary key (hrc_code);

create table org_tab
(hrc_code        number(4)     not null,
org_id    NUMBER(8) not null,
org_short_name varchar2(30) not null,
 org_long_name   varchar2(60) );
```

```
alter table org_tab add primary key (hrc_code, org_id);
alter table org_tab add constraint org_tab_uk unique (org_id);
alter table org_tab
add constraint org_tab_fk foreign key (hrc_code) references hrc_tab(hrc_code);

create table  org_site_tab
( org_id   number(8) not null,
  site_no        number(4) not null );

alter table org_site_tab add primary key (org_id, site_no);
alter table org_site_tab
add constraint org_site_tab_fk1 foreign key (org_id) references org_tab(org_id);
alter table org_site_tab
add constraint org_site_tab_fk2 foreign key (site_no)
references site_tab(site_no);

create table org_level
( org_id       number(8)     not null,
  org_level varchar2(1) not null);

alter table org_level add primary key (org_id);
alter table org_level
add constraint org_level_fk foreign key (org_id) references org_tab(org_id);
  alter table org_level
add constraint org_level_ck CHECK ( org_level IN ('C', 'E', 'M', 'L'));

create table sec_hrc_tab
(hrc_code   number(4)      not null,
  hrc_descr   varchar2(20) not null);

create table sec_hrc_org_tab
(hrc_code       number(4)      not null,
 hrc_descr   varchar2(20) not null,
 org_id    NUMBER(8) not null,
 org_short_name varchar2(30) not null,
 org_long_name   varchar2(60) );

create table  sec_hrc_audit
( hrc_code   number(4) not null,
  num_rows   number(8) not null );

create sequence hrc_org_seq minvalue 1;
```

You create the data for the tables by means of the following INSERT statements:

```
insert into site_tab values (1, 'New York');
insert into site_tab values (2, 'Washington');
insert into site_tab values (3, 'Chicago');
insert into site_tab values (4, 'Dallas');
insert into site_tab values (5, 'San Francisco');

insert into hrc_tab values (1, 'CEO/COO');
insert into hrc_tab values (2, 'VP');
insert into hrc_tab values (3, 'Director');
insert into hrc_tab values (4, 'Manager');
insert into hrc_tab values (5, 'Analyst');

insert into org_tab values
(1, 1001, 'Office of CEO ABC Inc.','Office of CEO ABC Inc.');
insert into org_tab values
(1, 1002, 'Office of CEO XYZ Inc.','Office of CEO XYZ Inc.');
insert into org_tab values
(1, 1003, 'Office of CEO DataPro Inc.','Office of CEO DataPro Inc.');
insert into org_tab values
(2, 1004, 'Office of VP Sales ABC Inc.','Office of VP Sales ABC Inc.');
insert into org_tab values
(2, 1005, 'Office of VP Mktg ABC Inc.','Office of VP Mktg ABC Inc.');
insert into org_tab values
(2, 1006, 'Office of VP Tech ABC Inc.','Office of VP Tech ABC Inc.');

insert into org_site_tab values (1001, 1);
insert into org_site_tab values (1002, 2);
insert into org_site_tab values (1003, 3);
insert into org_site_tab values (1004, 1);
insert into org_site_tab values (1004, 2);
insert into org_site_tab values (1004, 3);
insert into org_site_tab values (1005, 1);
insert into org_site_tab values (1005, 4);
insert into org_site_tab values (1005, 5);
insert into org_site_tab values (1006, 1);
```

Order Entry Application System

Here is the code for creating the tables:

```
CREATE TABLE region_tab
(region_id NUMBER(4) PRIMARY KEY,
 region_name VARCHAR2(11) NOT NULL);

CREATE TABLE region_tab_temp AS
    SELECT * FROM region_tab;

CREATE TABLE sec_region_tab
(region_id NUMBER(4) PRIMARY KEY,
 region_name VARCHAR2(11) NOT NULL);

CREATE TABLE supplier_tab
(supp_id NUMBER(6) PRIMARY KEY,
 supp_name VARCHAR2(20) NOT NULL
);

CREATE TABLE order_tab
(order_id NUMBER(10) PRIMARY KEY,
 order_date DATE    NOT NULL,
 total_qty  NUMBER,
 total_price NUMBER(15,2) ,
 supp_id  NUMBER(6) REFERENCES supplier_tab(supp_id));

CREATE TABLE order_items
(order_id NUMBER(10) NOT NULL,
 item_id  VARCHAR2(10) NOT NULL,
 unit_price NUMBER(11,2) NOT NULL,
 quantity   NUMBER);

ALTER TABLE order_items ADD CONSTRAINT pk_order_items
          PRIMARY KEY (order_id, item_id);

CREATE TABLE error_log
(order_id NUMBER(10) NOT NULL,
 error_code NUMBER NOT NULL,
 error_text VARCHAR2(1000) NOT NULL,
 logged_user VARCHAR2(30) NOT NULL,
 logged_date DATE NOT NULL);
```

```
CREATE TABLE order_tran_coming_in
(order_id NUMBER(10) NOT NULL,
 order_date DATE NOT NULL,
 tran_coming_in_date DATE NOT NULL,
 success_flag VARCHAR2(1) DEFAULT 'N' NOT NULL);
```

You insert the data for some of these tables by means of the following INSERT statements:

```
INSERT INTO region_tab VALUES (1, 'REGION1');
INSERT INTO region_tab VALUES (2, 'REGION2');
INSERT INTO region_tab VALUES (3, 'REGION3');
INSERT INTO region_tab VALUES (4, 'REGION4');

INSERT INTO supplier_tab VALUES (1001, 'Supplier 1001');

INSERT INTO order_tab VALUES (101, sysdate, 100, 750, 1001);
```

Also, you create individual tables with dynamically constructed names such as ORDERS_FOR_<region_name> and ORDER_ITEMS_FOR_<region_name> based on the structure of the ORDER_TAB and ORDER_ITEMS tables.

Index

FILEGETNAME() function, for
    BFILEs, 495
FILEISOPEN() function, for BFILEs,
    495
FILEOPEN() function, for BFILEs, 495
FINAL clause, 365, 404
FINAL object property, modifying,
    415
Fine-grained permissions, Java, 519
FIRST collection method, 449, 452
FIRST method (index-by table), 126,
    129–130
Flush procedure, 88–89
FOR EACH ROW clause (triggers),
    260, 264, 281
FOR LOOPs, 13–14, 127–128, 335,
    341, 475
FORALL statement, 355, 606–607
    for DML bulk binds, 334,
        336–338, 340–342
    with RETURNING INTO...clause,
        355–356, 606
    with SAVE EXCEPTIONS clause,
        342–344
    with USING clause, 26
FORALL statement attributes,
    344–346
FORCE option of DROP OPERATOR
    statement, 430
Foreign key constraints, specifying,
    298
Foreign key reference for object
    columns, 381
Form (HTML) to accept user input,
    570–573
Formal parameters, 187, 223, 602.
        See also Parameter modes
    as %TYPE or %ROWTYPE, 193
    data types of, 191–193
    declaring, 193
    default values for, 193–196
    explained, 53, 186
    with subtype of NOT NULL,
        192–193
Forward slash (/)
    command termination, 631

program ending, 178
statement-ending, 365
Fourth-generation language (4GL), 3
Fully qualified data type name, 518
Fully qualified Java type name, 518
Fully qualifying an object, 383
Function arguments, cursor expres-
    sions as, 87–94
Function bindings in operators,
    425–426
Function called from SQL, purity of,
    223–231
Function calls, chained, 373
Function names, unique, 222
Function parameter modes, specify-
    ing, 189–191
Function parameters, specifying,
    186–196
Function signatures, 207
Functions
    as call specs, 535
    calling, 182
    calling Java routines from, 228
    calling from a PL/SQL block, 181
    creating and using, 180–183
    cursor variables defined inside,
        219–220
    defined, 180
    executing, 183–186
    four parts of, 177
    overloading packaged, 242–248
    in packages, 426
    purity of, 230
    signature or header of, 181
    using in SQL statements, 220–231
    using synonyms for, 222

G
Gateway Configuration Menu page,
    560
GET_ADDRESS() method, 372
GETCHUNKSIZE() function, for
    BLOBs and CLOBs, 493
GETLENGTH() function
    for BFILEs, 496
    for BLOBs and CLOBs, 493

Apress Titles

ISBN	PRICE	AUTHOR	TITLE
1-893115-73-9	$34.95	Abbott	Voice Enabling Web Applications: VoiceXML and Beyond
1-59059-061-9	$34.95	Allen	Bug Patterns in Java
1-893115-01-1	$39.95	Appleman	Dan Appleman's Win32 API Puzzle Book and Tutorial for Visual Basic Programmers
1-893115-23-2	$29.95	Appleman	How Computer Programming Works
1-893115-97-6	$39.95	Appleman	Moving to VB .NET: Strategies, Concepts, and Code
1-59059-023-6	$39.95	Baker	Adobe Acrobat 5: The Professional User's Guide
1-59059-039-2	$49.95	Barnaby	Distributed .NET Programming in C#
1-59059-068-6	$49.95	Barnaby	Distributed .NET Programming in VB .NET
1-59059-063-5	$29.95	Baum	Dave Baum's Definitive Guide to LEGO MINDSTORMS, Second Edition
1-893115-84-4	$29.95	Baum/Gasperi/ Hempel/Villa	Extreme MINDSTORMS: An Advanced Guide to LEGO MINDSTORMS
1-893115-82-8	$59.95	Ben-Gan/Moreau	Advanced Transact-SQL for SQL Server 2000
1-893115-91-7	$39.95	Birmingham/Perry	Software Development on a Leash
1-893115-48-8	$29.95	Bischof	The .NET Languages: A Quick Translation Guide
1-59059-041-4	$49.95	Bock	CIL Programming: Under the Hood™ of .NET
1-59059-053-8	$44.95	Bock/Stromquist/ Fischer/Smith	.NET Security
1-893115-67-4	$49.95	Borge	Managing Enterprise Systems with the Windows Script Host
1-59059-019-8	$49.95	Cagle	SVG Programming: The Graphical Web
1-893115-28-3	$44.95	Challa/Laksberg	Essential Guide to Managed Extensions for C++
1-893115-39-9	$44.95	Chand	A Programmer's Guide to ADO.NET in C#
1-59059-015-5	$39.95	Clark	An Introduction to Object Oriented Programming with Visual Basic .NET
1-893115-44-5	$29.95	Cook	Robot Building for Beginners
1-893115-99-2	$39.95	Cornell/Morrison	Programming VB .NET: A Guide for Experienced Programmers
1-893115-72-0	$39.95	Curtin	Developing Trust: Online Privacy and Security
1-59059-014-7	$44.95	Drol	Object-Oriented Macromedia Flash MX
1-59059-008-2	$29.95	Duncan	The Career Programmer: Guerilla Tactics for an Imperfect World
1-893115-71-2	$39.95	Ferguson	Mobile .NET
1-893115-90-9	$49.95	Finsel	The Handbook for Reluctant Database Administrators
1-893115-42-9	$44.95	Foo/Lee	XML Programming Using the Microsoft XML Parser
1-59059-024-4	$49.95	Fraser	Real World ASP.NET: Building a Content Management System
1-893115-55-0	$34.95	Frenz	Visual Basic and Visual Basic .NET for Scientists and Engineers
1-59059-038-4	$49.95	Gibbons	.NET Development for Java Programmers
1-893115-85-2	$34.95	Gilmore	A Programmer's Introduction to PHP 4.0
1-893115-36-4	$34.95	Goodwill	Apache Jakarta-Tomcat
1-893115-17-8	$59.95	Gross	A Programmer's Introduction to Windows DNA

ISBN	PRICE	AUTHOR	TITLE
1-893115-62-3	$39.95	Gunnerson	A Programmer's Introduction to C#, Second Edition
1-59059-030-9	$49.95	Habibi/Patterson/ Camerlengo	The Sun Certified Java Developer Exam with J2SE 1.4
1-893115-30-5	$49.95	Harkins/Reid	SQL: Access to SQL Server
1-59059-009-0	$49.95	Harris/Macdonald	Moving to ASP.NET: Web Development with VB .NET
1-59059-006-6	$39.95	Hetland	Practical Python
1-893115-10-0	$34.95	Holub	Taming Java Threads
1-893115-04-6	$34.95	Hyman/Vaddadi	Mike and Phani's Essential C++ Techniques
1-893115-96-8	$59.95	Jorelid	J2EE FrontEnd Technologies: A Programmer's Guide to Servlets, JavaServer Pages, and Enterprise JavaBeans
1-59059-029-5	$39.99	Kampa/Bell	Unix Storage Management
1-893115-49-6	$39.95	Kilburn	Palm Programming in Basic
1-893115-50-X	$34.95	Knudsen	Wireless Java: Developing with Java 2, Micro Edition
1-893115-79-8	$49.95	Kofler	Definitive Guide to Excel VBA
1-893115-57-7	$39.95	Kofler	MySQL
1-893115-87-9	$39.95	Kurata	Doing Web Development: Client-Side Techniques
1-893115-75-5	$44.95	Kurniawan	Internet Programming with Visual Basic
1-893115-38-0	$24.95	Lafler	Power AOL: A Survival Guide
1-59059-066-X	$39.95	Lafler	Power SAS: A Survival Guide
1-59059-049-X	$54.99	Lakshman	Oracle9i PL/SQL: A Developer's Guide
1-893115-46-1	$36.95	Lathrop	Linux in Small Business: A Practical User's Guide
1-59059-045-7	$49.95	MacDonald	User Interfaces in C#: Windows Forms and Custom Controls
1-893115-19-4	$49.95	Macdonald	Serious ADO: Universal Data Access with Visual Basic
1-59059-044-9	$49.95	MacDonald	User Interfaces in VB .NET: Windows Forms and Custom Controls
1-893115-06-2	$39.95	Marquis/Smith	A Visual Basic 6.0 Programmer's Toolkit
1-893115-22-4	$27.95	McCarter	David McCarter's VB Tips and Techniques
1-59059-040-6	$49.99	Mitchell/Allison	Real-World SQL-DMO for SQL Server
1-59059-021-X	$34.95	Moore	Karl Moore's Visual Basic .NET: The Tutorials
1-893115-27-5	$44.95	Morrill	Tuning and Customizing a Linux System
1-893115-76-3	$49.95	Morrison	C++ For VB Programmers
1-59059-003-1	$44.95	Nakhimovsky/Meyers	XML Programming: Web Applications and Web Services with JSP and ASP
1-893115-80-1	$39.95	Newmarch	A Programmer's Guide to Jini Technology
1-893115-58-5	$49.95	Oellermann	Architecting Web Services
1-59059-020-1	$44.95	Patzer	JSP Examples and Best Practices
1-893115-81-X	$39.95	Pike	SQL Server: Common Problems, Tested Solutions
1-59059-017-1	$34.95	Rainwater	Herding Cats: A Primer for Programmers Who Lead Programmers
1-59059-025-2	$49.95	Rammer	Advanced .NET Remoting (C# Edition)
1-59059-062-7	$49.95	Rammer	Advanced .NET Remoting in VB .NET
1-59059-028-7	$39.95	Rischpater	Wireless Web Development, Second Edition
1-893115-93-3	$34.95	Rischpater	Wireless Web Development with PHP and WAP

ISBN	PRICE	AUTHOR	TITLE
1-893115-89-5	$59.95	Shemitz	Kylix: The Professional Developer's Guide and Reference
1-893115-40-2	$39.95	Sill	The qmail Handbook
1-893115-24-0	$49.95	Sinclair	From Access to SQL Server
1-59059-026-0	$49.95	Smith	Writing Add-ins for Visual Studio .NET
1-893115-94-1	$29.95	Spolsky	User Interface Design for Programmers
1-893115-53-4	$44.95	Sweeney	Visual Basic for Testers
1-59059-035-X	$59.95	Symmonds	GDI+ Programming in C# and VB .NET
1-59059-002-3	$44.95	Symmonds	Internationalization and Localization Using Microsoft .NET
1-59059-010-4	$54.95	Thomsen	Database Programming with C#
1-59059-032-5	$59.95	Thomsen	Database Programming with Visual Basic .NET, Second Edition
1-893115-65-8	$39.95	Tiffany	Pocket PC Database Development with eMbedded Visual Basic
1-59059-027-9	$59.95	Torkelson/Petersen/Torkelson	Programming the Web with Visual Basic .NET
1-59059-018-X	$34.95	Tregar	Writing Perl Modules for CPAN
1-893115-59-3	$59.95	Troelsen	C# and the .NET Platform
1-59059-011-2	$59.95	Troelsen	COM and .NET Interoperability
1-893115-26-7	$59.95	Troelsen	Visual Basic .NET and the .NET Platform: An Advanced Guide
1-893115-54-2	$49.95	Trueblood/Lovett	Data Mining and Statistical Analysis Using SQL
1-893115-68-2	$54.95	Vaughn	ADO.NET and ADO Examples and Best Practices for VB Programmers, Second Edition
1-59059-012-0	$49.95	Vaughn/Blackburn	ADO.NET Examples and Best Practices for C# Programmers
1-893115-83-6	$44.95	Wells	Code Centric: T-SQL Programming with Stored Procedures and Triggers
1-893115-95-X	$49.95	Welschenbach	Cryptography in C and C++
1-893115-05-4	$39.95	Williamson	Writing Cross-Browser Dynamic HTML
1-59059-060-0	$39.95	Wright	ADO.NET: From Novice to Pro, Visual Basic .NET Edition
1-893115-78-X	$49.95	Zukowski	Definitive Guide to Swing for Java 2, Second Edition
1-893115-92-5	$49.95	Zukowski	Java Collections
1-893115-98-4	$54.95	Zukowski	Learn Java with JBuilder 6

Available at bookstores nationwide or from Springer Verlag New York, Inc. at 1-800-777-4643; fax 1-212-533-3503. Contact us for more information at sales@apress.com.

books for professionals by professionals™

apress™

About Apress

Apress, located in Berkeley, CA, is a fast-growing, innovative publishing company devoted to meeting the needs of existing and potential programming professionals. Simply put, the "A" in Apress stands for *"The Author's Press™"* and its books have *"The Expert's Voice™."* Apress' unique approach to publishing grew out of conversations between its founders Gary Cornell and Dan Appleman, authors of numerous best-selling, highly regarded books for programming professionals. In 1998 they set out to create a publishing company that emphasized quality above all else. Gary and Dan's vision has resulted in the publication of over 50 titles by leading software professionals, all of which have *The Expert's Voice™*.

Do You Have What It Takes to Write for Apress?

Apress is rapidly expanding its publishing program. If you can write and refuse to compromise on the quality of your work, if you believe in doing more than rehashing existing documentation, and if you're looking for opportunities and rewards that go far beyond those offered by traditional publishing houses, we want to hear from you!

Consider these innovations that we offer all of our authors:

- **Top royalties with *no* hidden switch statements**
  Authors typically only receive half of their normal royalty rate on foreign sales. In contrast, Apress' royalty rate remains the same for both foreign and domestic sales.

- **A mechanism for authors to obtain equity in Apress**
  Unlike the software industry, where stock options are essential to motivate and retain software professionals, the publishing industry has adhered to an outdated compensation model based on royalties alone. In the spirit of most software companies, Apress reserves a significant portion of its equity for authors.

- **Serious treatment of the technical review process**
  Each Apress book has a technical reviewing team whose remuneration depends in part on the success of the book since they too receive royalties.

Moreover, through a partnership with Springer-Verlag, New York, Inc., one of the world's major publishing houses, Apress has significant venture capital behind it. Thus, we have the resources to produce the highest quality books *and* market them aggressively.

If you fit the model of the Apress author who can write a book that gives the "professional what he or she needs to know™," then please contact one of our Editorial Directors, Dan Appleman (dan_appleman@apress.com), Gary Cornell (gary_cornell@apress.com), Jason Gilmore (jason_gilmore@apress.com), Simon Hayes (simon_hayes@apress.com), Karen Watterson (karen_watterson@apress.com), or John Zukowski (john_zukowski@apress.com) for more information.